Build Me a Mountain

The MIT Press
Cambridge, Massachusetts, and London, England

Build Me a Mountain
Youth, Poverty, and the Creation of New Settings
I. Ira Goldenberg

This book is dedicated to those (particularly those within
the university community) who have yet to learn that
the questioning of traditions, far from symbolizing a rejection
of the past, constitutes its very affirmation in the service
of the future.

Foreword by Seymour B. Sarason

It would be sad, indeed, if this book were viewed within
the narrow confines of the so-called War on Poverty.
It is true that it deals with disadvantaged youth, the helping role of nonprofessional people, the orientation of
the mental health professions, and other matters of governmental and community policy. It is also true that this book
contains data supporting the conclusion that hard-core,
inner-city youth who were fortunate to live for varying
periods of time at the Residential Youth Center—which
was conceived and directed primarily by Dr. Goldenberg—
became significantly less "hard-core" than a control group
that did not live there. And like any good, self-respecting
contemporary action program, this book also has much
to say about race and sensitivity groups! Although all this
and more are contained in the book, its significance lies
elsewhere, and that elsewhere is an arena of thought that
is as fascinating as it is thorny and hardly recognized. In
this arena of thought the central problem or question has
two aspects: How *do* people go about creating settings
or organizations or programs? How *might* people go about
the creation of settings so that goals are not subverted by
processes of growth that usually produce what I like to term
"organizational craziness," i.e., administrative structures,
social atmospheres, and intra- and intergroup dynamics that
cause individuals to suffer and organizations to become
irrelevant to their purposes, or to become obsolete, or
to die. The recognition of organizational craziness has
produced a variety of related "consulting" professionals
who make more than a fair living trying to introduce a
note of sanity and reason into chronologically mature
settings beset with troubles. Like so many troubled individuals, the troubled settings need an external agent—the
fashionable term is *change agent*—to set them straight.
Since, as in the case of individuals, the ratio of setting to
consultant is extremely discouraging, it is obvious that the
therapeutic or remedial approach to troubled settings, how-

ever necessary and important, offers no practical societal solution to a problem of epidemic dimensions.

I hope the reader is as surprised as I was to discover that there are hardly any descriptions about how people do go about creating settings. We have some anecdotes, descriptions of aspects of the process, and some personal biography giving glimpses of the problem—but nothing resembling good description. It is as if one tried to understand the human adult with little or no knowledge of his development. The situation is worse yet because it is not even recognized as a problem by fields that one would expect to have something to say. For example, at one time I diligently looked through introductory and advanced texts in social psychology but found little, and that was not precious.

This book represents the most conscientious attempt I know to describe the creation of a setting, i.e., the specific experiences that brought the setting into existence, the problems anticipated, the built-in vehicles for recognizing and dealing with problems, the handling of crises, and the relationship of all this to the development of a general theory of setting creation and growth. Chapter 3, "Assumptions and the Creative Process," is alone worth the price of admission, so to speak, because it is such a seminal examination and critique of the verbalized and unverbalized assumptions determining the modal way in which settings arise. When Dr. Goldenberg suggests that the most important goal in the creation of a helping setting is to insure that the staff can change, learn, and grow—*not* to deliver services to a client population—the reader may at first react with surprise and then perhaps decide that such a goal is a virtuous one which is ordinarily taken into account. But Dr. Goldenberg persuasively demonstrates, in fact, that the primary goal is almost always to deliver help and services to "sick people" and that this effectively aborts or prevents necessary change in the helpers.

Candor requires that I tell the reader that my view of the significance of this book may be unduly influenced by personal factors. After all, the author was initially a kind of student of mine, he then became a colleague, he and his wife were married in our home, I tried in various administrative ways to make it possible for him to start the Residential Youth Center, and I am indebted to him for what he taught me about the creation of settings. With this *caveat* I must leave it to the reader to decide whether or not this is as pioneer a work and book as I am certain it is.

Although Dr. Goldenberg created the setting, he obviously did not do it alone. He chose a handful of some of the most remarkable human beings to help him. That they were nonprofessionals is no basis for attributing to them, as is too frequently done, a kind of folk wisdom usually denied to the highly educated and professional individual. They were highly effective individuals who had already demonstrated interpersonal competence, courage, and a disenchantment with established ways of acting. Dr. Goldenberg obviously knows how to select unusual people for unusual functions. Together they sustained one another and still continue to do so years after the venture began—a rather unique situation in this era of organizational craziness.

HU
1437
.N4
663

Acknowledgments

This book is the result of five years of work in the inner city of New Haven, Connecticut—a period of time that saw, among other things, the development of a Residential Youth Center as part of the city's attempt to deal with the problems associated with urban poverty. It tells the story of how a group of people from apparently different backgrounds and styles of life (e.g., professionals and nonprofessionals, blacks and whites, indigenous community people and transient academicians) joined together not only to develop what they believed to be an innovative and assumptions-questioning setting but to face the anxiety that invariably accompanies all creative enterprises. This book, therefore, belongs to many people, none of whose names appear on its cover.

First and foremost, this books belongs to that little band of rebels who comprised the original staff of the Residential Youth Center—specifically, to Wes Forbes, Ed Taylor, Ed Riggott, Bob Kellaher, Marlene Qualls, Leo Sherman, Jerry Jackson, and Sal Barrone. Without them there would have been no book to write because there would have been no story to tell. Thanks are also extended to Warren Kimbro and Ralph Paolillo, who joined the staff during the Center's first hectic year of existence and brought to the setting the kind of personal commitment which, together with the original staff's seemingly limitless energy, did much to increase the Center's chances for success.

Second, it was Seymour B. Sarason, Professor of Psychology and Director of the Yale Psycho-Educational Clinic, who created the conditions—both personal and professional —that made it possible for the author to become involved in what proved to be one of the most important experiences of his life. We are also grateful for the constant support and encouragement given by Murray Levine, Professor of Psychology at the State University of New York at Buffalo, who was Director of the Clinical Training Program at Yale University at the time the Residential Youth Center was being created and written up.

Questions of mutual trust and commitment were always central in the development of the Residential Youth Center. We therefore consider ourselves fortunate in having had Joseph Seiler and Harold Lewack as our "Feds" (Department of Labor Contract Officers), for they shared our dreams and helped turn them into realities.

Third, this book belongs to all the residents of the Center. Often under the most difficult of conditions, they and their families did much to create and maintain the setting during a period of time when its very existence was in doubt. We thank them for joining with us in what can only be called an "experiment in living," an experience from which no one emerged untouched and unchanged.

Finally, this book belongs to my wife, "Big Sue," who wore with such dignity the mantle of problems and pressures that defined our existence during the long months of the Residential Youth Center. Her ability to transform chaos into stability, her commitment to the project, and her unwavering faith that what we were involved in was "right" provided us with a source of strength whose meaning can only dimly be conveyed by words. And in this she was joined by the wives and families of the rest of the staff.

If the Residential Youth Center succeeded in providing the context within which there could develop a new kind of alliance between professionals and nonprofessionals, it also created the conditions under which it became possible (almost imperative) to question and change the nature of traditional student-faculty relationships. The demand characteristics of the Center, coupled with the energy and creativity that graduate and undergraduate students brought to the setting, made it impossible for us to indulge ourselves in, and to perpetuate, many of the self-defeating and archaic irrelevances that often so falsely separate faculty from students. We therefore thank our colleagues (or is it fellow students?) Bob Czeisler, Bob Garofalo, Dave Hoffman, Verne McArthur, Frank Neisser, Andy Schwebel,

Barney Brawer, and Ed Susskind both for what they contributed to the setting and for joining with us to prove that
it is indeed possible for people over and under 30 to
trust one another.

This book, perhaps like many others, was prepared for
publication in a manner that was far more efficient and
orderly than the process through which it was written. For
this and many other things we thank Anita Miller, the
secretary-mother of the Psycho-Educational Clinic. We also
wish to thank Mrs. Pat Cook and Mrs. Gail Brown for helping to review, criticize, correct, and otherwise prepare the
manuscript for publication.

I. Ira Goldenberg
September 1969
New Haven, Connecticut

Prologue

Never write a book about something you love, especially if you are or wish to be recognized as a member of the scientific community. One's perceptions of the love object often tend to be blurred and confused, invaded, so to speak, by the very passions that our scientific traditions have taught us, perhaps all too successfully, to view with more than a little suspicion, if not downright contempt.

The "loved one" in this book is something called the Residential Youth Center (RYC), and for a little while the author's affair with the Center was an all-consuming one. It is almost over now. The author and the RYC have, for the most part, gone their separate ways. This book, then, is as much in the nature of a farewell as it is intended as an introduction. Perhaps most love affairs end that way: old lovers part, first by trying to rekindle the past and then by moving away from it.

Chapter 1   Introduction and Organization

Each venture
Is a new beginning, a raid on the inarticulate
With shabby equipment always deteriorating
In the general mess of imprecision of feeling.
—T. S. Eliot

Each age writes its own epitaph—indeed, creates its own
eternity—with respect to how it conceives of man and how
it conceives of change. Man as the central figure in this
unending drama acts out these conceptions, implements its
attendant ideologies, and creates (or destroys) societies in.
terms of his changing images of himself and others. This is
but another way of saying that history is a series of continuing and vivid examples of the phenomenon that how
one conceives of a problem dictates how one tries to deal
with it. The specific societies that man creates, the means
he chooses to create them, and the ways in which he goes
about changing them are all concrete instances of how conceptions about man determine the form and content of the
societies he builds.

Many of the same things that have been said about the
development of societies could also be said about the development of institutions.[1] Societies are comprised of institutions—large and small, formal and informal—and it is
these institutions which, in their conception and development, both mirror the existing value systems of the society
and provide the foundations for future change. Despite
differences in scope and complexity there are, at least in
principle, great similarities between the attempt to create
a society and the attempt to create an institution. In both
cases we find ourselves confronted with the problem of
understanding the creative process; in both cases there is a

[1]In this chapter, and throughout the rest of this book, we shall use the
terms "institutions," "settings," and "programs" interchangeably. We
realize that these terms are often used to describe different kinds of
settings possessing different traditions, values, and histories. We
shall be employing these terms, however, to depict any formal organization characterized by explicit goals and possessing certain
internal processes and relationships, both ideological and interpersonal, to achieve those goals.

need to explore the relationship between the end product and the "builders'" original goals and aspirations; in both cases we, either as heirs to or as participants in the creative process, must assume the responsibility for defending, changing, or destroying that which we have inherited or wish to bequeath to others. It would not be unfair to state that in the final analysis, man defines himself through the institutions he chooses to allow to be born and to live, and those he decides he must kill or abort.

On September 16, 1966, a new institution was born in New Haven, Connecticut—an institution called the Residential Youth Center. Very little fanfare accompanied the birth of the new setting: ribbon-cutting ceremonies were conspicuous by their absence, and there were no speeches extolling its virtues or praising its yet unproved worth. It was a quiet beginning, almost a simple one, the kind of beginning one might expect for a setting whose very existence was symbolic of the uneasiness with which an apparently affluent society was finally committing itself to dealing with what had for so long been the muted, disorganized, and often-unheard demands of its disenfranchised citizenry . . . its "Other America."

The Residential Youth Center was funded as an experimental and demonstration project by the U.S. Department of Labor (the Office of Manpower Policy, Evaluation, and Research), administered through New Haven's community action agency (Community Progress, Inc.), and run in conjunction with the Psycho-Educational Clinic of Yale University. Its formal goals were both clear and misleadingly simple. They were as follows:

1. To evaluate the degree to which a neighborhood-based Residential Youth Center, developed within a manpower-oriented Community Action Program, could be utilized to facilitate the growth and rehabilitation of economically disadvantaged and/or disrupted adolescents and their families.
2. To explore the clinical and vocational potential of an indigenous nonprofessional staff with respect to their competence in dealing with both the psychological problems

associated with poverty and a population heretofore dealt with exclusively by professional personnel.

3. To explore the relationship between organizational structure and patterns of service, the purpose being to determine the kinds of structural and organizational changes that could facilitate the utilization, training and development of the nonprofessional.

4. To develop criteria by which new and different residential programs could be run more effectively and less expensively than existing programs.

5. To develop a setting in which both professionals and non-professionals could acquire the kind of training that would lead to a better understanding of the problems confronting disadvantaged youth and their families, and of the tools and techniques which might be useful in dealing with these problems.

6. To explore the possibility of establishing a viable and ongoing training, research and service relationship between the United States Department of Labor (Office of Manpower Policy, Evaluation, and Research) and Yale University. [U.S. Department of Labor, 1966; RYC Final Report, 1968]

But the goals of the program notwithstanding, the importance of the Residential Youth Center lies much more in the ideas that shaped it and the people who put it together than in the formal and seemingly explicit purposes for which it was funded. This book is about those ideas and people.

Although the Residential Youth Center formally came into existence on that September day back in 1966, it was neither conceived in a vacuum nor, as it were, "born yesterday." No new program or setting ever is. An institution is born at a particular time and place, but its conception and development are reflections of many things, not the least of which is how men think about and go about creating an institution itself. As soon as one begins to define the problem in this manner, two things become quite clear. The first is that the history of an institution extends much further back in time than we tend to realize. The second is that the development of an institution is, in the truest sense, an experiment in nature, an experiment that provides us with the opportunity of studying more general questions about man and about the ways in which his conceptions of himself and others determine his behavior. This is but another way of saying that one cannot fully understand an institution unless one is prepared to go beyond an assessment of the needs it was created to meet. One must, especially if one wishes to make a contribution to our understanding of the creative process, begin to focus attention on the question of how the institution itself is the product of a complex interaction between the ways in which men define problems and the techniques they devise to implement their solutions. From this point of view the study of institutions becomes a study of ourselves, and the Residential Youth Center is no exception.

Despite the aura of simplicity that surrounded its birth, there was, and continues to be, nothing simple about the Residential Youth Center. The creation of a setting is a complex human process, a process involving motives, values, ideas, and emotions. Unlike other human phenomena, however, it is a process about which we know precious little, for the creation of settings does not appear to be a problem contained in or derivable from existing psychological or social science theory. One who is contemplating the creation of a setting has little to turn to for help or support: there is no organized body of theory, few guidelines, and very little data. It is undoubtedly for this reason that the building of an institution is all too often a process in which the "builders" unwittingly become the prisoners of their own creations—the victims of their own conceptions, choices, and decisions.

This was a very difficult book to write, a book that from the very beginning presented us with great problems in organization. The reasons for these problems were many and varied, but in one way or another they could all be traced both to the difficulties usually associated with the creative process and to the particular problems that came to define what at this point we might call the "Residential Youth Center experience." For purposes of clarity we shall briefly describe these problems before turning our attention to the way in which this book was finally and formally organized.

We might begin by pointing out that this book is in many ways an intensely personal document, a book based on experiences that were extremely important in the personal and professional development of the author. The creation of the Residential Youth Center could not take place in the laboratory nor, for that matter, in any other setting that prides itself on its ability to maximize experimental control while at the same time holding constant or minimizing personal involvement. The Residential Youth Center, as we shall try to indicate throughout this book, was in large measure *built* by personal involvement, and for the author to have acted otherwise would have been to subvert the setting and its people. The Residential Youth Center had to be "lived," and living the RYC experience meant that one was continually confronted with oneself, with one's own values, problems, and emotions. It also meant that when the time finally came to communicate these experiences to others— to the reader, for example—the attempt to do so would inevitably suffer the fate of most deeply personal documents: either it would result in an empty echo of what was once so intensely moving, or it would appear as a splendid exaggeration of what might have been an almost commonplace happening. In either case, the mere fact that we were an intimate part of the very setting we shall be describing made the organization of this book more of a problem than it might have been had we been able (or willing) to assume the stance of the disinterested and uncommitted observer.

The final problem of organization had to do with the complexity of the phenomenon under consideration and the range of relevant material that had to be included if this book was to offer more than a hollow and surface understanding of the Residential Youth Center. The reader will recall that the Residential Youth Center was funded for a number of different reasons and was, therefore, from the very beginning a project with multiple goals. In retrospect, it would not be inaccurate to say that an entire book probably could have been written about any one of these goals, for they all involved variables that were at once both com-

plex and relatively unstudied. Thus, while we have chosen
to use the "creation of a setting" as the central and unify-
ing theme of this book, it should be clear that the development of the Residential Youth Center took place in a
context that provided us with a way of studying not only
ourselves and the creative process but also the variety of
forces, both social and historical, that shaped the experience
and gave it its meaning. Some of these forces and problems have already been mentioned in the brief listing of the
program's "formal" goals. They included such problems
as poverty and its effects (especially its psychological effects)
on the lives of inner-city youth and their families; the War
on Poverty and the role of that new mental health warrior
called the "indigenous nonprofessional"; the problem of
organizational structure and its implications for such issues
as the development of innovative services, human growth,
and the health and effectiveness of a setting; the relationship of research to the study and understanding of highly
volatile rehabilitative and action-oriented programs; and
the role of the helping professions in a society undergoing
acute social change. The story of the Residential Youth
Center could not be told unless attention was focused on
each of these problems, for they all, independently and in
interaction with one another, had an enormous impact on
the eventual development of the setting. Consequently, after
some deliberation it was decided that a *narrative approach
to the creation of the Residential Youth Center* would
afford us the kind of freedom and flexibility within which
we could deal with each of these problems both individually
and in terms of their relation to the development of the
setting as a whole. Having said this we shall now describe
the sequence in which our chapters have been organized.

The purpose of Chapter 2 is twofold: to place the Residential Youth Center in some historical perspective, and
to describe the variety of forces whose own histories coa-
lesced to form the ground out of which the RYC emerged.
Chapter 2 begins in very much the same way that
the RYC actually began, with a retelling of the events

of a trip that took a group of people from New Haven, Connecticut, to a Job Corps camp located atop a lonely mountain in Maryland. The trip took place in 1965, a year that will forever be remembered as the time that the programs and ideas, the *promise* of the New Frontier reached its zenith. The importance of that year is discussed at length, for it was a time when the War on Poverty and many of its constituent programs became a reality. Two of these programs, the Community Action Program and the Job Corps, played a crucial role in the eventual decision to develop the Residential Youth Center. Special attention, therefore, is focused on New Haven's Community Action Program (an agency called Community Progress, Inc.) from the point of view of how its own development made it possible for people with seemingly different backgrounds, experiences, and interests (e.g., professionals and nonprofessionals) to meet, begin to work together, and finally get to know and trust one another. The specific program that brought this about was the Neighborhood Youth Corps (in 1965 it was known as the CPI Work Crew Program), and it, too, is described in some detail. The remainder of the chapter is devoted to a discussion of the events that precipitated the trip, and the ways in which our experiences at a rural Job Corps camp formed the basis for the decision to develop the Residential Youth Center.

Chapter 3 can be considered, in the broadest sense, the book's "conceptual" chapter. In it we attempt to develop a framework for describing and understanding the process by which "helping settings" (i.e., settings devoted to facilitating human growth, development, or rehabilitation) are created. Specifically, the chapter deals with the assumptions and decisions that characterize the creative process, and wherever possible the particular assumptions under consideration are highlighted by the inclusion of specific examples taken from our experiences in the New Haven public schools, the Community Action Program, and the Regional Centers for the Mentally Retarded. The chapter's major thesis is that each decision in the creative process is predicated upon certain assumptions, and that the more aware we become of these assumptions (and their consequences), the more likely we are to be able to control for much of the irrationality and self-defeating behavior that plagues, and eventually undermines, so many programs dedicated to human "renewal." The description of the creative process begins with an analysis of the assumptions under which the decision is made to start a new program; it proceeds by explicating the conceptions underlying a program's choice of its staff, "treatment model," training paradigm, and social structure; and it ends by examining the assumptions under which a new program or institution defines itself both as an organization and in terms of its relationship to the community. In many important ways the manner in which the Residential Youth Center eventually developed was influenced greatly by our analysis of these assumptions; and, by way of introduction, we might point out that the RYC's development was in no small measure predicated both on a rejection of many traditional assumptions and on the attempt to develop alternative ones.

Chapters 4 and 5 are devoted to describing the Residential Youth Center and the people, programs, and ideas that shaped the setting and gave it its form and content. In Chapter 4 we discuss the setting in terms of its organizational structure, the way its staff was selected, the kinds of "clients" it served, and the manner in which its program was developed and defined. The chapter begins with an analysis of the state of the RYC's "mother organization" (Community Progress, Inc.) in 1966. The purpose of this analysis is twofold: first, to provide the reader with an acute understanding of the conditions surrounding the development of the Residential Youth Center; and second, to make clear, if only by comparison, the conceptual differences between the RYC and other action-oriented helping settings. We turn then to the question of its own social structure; the RYC is described as a "horizontal" setting, a conception of organization in which there is a significant alteration in the status, power, role, and decision-making responsibilities that usually define the relationships between people in a given setting. The RYC's horizontal structure represents an attempt to create the organizational conditions under which people can learn to share one another's problems and functions in an atmosphere of mutual trust and collective growth and not, as is so often the case, in a setting that views its staff as "replaceable" rather than "interchangeable." For purposes of illustration, the RYC's horizontal structure is described in some detail, and its ideas concerning the sharing of clinical, administrative, and programming responsibilities are compared and contrasted with the usual conceptions underlying most "pyramidally" structured settings. The remainder of the chapter describes the staff of the Residential Youth Center and the criteria by which they were selected; offers a picture of the youth and families that were to be served by the project; and discusses the general characteristics of the program itself.

In Chapter 5 we deal with the general question of training—its goals and processes—and with the particular pre-service and in-service training methods developed at the Residential Youth Center to provide the organization and its staff with a way of dealing with the problems that the setting would inevitably pose. The type of training utilized at the RYC was "sensitivity training," and the rationale behind its use is discussed at some length. The areas of concern for which this method of training was developed went far beyond the "usual" kinds of problems dealt with by T-group or T-group-inspired types of guided group interactions, and because of this the RYC's training paradigm is compared and contrasted with the T-group approach to laboratory education. At the Residential Youth Center, sensitivity training was initiated to meet a variety of different needs. These included the need to develop a vehicle for dealing with organizational and interpersonal problems; the need for clinical training; the need to develop a stable self-corrective and self-reflective mechanism for the setting as a whole; the need to handle problems of decision-making and growth; and the need to develop a system of feedback and research. The kinds of sensitivity training sessions held at the RYC varied both over time and as a function of the particular problems confronting the staff. In general, however, they fell broadly within what might be called three contexts: the "individual," the "interpersonal," and the "group." The chapter concludes with examples of each of these three types of sensitivity training sessions. The examples are taken from the verbatim transcripts of RYC sensitivity sessions and are included so that the reader will have a better understanding of the kinds of issues the staff was called upon to deal with, and the ways in which the sensitivity sessions were used to handle the very real and pressing problems of the setting and its people.

In Chapter 6 we turn our attention to the problems and issues a new program must deal with *before* the day arrives that it finally becomes a physical reality. In describing what might be called the RYC's "prehistory"—in detailing the variety of activities that became a part of that crucial period of time devoted to "community preparation and penetration"—our purpose is twofold: first, to dispel the myth that an institution is born on the day it opens its doors and starts "doing business"; and second, to indicate as clearly as possible the degree to which the eventual fate of the RYC may have been decided during the days and weeks that preceded its formal opening. Most of the "data" for this chapter are taken from a diary that the RYC's first Director kept during the period of time that he was a full-time member of the staff. It details the varying degrees of success (and failure) with which the Residential Youth Center was able to develop significant relationships with those segments of the community whose help and involvement were crucial to the future "health" and effectiveness of the new setting. The community groups involved included the residents living in the neighborhood where it was hoped the RYC might be located, the police, the mental health professions, and those low-income people who, because of the concept of "maximum feasible participation," found themselves to be members of what were called Resident Advisory Committees. In addition to a description of the nature of these early relationships with different community groups, special attention is focused on the ways in which the RYC's staff defined and implemented its thinking with respect to the involvement of its own potential clients in the development of the program. Briefly, this "involvement" consisted of two things: the continual sharing by the staff of the program's problems and "preoperational crises" with its clients, and the attempt to enlist client support in the resolution of these problems. In time this led to a major reconceptualization of the setting's basic orientation: the RYC became a "self-help" program. The chapter concludes by detailing the special problems that confronted the RYC by virtue of its being an integral part, both administratively and financially, of New Haven's community action agency. Such issues as autonomy and independence, on the one hand, and ac-commodation and coordination, on the other, are discussed from the point of view of how a new setting must, if it is to avoid being perceived as an internal threat to an al-ready established program, deal with the problem of its relationship to its "mother" organization.

Chapter 7 is perhaps the most "personal" of the book's chapters, for it tells, once again in diary form, the story of the Residential Youth Center from its chaotic opening days to the time some two weeks later when it began to look as if the setting would survive. The opening days of the Center were indeed days of stress and trial, and they are described as one of the RYC's staff members (its Director) experienced them. No attempt is made to "pretty up" the story, nor have the data been expurgated for purposes of publication. The diary presents, as concretely and honestly as possible, the Director's perception of and reaction to the range of problems that beset the setting and endangered its existence during those early crisis-filled days. Most of the problems described were "internally generated," that is to say, indigenous to the setting and its people. Some, however, were either created or exacerbated by the pres-sures and tensions that arose between the Residential Youth

Center and the larger organization (the community action agency) of which it was a part and to which it was "answerable." Following the diary, the remainder of the chapter is devoted to an analysis of some of the pressures and problems that defined the RYC's opening days. These problems are discussed in essay form, the purpose being to try to use the early experiences of the RYC as the basis for a preliminary exploration of such issues as the role of the clinician in the world of community action, the problem of leadership in helping settings, and the effect of established organizations (and their bureaucracies) on the development of new and potentially innovative programs.

Unlike many War on Poverty programs, the Residential Youth Center was funded as a research project. This meant that the question of assessment was, from the very beginning, of central concern to the program. In Chapters 8 and 9 we present some of the research that was carried out at the RYC during the first two years of its existence. Chapter 8 begins with a brief discussion of the problems associated with the attempt to evaluate highly volatile and complex settings—settings like the RYC, in which the criteria usually employed to define scientific "rigor" (e.g., control, replication) are either difficult (if not impossible) to apply or inappropriate as a means of understanding the phenomena under consideration. Following this discussion, the remainder of the chapter is devoted to the description of "a day in the life of an RYC worker," an observational record (not too dissimilar from the kind utilized by Barker [1951] in his book *One Boy's Day*) that attempts to make explicit the "blood and guts" of the RYC operation. Our reasons for wanting to present this chronicle were many and varied. Primarily, however, it is included not only because it provides the reader with an additional perspective from which to view the program, but because of what it says about the importance of observational records as a way of understanding settings that are less than perfect candidates for assessment by our more "accepted" empirical techniques. The chronicle itself follows an RYC worker from the time he enters the Center in the morning to the time he goes home at night. It records, as faithfully as possible, everything he did and said during the course of one working day.

In Chapter 9 we turn our attention to some of the results of the Residential Youth Center program with respect to the clients it served, particularly those youngsters who lived in and became a part of the setting. When the RYC first opened its doors, it took into residence 20 New Haven youngsters independently judged to have the greatest number of problems and the longest histories of social, vocational, educational, and personal failure. An additional 20 boys with similar problems were placed in a control group. Both groups were tested, assessed, and interviewed on a host of variables involving both behavioral (e.g., work attendance, difficulties with the police) and attitudinal (e.g., feelings of alienation, trust) functioning. Retesting of both groups was done between 6 and 12 months after the program began. Although the test-retest analyses indicated that participation in the program was highly correlated with a marked improvement in almost all the areas utilized for purposes of comparing the two groups, the results (and the limitations of the data) are discussed from the point of view of their implications, both methodologically and conceptually, for the application of research techniques to the study of action-oriented settings.

Chapter 10 is the book's "reflective" chapter, the chapter in which we look back over the RYC experience from a point in time when, for all intents and purposes, our own involvement in the setting had ceased; ceased, that is, being in the nature of a full-time commitment. The chapter focuses on two issues: first, the problems that have remained essentially unresolved even after the setting has emerged from its infancy and entered into the phase of its life when it has begun to be referred to as a "going concern"; and second, the implications of the program with respect to the broader question of institutional change. In terms of its unresolved problems, attention is once more directed toward the concept of "horizontality," this time however, from the point of view of how well (or poorly) it served the setting and its people. Similarly, the advantages and disadvantages of sensitivity training are discussed at some length. With respect to the question of institutional change, attention is focused on the potential of a setting such as the RYC to serve as a vehicle for altering the ways in which people (and professions) think about the problems associated with human renewal. This "potential" (or the lack thereof) is discussed not only with reference to the RYC's impact on conditions that define the quality of life locally (e.g., among the agencies that serve the people of New Haven), but in terms of its effects on the plans and policies of agencies whose power and influence extends far beyond the local level. The chapter concludes with a brief overview of the War on Poverty and the problems and conflicts that have defined its short life and now threaten its very existence.

It is in the book's last chapter, Chapter 11, that we finally come full circle, that we return once more to the journey that precipitated the development of the Residential Youth Center. This time, however, the journey is viewed in the context of its meaning for the helping professions as a whole, and for the continuing development of clinical psychology in particular. The chapter's central thesis is a relatively simple one: that professions, no less than individuals, are shaped by the same profound tendencies of history that mold the societies of which they are a part; that their orientations and practices are more often than not a reflection of the prevailing values and attitudes of the greater society in which they are embedded; and that they change as the needs of their societies change and accept as inevitable that through this process of change they continually will be defining and redefining themselves. In short, it was no accident that a clinical psychologist was one of the people who journeyed to that mountain in Maryland. Neither was it merely by chance that he became involved in the development of the Residential Youth Center. Therefore, his behavior is reviewed, this time, however, from the point of view of the developmental history of clinical psychology. The book concludes by pointing out the degree to which the present and future relevance of the helping professions, no differently than that of our society itself, is contingent upon an appreciation of the dynamics of change.

As indicated earlier, this book begins and ends with a trip, a trip that for many of us was no less exciting, disturbing, or personally meaningful than those currently being taken by so many of our alienated youth. The trip that began the story of the Residential Youth Center took place in the Fall of 1965, and it is with the events of this trip that the next chapter begins.

Chapter 2   The Trip

Gonn'a build a mountain, from a little hill
Gonn'a build a mountain, least I hope I will
Gonn'a build a mountain, gonna build it high
I don't know how I'm gonn'a do it, only know I'm gonn'a try.
—From the show *Stop The World I Want To Get Off*

It all began in the rain.

The rain started early that afternoon and some of the people riding in the station wagon had been lulled to sleep by the gentle surge of rain and road. But not the driver of the car. He was a man with a personal mission: come hell or high water he was going to cover the 120-odd miles between the Delaware Memorial Bridge and New York in under two hours. The miles along the New Jersey Turnpike flew by, and those of us who had not succumbed to sleep sat huddled in the car and began to reflect upon our experiences of the past few days.

We were now returning from a journey   en us from New Haven, Connecticut, to the top of a mountain in Maryland, where we had spent two days visiting a rural Job Corps Center. The visit was not in the nature of a pleasure trip (although there were many happy moments along the way), but was undertaken in order to find out what was happening to several of the youngsters with whom we had worked and who recently had left us to join the Job Corps. Because many of the things we saw and many of the people we met at this Job Corps camp had a great influence on the eventual development of the Residential Youth Center, it is important that we back   bit and describe who we were and how we had   gether to make this trip in the first place.

The New Frontier and the War on Poverty

The year was 1965, and it was a time when America was forcing itself to look inward toward its own problems, its own people, and its own institutions. The New Frontier, although born out of neither innocence nor empty idealism, was capturing the young and recapturing the old and providing both with a renewed sense of history. A country was stirring, beginning to move, and reawakening in its citizens those feelings of commitment and action that in preceding years had either lain dormant because of fear or been channeled into the frantic quest for security, sameness, or personal oblivion. But more than anything else there was a climate of hope, a feeling of identity, and a belief that man could again begin to control his own destiny and create a society that was more rational, liberating, and worthy of its people.

It was out of this climate of hope that the War on Poverty was born, and it was the War on Poverty that brought us all together on that trip. The War on Poverty was then (and may still be) a comprehensive attempt to marshal the human and material resources of a society to break the chain of hopelessness and helplessness that encapsulat   ny of its people. Because of the complexity of the problem and because the cycle of poverty involves the very young as well as the very old, the War on Poverty led to the development of a broad spectrum of programs, each one designed as a specific intervention to meet the needs of a particular group of people. For the very young there are child development centers, Headstart, and other preschool programs; for the adolescents there are Neighborhood Youth Corps, Job Corps, and other vocational training and remedial education programs; for the adults there are work training, retraining, and educational programs; and for the aged there are senior citizens' activities and a variety of part-time vocational placement programs. It was realized quite early that the development and administration of this vast complex of programs would necessitate a certain degree of local autonomy, since communities would vary with respect to both their specific needs and the availability of local resources. Consequently, the Office of Economic Opportunity (the central administrative agency in Washington) acted in concert with other federal and private agencies (e.g., the Department of Labor; the Department of Health, Education and Welfare; the

Ford Foundation) to authorize the establishment of local community action agencies to implement its general programs and to develop new ones.

Community Progress, Incorporated

New Haven's community action agency is called Community Progress, Incorporated (CPI); it was this organization which provided the setting in which those of us who eventually journeyed to the mountain in Maryland could meet, get to know one another, and begin to work together. We shall have much more to say about CPI as an organization (especially with respect to the development of the Residential Youth Center) in succeeding chapters, but for the present it is important to note that CPI, acting as an agency to fulfill the needs of New Haven's poor, also served as the vehicle by which a host of people working for the organization could themselves begin to feel fulfilled.

All of us riding in the car that day were, in one way or another, connected with CPI. Of the six of us, five were work crew foremen in CPI's Neighborhood Youth Corps program and one was a psychological consultant to the program. All of us had come to CPI from what would seem to be very different backgrounds and with very different experiences. Five of us were so-called nonprofessionals who, prior to becoming work crew foremen, had been employed variously as factory workers, an X-ray technician, a truck driver, a bank teller, and a singer with a local rock-and-roll group. One was a so-called professional who was on the faculty of Yale University and worked as a clinical psychologist at the Yale Psycho-Educational Clinic. Given only this information it would be far easier for one to dwell on the differences that separated us than to focus on the ideas and feelings that brought us together; for despite the differences in our origins we shared certain ideas and feelings as to where we were and where we wanted to go. As a group we were bound much more by the present and the future than by the past.

For all of us the present was the CPI Work Crew (Neighborhood Youth Corps) Program, and for some of us the future was to become the Residential Youth Center; and since it was the CPI Work Crew Program that brought us together initially, it is important that we describe it briefly at this point.

The CPI Work Crew Program is a prevocational training and remedial education experience for adolescents (between the ages of 16 and 21) who, for one reason or another, are both out of school and out of work. Whereas CPI's overall programs sought to break into and alter the cycle of poverty at many different levels, the work crew program was designed primarily to meet the needs of those adolescents who were the "heirs" to and the potential perpetuators of the previous generations' experience of vocational and educational deprivation (Sarason et al., 1966). When a youngster was placed on a work crew it was not only because he was unemployed but because he was, at least at that time, essentially "unemployable." And by "unemployable" we are not referring merely to the fact that he may not have had a marketable skill; we are referring to the fact that the youngster's attitudes toward himself and others, his feelings about himself in relation to the world, his conception of his own worth as a human being were such as to render him essentially unemployable. He was, in short, socially and psychologically unprepared to enter into, become a part of, and succeed in, the world of work. Within this framework, then, the work crew program could be described more accurately as a therapeutic experience in living—an experience that utilized the world of work as a therapeutic lever to alter, influence, and redirect styles of life that poverty and despair had already warped and misshaped. Consequently, when a youngster was graduated from a work crew and was successfully placed in a training or vocational setting, he actually had graduated from a position on the social and psychological periphery of life to a position more centrally located in the mainstream of a changing society.

A work crew is composed of from five to seven youngsters

and one work crew foreman. At the time the program was initiated, each youngster was paid 20 dollars per week for his participation on a work crew. The program consisted of 20 hours of work plus 8 1/2 hours of remedial education each week. Each crew has its own work site among any one of a number of settings in which the boys and girls are engaged in projects for a variety of public agencies. Each work crew has a particular job as its responsibility, such as painting, the care of greens, mechanics, carpentry.

The essential person in the work crew program is the foreman or forelady. These are indigenous, so-called non-professional workers—people who, for the most part, were either born and raised in, or have a personal knowledge and awareness of, the traditions, language, and problems of the inner city. Although his focus usually remained on the vocational setting, the work crew foreman—because of the nature and content of his involvement with the youngster—was often thrust into roles more aptly described by the terms "therapist," "father," "mother," "counselor," "teacher," "big brother," and "friend." The foremen and foreladies are, for the most part, mature, committed men and women who trust and respect the youngsters, who understand and have experienced their concerns, and who are, in their interactions with the boys and girls, relatively free of the usual stereotypes held about "dropouts." The youngsters, in turn, find it very difficult to perceive and react to the foremen and foreladies as "headshrinkers," "copouts," "Uncle Toms," or "sellouts" to the existing establishment. Needless to say, the positive changes that so often occurred in a youngster were more a function of his relationship with his foreman than of anything else (Goldenberg, 1967).

The work crew program had existed for some time before the advent of the Job Corps. It was and still is one of the most successful programs administered through CPI. The reason for its success rests almost completely on the nature, intensity, and duration of those particularly delicate relationships that foremen and foreladies are able to establish with many of the youngsters on their work crews.

And it was in great measure because of the enduring quality of these relationships that those of us who were now returning from that mountain in Maryland had undertaken the trip in the first place.

The Job Corps

The trip actually began—although we did not know it at the time—when the Job Corps ceased being an idea and became a reality. It is difficult even now, scarcely five years later, to recall and describe accurately the atmosphere that accompanied the arrival of the Job Corps. To call it one of frenzied reawakening probably would be erroneous, because it would both overestimate the historical impact of the program and understate the feelings that it liberated. Nevertheless, those are the only words that even faintly begin to describe what those of us in New Haven felt when we first learned of the birth of the Job Corps, or later experienced when we finally understood the full impact of the program. To some degree, frenzied reawakenings were the order of the day—and the Job Corps was no exception.

The birth of the Job Corps came as a signal that suddenly linked two generations of Americans. For those of us too young to remember the dust bowls and Hoovervilles and CCC Camps of the 1930s, the Job Corps became a tie with the past. It was a time when the long-dormant voices of Woody Gurthrie and Cisco Houston once again rose up, swept across the years and the miles, and spoke to a new generation of Americans. Only now their voices were translated into the idiom and style of the 1960s, for it was a time when the voices of the Motown Sound, Murray the K, and James Brown joined with those of Hubert Humphrey and R. Sargent Shriver in a chorus of "You're What's Happening, Baby," each singing in his own key and to his own audience but all combining on the same basic theme of Right Now, the future . . . and hope. At long last, Michael Harrington's youthful "Other Americans" were going to camp. Only now it would not be because of the well-intentioned noblesse oblige of some Fresh Air Fund, but because the United States government had committed itself to and was making a vast investment in its young people.

Job Corps came into New Haven with little advance notice, much like a child born before full term. Its needs had to be met quickly, and there was precious little time for adequate preparation. CPI, finding itself caught almost unaware by the premature birth of the Job Corps, rapidly shifted gears and nobly set itself to the task of meeting its responsibilities to the new program. There then followed a frenzy of activity that would leave an onlooker, much less a participant, breathless and exhausted. The next few days saw more than 100 potential Job Corps enrollees processed for the initial 20 openings that had been earmarked for New Haven. Processing any one youngster involved interviewing him; testing him; getting him to take a complete physical examination; dickering with his corrections officer if he was on probation, or bargaining with the police in case he had a previous record; getting his parents or guardian to sign a consent form; and finally, screening him before a makeshift board of CPI personnel. We can only leave it to the reader's imagination to conjure up a picture of the effort required to process more than 100 applicants.

Needless to say, the conditions created by the requirements of the situation brought with them the guarantee that many youngsters would be bitterly disappointed and that their foremen and other CPI employees would share in their grief. Now, some years later, one of the people who took part in those days of turmoil could look back and say:

It was a madhouse. It was like they say, a typical federal program moves in. Congress voted the Job Corps its money and it had to be used before the end of the fiscal year.

I was appalled by the amount of stuff that had to get done in a short period of time. It was like someone on topside saying: "If I had had a chance to tell you a couple of months ago it would have been that we wanted the program to start tomorrow."

At the time, although we were acutely aware of our

mixed feelings with respect to the lack of preparation and communication that surrounded the advent of the Job Corps, most of us went about our task of processing youngsters with the same missionary zeal that had come to be accepted as the order of the day. Regardless of the difficulties and the momentary panic, we saw ourselves as part of a great human adventure; and it was that experience, more than anything else, that guided our actions and gave us comfort.

It finally ended. Those of us who were not too fatigued went down to the ceremonies in which the 20 youngsters who had finally been selected for the program were formally inducted into the Job Corps. The swearing-in ceremony took place at CPI's central office, and many of the youngsters' parents and foremen looked on as New Haven's first contingent of Job Corpsmen solemnly lifted their right hands, repeated the words of the Job Corps oath, and prepared to leave New Haven for their assigned camps. The youngsters left amid a host of good wishes, farewells, and not a few silent tears. It was over—or so we thought—and some of CPI's staff went out for a well-deserved drink . . . or should have.

But it wasn't over; in fact, it was just beginning. The relationships that many of the foremen had so painstakingly established with their youngsters would not allow them to adopt the position that "out of sight" meant "out of mind." Although the youngsters had left New Haven and were now scattered in camps all over the country, they and the foremen continued to communicate with one another. Letters started coming in to foremen, and the foremen, in turn, answered the letters and kept their youngsters apprised of what was happening in New Haven. At first the letters were filled with only slightly disguised wonder and awe—the kind of wonder that only a youngster who has never been very far from New Haven can experience when first confronted with a country that now seems infinite and really does not end in New York or Hartford, and the special awe that only a boy from an overcrowded and underfed family can feel when food is free and plentiful and when living space becomes his ally and not his arch-enemy.[1] These were letters of hope, of a new beginning and a different future.

But after a while the letters changed. They came less often, and the feelings they communicated were quite different. They became letters of discontent and disillusion; the boys spoke of missing New Haven, of feeling "conned," or of feeling lonely and isolated in an alien land. At first most of us reacted to the letters as "natural." The initial feelings of euphoria and excitement were over and we saw the boys as now having to deal with the inevitable problems of homesickness, separation, and the new demands that were being made of them in their new settings. The foremen tried to make this clear to their youngsters, and their letters began to urge them to "stick it out," "settle down," and "get on with the work at hand." In some cases the advice was taken, and with rather happy consequences. But in too many other instances the situation did not get better with the passage of time; it got worse. Finally, one youngster and then a second returned to New Haven and made it quite clear that they had no intentions of ever going back to their respective camps.

Those of us who had worked with the youngsters and were now following the situation were frankly perplexed and not a little curious as to what was really going on. The boys spoke of fights, military rule, and the disparity between the kinds of vocational skills they had been led to believe they would be learning and the training they were actually receiving. They also talked a great deal about the kinds of people who were working with them and of the negative feelings toward them both from people employed at the camps and from those living in the sur-

[1] In a 1965 speech to a group of returned Peace Corps volunteers, R. Sargent Shriver recalled his experiences at a Job Corps camp in the following way: "I saw young men up there who had never slept in their own bed in their entire lives. And when they were ushered into a little room and a bed was pointed out to them and we said, 'That's your bed,' a lot of them said, 'You mean that I'm going to be able to sleep in that bed by myself, that's my bed and nobody else's bed?' " (Fox, Nicolau, and Wofford, 1965, p. 40)

rounding towns. Despite the vivid—often lurid—descriptions that we were given by the youngsters, most of us felt that they were either overreacting to the situation or purposefully painting a picture so dismal and foreboding as to justify their own failure to perform once the initial excitement had died down and the going got a little rough. This is not to imply that we completely discounted what we were being told, for we believed that the truth lay somewhere between the extremes of joy and despair that had been communicated to us through the boys' letters and their narratives.

There seemed to be only one way of finding out what was really going on, and that would involve getting some firsthand knowledge and experience in the Job Corps setting. Most CPI foremen are not passive people. If there is a problem "out there," then "out there" is where it should be confronted. The trip was planned and undertaken as a sort of modern sequel to an ancient legend: the Job Corps camp where we wanted to go was located on a mountain and, since the mountain would not come to the foremen, the foremen would go to the mountain. In this case, the mountain stood somewhere in Maryland.

The Trip and Its Consequences
The journey began in an atmosphere of expectation—even adventure—and, perhaps in keeping with the spirit of adventure, we got lost several times along the way. What should have been a 7-hour trip took us almost 12 hours, and we arrived at the Job Corps Center late at night, very tired. Although we could not see very much, we had begun to "sense" the mountain's presence on the last few miles of our trip, for the road began winding ever upward, it got colder, and the air seemed to become cleaner and crisper. In the morning we would see the campsite and find that it fell well within the description given of rural camps by a resident counselor from a different Job Corps Center in another part of the country:
. . . a series of old, renovated, and new prefabricated

buildings huddled together on a lonely mountain side, a wooded forest or on the wind-blown, sandy wastes of Cape Cod, Massachusetts. [Germano, 1967, p. 8]

Despite the lateness of the hour, one of the camp's staff members was still awake; we found him sitting hunched over, talking quietly to a youngster who was lying on a cot that had been placed in the counselor's room. After acknowledging our presence and introducing us to the young Corpsman, he asked us to wait outside. A few minutes later he emerged from his room and joined us in the hallway. This was our first encounter with a man whose feelings, ideas, hopes, and resentments were, in the long run, to prove so consequential in the eventual development of the Residential Youth Center. It is for this reason that it remains so firmly fixed in memory.

The remainder of the night was spent in talking with (mostly listening to) this resident counselor. He began by explaining to us why he had placed the extra cot in his room and why the youngster was there. The young Corpsman, it seems, was having a rather difficult time adjusting to the camp situation. He was an effeminate-looking boy from the hills of Mississippi, and some of the other youngsters had begun taunting and teasing him. Since this had happened late at night, and because the counselor did not feel that the situation could be used as a stimulus for group discussion, he had decided to let the boy sleep on a cot in his room. This was what the counselor was explaining to the boy when we had first walked into his room.

The counselor used this incident as a way of beginning an extended monologue that kept our attention until dawn broke a few hours later. He was a big man with sad eyes, a tired face, and the hint of what would soon become a roll of excess weight around his belly. He had a manner of talking that made us feel as if we had known him for many years, as if the present discussion had started a long time ago and could easily be picked up at some point in the future. He was humorous, hopeful, bitter, and totally committed to the concept and ideals of the

Job Corps. But what was most impressive was his honesty and candor; he "told it like it was." He spoke at great length about the five youngsters from New Haven whom we had come down to see and about the Job Corps in general. Because of the overwhelming impression that he made on us personally, we all silently decided during the course of our conversation that we were listening to a man eminently qualified to be talking about our boys and the Job Corps, a man to be taken seriously, to be heeded, and to be leveled with. He spoke to us as though we were there to help, as friends of the Job Corps, not as its enemies. As the hours passed we found out a great deal about this man, and what we learned only increased our feeling that we were listening to an "expert" in the field. He had graduated from a Negro college in the South, had toured the country as a member of the Globetrotters basketball team, and had worked for several years as a street-gang counselor in the slums of Washington. He lived with his wife and children in Washington during the time that he was able to get away from the camp. His knowledge of the problems of adolescence and poverty was great, and his discussion of "our five boys from New Haven" was filled with such a sensitive awareness of the feelings they were experiencing that we could hardly accept the fact that he had known them only for a few weeks.

He spoke of the problems he was having at the camp and of those that were, or would soon be, confronting the Job Corps in general. He himself had been caught up in the frenzy with which the program was started, and he felt that the camp had been opened prematurely and with precious little foresight. He was deeply concerned with the nature and content of the terribly insufficient pre-service and in-service staff training. He questioned the wisdom of the way the staff had been selected and the manner in which the camp had been both structurally and functionally organized. He was especially bitter about the ways in which youngsters were being prepared for their entry into the Job Corps and had grave doubts regarding the wisdom

that lay behind transporting them so quickly, and with
so little regard for the psychological problems associated
with transition, from one part of the country to another,
or from one kind of setting (i.e., urban) to another
(i.e., rural). He had already experienced some of the racial
and social difficulties that were directly related to having
the camp located near a community which had had little
or no prior contact with Negro youngsters and even
less preparation for such contact. He felt that with the
passage of time the situation would get even worse. He spoke
at great length about the problem of developing relevant
skill-training experiences, the problems of staff communication, and the problems surrounding the development of an
appropriate remedial education experience. The longer
he spoke, the more we began to sense that we were listening to a man whose personal and intellectual commitment to
the goals of the Job Corps were unassailable, and yet a
man who was experiencing an almost unbearable feeling of
powerlessness regarding his ability to effect any meaningful
change in the program. He was another nonprofessional,
verbally honored for his supposed "indigenousness" and
"earthiness" but quite ignored when it came to matters of
policy-formation and decision-making: much like a child,
he was supposed to be seen but not heard . . . and
certainly not heeded.

He was still talking when the sun's first rays broke across
the room and signaled the start of another day. Although
he had stayed awake all night, the resident counselor
seemed quite prepared to start a new day. His energy and
enthusiasm were infectious; the rest of us suddenly found
ourselves no longer tired, almost as though we were
responding to a challenge that had been thrown our way.
We poured out of the room and prepared to meet the
youngsters whom we had come to see.

If a mountain ever needs a time to show itself off and to
enchant its guests, it should always choose the dawn.
No mountain should be without one. We emerged from the
barracks and were immediately enveloped by all the things

we could not see the previous evening. The camp itself was, as they say, "nothing to write home about," but the impact of the setting as a whole was spectacular. The contrast between the stark simplicity of the barracks and the natural richness of the surroundings did little to detract from the overall effect of the situation. It was beautiful—stunningly so—and "clean" as only a mountain setting can be.

The counselor led us to the barracks that housed our boys. The reunions took place: at first timidly, but soon with more and more abandon, and it was very hard to tell whether the foremen were happier to see the boys or vice versa. In a little while the initial greetings were at an end, several of the foremen and youngsters who had been wrestling picked themselves up off the floor, and we all went to the mess hall for breakfast.[2] After breakfast the youngsters showed us around the camp and we were able to remain with them for the better part of the day. During the tour they pointed with pride to the isometrics and weightlifting gym that they had built and to the many physical improvements in the camp that they were working on.

A day in the life of a Corpsman at a rural center is a complex and relatively scheduled affair; and since, as we shall later indicate, we happened to be at this particular camp on a very atypical day, it is important that we provide the reader with a brief description of a more-or-less routine day. The account that follows (Germano, 1967, pp. 5–8) is once more taken from a rural Job Corps camp set in a different part of the country, but our own observations would indicate that the day described would be essentially the same in the camp we were visiting.

The day at a rural Job Corps Center begins haltingly

[2]The food served at breakfast—and this was true of all the meals we ate at the Center—was superb. It was available in abundance and tastefully prepared by the Corpsmen and their supervisors. One of the men in our party was so impressed with both the quality and quantity of food that he remarked that it was the first time in his life that he could enjoy the luxury of guiltlessly eating only the yolks of the eggs and discarding the whites.

at 6:30 a.m., when the sleeping Corpsmen are awakened by a sleepy Corpsman Supervisor (Dorm Supervisor). The Corpsmen, with some variations from center to center, live in semi-barracks set-ups. At Camp W there are six barracks; each holds between 16 and 18 Corpsmen. A Corpsman sleeps in a bed which closely resembles a hospital bed. Each barrack has about four showers and the same number of washbowls and toilets. The dorm supervisor, or resident youth worker, as he is formally titled, may range from the age of a 23-year-old college graduate to a 45-year-old retired army sergeant. In general, his duties are to keep order in the dormitory, supervise Corpsmen in the maintenance of the dormitory, and to give the Corpsmen informal but special counselling. For the most part, he also supervises and takes part in all Corpsmen activities after working hours through to "lights out".

Breakfast is served from 7:00 to about 7:30. Breakfast and all the other meals are prepared by professional chefs with the able assistance of those Corpsmen who are serving as cook-trainees. It should be noted, with much chagrin on the part of the Corpsmen, that Corpsmen are responsible for the maintenance of the mess or dining hall. This means "K.P." for all Corpsmen on a rotating basis.

From 7:30 to 8:00 a Corpsman will complete his daily grooming, and if it is his turn, take part in the cleaning of the dormitory. At 8:00 the Corpsman reports for work or school. School begins with a brief assembly, which consists of either a discussion period or a brief educational film. The Corpsmen then go to reading or math rooms. In some camps the Corpsmen will spend a day in school and a day at work. In other camps, he will spend the morning in school and the afternoon at work. Most of the work done in school, reading and math, the Corpsman does by himself with the use of programmed reading and math materials. A teacher is always near at hand to help him over some rough spots he does not understand.

The work projects which the Corpsmen must attend and whose object it is to improve the camp or the conservation project of the Federal Government (while at the same time give the Corpsmen good work experience and good work habits), fall into a number of categories. Work projects do not vary that much from camp to camp. The average camp will have two conservation projects in the works; a vehicle maintenance shop, which struggles to keep ancient trucks and cars on the road (this is a poverty program); and a carpentry shop which on its own, or assisted by private contractors, attends to and adds to the camp maintenance. The combination work-school day begins at 8:00 and ends at 5:00, with an hour off for a good lunch. There are two 15-minute coffee breaks—one at 10:00 and one at 3:00 in the afternoon.

As noted previously, a small group of Corpsmen, each day, are in the kitchen on K.P., and a second group serves as cook-trainees. As a cook-trainee, the Corpsman assists the cook in learning the rudiments of buying, storing, and preparing food. A few Corpsmen have come to their center unable to boil water, and have left after 7 or 8 months able to prepare and cook an elaborate meal for some 100 Corpsmen, staff, and guests.

From 5:00 to 11:00 p.m., the Corpsmen have leisure hours in which they may do a number of things. They may go to the rec hall and watch TV, play pool, ping pong, or cards. Gambling is illegal but it does pose a sporadic problem for some Corpsmen and staff members. Two or three movies are shown at the camp weekly, and the Corpsmen have also been invited to watch a movie at the Air Force base nearby. The town closest by is W. In the winter it has a population of 1600 and it literally rolls up its sidewalks at 6:00 p.m. To a Corpsman who has just arrived from Manhattan, Boston, South Chicago, or West Philly, etc., this is a shock which he really never overcomes. There is also some opportunity for the Corpsmen to enter sports—baseball, basketball, football, etc., but at Camp W., unlike other camps, there has been a very meager interest in sports. Just why this is so, it is difficult to say. Finally, the Corpsmen has the choice of going back to his dorm to write a letter, shoot the bull, or sleep. Occasionally a group of Corpsmen will find an inconspicuous spot to have a drink. Drinking is illegal on the center and no Corpsman is allowed to purchase liquor off the center unless he is 21. Fortunately, or unfortunately, there is a liquor store within walking distance from the camp. Corpsmen have been known to buy liquor at this store.

On a Friday night, a few Corpsmen may be invited to a local dance. Camp W. is fortunate, for some 35 miles away there is a town of some 35,000 people where there is some activity. At least it has an old familiar diner where the Corpsmen can buy coffee and hang around as they did back home. Most rural centers are not that fortunate, and the closest city of 35,000 or more may be hundreds of miles away.

Here briefly you have a picture of what it is like to be at

a Job Corps Center from day to day. Not only are the physical areas where the camps are located rural, but so are the people who inhabit these areas. They are suspicious of new people and new ideas and may be very slow to accept the outsiders and any new-fangled ideas they may bring with them—like integration, for example. They may be quick to tell you of their virtues and just as quick to tell you of your inevitable faults. Even worse, they can spot you at a mile's distance. Thus, because of the lack of social and recreational facilities in surrounding hamlets, and because of the passive resistance in being accepted in the community, life tends to evolve and revolve around the center for Corpsmen, the staff, and the staff's families.

What made our stay at the Job Corps Center atypical was the fact that we were there at a time when the camp was in the midst of making itself ready for its own "ribbon-cutting" ceremonies. Although the camp had been operating for several weeks it was now awaiting anxiously the arrival of a number of U.S. Senators, Representatives, and members of the President's Cabinet for its formal opening. There was even the rumor that the President, vacationing at the time in nearby Camp David, would make an appearance at the ceremonies, and the camp's staff and residents were furiously involved in last-minute preparations and arrangements.

The time for the ceremonies arrived and the Corpsmen, all dressed up for the occasion, took great pride in showing the visiting dignitaries around and pointing out to them the fruits of their labor. The camp became a beehive of activity and we, along with the other visitors, were swept up in the swarm of movement and spirit that marked the occasion. With flashbulbs bursting and reporters bustling, the ceremonies took place in the atmosphere of gaiety and solemnity that so often surrounds a christening. When at long last it was over and the dignitaries were gone, many people— Corpsmen and staff members alike—gave audible sighs of relief and returned to the work at hand.

When the storm of the ceremonies was over, we had a chance to spend several hours with our youngsters, talking quietly with them and listening to their feelings about the camp and their experiences. We found out, after taking into consideration their inevitable and predictable feelings of homesickness and separation, that their overall reactions to the camp setting were surprisingly similar to those of the resident counselor. The kinds of problems they were having closely paralleled those that had been described to us earlier. They felt unwanted—at best, tolerated—by the community; they saw very little connection between the training they were receiving (forest conservation) and the training they wanted (automobile mechanics, industrial and heavy machinery skills, etc.), and even less relevance between what they were learning to do and the realities of the job market back in New Haven; they resented most of the staff (with the significant exception of the counselor whom we had met) and felt that they (the staff), having mostly been recruited from the surrounding towns and colleges, were either racists or ignorant of the differences between "farm boys and city boys" (what they were really saying was that the people working with them were very much unlike the foremen from CPI); and they felt hemmed in, restricted, and lonely. More than anything else they felt "conned." To be sure, they had many positive feelings about the camp— feelings which, at that time, revolved around the material advantages of the setting (the food, money, accommodations, etc.) and the sense of adventure they were experiencing. In other words, the image of Job Corps life that they projected was certainly not totally one-sided, dismal, and dark, but the balance was certainly—both implicitly and explicitly—of a kind that left us feeling somewhat doubtful of their willingness or ability to stay there long enough to "make it."

All too quickly our visit came to an end, and we prepared to leave the Job Corps Center, our youngsters, and the resident counselor whose presence had affected us so deeply. Some of us left with the uneasy feeling of having been present simultaneously at the birth and death of the Job Corps, of having witnessed the beginning and the end of a program whose noble intent was in the process of being undermined—and eventually destroyed—by both the exigencies of the situation and the technological gap between the questionable assumptions underlying the program's conceptualization and the techniques developed to implement it. We had arrived with a feeling of expectation; we were leaving with a feeling of deep apprehension.

It is important that we interrupt our narrative at this point so that we might make the reader acutely aware of the context in which we hope he would *avoid* placing our criticisms and feelings about the Job Corps. From the very beginning, the Job Corps—indeed, the whole War on Poverty—has heard from more than its fair share of cynics and carping critics. Any new program—especially one whose goals and ideals are perceived as a threat to the status quo—rapidly becomes the focus of unrelenting concern and scrutiny. In part this is appropriate and understandable. All too often, however, the greatest concern is shown by those who use their concern as a cloak for selfish interests: their intent is not to participate constructively in the development of a program, but to discredit and bury it. The War on Poverty and the Job Corps in particular have been the recipients of a great deal of this type of criticism. There are those who, from the very beginning, have reacted to the program in ways which have become almost characteristic of their response to anything innovative or faintly progressive. Their fear and anxiety about the program—and its real or imagined implications—are surpassed only by the amount of venom they employ to kill it. But there are also those—let us call them the "chronically unpleasant Utopians"—whose unrelenting opposition to new programs is no less destructive. For them changes in the fabric of society, be they large or small changes, are invariably either "not enough" or "too little, too late": they themselves rarely offer any viable suggestions and seem to relish their roles as modern-day prophets, forever "crying in the wilderness." Schlesinger, for example, in describing Paul Goodman's manifesto for ameliorating the ills of a high-technology society, rightly calls it "whimsical," and leaves little doubt that he views Goodman's "program" as little more than an exercise in personal catharsis. According to Schlesinger (1965, p. 746):

Goodman thus summarized his program: "An occasional fist fight, a better orgasm, friendly games, a job of useful

work, initiating enterprises, deciding real issues in manageable meetings, and being moved by things that are beautiful,
curious, or wonderful."

It should be clear that both sources of criticism—the one
characterized by its unremitting hostility, and the other by
its insatiable idealism—are neither more nor less than a
series of blanket indictments relatively devoid of any attempts to understand the historical context of a program,
and bereft of any constructive attempts to render it assistance. The poet Yevtushenko (1963, p. 40) writing with reference to other problems and other settings, expressed a
condemnation of the empty cynic that best summarizes our
own feelings on the issue. He wrote:

I hate the cynics with their lordly view of history, their
scorn for the heroic labors of my countrymen, whom they
try to represent as a lost flock of sheep, their skills for lump-
ing the good with the bad and spitting on the whole thing,
and their utter inability to offer any constructive alternative.

Despite the fact that the eventual development of the
Residential Youth Center was based on a sympathy with,
rather than an antagonism toward, the overall goals of the
Job Corps, it would be all too understandable if it were now
viewed as a program whose aims are antithetical to those
of the Job Corps, especially if it were seen through the eyes
of the Job Corps itself.[3]

Now, as we left the Job Corps Center and began the long
ride home, each of us became prisoner of his own thoughts
and feelings about the camp. We had seen and heard much,
and the experience was still fresh in our minds. It was now a
time to reflect and think, to sift through the myriad impres-

[3]To say that the attacks on the War on Poverty—and particularly
those aimed at the development of the Job Corps—from either the
extreme Right or the extreme Left were both predictable and irrational
should not be accepted as evidence that they did not take their
psychological toll of the programs. In time the Job Corps reacted to
this constant harassment by becoming understandably defensive and
suspicious of any and all criticism of its program. For example, when
in the process of developing the initial proposal for the Residential
Youth Center we visited the offices of the Job Corps in Washington,
we were given a decidedly cool reception. We were treated as people
who, since we didn't agree with everything the Job Corps was doing,
were either enemies, outsiders, or at best, persons of little faith
and questionable motives.

sions and images that were flooding our consciousness. It was a time for silence . . . and rain.

But it is difficult for men such as we were to remain silent for very long. In a little while, as the rain continued to fall and the miles flew by, we began to share some of our feelings and ideas about the last few days. One by one, each in his own way and from his own perspective, we began to talk about the things that had both impressed and concerned us about our stay at the Job Corps camp. Some of us were most concerned about the rationale underlying the decision to shift youngsters from one part of the country to another;[4] others focused their attention on the obvious problems of staff selection and training; and still others zeroed in on the interpersonal and communication problems that seemed to characterize the relationships among many of the individuals working in the setting. As the discussion continued, some of us became dimly aware of the fact that many of the questions and concerns we were raising were directed not so much at the aims and ideals of the program as they were at the Job Corps itself as a complex system or organization. In other words, our attention began to shift from questioning the goals of the program (we were in obvious agreement with the Job Corps' nobility of purpose) to considering the relationship between these goals and the systematic mechanisms employed to achieve them. Somehow the Job Corps was creating the conditions for its own destruction, and the seeds were being sown within the organization itself.

It would be only much later in time that we could begin to conceptualize the kinds of organizational problems that invariably affect the course a new program would take; or to understand the power of the notion that new institutions

---

[4]Levine (1967), in a paper describing some of the principles involved in the practice of community mental health, has focused attention on the very problems that we were experiencing in what was then an amorphous, diffuse, and unorganized manner. According to Levine: "Help should be located strategically to the manifestation of the problem, preferably in the very situation in which the problem manifests itself. The goals or values of the helping agent or service must be consistent with the goals and values of the setting in which the problem is manifested."

are born out of a legacy of institutional thinking; or to appreciate our observations that the birth of new and apparently innovative programs offers no guarantee that they
will similarly give life to new and innovative techniques of
implementation. At this point in time we were only dimly
cognizant of the fact that there was something "sick" about
the Job Corps, that there was a cancer beginning to eat
away at its organizational insides. And the cancer had something to do with the assumptions underlying the conception
and organization of the Job Corps, and with the relationship
between the goals it wanted to achieve and the mechanisms
it had developed to achieve these goals.

It was probably around the time that we hit the New
Jersey Turnpike that some of us began to play the game of
Monday-morning quarterback and to second-guess the "calls"
the Job Corps was making in running its program. From the
luxury and relative safety of our position as onlookers we
began to fantasize how, if given the chance, we would think
about, organize, and run our own Job Corps Center. It was
all done in a lighthearted manner, and it was amusing to
notice how quickly we would gang up to "put down" someone's ideas, push our own, and then find everyone ganging
up against us. But despite the obvious delight we took in
needling one another, a number of ideas were being presented, and, out of necessity as well as self-defense, we had
to consider the possibilities of each one. Consequently, we
found ourselves thinking about the variety of issues surrounding the running of a Job Corps camp—issues of personnel, training, community relations, programming, and the
host of problems one might expect to encounter in such a
venture. It was soon evident that what had started as a
game, as an exercise to pass the time, was now assuming
the appearance of a half-serious attempt to formulate a program. Despite the laughter and the needling (or maybe because of it), a project was beginning to take shape.

Our trip was over, and what had begun in the rain was
ending in the rain. We entered New Haven and found it
wet and cold, almost as if the rain had followed us, over-
taken us, and beaten us home. We were now very much

like the counselor we had met at the Job Corps Center—
tired but somehow looking forward to the next day with
great anticipation. We had journeyed to a mountain and
found it wanting. Some of us would now use the experience
to begin to build a new one, and it would come to be
called the Residential Youth Center.

In this chapter we have described both the events that
led up to and the conditions under which a group of people
began to think about the creation of a new setting.[5] In the
next chapter, we shall turn our attention to the paths this
thinking took and the problems it encountered.

[5]As already indicated, one of those people was a clinical psychologist,
and while it would be going too far afield to describe in detail the
particular manner in which he became a part of that group, it is
important for the reader to know that his involvement in the
subsequent development of the Residential Youth Center was a direct
outgrowth of his being a member of the Psycho-Educational Clinic
of Yale University. This Clinic, developed and directed by Dr. Seymour
B. Sarason, was begun because of a lingering dissatisfaction with the
felt limitations of traditional clinical practice, training, and research.
Its own evolution was predicated on the realization that the mental
health professions would have to develop new and different models
of help if they were to remain (or become) relevant in a society
characterized by acute social change. While the "adventures" of the
Psycho-Educational Clinic are detailed elsewhere (Sarason et al., 1966;
Goldenberg and Levine, 1969; Goldenberg, 1965), it is important
for the reader to be aware of the role the Psycho-Educational Clinic
played in the development of the Residential Youth Center. First, and
perhaps most important, it was in the context of the Psycho-Educational
Clinic's commitment to the inner city that we "left" the Halls of
Ivy and became directly involved in that multifaceted cauldron so
simplistically defined as "the community." By entering into and
becoming enmeshed in New Haven's community action agency (CPI),
inner-city public schools, and regionalized services for the mentally
retarded, we became a part of the settings and people whose
problems could no longer be explored solely in laboratories or
understood in books. These experiences in the ghetto (some are
described and summarized in Chapter 3) signaled an end to both
innocence and the myth that the tentacles of poverty and institutionalized racism did not, indeed, reach into our own lives. Second,
and as a direct consequence of our involvement in community
settings, we were confronted with the reality that, as Sarason (1967)
put it, "the craziness of people in a very important way reflects the
craziness of the setting or systems or organization in which they
have been or now are." This realization—this frightening correlation
between sick settings and sick people—formed the basis for the
decision to attempt to create a setting (the RYC) whose goals and
values would not be subverted (and eventually destroyed) by the
dehumanizing effects of organizational pathology.

Chapter 3   Assumptions and the Creative Process

A man builds a fine house; and now he has a master, and
a task for life; he is to furnish, watch, show it, and keep
it in repair for the rest of his days.
—Ralph Waldo Emerson

Introduction

In this chapter we shall attempt to describe some of the
assumptions that, at least in terms of our own experiences
and observations, seem to influence the creation of certain
types of settings. Our goals are to indicate how each decision in the creative process—whether verbalized or not—is
predicated upon certain assumptions; and to illustrate how
these assumptions inevitably influence or have consequences
both for what one *does* in the present and for what one
contemplates doing in the future. Our concern in doing
this is simple: until we begin to make explicit the process by
which settings are created, we will be confronted by and
asked to deal with "sick" settings—settings whose goals are
either defeated or substantially diluted by internal and organizational malfunctions. If institutions are indeed both
reflections of existing values and vehicles for societal change,
it becomes imperative for those of us who deal with the
creation of settings (i.e., those of us who are, in one way or
another, in the business of social change), to begin to describe our experiences in ways that lead to formulations
relevant to the issue of understanding *man in society*.

It is important for the reader to understand that this chapter constitutes little more than a first step in the process of
describing and examining the problem of how one goes
about creating a setting. It should be viewed, almost by
definition, as a preliminary statement that is both tentative
and incomplete. Our discussion will be limited to the kinds
of settings with which we have had some experience. It will
focus, therefore, on institutions in which "people are our
most important product" (e.g., human service programs in
the War on Poverty, education, and mental health) and not
on organizations that produce "things" or provide "services"
in the usual commercial-commodity sense. Finally, we should

point out that our description of many of the problems and conflicts that are created by some of the basic decisions and assumptions of "institution-builders" should not be taken to mean or to imply that we, in the process of developing the Residential Youth Center, did not make some of the same mistakes. Nothing could be further from the truth, and wherever it is appropriate we shall give illustrations of how we, too, were the victims of our assumptions, conceptions, and decisions. Our sole purpose in writing this chapter is to make explicit some of the variables that influence the creative process. *Our own "assumption" is as follows: the more aware we become of the consequences of our assumptions and conceptions (to the degree that that which is "unconscious" becomes "conscious"), the more able we will be to control for much of the "irrationality" and self-defeating behavior that plagues so many programs, new or old.*

Assumptions and Decisions

I. *A new institution, agency, or setting is needed to meet some need (new or old) that has been identified in the community or society.*

It seems only natural that our description of the creation of a new setting start with that point in time at which the actual decision to undertake such a venture is made. What is rarely made explicit, although it has definite consequences for the future development of the organization, is the fact that the decision to create a new setting is, in and of itself, a decision born out of the combined feelings of *hope* and *frustration*. To be sure, this seems to be a glimpse of the obvious. What is less obvious, however, are the ways in which these emotions, particularly that of frustration, facilitate or impede the creation of a truly "new" or "different" type of setting.

In the decision to create a new setting, the element of *hope*, although certainly a complex emotion, is relatively easy to understand. It is the feeling of adventure and singleness of purpose shared by a group of people who are about to embark on a project whose goal is "finally" to meet certain identified human needs. Although hope serves to bind the "setting-builders" in the present, and to symbolize a unity of goals, it does not insure any communality or agreement as to how these goals should be achieved. The element of *frustration* in the decision to create a new setting is even more complex and, in the long run, perhaps even more significant in determining the course of future events. When we refer to the "element" of frustration we are referring to the fact that more often than not the decision to create a new setting represents the thinking of a group of people whose previous attempts to deal with a problem have resulted in failure, disillusion, and/or disappointment. In other words, in one way or another, the idea for the new institution is the product of the combined frustrations of a group of well-meaning and highly motivated individuals who already have been unsuccessful in trying to meet "the need" in a relatively uncoordinated and, for the most part, noncooperative manner. More often than not these people come from different backgrounds and different disciplines, but it is "assumed" that their differences in orientation and perspective will be less important than (and will certainly remain subservient to) their newfound union. *In short, the implicit assumption is that a unity born out of collective hope and shared frustration is strong enough to transcend differences between individuals and professions.*

The situation described is all too often a temporary condition. It is a unity that is achieved not through the mutual exploration of new or different orientations but through the much simpler process of combining established points of view and trusting to fate or to the intervention of some Divine Providence that interpersonal and, more important, interprofessional conflicts either will never arise or will never pose a serious problem to the organization. No one is asked to give up any of his personal or professional autonomy, and there is usually no attempt to explore the problem of "vested interests" (i.e., the particular and cherished theoretical or organizational prejudices that the participants bring with them by virtue of their membership in different professions possessing different orientations and ways of functioning). And yet, more often than not, conflict does indeed arise, usually when the "halo effect" has begun to wear off and the organization is confronted with the "crisis" of having to operate on a routine basis.

Example 1: The "regional concept" with regard to providing services to the mentally retarded is a relatively new and apparently innovative one. It is predicated on two main assumptions. The first is that the problem of mental subnormality is a community problem and can be dealt with most effectively on that level. The second is that by regionalizing or decentralizing services (i.e., by replacing the older and larger institutions with community-based Regional Centers that can more efficiently utilize and coordinate local resources), new and different patterns of service can be developed through which the mentally retarded individual and his family can live a healthier and more productive life in the community. Implicit in the regional concept is the notion that the Regional Centers, by virtue of their greater autonomy and community "based-ness," will be able to be more responsive both to the individual needs of their clients and to the need to develop community-oriented patterns of service.

The basic staff of one particular Regional Center was assembled and had begun functioning long before the building that was eventually to house them and their programs was ready for occupancy. For the most part the staff was drawn from existing state institutions where they had been employed for varying amounts of time. Every member of the staff had, in one way or another, felt stifled by the restrictions, policies, and orientations that characterized the institutions from which they had come. Regardless of the differences between them with respect to their personal or professional allegiances, they shared the hope that they would now be able to develop patterns of service that not only would better meet the needs of the retarded but would also lead to a greater feeling of personal and collective competence. The early days of the organization seemed to be doing just that. The staff, under dynamic leadership, was able to experiment with a variety of patterns of functioning and to suspend temporarily their own traditional conceptions of what was the "best way" of providing service. There was a great deal of sharing of experiences and a heightened awareness of the importance of open communication.

With the formal opening of the Center, and even for a

period of time before that, subtle and then pronounced changes began to occur. Confronted with the day-to-day problems of the clients and the developing programs, the staff, without talking about what was happening to them, began to change, began to "regress" or revert to what seemed like much more traditional ways of functioning and of looking at problems. There began a growing isolation between people, and one could sense the development of an essentially unhelpful professional parochialism. The old "minor kingdoms" began to appear; there was less communication, and there was a decrease in the sharing of experiences. There was now the Social Work Kingdom, the Psychology Kingdom, the Day Care Program Kingdom, and the Teacher Kingdom. Responsibilities were divided, the client was "cut up"; there was less and less willingness by the staff to venture beyond the limits of their supposed areas of professional concern and expertise. The "new" institution began to look more and more like the "old" institutions from which the staff had come.

At the present time the particular Regional Center we have described is still in its infancy. It is still a somewhat "innovative" organization and certainly seems to be providing services that are at least as good as and probably superior to those offered by the state institutions. But the organization as a whole has "lost something," something it had for a little while, something that made it an exciting place to be and to work. Despite the fact that ideal goals are never attained, it seems safe to say, at the present time at least, that this Regional Center seems to be functioning in a manner that suggests that the hope of ever approaching these goals has been abandoned.

This is only one example of the assumption (or myth) being made that people, professions, and agencies—each with a different history, value system, and way of functioning—can be brought together easily, and that simply by being brought together they will be able to combine their talents in non-self-defeating ways to deal with a given problem. What is overlooked is the fact that the effective pooling of resources is neither an easy nor a self-evident process. What is more often the case is that the assumption itself (i.e., the automatic cooperation between professions with different traditions) becomes the genesis of the "everybody's got a piece of the action" phenomenon, a phenomenon in which the needs to maintain professional autonomy soon preclude and transcend the goals of developing truly innovative patterns of functioning.

There is also the situation in which the decision to create a new institution carries with it little or no pretense that the new institution will even try to coordinate the efforts of other agencies involved in similar areas of concern. This does not mean, however, that the new institution will not seek or need the help of agencies that already exist. All it means is that the new institution will function independently of, and will not try to coordinate in any formal sense, the efforts of existing agencies that are, and have been for a long time, trying to meet certain human needs in the same area. *What is usually overlooked in this decision, however, is that the rise of the new organization is in many ways an indictment of the ways in which the more traditional agencies have been meeting (or, in reality, not meeting) the needs they were originally intended to serve.* What often results, regardless of public protestations to the contrary, is that the new institution is perceived both as a condemnation of previous attempts to render service and as a distinct threat to the future existence of the more established agencies. Under these conditions, cooperation of any sort, formal or informal, is highly unlikely. More important, the overlapping and duplication of functions that inevitably result once the new agency begins operations guarantees the development and perpetuation of greater conflicts—the kind of inter-agency conflicts that are, in the long run, not only harmful to *all* the agencies involved but cruelly detrimental to the clients who hope to receive service. It is, in the final analysis, a situation in which "cooperation" becomes little more than a slogan to be used for purposes of public consumption, and political maneuvering and undermining become the accepted order of the day.

Example 2: There is little doubt (at least now and in our own minds) that the creation of the Office of Economic Opportunity (OEO) was as much a reaction against the ways in which existing agencies were waging their "undeclared" War on Poverty as it was a response to the newly grasped needs of the poor. The implied indictment was a simple and clear one: had the existing agencies (e.g., the Office of Education, the Department of Health, Education and Welfare, the Department of Labor) met their responsibilities and obligations to the poor in an appropriate and relevant manner, there would have been much less need for the launching of the War on Poverty in general, and for the creation of a new super poverty agency (OEO) in particular. From the very beginning, then, one might say that the War on Poverty, at least in terms of those already engaged in efforts to provide services to the poor, could have been perceived as a criticism of existing programs and agencies. Again, this may seem to be a glimpse of the obvious, but what is less apparent are the ways in which these perceptions can influence the development of new programs and the motivations behind them.

The reader will recall that in Chapter 2 we described as "decidedly cool" our reception at Job Corps headquarters (OEO) in Washington when, in the process of developing the initial proposal for the Residential Youth Center, we visited them seeking information and assistance. In actuality, we now feel we were being rather gracious in describing our reception as "decidedly cool." In point of fact we were treated more as interlopers, meddlers, even spies, rather than as people who were genuinely interested in the problem and wanted to be of some help. But this reception was almost "warm" compared to the one we received some two months later when we returned to OEO to ask them to fund the RYC, which was now in proposal form. This time we received no reception at all. We were told, in no uncertain terms, that our proposal would not be considered, that the idea for the RYC was at variance with Job Corps philosophy, and that we should "go elsewhere to peddle the project." Somewhat shaken, we did just that. We walked two blocks to the Department of Labor (Office of Manpower, Policy, Evaluation and Research), where we recounted our experiences and presented our proposal. Within 20 minutes we found, to our utter amazement, that our proposal not only was being listened to with much enthusiasm and delight but also was almost guaranteed its funds. We left the Department of Labor feeling, quite naïvely we now believe, that at least someone understood our program, shared our belief in its values, and was willing to support it all the way. Only later were we to realize that there may have been many other reasons for the speed with which we were funded by the Department of Labor, reasons having at least as much to do with the relationship and conflicts between OEO and the Department of Labor as with the particular merits of the RYC proposal. On the basis of this kind of experience, as well as a variety of others to be described in later portions of this book, one wonders—or at least has a right to speculate— about the motivations that lie behind the funding of a variety of antipoverty programs. Put simply, to what degree are programs funded because of their inherent or potential value as opposed to reasons (i.e., motives that are politically inspired and reflect the machinations caused by interagency conflict) that have, at best, little to do with the goals of the War on Poverty?

Another assumption behind the decision to create a new institution is that this decision has taken place only after the attempt has been made to explore a variety of alternatives. Again, this may seem to be little more than a glimpse of the obvious, but our own experience indicates that there is more to this assumption than meets the eye. All too often, as is the case with anything "big" and "new," like the War on Poverty, the knowledge that great sums of money are available for a variety of experimental and demonstration programs has serious consequences for the exploration of modes of functioning that might preclude or make less desirable the creation of a new setting. In some cases the sudden availability of "easy money" acts as a signal that primary and tertiary preventive thinking should cease because what's "in" are new programs in remediation. In other cases the awareness that capital is available acts as a deterrent to efforts to improve existing programs, and facilitates the kind of thinking and planning for which there will almost certainly be financial support. In short, "new" money makes the development of new programs attractive and increases the tendency to turn away from "older," more troubled programs. The conceptualization and development of the RYC is a case in point.

Example 3: Now, in retrospect, it is clear to all of us that virtually no attempt was made to explore alternatives to the development of the Residential Youth Center before the decision was made to create a new facility. It seems apparent that the unverbalized, perhaps unconscious, assumption (or wish?) was that nothing of significance would come of any attempts to modify or render assistance to existing residential (e.g., Job Corps) programs. In point of fact, however, there were at least two alternatives to the development of a new program. We could have decided, for example, to spend our time and energy developing a program within CPI (at no cost to anyone) to prepare and orient youngsters better to the life and realities of the Job Corps. Had we done this, we might have been able to help a number of youngsters deal with the kinds of problems that the Job Corps would present (e.g., separation, loneliness) in a way that would facilitate their transition from urban to rural life. Or, instead of deciding on an *a priori* basis to start a different kind of residential program, we could have shared our observations and misgivings with the Job Corps more directly and tried to help them develop a more appropriate preservice and in-service program, the kind of program that would help their existing staffs understand and deal with the problems of inner-city youth. But clearly, we chose neither of these alternatives. More important, however, we cannot honestly say that we ever entertained seriously either of these alternatives. In the final analysis, we were responding to the fact that money was available for experimental programs of various kinds, and the strength or attractiveness of this knowledge was sufficient to influence and, indeed, preclude the exploration of any viable alternatives to the creation of a new program.

II. *A new and separate facility should be built (i.e., the new program requires its own physical plant) in order to meet the identified need.*

Once the decision to create a new setting has been made, for whatever reasons and on whatever bases, it almost inevitably follows that attention is immediately focused on the need or desirability of housing the new program in its own physical facility.[1] The underlying assumption is that possessing one's own physical facility increases the probability of developing a program that will reflect more faithfully the goals it was intended to meet by providing the setting-builders with a greater sense of freedom and ownership. To a large extent this is true. One need only mention once more the "identity crisis" that still plagues clinical psychology to appreciate more fully the importance of "owning," rather

[1]Many Operation Headstart programs are exceptions to this process. They are, for the most part, housed in existing community facilities such as schools and community action agencies.

than being a "tenant" in, a particular facility. What is often overlooked, however, is that the source of funds (i.e., who finances the program and in what manner they choose to finance it) almost invariably influences the nature of the resulting institution in a variety of physical and practical as well as theoretical ways. The inability or unwillingness to recognize this fact—the ease with which we all seem willing to indulge our delusions of complete autonomy—often results in program expectations and aspirations that are unrealistic and that, when shattered by the ever-present reality, all too quickly lead to despair.

Example 4: The Job Corps counselor we described in Chapter 2 was a despairing and angry man. Despite his continued hope for the eventual success of the program he was, at least when we met him, a man who would soon approach that point of disillusion from which there is no return. His anger may have been misplaced. He was reacting to the situation around him in his own camp. The basic problem, however, seemed to reside not in his camp, but further away in the curious or perhaps not-so-curious federal-state relationship through which the Job Corps was born.

From its very beginning the War on Poverty was conceived as a "partnership" between the federal and state governments. The Job Corps Centers, for example, while financed primarily through federal moneys, were often housed in and "responsive" to state facilities and needs; or while Job Corps camps might be situated on "federal" facilities, their development, staffing, and administration were often under local authority. To be sure, this situation resulted in the creation of employment and increases in income for the local community surrounding the Job Corps Centers. What it also did, however, was to place certain local appointees in positions of power to determine at least some of the content and policies that were to govern the camp. Even this would not have been so bad if it were not for the fact that all too often these people, well-intentioned and well-meaning though they may have been, had very little experience with the kinds of problems presented by inner-city youth who had been uprooted and thrust into their communities. As was the case in the Job Corps camp high on that mountain in Maryland, the nature of the relationship between the federal and state governments almost guaranteed both the creation and exacerbation of camp problems.

Example 5: Although the Residential Youth Center was funded by a federal agency, it was not financed as an independent and autonomous program. The actual funds for the RYC went to Community Progress, Inc. (the local action agency). The RYC itself, therefore, was a program that, from the very beginning, had to function within the framework and context of the other programs under CPI's jurisdiction. At the same time, however, it had to be responsive to the particular needs and research interests of the Department of Labor. In much the same manner as Freud's ego had to serve two "harsh masters," so did the RYC have to be responsive to two different sources of influence, each with its own particular (and understandable) needs, concerns, and problems. Although both CPI and the Department of Labor were for the most part helpful and supportive to the program, there were times, especially during the early days of the program, when the particular needs and interests of each of the two agencies created a great deal of difficulty in the RYC's attempts to get its own program off the ground. Interestingly enough, one of the points of greatest difficulty occurred during the time when we were trying to obtain and renovate a building to house the program.

The problem arose in the following manner. Soon after it became apparent that the RYC would be funded, we were approached by one of CPI's directors and asked if we had thought about or decided on where the RYC would be housed. We told him that we would soon be looking for a rooming-house type of building that could be renovated to meet the needs of the program. He then proceeded to tell us (as if we needed to be reminded) that the RYC was only one of the many opportunity programs under CPI's "umbrella" and that our particular needs should be seen in the context of CPI's problems and concerns as a whole. What he was leading up to was the fact that at that time CPI was contemplating moving part of its operation (and some of its programs) into a larger office building in New Haven. In order to justify this move to the federal government, however, CPI was in the position of having to guarantee that they could "fill up" the space that would be provided by this new and bigger building. From this director's point of view, the RYC program should be willing, if called upon, to occupy the top two floors of an office building, especially if this would result in broader gains to CPI as a whole. In other words, it was his feeling that any program, of necessity, had to view itself in terms of the "big picture," independent of its own particular needs, goals, and processes.

It would be all too easy for the reader to get the impression that this particular director was unaware of or had little concern for the aims and problems of the infant RYC. Nothing could be further from the truth. He was, in point of fact, a man deeply committed to the ideas behind the RYC, a man who had been more helpful than anyone else in getting the RYC funded. The point we are trying to stress is that his perception of the RYC and his response to it was, in part, necessarily determined by a wide variety of pressures (i.e., considerations having to do with the current and future status of CPI as a total organization) that he was responding to; pressures that we were relatively unaware of and about which we could only speculate. Be this as it may, what became clear to us was the fact that CPI as the official source of the RYC's funds was in a very strong position to affect the course of our program. More important, however, was the realization that this influence could be brought to bear for a variety of reasons having little if anything to do with the goals of the RYC program itself. The situation described ended on what, at least from our point of view, was a happy and perhaps lucky note. CPI, for a variety of reasons (most of which we still do not understand), decided to give up its quest for a new facility in which to house some of its programs. Consequently, the RYC was "spared" from having to occupy a physical plant which would have been ill-suited to its purposes. To this day, however, many of us wonder what would have happened had we been put, or had we allowed ourselves to be put, in a position where the future of the infant program would have been so closely tied to the more global concerns of the funding agency.

Approximately one month after this incident, the RYC was officially notified by the Department of Labor that the program would receive its funds. We were also told that we would be funded as a one-year experimental and demonstration project for the fiscal year beginning July 1, 1966, and ending July 1, 1967. This was in June of 1966. The mandate was clear: we should open our facility on July 1, 1966. At this point in time, however, we were faced with at least two problems that we felt we had to deal with *before* opening the RYC. The first was that we had just found a place that seemed to be suitable for the purposes of the program. It was clear, however, that extensive renovations would be necessary before the program could, or should, become functional. The second was that we had just finished recruiting a staff and felt very strongly that the staff needed at least two months to get to know one another, to develop policies and processes relating to how we would work with the youngsters and their families, and to implement important preservice and in-service training programs. Although we made these views clear to the Department of Labor, we were told that any delays in initiating the program would create problems regarding the fiscal-year appropriations under which the RYC was funded. We were also told that such delays might have consequences with respect to re-funding in the next fiscal year. The dilemma posed was a clear one. If we opened "on time" (i.e., July 1, 1966), we knew that we would be beginning the program prematurely with respect to problems we felt had to be resolved prior to the formal initiation of the program. If, on the other hand, we postponed the formal opening until such time as we felt reasonably sure that we had at least tried to cover some of the issues that we felt had to be resolved before we became operational, we would be jeopardizing our chances of "proving" what we wanted to prove and thereby of being re-funded. We chose the latter course; but still, as we shall indicate in the succeeding chapters, we found ourselves opening the facility before we felt ourselves "ready." The point we are trying to make, however, is that once again the source of funds had a definite influence on the resulting institution in a variety of direct and indirect ways, ways that had little to do with any understanding of the ideas and goals of the program.

What is rarely made explicit in the decision to start or, more important, to *build* an institution is the fact that all institution-builders operate within the framework of a certain *time perspective* concerning both the nature of the problem they are dealing with and the amount of time that will be necessary to deal with that problem in a relatively effective manner. The problem of one's time perspective is crucial for a number of reasons, the most important of which seems to be its influence on the nature of the resulting physical facility and/or its effects on the kinds of programs one tries to develop.

Implicit in the decision to build some institutions is the assumption that the remedial nature of the institution's functioning is great enough that a long life for its physical plant can be envisioned. *Rarely does an institution see as one of its primary functions the development of programs* and patterns of service which, if successful, would result in the institution's putting itself "out of business." Much more often quite the opposite is true. An institution is built on the assumption that the problem with which it is being created to deal will exist both now and in the foreseeable future to a degree that is relatively predictable, if not stable, and in a manner that requires a certain kind of intervention. What is often overlooked is the possibility that this assumption, predicated as it is on what might be called an infinite time perspective, may lead to the phenomenon of institutional self-perpetuation and the genesis of a kind of situation in which the goals of functional innovation become subservient to visions of structural longevity. The poet Robert Louis Stevenson (1894) put it perhaps better than anyone else when he wrote:

When a road is once built, it is a strange thing how it collects traffic, how every year as it goes on, more and more people are found to walk thereon, and others are raised up to repair and perpetuate it, and keep it alive.

Example 6: The growth and development of the Veterans Administration Hospitals is one example of how the creation of an institution can be governed by the assumption that the institution will reflect and be responsive to a problem that exists in the present and will continue, in much the same way, to exist in the future. This is in no way meant to derogate either the worth or importance of the V.A. Hospital complex. Were it not for the V.A. Hospitals and for the training experiences they provided to countless clinical psychologists, it would be very difficult to imagine what the field of mental health would look like today. What is important, however, is the point that the time perspective under which it was created also served to limit the ways in which the institution could be altered (in terms of goals, training practices, and internship programs) to meet the new and different problems that were to become manifest in the society as a whole, problems involving a different population from the one it was originally created to serve.

But just as some institutions and programs are created with implicit time perspectives that are almost infinite in length, others are born with unrealistically short time perspectives or none at all.

Example 7: The War on Poverty itself is perhaps as good an example as any of a program whose birth was based on the assumption that an exceedingly complex human problem (i.e., poverty) could be dealt with and overcome in a relatively short period of time. The speed with which it was inaugurated and the fanfare that accompanied its birth—despite the obvious and understandable political implications—seemed to indicate that, as is presumably the case in any major military conflict, if only enough resources could be marshaled quickly and deployed appropriately, a war could be won in a relatively short period of time. The implicit time perspective was one that assumed that the problem of poverty could be eradicated in the foreseeable future (i.e., five, ten, or twenty years) by enlarging certain existing programs and creating some new ones. Despite some of the obvious and tangible positive results that we see about us, the possibility remains—and grows stronger with each passing day and each passing riot—that such a relatively short time perspective was guaranteed to create many new problems and perpetuate some old ones. Not the least of these problems is the fact that aspirations (especially the aspirations of the poor) buoyed up so quickly by the hope of immediate change were likely to turn to anger and then rage once the anticipated payoff was slow in coming. What is now clear, and what was clear to many people at the very time the War on Poverty was launched, is that this war, if it is to be at all successful, must involve and must eventually lead to basic structural changes in the systems and institutions that influence and regulate life in our society. But such changes cannot be expected to occur with any regularity or predictability in a relatively short period of time. A time perspective that envisions such change as occurring quickly, and that predicates its programs and interventions on this assumption, can only result in the kinds of immediate payoffs that fall far short of the expectations engendered in the target population.

One of the most striking characteristics of most new programs—especially those which, from the moment of birth, are to be "housed" in their own buildings—is the degree to which they are affected, sometimes irrevocably, by their own formal "ribbon-cutting" ceremonies and the early days that follow. In some ways the situation can be likened to the feelings of a young couple the day before and the first days after the birth of their first child. Life changes drastically, and expectations held the day before the child issues his first cry are soon forcibly submitted to the first of what will be many "agonizing reappraisals." Expectations of what life will be like change, and the experiences are often so disruptive as to result in patterns of functioning that bear little resemblance to the ways in which the institution saw itself functioning almost to the very moment of its formal opening. Reiff (1966, p. 543), in a paper dealing with the problems of institutional change, provides a good example of this phenomenon in his description of the "walk-in clinic":

Witness what is already happening in many instances to the walk-in clinic. The idea of the walk-in clinic was a bold attempt to deal with the problems of delay in providing service. It was to be the means of doing away with the problems of waiting lists, delayed referrals, etc., and its primary purpose was immediacy of service. It was to be the means by which the mentally ill could enter and be routed without delay to whatever kind of service was needed. It was to be the open door to a full array of comprehensive services.

But for the most part the new walk-in clinics have become brief psychotherapy clinics. The idea of an open door to comprehensive mental health services has already in many instances been converted into the old revolving door. They have become brief psychotherapy clinics because that is what the professionals who man them know how to do.

Comprehensiveness, an important aspect of the new programs, is slipping away. In some instances, the situation has developed where the kind of treatment patients get depends on which door they walk into. If they come to the walk-in clinics they get brief psychotherapy, if they come to the emergency room they get drugs, or are hospitalized.

The formal opening of a facility often signals the death knell of whatever preoperational patterns of functioning have been developed, and the reintroduction of more traditional patterns of service. It is a situation in which attempts at functional innovation succumb to more or less "institutionally" oriented ways of thinking and patterns of behavior.

Example 8: The staff of one Regional Center for the Mentally Retarded began working with some of its clients several months before the buildings being constructed to house the program were ready for occupancy. Because of this situation, as well as the willingness and desire on the part of the staff to develop "noninstitutional" patterns of functioning, a variety of rather innovative models of service were explored. Having no physical plant to use as a base of operations (i.e., no offices in which to see clients), the staff spent most of its time in the community working with clients in settings bearing little or no resemblance to the institution under construction. Clients were seen and worked with in the context of whatever community facilities the clients were already a part of (i.e., their homes, schools, places of business, etc.). In addition, case loads were assigned to staff members on the basis of interest and experience rather than in terms of formal credentials, status, "job description," or position in the organizational hierarchy. The results were quite impressive. Clients seemed to be receiving better and more intensive service than was the case in most established institutions, there was a high degree of staff cohesiveness, and a productive situation of mutual learning for the staff seemed to be developing.

Once the physical facility was ready, however, marked changes began to take place. The amount of time spent in the community diminished greatly as people began spending more and more of their time seeing clients within the confines of the new offices they had been provided with. Even more important, however, was the change that came about in the practice of case assignments. No longer were cases assigned on the basis of interest, and there was much less experimenting with the sharing of functions and responsibilities. People began functioning much more in terms of how their job descriptions said they should function rather than in the ways in which they had been working prior to the day they moved into the new building. In a relatively short period of time, much of the staff's "pre-opening day" attempts at service innovations gave way to patterns of functioning much more reminiscent of the accepted institutional ways of doing things.[2]

III. *The need can best be met in a situation different from, and usually removed from, the setting or conditions that produced the need.*

[2] The Residential Youth Center learned much from the experiences of the Regional Center. We became acutely aware of the relationship between the nature of a program's physical plant and the patterns of service that are developed. Simply put, what we learned was that if a program is oriented toward the community (i.e., it sees the major portion of its work time as being spent outside the physical plant),

In a traditional and historical sense, most institutions have been founded on the assumption that the kinds of services, interventions, or restorative processes needed to deal with a certain problem cannot be maximally helpful until the client is removed from the setting in which the problem either was created or became manifest. Implicit in this assumption also is the notion that the institution, presumably being a very different and "healthier" setting, is itself an important ingredient in the therapeutic process.

On the basis of this kind of thinking, as well as for a variety of other reasons, most institutions in the past (and, as we shall indicate, many newly created institutions) have been built and located some distance from the communities and settings from which their clients come. Thus, for example, most early state mental hospitals, institutions for the mentally retarded, and V.A. facilities were located far away from large communities and areas of high population density. Even today many large institutions and programs (e.g., Job Corps Centers) are being built in places far removed from the environs of their clients. As was the case in the past, people come or are brought to these facilities, stay there, get "cured" (hopefully), and, after a specified amount of time, return to the communities from which they came.

The assumption that people can best be helped in a situation different from the one in which they supposedly became sick rests on a number of conceptions not the least important of which is the notion that the problem is one that exists primarily "in the client's head" and, this being the case, treatment should occur in a setting that is either most conducive (theoretically) for change or more comfortable (actually) from the point of view of the therapist. Our concern about

---

then it should make certain that the program never becomes the prisoner of the building that houses it. To guard against this situation, the RYC ordered only half the number of desks it needed. As simple a move as this may seem, it did result in greater time being spent by the staff in the community. The underlying assumption was that if one does not, and cannot, "own" a desk or an office, he is much more likely to spend his time "in the field," working with clients in their settings, than to become wedded to, and increasingly dependent upon, "his" office.

the implications of this assumption has little to do with the actual physical location of institutions, for, as we shall indicate, it does not necessarily follow that moving an institution closer to the community offers any guarantee of better or more appropriate service. The real question is the degree to which the "assumption of separation" and the conceptions that lie behind it facilitate or impede the development of new and truly innovative models that lead to basic changes both in the ways we think about problems and in the techniques we devise to deal with them. The current community mental health movement and its relationship to the problems of the poor is a case in point.

It appears, at least on the surface of things, that the emergence of the community mental health movement in this country signifies a fundamental change in our ways of thinking about and dealing with the problems of mental illness and health. The movement has been called "innovative," a term used to place the stamp of both newness and fundamental or lasting change on a phenomenon that has only recently made its presence known or felt in our society. Smith and Hobbes (1966, p. 500), in a paper that describes the "movement" and places it in some perspective, put it in the following way:

The comprehensive community mental health center represents a fundamental shift in strategy in handling mental disorders. Historically, and still too much today, the preferred solution has been to separate the mentally ill person from society, to put him out of sight and mind, until, if he is lucky, he is restored to normal functioning. According to the old way, the community abandoned its responsibility for the "mental patient" to the distant medical hospital. According to the new way, the community accepts responsibility to come to the aid of the citizen who is in trouble. In the proposed new pattern, the person would remain in his own community, often not leaving his home, close to family, to friends, and to the array of professional people he needs to help him.

With respect to the relationship between the community mental health movement and the problems of the poor, however, Reiff (1966, p. 543) is quick to point out:

It has been proclaimed that the community mental health

development signals a revolution in mental health. Such a view is a gross exaggeration. The concept of community mental health has the potential for introducing revolutionary innovations, but a sober look will reveal that institutionalized community mental health under the Federal programs tends to become an extension of current professional ideology with modified goals, tactics, and techniques, over that part of society from which it has been hitherto alienated. It is in fact a process of consolidation rather than revolution, a consolidation motivated by the realization of the failure to adequately perform the social function of restoration of those whose needs are greatest. Such a consolidation may be a step forward. But it must be kept in mind that it solves none of the ideological problems but rather perpetuates them.

The issue, indeed, seems to be an "ideological" one. Whether or not the client is physically removed from his setting (i.e., transported to some spot far away from home as is the case in the Job Corps, or treated "in the community" as is the case under the aegis of the community mental health movement) is of greater symptomatic than causal significance. It is symptomatic of a state of affairs which in effect says: "There is no need for us to alter our conceptions of what constitutes illness, nor is there any overriding reason to question the assumptions underlying the forms of treatment we have to offer. All that is necessary is that we make our services more available to those who need them." What is overlooked in this formulation is the fact that "availability" has little if anything to do with the question of physical proximity. The fact that certain human services are more available in a physical sense does not necessarily mean that they are more available in a psychological sense. *The real issue, the ideological problem, has to do with the distance— the psychological distance—between the orientations and assumptions of the helping agency or institution on the one hand, and the needs of the target population on the other. For as long as the psychological distance between them remains great, "treatment" will always tend to separate the individual from his setting, will always tend to inhibit real attempts at innovation, and will aways function to solidify professional orthodoxy.*

Example 9: The Job Corps program is explicitly founded on the assumption that people can best be helped in a setting that is different and removed from the kinds of settings from which they came. Perhaps more than any other program in the War on Poverty, the Job Corps exemplifies the notion that individual change can best be accomplished under conditions of extreme environmental manipulation. Youngsters are taken out of ghettos—rural or urban—and sent to Job Corps Centers, where they are trained and counseled; after a period of time they leave the camp either to return home or to seek employment in some other city. So far, so good. What is often overlooked and rarely planned for, however, are the consequences and implications of a program predicated on the assumption that there is something inherently good about first separating an individual from, and then returning him to, an environment that is markedly different from the one that exists at the Job Corps Center. More often than not, as was supposedly the case in days of old, the "referring" community abdicates its responsibility to the Job Corps-bound youngster at that point in time when it learns of his imminent departure. No provisions are made to facilitate the transition from the community to the Job Corps camp, and there is no planning for his eventual return. The "community" (i.e., the agencies that have had contact with the youngster) does little by way of preparing him to leave, does less in the way of staying in touch with him while he is away, and usually does nothing by way of preparing for his return. It is, in short, a situation in which the community takes the position, as Wechsler (1967) has pointed out recently, that the youngster is "out of our conscience and consciousness." One youngster who returned to New Haven from a Job Corps Center in Arizona put it the following way: "I felt like everybody was getting rid of me. Like nobody gave a damn anymore what the hell happened to me. I'd of even felt better if my damn probation officer would have kept in touch with me."

The problem lies not so much in the physical separation of an individual from his environment. Few people would argue with or question the fact that the Job Corps was developed with the best of intentions and motivated by the most humane of considerations. The real problem lies in the kind of thinking that assumes that separation, in and of itself or coupled with "treatment," is a relevant way of dealing with the problem. It is the kind of assumption that makes thinking about problems of transition and reintegration at best of secondary concern and at worst of no concern at all.

Example 10: Unlike the Job Corps camps, community mental health centers are situated much closer to the settings from which their clients come. In some cases they are even located in the neighborhoods where their clients live. It does not follow, however, that having dealt with (and apparently resolved) the problem of physical proximity guarantees, in any way, shape, or form, that community mental health centers are any closer *psychologically* to the people they wish to serve. "Psychological closeness," as we have indicated previously, may be more a matter of clinical orientations and practices than of physical location. In some cases it may even be true that the mere fact that the institution *has* been moved closer to the community acts as a force that inhibits rather than facilitates the development of the kinds of orientations and practices that could serve truly to decrease the distance that separates the institution from the people with whom it wishes to work. In other words, defining the problem of service in terms of physical proximity may be a most exquisite form of "copout," for it enables the institution to retain (often not even to question) its basic clinical orientations and, at the same time, to delude itself into believing that it has already effected some fundamental change in its patterns of service. The following example, only one of several that we could have presented, illustrates the point.

Early in the life of the RYC we received an invitation from one community mental health center to discuss the possibility of working out an arrangement under which several of our youngsters could receive treatment (psychotherapy) at the mental health center. We arrived a bit early for our appointment and took a seat in one of the waiting rooms while the doctor whom we had come to see was told of our arrival. While waiting for him we witnessed the following incident.

It was about ten minutes past the hour. The elevator door opened and a woman, obviously in a great hurry, made her way to the reception desk. Behind the desk there was a young woman, and behind her, some five yards away, a man was seated at a desk. He was typing and looked up briefly as the woman approached the receptionist, but then returned to his work. The patient, a rather obese Negro woman, was quite disheveled and seemed somewhat flustered and agitated. She was obviously late and gave the receptionist her appointment card without even glancing around the room. Had she looked about her she would have seen a pleasant room with furniture of modern design. The furniture was certainly not "extreme" in design and it was quite comfortable. A few plants were situated in the center of the room and some "op" and "pop" art paintings and pieces of sculpture dotted the walls of the waiting room. A few other people were sitting around, apparently waiting to see their doctors. The receptionist smiled as the woman gave her the card and immediately picked up the phone to dial the woman's doctor. The phone rang on the desk where the man was typing. He picked up the phone, said a word or two, and then got up and came and stood next to the receptionist. He was the woman's doctor, and I recalled, much to my amazement, that he had seen the woman enter but had not bothered to come to greet her until the receptionist had buzzed him at his desk. Now, standing next to the receptionist, he proceeded to tell the woman, almost beratingly, that he would not see her that day because she was late. Although he did not shout at the woman, he spoke in tones loud enough for the other people sitting in the waiting room to look up from whatever they were doing and to watch and listen to the interchange. The woman, now even more flustered, looked about her in an embarrassed way and mumbled something about not having been able to get a babysitter. The doctor reiterated his statement and made some comment about the woman "resisting treatment," adding that they would discuss the matter at their next session provided that the woman showed up on time. The woman, more embarrassed now than ever before, looked about the room once again and returned her gaze to the doctor. He stood silently and looked at her. Suddenly the woman grabbed the appointment card from the receptionist's hand, threw it at the doctor, and told him in no uncertain terms to "go shove it." She then turned and hurried back to the elevator. As she left, the doctor shook his head a little sadly and immediately returned to his desk and to his typing.

Although it is only a guess on our part, we believed it highly unlikely that the woman would ever return. The point of this example, however, has little to do with this particular woman and her particular therapist. From our point of view, the example is illustrative of a situation in which the helping agent's "availability" to a client—his psychological availability—is determined more by the theoretical framework from which he works than by his physical location in the community. Ludicrous as it may sound, this doctor and the particular community mental health center in which this situation occurred could have been located in the woman's living room and it would have made little or no difference in the way the situation was handled or turned out. In short, the overall orientations and conceptions of treatment had neither changed nor been influenced in any meaningful way as a function of the health center's new location in the community. The degree of psychological distance between the institution and the conditions of life surrounding the client were relatively unaffected by the "revolutionary" shift in location.

IV. *A certain kind of person is best equipped to render the kind of service that the institution wishes to offer or make available.*

An institution is rarely better than the individual and collective competence of its staff. The ways in which an institution selects its staff (i.e., the criteria and procedures it develops as to what constitutes a potentially effective staff member) play an undeniably important role in determining, for better or worse, the future of that institution. Most institutions are founded on the assumption that only people with certain kinds of training experiences and backgrounds can (or should) be trusted with the responsibility of meeting the kinds of needs for which the institution was created. This assumption, coupled with the fact that most institutions pride themselves on the "professional quality" of their services, has certain consequences for the criteria and procedures developed with respect to the hiring of staff. One of the most important of these consequences is the tendency to evaluate (and to value) an individual more in terms of his formal credentials than his personal characteristics. It is a situation in which primary emphasis is placed on an individual's "professional" preparation, the assumption being that there is a direct relationship between one's level of competence and the nature of one's formal or academic training. It is also, almost by definition, a situation in which present and future competence is gauged not in terms of any assessment of an individual's inherent potential for growth but in terms of his past performance and preparation in an area that is presumed to be related to the particular goals of the institution. And finally, implicit in the situation is the notion that a certain kind of formal training (i.e., academic experiences, professional degrees) is inherently better than other less formal types of preparatory experiences.

The realization of the extent to which our society's needs for services have not been met by our traditional reliance on professionally trained and accredited personnel has exposed, at least in a symptomatic form, some of the problems created by the "credentials crisis." The assumption that only certain individuals (i.e., those with particular kinds of formal credentials) are equipped to deal with complex human problems has resulted in the "numbers problem," in the realization that we do not have now, and probably never will have, enough professional manpower to deal with the mental health needs of our society. To some degree the creation of the War on Poverty and the development of the community mental health movement represent both a realization of and a response to the implications of this situation.

One of the most significant results of the War on Poverty (and to a lesser extent of the community mental health movement) has been the emergence of the nonprofessionals (variously termed the "subprofessionals," "paraprofessionals," "indigenous workers," "facilitators," or "advocates") into the fields of mental health and community action. These are people generally recruited directly from the ranks of the poor, who live in the neighborhoods in which they work and who have at one time or another in their own lives been faced with many of the same problems and crises as the people with whom they now work. It should be pointed out, however (for it bears some significance on the question of how nonprofessionals are perceived and "used"), that the decision to include these people in the ranks of the "mental health workers" (however broadly defined) was motivated more by conditions of necessity than by choice.

It would seem, at least on the surface, that the admission of a whole new population—a group of people with different "credentials"—into the mental health labor force is a signal that the assumption concerning what constitutes "being equipped" to deal with complex human problems has undergone some significant change. Such was neither the case nor apparently the intent behind the move that brought the nonprofessional into prominence. If anything, the move seems to have done more to solidify than to change professional orthodoxy. With respect to the field of mental health, Reiff (1966, p. 546) puts it the following way:

There is no question that the use of these new nonprofessionals opens up a great reservoir of manpower for mental health activities. But, unless this manpower is used effectively they can become nothing more than wardens and nursemaids tending the mentally ill who are waiting for the professional to serve them. They can also become a garbage heap where the professional dumps the patients he feels he can do nothing for. And, finally, the nonprofessional can become the menial who performs all the "dirty work" that the professional resents and wishes he could get rid of so that he could have more time to do the same old things. Used this way, the nonprofessional will reinforce all the tendencies in institutionalized mental health practice that mitigate against change.

The situation in the War on Poverty is even more complex and not a little curious. In the first place, the criteria as to what constitutes a "professional" (not to mention a nonprofessional) are vague and somewhat paradoxical. Almost by fiat, people who are identified as mental health workers (e.g., psychiatrists, psychologists, social workers, and vocational counselors) have been perceived as the "experts," and if they have not officially assumed the mantles of leadership, they are increasingly consulted for advice on how to wage the war against poverty. It is a curious situation in many ways, not the least of which is that the "professional" (i.e., the individual with formal credentials) has already either proved himself to be a failure when it comes to dealing with the problems of poverty or has heretofore never shown any interest in becoming involved in the problem at all. In point of fact, the mental health professional's previous experiences in the area have been little more than minimal, his interest less than that; and, perhaps most important, he has "distinguished" himself by developing theoretical conceptions and models of clinical functioning that are highly suspect with respect to their relevance and applicability to the problems of the poor. Reiff (1966, p. 545), we believe, is quite correct when he states:

The Community Action Program of the Office of Economic Opportunity is in much better position to succeed where the mental health professionals have failed because it is not bogged down by the difficulties inherent in the ideology of mental illness.

The Community Action Program addresses itself to the normal. The poor are not considered sick. The goal of the poverty program, particularly the Community Action Program, is self-determination not self-actualization. Its focus is on coping techniques, not on psychodynamics. In brief, it is free from many of the characteristics of the mental health professionals' ideology which makes for alienation.

A second aspect of the problem has to do with the ways in which nonprofessionals are perceived. Here, too, the situation is a somewhat curious one, for no sooner did the nonprofessional, via the Community Action Program, get into the "business" of delivering what for all intents and purposes were mental health services—and begin to show that he could do the job—than great pains began to be taken to indicate that he was, indeed, ill-equipped to perform that function with any high degree of competence. Iverson (1965, pp. 12–13), for example, in a paper dealing with the "use of the nonprofessional" puts it the following way:

The untrained worker, because of his need to achieve quick, tangible successes, may settle for short-range goals in effecting changes in behavior, neighborhood conditions, and so forth, instead of pushing toward the long-range permanent goals. It is important, however, in working with the nonprofessional, to encourage as many immediate successes as possible, especially in the beginning stages of his work. With adequate supervision he can be helped to sustain his efforts toward long-range goals and achievements.

Another problem for the nonprofessional worker is becoming too personally involved and overly identified with the problems of the poor. In many instances action is based upon emotional involvement rather than rational consideration of alternative solutions, community resources or legal rights.

It is well to point out some dangers which need to be considered in the hiring of such persons. The following are worth note.

1. Because of his success motivation, the untrained worker may be impatient with, or misunderstand a person's right to self-direction and decision. Some workers have been punitive toward their peers and toward persons having less motivation and have been too ready to condemn them as lazy and apathetic.

2. The untrained person may not be able to listen. In his eagerness to deliver services, he may ignore the facts, feelings, and attitudes necessary to provide appropriate help. The need to tell people what to do about their problems is an urgent one to many nonprofessionals, and they may become frustrated with persons who do not respond.

3. All too quickly the nonprofessional will give the illusion of being trained and will take on the mannerisms and the language of the professional. While this may be fulfilling to the worker, it may render him hollow and ineffective.

4. Neighborhood leadership may be drawn off into the so-called establishment, thereby limiting the degree to which local energy can effectively negotiate with the power structure in matters involving political or civil rights. As the saying goes, "You don't bite the hand that feeds you."

5. As the indigenous, lower-class person takes on the mantle of middle-class status, he may look with disdain or criticism upon his former lower-class neighbor who may be less motivated to achieve middle-class status. Again, the feeling is "I made it; why can't you?"

Similarly, Riessman (1967, p. 104), in a paper with which we are otherwise in total agreement, writes:

Frequently, professionals assume that NP's (nonprofessionals) identify with the poor and possess great warmth and feeling for the neighborhood of their origin. While many NP's exhibit some of these characteristics, they simultaneously possess a number of other characteristics. Often, they see themselves as quite different from the other members of the poor community, whom they may view with pity, annoyance, or anger. Moreover, there are many different "types" of nonprofessional: some are earthy, some are tough, some are angry, some are surprisingly articulate, some are slick, clever wheeler-dealers, and nearly all are greatly concerned about their new roles and their relationship to professionals.

While nonprofessionals may be selected because of certain characteristics they possess, such as informality, humor, earthiness, neighborliness—in other words some of the "positive" characteristics of the resident population—the other side of the coin cannot be ignored. That is, they may possess characteristics of low-income population that interfere with effective helper roles. For example, they may possess considerable moral indignation, punitiveness, suspicion, or they may be so open and friendly on occasion that the significance of confidentiality escapes them.

Now, if the points being made by these authors are that there are potentially both "good" and "bad" nonprofessionals, or that nonprofessionals need to learn certain psychological skills (whatever that means), or even that nonprofessionals should have further training, well and good. But implicit in many of the descriptions of the nonprofessional—and even more explicit in some of the "cautions" that have been expressed with respect to what the nonprofessional can or cannot (really, should or should not) be allowed to do—is the notion that when it comes to the nonprofessional, we are dealing with a very different kind of animal than, for example, when we are discussing the professional. *What is most intriguing about the points made by Iverson and Riessman is that if one erased the word "nonprofessional" from their statements and replaced it with the terms "psychiatric resident" or "psychological intern," the meaning and implications of their statements would assume a different perspective and be seen in a different context.* Anyone who has ever supervised the work of prospective clinicians (e.g., psychiatric residents, clinical psychology interns, etc.) has had to deal with many of the same problems that supposedly characterize the nonprofessional. In other words, problems of "becoming too personally involved," affecting "the mannerisms and the language of the professional," the "need to achieve quick, tangible successes," and reacting to the client "with pity, annoyance, or anger" are not problems particular to nonprofessionals: they are issues that confront anyone who is contemplating training for a career in human service.

The basic point we are trying to make is that the emergence of the so-called nonprofessional into a position of some prominence in the field of human service has not, at least until the present time, been accompanied by any basic change in the assumption of what constitutes "being equipped" to deal with complex human problems. Despite calls for "new careers," perhaps even because of them, the need to maintain and enhance professional orthodoxy has been safeguarded. The rather premature judgment of what the nonprofessional is supposedly capable of doing is symptomatic of this state of affairs. What follows—what is happening to the nonprofessional at the present time—is that he is viewed as almost innately different from professionals and is given the kind of training (if he is trained at all) that is often a watered-down version of what has failed in the past. The criteria for what constitutes adequate preparation remains unchallenged and unquestioned, and the world has been kept safe for the professional.

Example 11: In its early days, Community Progress, Inc., was very much like an experimental laboratory; it was a place where a variety of ideas, processes, and programs were tried out—all of which were focused on the problem of developing new and better services for the poor. In time, many of these experimental programs were adopted for use on a much broader scale once the War on Poverty became a reality.

One of CPI's most successful programs was its work crews (now called the Neighborhood Youth Corps program). As we indicated in Chapter 2, the success of the work crew program was primarily due to the quality and motivation of its staff. The staff (work crew foremen and foreladies) was composed entirely of indigenous nonprofessionals most of whom were recruited from the neighborhoods in which CPI had established employment centers. Some of these people had finished high school, but many had not; and none had ever had the kind of formal training usually associated with mental health workers. They were selected for the job not on the basis of any formal criteria but in terms of how motivated and interested they seemed to be in getting involved in the kinds of problems to which the work crew program was addressing itself (i.e., the problems of how to prepare out-of-work and out-of-school youth for full-time employment).

In a relatively short period of time it became clear to

almost everyone that the work crew program was one of CPI's shining successes. The foremen and foreladies were, indeed, able to reach and work with youth whom most people felt to be "beyond help." Although the terms were never used, it was clear that these people were doing what, for all intents and purposes, could be described as psychotherapy, group counseling, and social work. In the course of developing a relationship with a youngster, the foremen would usually enter the youth's home, work directly with his parents, and often use his relationship with the family members to try to get them to a point where they, too, could begin to get involved in opportunity programs. More often than not the homes were "multiproblem" ones, and the families were known to a variety of public and private agencies over long periods of time. Despite their lack of formal preparation, it was apparent, especially from some of the results they achieved with families having long-standing difficulties, that the foremen and foreladies were playing an important and helpful role in the lives of many people. In short, there was every indication that the foremen and foreladies were doing as good a job and in some cases better, as were the more "trained" people from some of the traditional helping agencies.

As CPI grew older and began to receive some national recognition, changes started to occur in some of its programs and orientations. One of these changes involved the organization's increasing professionalization. Within CPI, a new program was born (Unified Social Services) whose goal was to provide a broader and more coordinated set of social services to inner-city people. The program was developed and administered by professional social workers who now assumed the responsibility for training and supervising the work of neophyte social workers and nonprofessionals. In a short time the foremen and foreladies were told, both formally and informally but in no uncertain terms, that they "ought to stop doing social work and concentrate on being work crew leaders." Implied in the message was the notion that they were "getting in over their heads," were not sufficiently trained to do the job, and should step back and "let the pros take over." The foremen and foreladies did step back; they had to. But the effects of the situation, especially the cavalier manner in which it was handled, seemed, at least to those of us who were watching the drama unfold, to have a number of consequences. The most important consequence was a visible diminution in the amount of commitment and involvement that foremen now showed toward their jobs as a whole. Despite the fact that they were increasingly lauded for their "indigenousness" and praised for their "good work with kids," it was clear, at least to them, that for some reasons (the reasons never being made explicit or understandable) they could no longer be trusted with the kinds of responsibilities that they had been handling informally for some time. The overall result was a noticeable decrease in their feelings of worth; a decrease that, in one way or another, could not help but have implications for their feelings about CPI as a whole. Despite the fact that the Unified Social Services program failed and was discontinued within two years, the foremen never, at least officially, resumed their "home visits."

The particular dynamics of the War on Poverty have, in a somewhat different but no less important way, placed the professional in as difficult a position as anyone else with respect to the definition of his role. The War on Poverty, like most institutions and programs, has not been spared the effects of the increasing emphasis on specialization that characterizes our society as a whole. It is a situation in which roles, rather than being broadened conceptually or becoming more generalized, are being defined in narrower and narrower terms. This tendency to restrict the scope and definition of one's role mitigates against the creation of the kinds of conditions under which any basic change in professional outlook can occur or even be contemplated. All this has occurred despite the knowledge that the mental health professions, if they are to begin to play a more meaningful and helpful role in our society, will have to undergo some basic ideological and functional change. Reiff (1966, pp. 544, 546), for example, puts it in the following way:

What is needed is a new profession of experts in changing social systems for the prevention of mental illness and for the improvement of the psychological effectiveness of all individuals in society to deal with the problems of living. It is an exciting prospect but it also contains the same problems of manpower and institutional change.

The role of the professional will change. He will need to be more of a consultant, supervisor, and administrator. And if he should venture into primary prevention or become involved in community action programs, he will probably also be required to play the role of organizer, politician, and educator. All of which will compel him to face new conceptual problems, such as when does community action become political action, how shall he differentiate his citizen role from his professional one, etc. One thing he will have to learn for certain is the harsh reality of power struggles. In a similar fashion, Yolles (1966, p. 40) points out:

In exploratory conferences on training psychologists in community mental health—such as the one held recently in Boston—the psychologist is being discussed as the "creative generalist" of the community mental health center, and as such, some aspects of social psychology, behavioral psychology, and other specialties may become part of the community psychologists' skills.

The calls and needs for change are clear. What is less clear is the fact that change will not occur unless and until the mental health professional is liberated, and liberates himself, from what have become the traditionally accepted definitions of his role, areas of expertise, and limits of responsibility. Much of the mental health professional's currently "maladaptive" behavior in the War on Poverty is no more than an example of the kind of behavior that could be expected to result from a situation of "role ambiguity." Despite the fact that the dynamics of both poverty and poverty programs confront the mental health professional with the need to develop new conceptualizations and patterns of help, he will continue to function in the "same old ways" so long as he remains insulated and isolated by what he and others have defined as his role. What usually follows is that the mental health professional, faced with the demands of a new and oftentimes unfamiliar situation, falls back on his repertoire of traditional behaviors and, by so doing, succeeds in turning the new situation into what for him is a more comfortable one, one much more like the kinds of situations he has experienced in the past.

Example 12: Some time after CPI's Neighborhood Employment Centers had been opened and had become fully functional, several local psychiatrists were hired to participate in some of the disposition meetings regularly held at each center. The decision to utilize the psychiatric consultants was motivated by two factors. On the one hand, several psychiatrists wanted very much to become involved in CPI's work and to be as helpful as they could. They were sincerely interested in the War on Poverty and wanted to become a part of it. The second reason seemed to involve CPI's growing tendency to become more professionally oriented.

In a relatively short period of time, the disposition meetings at one employment center began to look more and more like the case conference usually associated with the mental hospital. The psychiatrist would appear at the appointed time and a number of "cases" would be presented to him for his comments and suggestions. He, in turn, would try as quickly as possible to come up with some reasonable "diagnosis" and would then offer suggestions as to how to handle the "case." The character of the meetings changed in a number of ways. More and more time seemed to be spent dwelling on the dynamics (usually the psychodynamics) of each case, and more suggestions were made that the client be referred for individual treatment. In addition, there was a change in the pattern of staff participation. The more "professional" members of the staff (i.e., vocational counselors) seemed to be contributing much more to the discussion, while the participation of the more "nonprofessional" members of the staff (i.e., neighborhood and community workers) decreased.

Oftentimes, usually after the psychiatrist had left the meeting, there was some grumbling by the nonprofessionals about the way in which things were going. Many of them felt that the psychiatrist's contributions were not very helpful, and their concern focused on the fact that "he comes down here once a week and tells us what to do." They also felt that "he doesn't know this neighborhood, never spends any time in the community and probably is afraid to, and doesn't really know the people that he's making book statements about." The overall feeling was that the psychiatric consultant was not really involved in what they were trying to do, and that he knew very little (and seemed not to want to increase his knowledge) about life in the ghetto. He was perceived, and seemed to be perceiving himself, as someone whose function was to focus on whatever "clinical" problems were presented to him at the center in much the same fashion as he functioned at the mental hospital.

In short, the feeling was that the psychiatrist's suggestions would be more appropriate—and would certainly fall on more willing ears—if he "knew more" about the setting (i.e., spent more time in the streets) and stopped viewing it as little more than an extension of the mental hospital.

The most important point about this example has little

to do with the question of the actual validity of many of the psychiatrist's "diagnoses" and suggestions, although that is certainly an important consideration. The more important point has to do with the degree to which the psychiatrist (well-meaning though he was), when confronted by a new and different situation, acted in such a manner as to turn this relatively unfamiliar situation into one in which he felt more comfortable and certainly more confident.

V. *A certain kind of treatment or intervention is most appropriate to meet the needs the institution was created to serve.*

The particular form of help an institution adopts as its "preferred mode of treatment" (i.e., the kind of intervention it will try to make available to a degree heretofore nonexistent) is assumed to be intimately related to the way in which that institution has diagnosed the problem it wishes to deal with. *Inherent in this assumption, however, is the notion that, in a way, each institution is born a "tabula rasa," that its decision to adopt or develop a particular therapeutic strategy (and then to call it its own) is a free and open one, that it is a decision-making process relatively unencumbered by any "treatment legacies" or "problem diagnoses" inherited from the past. In point of fact, however, this is rarely the case.* More often than not, the birth of a new institution is not accompanied by the exploration and development of new treatment modalities. What usually occurs is that the new institution succeeds in expanding and extending the kinds of services that have become traditional in the field. It is apparently much easier and certainly much less disruptive of a profession's sense of continuity to build new institutions than it is to question some of the basic assumptions underlying its established treatment modalities.

Nowhere is this more apparent than in the situation that currently exists both in the community mental health movement and in the War on Poverty.[3] In both instances it is

³Although the community mental health movement and the War on Poverty share a common interest in providing services for the poor, it would be a mistake to view them as inherently joined or united in this effort. Whatever relationship exists between the two programs is of fairly recent vintage. Reiff (1966) makes clear the fact that they developed—and in some ways continue to develop—both independent of and isolated from each other.

becoming clearer and clearer that individual remediation, not basic institutional change, is the primary focus of concern. The fact that in neither case has there been any concerted effort to question or change what Reiff (1966) has called "the set of integrated assertions, theories, and aims, primarily psychoanalytical, which constitutes the individualistically oriented program for restoring to society the mentally sick and socially deviant" is, at least from our point of view, symptomatic of the state of affairs. Both the community mental health movement and, to a lesser but no less important degree, the War on Poverty have adopted the kinds of treatment modalities that could best be described as psychotherapeutic in nature. Both programs have come to rely on treatment techniques that uphold the "doctrine of intrapsychic supremacy," assume that the "treatment" in and of itself transcends extrasymptomatological variables, and view other possible forms of interventions as having less "depth" and hence less importance than treatment of an individual psychotherapeutic nature. Finally, both programs seem to be becoming increasingly tied to the assumption that the best way to meet the "numbers problem" is to modify and extend the psychotherapeutic model rather than to search for alternatives involving general principles of clinical functioning that could be used in a variety of different ways and by a variety of different people.

Several writers have begun recently to question the wisdom and efficacy of new programs (i.e., the community mental health movement and the community action agency) that base their intervention strategies on the traditional psychotherapeutic model of help. Kelly (1966), for example, sees the "provision of professional help which is divergent from the client's culture" as an important ecological constraint on mental health services. Others have begun to stress conceptions of help that differ markedly from the current "intrapsychic" view; these conceptions, if translated into strategies of help, would result in the development of different intervention techniques. Gladwin (1966), for example, has proposed a "competence" model, and Reiff (1966) has pointed to "self-determination" as opposed to "self-actualization" as the most important issue in the development of a viable treatment program involving the poor.

Despite certain differences, there are important similarities in the viewpoints and suggestions of those who have come to question the appropriateness of the psychotherapeutic model of help as the "preferred treatment modality" for the psychological, social, and vocational problems usually associated with poverty and poor people. Common to all of these viewpoints is the observation that the problem has less to do with the "kinds of people" being treated as with the basic assumptions inherent in the treatment model itself. *The basic point, however, is that rarely does an institution— at that point in its development when it is deciding on a philosophy of treatment—take seriously the fact that it does, indeed, have a variety of choices available to it. To take this fact seriously would imply two things: first, that alternatives are worthy of consideration; and second, that the institution is willing to undertake a critical evaluation and assessment of the assumptions underlying current treatment strategies.* Both courses of action involve a willingness to break with tradition; therefore, both are, almost by definition, not only exciting but also very threatening . . . to say the least. It is for this reason that most institutions content themselves with extending the availability of existing treatment modalities (making the assumption, often without "hard" data, that they are appropriate) rather than searching for or developing new ones.

Elsewhere (Goldenberg, 1966) we have attempted to examine some of the assumptions underlying the psychotherapeutic model of treatment in terms of its appropriateness for dealing with the problems of poverty. Because, as we have already indicated, most existing poverty and mental health programs seem to be developing their services within a remedial psychotherapeutic framework, it is important that we describe, at least from our point of view, what seem to be some of the problems and implications of such a decision.

The field of clinical psychology is trying now as perhaps never before to fulfill its social and professional responsibilities to that segment of the population—namely, the poor, the disenfranchised, or those we now label the "inner-city" poverty population—who heretofore have been almost curious by their absence from the mainstream of clinical thinking and professional concern.

The major task that confronts the mental health professions in this day and age is essentially no different from what it always has been. It is the task of developing models of clinical functioning that hold the promise of rendering help. Today, as in the past, we rely on psychotherapy as the single most important tool for offering such help. It is the primary pattern of clinical functioning that we have developed, and consequently, it is the major form of treatment that we offer the public.

To be sure, psychotherapy has earned the right to be viewed with warmth and affection. It has, with its various orientations and in its myriad forms, brought relief to many, and it need not cringe before its .05 critics. However, just as psychotherapy need not apologize for the nature of its current esteem, so, too, must it not overestimate the impact it has had on that segment of society which has needed it the most.

Psychotherapy has been, and still is, basically a middle- and upper-class phenomenon. Having said this, let us quickly add that our labeling it in this manner should not be interpreted as an indictment of psychotherapy as a model of help. It should also be made clear that we are not implying that psychotherapy has not been offered or made available in a physical sense to the so-called poverty population, for such is neither the case nor our intention. What we are saying is that both the assumptions underlying psychotherapy as a form of help and the explicit demand characteristics that comprise the psychotherapeutic situation may have led, albeit unwittingly, to the systematic exclusion of a significant portion of our society from its potential benefits.

The War on Poverty has placed dramatically before this nation the nature and extent of the problems confronting the poor. It has made visible that "Other America" that remained silent, romanticized, and unseen until Michael Harrington turned the pen into a sword and until President Kennedy used that sword to start a modern-day crusade. Part of that crusade has involved the mental health professions and has resulted in the Community Mental Health Act of 1963. As a consequence of this Act community mental health centers are being established with the aim of making help physically available to any and all members of the community who wish to take advantage of that help. We stress the term "physically available" to make quite clear that services may be physically available, on paper, while at the same time they remain "psychologically unavailable" to the client. At the present time, treatment (i.e., psychotherapy of varying kinds) is or will soon be available physically to everyone in the community, and the ability to pay is of no consequence in determining one's eligibility for treatment. It remains to be seen whether, even under these conditions, inner-city people flock to our centers and clamor for our services. Our own feeling is that they will not seek us out now any more than they have in the past, and the reason for this is to be found in the paradoxical situation of a form of treatment being made available to people who are psychologically unavailable to take advantage of that treatment. This situation is further complicated by that fact that clinicians—far from understanding the psychology of poverty, and far from using this understanding to develop truly innovative models of help—have taken the democratic and conscience-absolving position that psychotherapy, in and of itself and with no significant modification, will achieve its purposes as soon as it is made available to people of all races, religions, and social classes. To make this point clear, it is important that we examine some of the assumptions underlying psychotherapy and relate these assumptions or conditions to some of the psychological characteristics of poverty.

A colleague of ours has defined psychotherapy as "the sustained talking cure," a definition that, from our point of view, is as good as any and better than most. It is a definition that most therapists, regardless of their particular theoretical predilections, could probably live with.

Defining psychotherapy as the "sustained talking cure" clearly indicates that in order for psychotherapy to occur, the client must agree to a minimum of at least two conditions. First, he must accept the condition that he appear regularly for his appointed hour or hours each week. In other words, he must accept the responsibility of making himself available during those specified times of the week when he and the therapist have agreed to meet in the latter's setting (i.e., the clinician's office). Similarly, and implicit in this situation, is the assumption that the client both accepts and experiences the relevance of the patient-doctor relationship. These are, in short, the behaviors, responsibilities, or demand characteristics that we assume when we use the term "sustained."

The second condition of psychotherapy, at least as we have defined it, is that the patient eventually talk. For Freud, as for all subsequent clinicians regardless of their particular theoretical predilections, talking was and is the basic rule of treatment. Thus, we include the term "talking cure" in our definition of psychotherapy. However, implicit in the demand or condition that the client talk are some additional assumptions about the role and importance of verbal behavior in the client's life. First, it assumes that the client experiences verbal interactions as a personally relevant way of communicating. Second, it assumes that the client perceives talking as a reasonable vehicle for personal change. In short, the condition of talking assumes that the client is comfortable in and has confidence in the world of words.

To say that the conditions of treatment we have described are obvious is one thing; but to say that we comprehend fully the implications that these assumptions make about the human condition is another. For an individual to accept the conditions of psychotherapy implies one additional thing:

that the individual experiences himself to be a human being who has a definite stake in, concern for, and place within the total societal process. It implies that the client sees his life as integrally bound to his society's, and that he views himself as a functional part of that society from which he now seeks help. In other words, in order for an individual to accept the conditions of treatment, he must already be at a point where, to one degree or another, he both accepts and feels accepted by his society. He must already have identified his goals and needs as somehow relevant to, and attainable through, his participation in the societal process.

To carry what we have just said to its logical conclusion, we would have to add that psychotherapy seems to be the treatment of choice for those people who need treatment least. Thus, for example, psychotherapy has been most effective with individuals whose problems do not significantly interfere with their ability to accept the conditions of treatment (e.g., psychoneurotics and persons with certain character disorders). Similarly, psychotherapy has been least effective with those patients whose problems have manifested themselves in an inability to accept the responsibility, regularity, and commitment to the world of words that characterize the treatment situation (e.g., schizophrenics, addicts, and the poor). To clarify this point, it is important that we discuss briefly some of the psychological characteristics of poverty and relate these characteristics to the assumptions underlying the psychotherapeutic situation.

Poverty—psychological poverty—is, perhaps more than anything else, a condition of being, a stance one assumes with respect to oneself and the world. It is a stance through which one views oneself as static, limited, and irredeemably expendable. People enter or become a part of the world of psychological poverty only when they have succumbed (usually involuntarily) to that insidious process that undermines hope and subverts the desire to "become." This process, which is both self-perpetuating and self-reinforcing, leaves in its wake the kinds of human beings who have learned to view themselves and their world as chronically, almost genetically, poor. The end product of this state of affairs is an individual who is, in fact, alienated, isolated, and insulated from that very society of which he nominally remains a member. He and his society are spatially joined but psychologically separate: they inhabit parallel but non-reciprocal worlds.

If what we have described has any validity to it, then there is reason to wonder how or why the poor (the psychologically poor) should experience psychotherapy as a form of treatment whose conditions are relevant to their needs and appropriate to their interests. There is no compelling reason to believe that those who experience themselves as inhabiting a world that is psychologically removed from the world of their fellow citizens should suddenly embrace a form of treatment which, for all its noble intents and purposes, comes from an alien culture.

If a person does not perceive himself to have a stake in his society, and if he does not experience his society as uniquely concerned with him as a human being, then the assumptions underlying the "sustained talking cure" are, at least for him, both irrelevant and inappropriate. It is meaningless to expect this person to accept the responsibility of regularly keeping his appointments at the therapist's office. For him to do so would be inconsistent with the very dynamics that define psychological poverty. It would be just as meaningless for him to feel comfortable in the world of words, for there is no reason to assume that he shares our faith in the power of the spoken word. In short, the fundamental assumptions that psychotherapy makes about the human condition may be invalid when applied to that large segment of the population we now know as the "Other America."

VI. *The institution as a social structure should be organized in a way that reflects the orientations and values of its leaders and their techniques.*

One of the most important but least studied problems in the creation of institutions is the "how and why they get to look and act the way they do" problem. The importance of this problem is underscored by the fact that many now take seriously the notion that there is an intimate relationship between the way in which an institution is organized and the effectiveness with which it meets the needs it was created to serve.

The thesis we shall advance is a simple one: that the social structures of most institutions are determined by the ways in which their "builders" have dealt with (or avoided dealing with) the implications of Assumptions IV and V. *In other words, an institution's internal organization (i.e., the way it defines and distributes power and responsibility, the kinds of channels of communication it develops, and the decision-making processes that come to characterize the organization) is a reflection of the kinds of assumptions and decisions that have already been made with respect to the question of "credentials" and the selection of a "treatment model."* It is in this manner and through this process that almost every new institution and program, at least in terms of its social organization, comes to mirror the orientations and values of its leaders and their techniques.

The assumption that an organization's social structure should reflect the values, goals, and methods of certain of its members to the exclusion of others has a number of consequences not only for the growth and development of the organization but also for the manner in which it goes about its task of fulfilling its responsibilities. One of the most important of these consequences is that the institution's internal structure is, in a very real sense, "preordained"; that is to say, the particular ways in which it is organized precede rather than grow out of the natural evolution of the institution as a social setting. Of equal importance is the fact that implicit in this situation is the notion that the institution's organizational pattern is basically unchangeable, that whatever problems the organization is confronted with are soluble within and only within the context of its existing social structure. The social structure itself is more or less "out of bounds" with respect to the question of basic change. And finally, inherent in the preordained quality of the social structures of most institutions is the assumption—rarely verbalized and never discussed—that not only is there a logical rationale for its being the way it is, but there is also a body of data to support the wisdom of the particular way in which that institution has been organized.

More often than not, the assumption that an institution should be organized in such a manner as to reflect the orientations and values of its leaders and their techniques results in the institution's being structured in a pyramidal fashion. The pyramidal organization has a number of characteristics that distinguish it from organizations structured along different lines; the most important one is that it rests upon certain conceptions of man and of what people are capable of doing both now and in the future. We shall have much to say about these conceptions about man (especially in terms of how they affect individual, group, and organizational growth) in this and later sections of this book. For the present, however, all we wish to stress is the fact that the decision to organize an institution in a pyramidal fashion is, in and of itself, a decision that can only be made if one makes certain assumptions and holds to certain conceptions about the human condition.

When we refer to the "pyramidal" structure, we are referring to an organization whose internal structure is characterized by certain vertically ordered power relationships, communication patterns, and decision-making processes. It is an organizational structure in which an individual's role, responsibilities, and influence are clearly defined by the position he occupies in the institution's hierarchy. At any given point in time, the individual's "job description" can be used as a convenient index both to locate him within the total organization and to get some clear indication of the nature of his duties, rights, and obligations. *Most important, the pyramidal structure is one in which people and roles are always replaceable but never interchangeable.*

From our point of view, the importance of the pyramidal structure arises from the fact that it is the prepotent model and philosophy of organizational structure currently employed by most agencies, institutions, and settings involved in what can be defined broadly as the area of human service. Almost all educational institutions (school systems), community action agencies (War on Poverty programs), and mental health settings (community mental health centers) are internally structured along organizational lines that are basically pyramidal in form. Common to all these social institutions is the assumption (one could more accurately call it the faith) that their goals and objectives can best be achieved within the framework of a pyramidal or vertically ordered organization. In other words, implicit in the way each of these helping agencies is organized is the belief that there is a positive relationship between their particular organizational philosophy (i.e., the pyramidal structure) and the efficacy with which the organization as a whole meets the needs it was created to serve. Thus, for example, children will supposedly learn better, poor people will receive better service, and emotionally disturbed individuals will get better treatment when the services offered are made available in and through a social system that is governed by the dynamics of pyramidal organization.

But what is a pyramidal organization? What does it look like? What are some of its inherent dynamics and self-defining characteristics? And what internal processes does it produce to confirm or deny the assumption that it is, indeed, the most appropriate organizational model for delivering the kinds of services that define the goals of most educational, social-rehabilitative, and individual-therapeutic institutions?

In Figure 3.1 we have outlined, in very schematic form, the formal organization of three human service subsystems: the ward of a mental hospital, the Neighborhood Employment Center of a community action agency, and an elementary school. Rather than try to describe the overall "systems" (i.e., the psychiatric hospital, the community action program, and the school system) to which each subsystem belongs and of which each is a part, we have limited ourselves to describing the social structures of those subsystems whose primary responsibility is to deliver the services

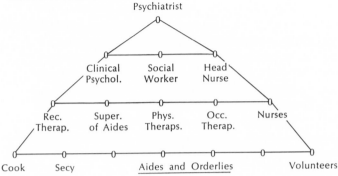

Psychiatric Hospital Ward

Psychiatrist

Clinical
Psychol.

Social
Worker

Head
Nurse

Rec.
Therap.

Super.
of Aides

Phys.
Theraps.

Occ.
Therap.

Nurses

Cook   Secy   Aides and Orderlies   Volunteers

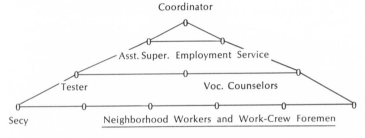

Neighborhood Employment Center

Coordinator

Asst. Super. Employment Service

Tester   Voc. Counselors

Secy   Neighborhood Workers and Work-Crew Foremen

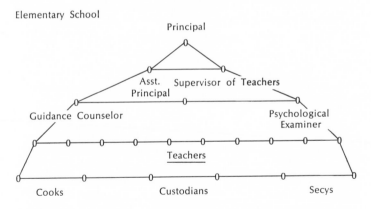

Elementary School

Principal

Asst.   Supervisor of Teachers
Principal

Guidance Counselor   Psychological
Examiner

Teachers

Cooks   Custodians   Secys

FIGURE 3.1 THE FORMAL ORGANIZATION OR SOCIAL STRUCTURES
OF THREE HUMAN SERVICE SUBSYSTEMS

of the larger system to a particular circumscribed group of people.[4] We have done this for two reasons: first, because each subsystem or organization can, in one way or another, be viewed as a self-contained unit, thus making it easier to describe the dynamics and processes that are characteristic of that particular setting; and second, because each subsystem, in terms of its own organization, mirrors the social structure of the system as a whole. In other words, each subsystem both occupies its own position in the pyramidal hierarchy of the system as a whole and, at the same time, is itself structured in such a fashion as to replicate, albeit in smaller form, the pyramidal organization of the larger system to which it belongs. Consequently, there is reason to believe that some of the dynamics and processes that occur *within* each subsystem are similar to those that occur *between* each unit and the system as a whole.

Despite certain differences, there are a number of characteristics common to all the subsystems described in Figure 3.1. It is these communalities in which we are most interested, because they define both the meaning and implications of the pyramidal structure in human service organizations.

The most obvious characteristic common to all the subsystems is the fact that the number of people accommodated by each stratum or level increases as one descends from the leader's position at the apex of the pyramid. Each subsystem has only one official leader and (with the situation in the public schools providing the only exception) the number of people in low-power positions increases as one

[4]The fact that our outlines of each of the human service subsystems do not include the recipients of these services should not be taken to mean that we do not consider them to be an important and integral part of each institution. A number of writers, such as Caudill (1958), Polsky (1962), and Levinson and Gallagher (1964) have pointed out how, in one form or another, the "clients" of institutions both influence and are influenced by the organizational and social structures that characterize different settings. The mere fact that the recipients of an institution's services generally have little or no voice in the decision-making processes that ultimately affect their lives is as important a characteristic and consequence as any other of the ways in which institutions are usually organized, and of the relationship between organizational philosophy and patterns of service.

approaches the base of the organization. It is a situation in which the few govern the many. The positions at every level of the organization are clearly defined with respect to role specification and role responsibility. There is very little overlapping of official duties. Thus, for example, the psychiatrist who administers the inpatient ward will not be expected to herd patients to and from recreational activities; the neighborhood workers in the employment center will not do any testing; and the custodians in the elementary school will not supervise the work of teachers. The roles people fill can be replaced or realigned on the organizational hierarchy; but there is no role interchangeability between echelons, and there is very little role interchangeability even within a given level except for people having the same job descriptions. Another characteristic is that the degree of professionalization (i.e., the kind and number of credentials) increases as one ascends the pyramid. Those occupying the base of the pyramid have the least amount of "professional training" and hold the fewest relevant "credentials" in terms of the kinds of services that the organization defines itself as offering its clientele.

In each of the subsystems there is a direct relationship between an individual's power, status, and overall responsibility and the position he occupies in the organization's hierarchy. In similar fashion, one's income and sphere of influence are governed by one's standing in the pyramid. The decision-making process is governed by the same dynamics that characterize the system as a whole. The leader of each subsystem has the final say in any and all decisions concerning basic policy as well as in those affecting the "course of treatment" for any single individual (patient, client, or student) served by the organization. In addition to this power, he must also assume the responsibility for whatever decisions have been made. Under these conditions, and because the leader's decision is only as good as the information he has available to him, it becomes important that channels of communication be established which are helpful in the decision-making process.

In most settings (including the hospital ward, the Neighborhood Employment Center, and the elementary school) the decision-making process occurs through what is called a "team approach." The team approach (variously termed a team meeting, disposition meeting, or case conference) has as its purpose providing the leader with the kinds of information, opinions, and ideas held by the various members of his staff with respect to a specific issue. More often than not, however, the "team" quality of the decision-making process is usually very difficult to perceive; this is partly explained by the dynamics inherent in an organization in which valuation is based primarily on the nature of one's credentials and position in the organization's social structure. The opinions of certain staff members will be solicited and given some degree of thought and attention, while the opinions of others will rarely be solicited and hardly ever be considered. This differentiation occurs not because of some premeditated plan to exclude or inhibit the behavior of certain individuals: it is the natural result of a situation predicated upon certain assumptions and conceptions regarding the criteria that designate someone as a person whose opinions are worth soliciting and considering. In the psychiatric setting, for example, the concept of the team approach is often little more than a euphemism. It is a way of describing a meeting in which, whether or not nonprofessionals (i.e., aides, orderlies, etc.) are present, the primary purpose is to provide the professional staff (i.e., the psychiatrist, the clinical psychologist, the social worker) with a forum through which they can present, discuss, and defend their own ideas about diagnosis and treatment, all in the hope that such an interaction will enable the "team leader" (the psychiatrist) to plot a course of action, which each person will then implement in his own circumscribed area of responsibility and alleged competence. Rarely if ever are the opinions of low-power, low-prestige staff members solicited, and almost never do their ideas, if voiced, constitute a basis for any action that would represent a significant departure from the orientations of the more professional members of the staff, especially the team leader.

Example 13: Although CPI's Neighborhood Employment Centers began as rather free-wheeling operations, it was not very long before they assumed many of the structural and interpersonal characteristics of most pyramidal organizations. Nowhere was this more discernible than in the weekly disposition meetings held at each center.

The disposition meeting was the vehicle that brought together the entire staff of the NEC for the purposes of first evaluating and reviewing the status of a particular client, and then using this information to plan whatever future interventions seemed appropriate. Each meeting was attended by the NEC Coordinator, his assistant, the vocational counselors, a staff member from the State Employment Service, a testing specialist, the NEC secretary, and the NEC's neighborhood workers and work crew foremen.

In one NEC the disposition meetings were held in a rather small room around a long, rectangular table. It was clear that the table was not large enough to accommodate all the staff members of the NEC. Over a period of time the seats people occupied took on a regular, distinctive, and predictable pattern. Although no particular seating arrangement had been discussed or agreed upon, week after week one would find the relatively higher-status, higher-power staff members (i.e., the NEC Coordinator, his assistant, the vocational counselors, the tester, and the State Employment Service personnel) occupying the seats around the table. The less "prestigeful" members of the staff (the neighborhood workers and work crew foremen) were relegated, or relegated themselves, to chairs at the back of the room a few feet from the conference table.

The pattern of verbal interaction at each disposition meeting soon began to mirror the seating arrangement. Most of the talking, suggesting, and arguing was done by those who had seats around the table. Rarely were those seated at the back of the room asked for their opinions. Even more rarely would they volunteer unsolicited suggestions or ideas. Although the neighborhood workers and foremen "knew" the client more intimately than most of the other members of the staff, their judgments and assessments of a particular client's situation carried very little weight in the final "disposition" of the case. More often than not, the Coordinator's decision reflected some agreement or compromise reached between the vocational counselors, the tester, and the State Employment Service personnel.

In time, the foremen and the neighborhood workers began coming late for, or even missing, some of the meetings. Whenever they came they would automatically take up positions on the periphery of the room. Although they grumbled a great deal about their feelings of being "left out" of the decision-making process—the grumbling usually taking place outside the NEC—neither they nor the more "powerful" members of the NEC ever brought the issue up for general discussion. After a while the situation became accepted as "traditional."

One of the more interesting consequences of the pyramidal structure is the phenomenon that those who "know" the client best (knowledge being defined in terms of concrete experiences rather than formal education) have the least to say about what happens to the client. In most pyramidal organizations, power, status, and influence in the decision-making process are inversely proportional both to the absolute amount of time spent with the client and the number of settings in which one's experiences with the client have taken place. On the mental hospital ward, for example, the psychiatrist's contact with a given patient is usually confined to periodic ward rounds and, at best, one hour of weekly treatment in the psychiatrist's office. The clinical psychologist usually knows the patient only from the diagnostic situation or from the therapeutic situation if he happens to be in charge of treatment. In similar fashion, the social worker may have visited the patient's home and worked with the family. The aides and orderlies, on the other hand, spend approximately eight hours every day in situations through which they have direct access to the patients. In addition, their interactions with the patient occur in a variety of different settings (e.g., the day room, the dining room, the hospital grounds) and are not confined to the kinds of situations (e.g., the "treatment" situation or the diagnostic situation) whose demand characteristics and ecology may produce more "atypical" kinds of behaviors. The situation in the NEC is no different. The NEC Coordinator may or may not have met the client personally, and the vocational counselors and tester must base their opinions about the client's behavior on data obtained from very specialized and limited interview or evaluation situations. The foremen, on the other hand, usually work with the client (if he is an adolescent) for about five hours a day, and the neighborhood worker usually knows the client from many hours spent with him in the streets, at home, or in whatever neighborhood settings the client frequents. In the case of both the psychiatric ward and the NEC, however, the power to make "client decisions" and the responsibility for these decisions rest in the hands of those staff members who have had the least amount of direct contact with the client himself. This situation can only exist in settings that define expertise (and by implication, power, worth, and responsibility) in terms of certain criteria (i.e., professional degrees, formal training in a specific treatment model, etc.) and not others (i.e., the personal qualities of an individual, his potential, and the nature of his experience and contact with the target population). McIntyre (1969), in a paper describing some of the characteristics of the pyramidal structure in the school system, has focused attention on the relationship between organizational structure and individual behavior. Many of his observations are relevant here for they offer a vivid picture of some of the consequences and problems that are either inherent in, or emanate from, this conception of organizational structure. According to McIntyre (pp. 123–129, 132–133):

The administrative power hierarchy of the Sheffield school system can be compared, with some success, to that of the military, as quite probably can that of most school systems or that of any other system based on a pyramidal structure. The military system is designed to meet the ultimate exigencies of combat and, of course, is more exaggerated in its authoritarian characteristics than a school system, but I think there are some essential similarities.

The military decision-making process is moved by the necessity to organize large numbers of people as quickly as possible into effective action. Speed and control of organized action is the overriding concern, and concern for the wisdom of decisions cannot be allowed those beneath the decision-making point on the pyramid of command. The structure is based, necessarily, on individual judgment and absolute authority. There is no time for free discussion of alternatives, and the wisdom of decisions must be assumed. Innovation is permissible only in the interest of already-established goals and courses of action. The feelings and welfare of individuals down the line are of no importance, except in so far as they affect ability to carry out orders. Corrective and punitive measures are swift and often without much mercy; again by necessity, conformity, as it affects organized impact, is more important than individual justice. The welfare, security, and worth of an individual within the military establishment is based almost wholly on approval by higher authority rather than by a standard judgment of competence. As there is absolute authority, there is absolute responsibility; a military commander is ultimately responsible for all the relevant actions of every individual beneath him, as is everyone else down the line.

Obviously, the above falls far short of a complete description of military organizations. It is interesting, though, how many of these characteristics seem to fit, in some measure, almost any pyramidal social structure whose function is primarily operational efficiency.

Since organizational efficiency depends largely on control, which, in turn, depends on the sharing of ideas, which, in turn, depends largely on equality of voice, most social organizations will experience a conflict between efficiency and innovation, between authority and freedom to share ideas. To the extent that one kind of characteristic is in evidence, the other will be inhibited.

Authoritarian structures seem to contract communications problems. Those people with the most authority are furthest from the "front lines." For decisions made at the top of the pyramid to be relevant to the situations occurring at the bottom, there must be considerable feedback of accurate information from bottom to top. The more authoritarian the social structure, the more difficult it is for this feedback to occur, since it involves the sharing of ideas. The only other way for this information to get from bottom to top is by filtering upward. In an authoritarian system, where an individual's security depends on approval by higher authority, information not certain of approval tends not to filter upward. The unfortunate result is that the more authority you have the less likely you are to be informed.

A serious consequence of increasing upward selectivity of information is conflicting demands issued by different levels of authority, based upon differing amounts and kinds of information at each level. Another is the non-relevance of top-level decisions and directives, creating the eternal problem for subordinates to safely work around them without incurring top-level anger.

For the most part, the concerns of individuals move from the general to the specific as they move from the apex of the pyramid toward the base. A large number of specific, circumscribed concerns fill the heads of individuals at the base. Neither time nor head size permit an individual at the top of the pyramid to be aware of all the specific concerns of all individuals at the bottom. This results in the delegation of authority and responsibility. Spheres of responsibility descend from the apex in decreasing scope and increasing specificity, and a pyramidal network of procedural protocol organizes the chain of command into a workable structure. Because of increasing upward selectivity of information, it becomes a serious matter of individual security that this procedural protocol specifying the chain of command not be violated. In a system where welfare depends largely on approval by higher authority, the security of an individual at a particular level hinges critically on his having immediate responsibility to and immediate contact with only those individuals on the next highest level, who have the best information on which to judge his performance. Likewise, the security of that next highest level hinges critically on its being the sole filter through which information passes further, and any short-circuiting of the ascending communication network ("going over the head" of one's immediate superior, the chief's inspection tour of the lower level, "gripe sessions" at which higher levels are present, etc.) jeopardize those levels caught between. In this way, authoritarian structure tends to rigidify itself, and as procedures and areas of responsibility become more rigid, the more security becomes dependent on that very rigidity. As this occurs, the less likely is open communication between levels, and the less effective is inter-level sharing of ideas.

In systems focusing primarily on operational efficiency, where authority and rigidity of function are dominant characteristics, individual frustration often involves a conflict as a result of the fact that different levels in the hierarchy have different information about the same issues. Since these differing points of view rarely are dealt with by open confrontation, the resulting conflicts are easily blamed on the stupidity of those in higher positions, the incompetence of those in lower positions, and the idiocy of the system itself. Frustration, though keenly felt, is much more likely to be felt impersonally, in the sense that it is much more easily directed outward.

The more authoritarian a structure is, the more rigid are the policies and procedures that relate to the way one functions. What this amounts to is fewer action alternatives from which to choose. The more one feels that one's actions are prescribed, the less personally responsible one can feel for their consequences, and in this sense authoritarian structures can offer considerable security in their lack of freedom. One can safely predict great resistance in any authoritarian structure and at any level on the pyramid toward freer discussion of alternatives and toward greater power to choose among them, however frustrating the lack of freedom might have been. Furthermore, the greater the weight of tradition behind authoritarian security, the greater will be the resistance to change. Individuals in positions of higher authority can protect themselves from the awesome feeling of personal responsibility by barricading themselves against hearing alternatives and against hearing information about the results of their decisions. Individuals toward the bottom of the pyramid can protect themselves by believing in their own powerlessness to choose alternatives.

In trying to understand such a complicated human network as a school system, it is insufficient to characterize its organizational structure as more or less authoritarian. There can be many variations in organizational structure, and these variations are important in terms of the pattern of human functioning. Likewise, similar organizational structures can be inhabited by different kinds of people, and this too is important. The interaction between structure and individual must be our focus. Furthermore, to make matters even more complicated, it is precisely this kind of interaction, occurring over long periods of time, that results in something we call a subculture, and which is held together by a force not much different and no less powerful than the feelings of morality that bind our larger western culture.

We shall have much more to say about some of the other consequences of the pyramidal structure—especially in terms of its implications for clinical functioning and individual growth—in later sections of this book. For the present, however, all we wish to stress is the fact that as a model and philosophy of organization, the pyramidal structure is predicated upon certain conceptions and assumptions about people and the relationship of people to the goals and processes of the institution of which they are a part.

VII. *The institution's concern should be focused on the external needs it was created to meet, not on itself as a social organization.*

It would be highly demoralizing, to say the least, for an institution to view itself as a potential candidate for the kinds of services it wishes to offer to others. From almost the very moment of conception, most institutions accept as fact the assumption that they are, and will continue to be, "healthier" than the clients whose needs they were created to serve. This attitude seems to be especially prevalent among institutions involved in the area of human service. It is a striking phenomenon for a number of reasons, not the least of which is that one might expect institutions dealing with clinical or clinical-related problems to accept the reality of their own vulnerability to the kind of organizational problems which, though different phenotypically from the kinds of problems presented by their clients, may have similar genotypic bases. In most cases, however, the reverse is true. Most institutions, while recognizing that they may have certain internal problems, persist in viewing these problems as inherently different (and, by implication, less serious) than the problems of their clients. It is the assumption of "agency-client disparity" that enables an institution to maintain the stance that most, if not all, of its efforts should be focused solely on the external needs it was designed to meet, and not on the dynamics and problems of its own social organization.

The fact that an institution tends not to see its own "mental health" as a problem important enough to merit a high priority of concern is perhaps the best guarantee that serious problems will almost inevitably occur. There is by now a vast literature indicating how and why many different kinds of service institutions are, in reality, not very much healthier than the clients they serve. The works of Goffman (1961), Stanton and Schwartz (1954), and Street, Vinter, and Perrow (1966) offer classic and frightening descriptions of the craziness and sickness that can become an integral part of so many institutions dealing with problems of human welfare. In each case, whether the description is of an "asylum," a mental hospital, or a correctional institution, the picture is of an organization suffering from many of the same problems (e.g., interpersonal difficulties, communication conflicts, patterns of individual and group deviancy, pathological behavior) as the clients they are supposed to serve. The most discouraging aspect of the situation is that sooner or later these internal problems seriously impair the institution's attempts to render the kinds of service that would be helpful to its clients. In the more extreme cases it becomes difficult to distinguish who is "sicker," the client or the helping agency.

The assumption of agency-client difference carries with it a number of conceptions about the nature of the institution and the needs of its staff. One of these conceptions involves a view of the organization and its staff as relatively "finished products"; that is to say, not only is the institution a fixed entity, but the people who become a part of it enter the setting in an assumed state of relative personal and/or professional completion. This being the case, it need not be an institution's goal to focus undue attention on the individual and collective growth of its staff, for the needs for self-actualization either are no longer an issue or are assumed to have been dealt with prior to entry into the organization.

By far the most important consequence of the assumption that the institution need not overly concern itself with its own mental health is that the institution rarely attempts to develop or build into itself any viable mechanisms for preventing or dealing with its own problems. By "viable mechanisms" we mean any processes that would enable the institution systematically and regularly to take a long, hard look at its functioning, its growth, and its conflicts. The fact that few institutions or institution-builders ever develop such vehicles for self-scrutiny should not be taken as evidence of bad faith, poor judgment, or questionable motives. It is the inevitable result of a situation in which an organization does not view itself, its staff, and its problems as legitimate and important areas of concern. Once the assumption has been made that there is something inherently different between its own life and the lives of its clients (between its own needs and the needs of those it wishes to serve), a pattern of thinking is born which inhibits or stamps as irrelevant the de-

velopment of vehicles for self-study and self-correction. In
short, once the institution accepts as fact the alleged dichotomy between its own existence and those of its clients—
a dichotomy which then allows the institution to rationalize
and justify its being solely in terms of "helping others"—
the institution need no longer "trouble" itself with questions of internal self-actualization or problems of self-
confrontation.

As we already have pointed out, the tendency of an institution to avoid looking at itself and to refrain from the
often agonizing search to develop internal mechanisms for
dealing with its own problems does not bring with it any
guarantee that serious problems will not occur. All it does
is guarantee that when such problems arise they will be
dealt with haphazardly, instinctively, and reflexively; in short,
they will be dealt with in precisely the kinds of ways that
the institution would never condone or allow to happen
were it dealing with a problem of any of its clients.

Example 14: One of the primary reasons for CPI's success
in working with the disadvantaged and the Regional Center's success in working with the mentally retarded was the
concern and involvement that each of these agencies brought
to the problems of their respective clients. Both agencies
prided themselves, and rightly so, on their ability to develop programs for, and to work closely with, populations
that had so often been either neglected or served in more
or less haphazard and "token" ways. One of the most important characteristics of the services that these agencies
provided their clients was the time and energy that were
expended in planning and following through on any dramatic changes that would involve the lives of their clients.
Nowhere was this more obvious than in the ways these
agencies dealt with the interrelated problems of dependency
and termination.

In both cases, whenever a client was ready to "leave the
institution" (either because he had gained employment after
having been through one of CPI's opportunity programs, or
because he was ready to reenter the community after having
been worked with at the Regional Center for the Mentally
Retarded), a great deal of time was taken to prepare the
client for termination. Many of his feelings (e.g., dependency,
separation anxiety) were "worked through"; help was given

in planning for the future; and the attempt was made to provide for a period of transition that would help both the client and his worker adjust to the possibility of a new and different kind of relationship. The one thing the worker would *not* do was to "pull out" of the relationship with little or no explanation of his behavior, or to leave without enabling the client to understand or adjust to the situation.

But just as this way of thinking and planning was almost second nature to anyone working with a client in either of these agencies, the exact opposite appeared to be true in cases involving a change within either of the two agencies. In other words, neither agency perceived the importance of working with its own staff in the same kinds of ways that it worked with the problems of its clients.

Both CPI and the Regional Center underwent changes in leadership at a point fairly early in the life of each agency. In both cases the leaders of the organization left to take other positions. Both men were dynamic leaders, the kind of men who were able to inspire and motivate a group of people to share their dreams, to work tirelessly to fulfill certain ideals, and to join with them in the great adventure of human renewal. Each, in his own way, was a charismatic leader capable of eliciting trust and confidence—as well as a certain degree of dependence.

Each leader handled his departure from the organization in a manner that guaranteed problems, and in a way that was totally at variance with the manner in which he had helped the members of his staff to conceive of their relationships with the clients whom they had served. Neither leader seemed to expend even a minimum amount of time to prepare his staff for his departure, to help them handle their feelings, or to provide for a period of relatively peaceful transition. In one case the leader simply announced his imminent resignation, withdrew, and allowed his successor to begin his own "term of office" with little assistance or active guidance. In the second case the leader allowed the question of his resignation to drag on for a period of several months, continually hedging as to whether or not he would leave, and never consulting with the staff to plan for a successor. The result in both agencies was predictable and not a little disorganizing. There was a serious problem with morale; people seemed to be much less involved in what they were doing; there was a drop in service and an increase in feelings of anxiety, anger, and depression. But the soon-to-be-departing leaders seemed almost oblivious to what was going on around them. Even when it became apparent that their imminent departures were having a serious effect on their staffs, neither leader seemed inclined to help deal with the problems that were, and would continue to be, related to their leaving the organization. In short, the leaders, in terms at least of how they dealt with the problems of their own staffs and their own organizations, approached the situation in precisely the way that they would never have allowed to happen were it a case involving the life of a client.

Example 15: There are certain assumptions that most people involved in poverty programs (or, for that matter, in any program of service) make concerning the kinds of issues they will have to deal with in working with a client. Thus, for example, the problem of race is almost guaranteed to come up in the course of most encounters that poverty workers have with members of the target population. Similarly, problems of status and power are almost sure to arise in any interpersonal situation. Most workers in the area of human service accept the fact that these problems— especially if they remain below the surface, unverbalized, and undiscussed—can have a variety of potentially unhelpful consequences for the client's attempts to seek, obtain, and hold employment in any situation involving people of different races. Once again, this way of thinking is almost second nature to anyone involved in work with members of minority groups. This does not mean, however, that poverty workers will automatically transfer this orientation to the settings of which they themselves are a part.

Over a period of time a number of CPI's Neighborhood Employment Centers became known as places of great unrest. Each of these NEC's seemed to be in a state of perpetual tension and dissension. A number of cliques had formed and it became more and more difficult for people to cooperate with one another. The cliques that had formed seemed to be based on race and status. Thus, for example, the whites tended to form a clique, the Negroes had their own group, and the professionals comprised a third group. At times it became so bad that there was little if any communication between any of these groups of people.

The importance of this example does not lie in the fact that people working together (supposedly regardless of race or status) in an antipoverty program could fall victim to the same kinds of prejudices and problems as the clients with whom they worked. All that it would indicate is that people in the War on Poverty are only human. The significance of the example is that no provisions were made within the organization for the discussion of some of the very same issues that each worker would almost automatically discuss with his client. In other words, the organization could not think in terms of developing any internal mechanisms through which such issues as race, status, and power could be brought out into the open, discussed, and dealt with in any meaningful way.

Since most institutions, because of their acceptance of the assumption of agency-client difference, do not usually develop any internal mechanisms for dealing with or preventing problems, the question arises as to how problems are dealt with once they have become manifest. The answer will vary, of course, from agency to agency depending on the nature of the agency's problems and the rigidity of its organization. The safest thing to say, however, is that regardless of the specific agency, whatever problems arise will have to be either ignored or dealt with in a remedial fashion. One thing remains clear. Once an agency views the development of self-reflective mechanisms as unimportant or irrelevant to its goals of providing service, the number of alternatives available to the agency when a problem manifests itself are severely limited. If the agency recognizes its problems and chooses at all to deal with them (a situation that is far more often the exception than the rule), it will generally seek relief by involving itself with some consultant external to the situation. In other words, it will present itself as a client or as a patient to a different agency or individual. It will invite a "therapist" (the current terminology is to call them "organizational consultants" or, even more euphemistically, "change agents") into the organization for the purpose of "fixing" whatever the consultant feels has gone awry. The hope is that by presenting its problems in typical clinical fashion to an outsider the institution will obtain relief, at least some symptomatic relief. The fact that this hope may or may not be realized—and that if it is realized there is no guarantee, as is the case in any psychotherapeutic situation, that problems of a similar nature will not appear in the future—is irrelevant at this point. The major point we wish to make is that the entire situation arises as a consequence of the assumption, made early in the life of the institution, that the institution was designed to meet certain external needs and that it was not meant to focus undue attention on itself as a social organization.

VIII. *The institution is a part of, yet apart from, the community in which it is embedded.*

The final problem we shall consider concerns the assumptions an institution makes with respect to its overall relationship to the community. This is perhaps the most difficult and sensitive problem confronting any institution, for it involves such basic and crucial issues as power, control, and autonomy. It is also, therefore, almost by definition, the most important issue with which the institution must deal; for the manner in which the institution resolves these questions both determines the kind of relationship that will exist between the institution and the community and provides the institution with an identity of its own.

Although the problem of "community relations" is a general one that affects virtually all human service institutions, it is a particularly crucial problem in the War on Poverty. Consequently, although the descriptions offered in this section are theoretically applicable to any service-oriented institution, we shall confine most of our observations to those agencies (e.g., Community Action Programs) which owe their existence to the current attempts to eliminate poverty in our society.

Most institutions (poverty programs are not exceptions) make the assumption that they are a part of and, at the same time, apart from the communities in which they are embedded and the clients with whom they are involved. This assumption is important not only for theoretical reasons but also because it enables the institution to provide itself with a rationale for dealing in certain, specified ways with many of the practical realities having to do with questions such as who defines the institution's basic policy, who decides and plans the kinds of programs that will be developed, who controls these programs, how the programs will be administered, and so forth. In a most basic sense, the manner in which these questions are dealt with determines the degree to which, if at all, the institution is willing to accommodate its orientations and its programs to forces and influences external to itself. In short, the ways in which an institution defines its relationship to the community it serves have a variety of consequences for how the institution both perceives and deals with such issues as power, autonomy, and control.

The traditional assumption of being a part of, yet apart from, the community enables the institution to take a stance whereby it is both responsive to certain needs as it (the institution) defines these needs, while at the same time it retains the right to determine how these needs should be met. It is a situation in which the institution makes clear its desire to be of help but couples this desire with a communication that says, in effect: "We will be helpful in our own way and on our own terms, and are not willing to surrender to others (i.e., the recipients of our help) the power to decide what form this help should take." There is rarely any doubt that while the institution may, indeed, be "responsive" to the needs of the community, its primary allegiance is, must be and will continue to be the overall orientations and goals of some other reference group (e.g., its source of funds or its institutional ideology).

The issues of control and power are probably the two most crucial issues involved in the War on Poverty. The Economic Opportunity Act of 1964 carried with it some vague mandate to "involve the poor" in the planning and implementation of antipoverty programs. This concept of "involvement" was subsequently defined (and refined) as something approaching the "maximum feasible participation" of the poor in the development and administration of opportunity programs. Despite the ambiguity and vagueness that surrounded the wording (and possibly even the intent) of this mandate, it is important from the point of view that it established a precedent: for one of the first times in history the recipients of a service were given the right to determine, in one fashion or another, the content of the service they were to receive. Whether by accident, choice, or political expediency, the Economic Opportunity Act of 1964 set in motion a process which, at least on the surface of things, could be interpreted as an attempt to redefine and change the traditional relationship between the helping agency and the community.

But if there is anything that we have learned from the War on Poverty, it is that it is almost impossible, at least within a short period of time, to legislate change. This is particularly true in a situation where one is dealing with institutions whose entire histories and traditions make change virtually "unlegislatable." An institution's assumption that it is a part of, yet apart from, the community in which it is embedded is predicated upon conceptions and ideologies that have grown and been reinforced over a long period of time, a period of time long enough to permit the institution to view its orientation with respect to the community as based no longer on assumption but on self-evident and consensually validated reality. In short, despite the wording of the Economic Opportunity Act of 1964, most helping agencies (including many whose parentage can be traced directly to the launching of the War on Poverty) have maintained the traditional position of being responsive to, but never under the control of, the people they are supposed to serve.

Like all the assumptions discussed in this chapter, an institution's assumption that it can be a part of, yet apart from, the community in which it is embedded has a number of different consequences. One of the most important of these consequences is the gradual emergence and eventual supremacy of the orientation that the institution must do something *for* rather than *with* the people it serves. As long as the institution is able to view itself and to function as if it were free from the direct influence and control of its clients, the institution can maintain the position that it alone "knows" the needs of the community, and that it alone is capable of designing and implementing programs to meet those needs. What often results is a sort of "institutional noblesse oblige": a conception of the client as someone for whom things must be done, as someone who is, almost by definition, incapable of being trusted and unworthy of treatment as an equal. The tragedy of the situation is that sooner or later patterns of service are developed that mirror this conception. The client is addressed as though he is, indeed, basically passive, dependent, and incompetent, and as though he is an individual for whom things must be done and to whom things must be given if he is to be maintained. *In its most extreme form, the situation can lead to the mutual and permanent estrangement of the helping agency and the client. What may have begun as a desire to help often ends in a self-fulfilling prophesy: the client and the helping institution learn to view each other as inhabitants of different and nonreciprocal worlds.* The situation in the field of public welfare is perhaps the most tragic example of this state of affairs. In his book *Nigger,* Dick Gregory (1965, pp. 28–29) describes his mother's encounters with the Welfare Department:

I wonder how she kept from teaching us hate when the social worker came around. She was a nasty bitch with a pinched face who said: "We have reason to suspect you are working, Miss Gregory, and you can be sure I'm going to check on you. We don't stand for welfare cheaters."

Momma, a welfare cheater. A criminal who couldn't stand to see her kids go hungry, or grow up in slums and end up mugging people in dark corners. I guess the system didn't want her to get off relief, the way it kept sending social workers around to be sure Momma wasn't trying to make things better.

I remember how that social worker would poke around the house, wrinkling her nose at the coal dust on the chilly linoleum floor, shaking her head at the bugs crawling over the dirty dishes in the sink. My Momma would have to stand there and make like she was too lazy to keep her own house clean. She could never let on that she spent all day cleaning another woman's house for two dollars and carfare. She would have to follow that nasty bitch around those drafty three rooms, keeping her fingers crossed that the telephone hidden in the closet wouldn't ring. Welfare cases weren't supposed to have telephones.

But Momma figured that some day the Gregory kids were

going to get off North Taylor Street and into a world where they would have to compete with kids who grew up with telephones in their houses. She couldn't explain that to the social worker. And she couldn't explain that while she was out spoon-feeding somebody else's kids, she was worrying about her own kids, that she could rest her mind by picking up the telephone and calling us—to find out if we had bread for our baloney or baloney for our bread, to see if any of us had gotten run over by the streetcar while we played in the gutter, to make sure the house hadn't burnt down from the papers and magazines we stuffed in the stove when the coal ran out.

Even granting the possibility (remote though it may be) that Gregory's experience may have been an extreme and, hopefully, an atypical one, what remains is the feeling that what he is describing is a situation in which both the helpers and the helped are eventually corrupted and dehumanized by a process of institutional noblesse oblige—a process founded upon certain conceptions of the client, which in turn are themselves little more than a reflection of the assumptions underlying the agency's view of its relationship to the community.

Another consequence of the institution's assumption that it and it alone "knows" what is good for the client is the situation in which change, often of a massive and far-reaching nature, is "imposed" on the community with little or no attempt either to involve the community or to prepare for the problems that this change will generate in terms of the existing values and culture of the community. The problem of slum clearance (now called "urban renewal" or "area redevelopment") is a case in point. Salisbury (1958) provides a vivid description of how a particular conception of help (i.e., that the immediate and forcible removal of inadequate and substandard housing will, in and of itself, be both acceptable and beneficial to the ghetto-dweller) can lead to the perpetration of old problems and the creation of new ones. All the cases cited by Salisbury share a common theme. Someone, somewhere, decides what the "people need" (in this case, new and better high-rise apartments to replace old and delapidated tenements). With

little or no consultation and usually without the involvement, let alone the active participation, of the community,
a "helping project" is begun. In a relatively short period of
time the bulldozers move in: people are dislocated and
relocated; slums come down, and new buildings burst
forth from the ground on which the old tenements once
stood. Almost overnight a new neighborhood is born. The
fact that something "new" has been created is incontro-
vertible. But is it a "neighborhood"? Is it a "community"?
In short, is it a setting with a culture, a tradition, and a
history that it can point to as its own? Salisbury's observations
are that all too often the process of change (in this case,
the creation of what most people would agree are physically superior conditions of living) is accompanied by a
degree of destructiveness that is both needless and avoid-
able.[5] In the case of slum clearance, the creation of better
housing often brings with it the destruction of that continuity which, for all its problems and difficulties, once
gave a neighborhood a certain viability and identity of its
own. In almost no time at all the architects of change are
confronted with the fact that the reward for their work is
nothing more nor less than a new "instant slum"; that the
recipients of their efforts feel no gratitude for what has
been done for them; and that conditions of life in the

[5]The self-defeating character of so many "helping" projects seems to
be founded, among other things, on what might be termed the
"simplistic" view of change. It is a view which, despite it's presumed
nobility of purpose and good intent, is based upon a conception of
change that is both circumscribed and self-limiting. In their work on
minority groups in New York, Glazer and Moynihan (1963) describe
some of the variables that are inevitably involved in any attempt to
reconstruct a community. Their observations indicate that a project of
such a magnitude must, of necessity, focus attention on "involving the
people of the projects in their management and maintenance, encouraging and strengthening forms of organization among them (even
when the purpose of these organizations seems to be to attack the
management), encouraging forms of self-help in them, varying their
population occupationally as well as racially by greater tolerance in
admissions, reducing the stark difference of the projects from their
surroundings by changing their appearance, [and] considering more
seriously the impact of their design on the social life that they en-
fold . . ." (p. 63). The model that Glazer and Moynihan present is, in
short, a much more complex one than those previously associated
with slum clearance.

ghetto are no better, and possibly even worse, than they were before the project was begun. In the cruel light of the morning-after-the-night-before, the "helpers" and the "helped" view each other with the same desperation that has always marked their relationship with each other. The "helpers" are frustrated and depressed by what they interpret as new evidence that the community and its people "don't want to improve themselves no matter what you do for them." The "helped" view the situation as another in a series of cruel deceptions in which, in the name of assistance, they were robbed of whatever shred of individual and communal relatedness they had been able to preserve. It is a situation in which mutually held attitudes and stereotypes become more rigid and less susceptible to change. However, what is overlooked, especially by the agents of change, is that a good deal of the problem was there long before the project was ever begun, and that it was rooted, at least in part, in the traditional assumptions that the agency made long ago regarding its formal relationship to the community it served.

In the long run, the most important consequence of the institution's assumption that it is a part of, yet apart from, the community in which it is embedded has to do with the question of institutional change. This question has at least two aspects to it. The first involves the issue of the degree to which the institution itself is open to change. We have, at least in part, already tried to deal with this aspect of the problem. Our observations have led us to believe that the assumptions underlying the institution's traditional relationship with the community are of such a kind and quality that, barring any unforeseen or dramatic circumstances, they serve to protect and insulate the institution from any meaningful dialogue with the community concerning the question of direct community or "recipient" control of the programs, policies, and orientations of the helping agency.

The second aspect of the problem has to do with the institution's view of itself as a vehicle for potentially influencing or altering the practices of other institutions. But here again, as was the case with the notion of the institution itself being open to change, basic change cannot and will not occur unless and until the institution conceives of the problem as an institutional one in the broadest sense of the term, rather than as a problem involving or necessitating the change of specific and isolated aspects of institutional functioning. Nowhere is this clearer than in the War on Poverty. The conception of poverty as an institutional problem will not become a meaningful reality or lead to the development of programs predicated on that reality until our concern shifts from an orientation toward the presumed needs of the poverty-stricken person to one that focuses attention on the institutional constraints that define such needs. This shift in orientation is far more difficult and threatening than is the process of perpetuating old institutions and creating new ones through the development of "opportunity programs" based on the traditional assumption of "service." Cloward (1965), in testimony given before a Senate subcommittee on poverty, put it as follows:

The chief target of the federal anti-poverty program is the victim of poverty, not the *sources* of his victimization.

If fundamental *institutional change* is not the primary object of the anti-poverty program, massive individual remediation is, and this is the sense in which the program does not constitute a plan to attack long-standing social and economic inequalities in our society.

Nothing being said should be taken to mean that casualty programs are not needed—whether the existing ones or the new ones to be created with poverty funds. No humane society can abandon those who have already experienced the ravages of prolonged deprivation. The point is, however, that low-income people *as a class* cannot expect to benefit from the anti-poverty program as it is currently conceived. A guaranteed annual wage would eliminate poverty, even a system of children's allowances would raise whole groups from poverty. But if we fail to make a broad spectrum of institutional changes, new casualties will steadily fill the vacuum left by individuals who are helped by the anti-poverty program, for the causes of economic deprivation will continue to be at work.

At present, political pressure for basic economic change does not appear to exist in American society. The broad consensus favoring the anti-poverty program is hardly proof of a national determination to wipe out economic deprivation. It is true that a consensus exists, including business and labor, Republicans and Democrats, rich and poor. The very breadth of this consensus, however, merely lays bare the fact that no vital institutional interests are threatened by the program. For this reason, it is relatively easy to develop support among groups whose political and economic interests are fundamentally divergent.

Although Cloward's remarks were directed toward "institutions" defined in the most general sense (i.e., as sources of pervasive social, economic, and political power), similar observations could be made with respect to the community agencies (i.e., the educational, welfare, and mental health institutions) that represent those power systems on the local level. The fact that most antipoverty programs have not been able to effect any meaningful and lasting change in the basic orientations of established community institutions is a testament not only to the ambivalence with which most anti-poverty programs have approached the problem, but also to the powerful resistance to change that is characteristic of traditional ideology. In some instances change has occurred, but it has been of the superficial or short-term variety.

Example 16: CPI's Neighborhood Youth Corps program, like most NYC programs, is made up of two components: a medial education component. When the program first began, work experience, or prevocational, component; and a re-CPI accepted the responsibility of running the work experience aspect of the program but delegated to the public school system (in accordance with agreements made between CPI and its source of funds) the responsibility of co-ordinating and administering the remedial education component of the program.

It appeared, at least on the surface, that the school system, by joining with CPI to devise and implement a program for school dropouts, was moving in a direction that would open up the educational system to new and potentially helpful influences from sectors of the community (e.g., community action personnel, inner-city people) that had heretofore had little to say about the structure and content of the educational process. This feeling was reinforced when the public schools agreed, in principle, that one of their goals in joining with CPI was to explore new ways in which the learning situation could be adapted and made meaningful to the needs and interests of a population (high school dropouts) that had been "turned off," in one way or another, by their previous academic experiences. The most tangible sign of this willingness to explore new avenues of the learning experience was the schools' decision that the remedial education aspect of the NYC program should be held in a setting as far removed and different from the school as was possible. In addition, it was felt that the major focus of the remedial education component of the program should be "preparing the enrollees for the world of work" in a manner no different from the prevocational aspect of the program.

Despite these formal and public goals of the educational program, it soon became clear that no real or basic changes were being contemplated in either the structure or content of the learning situation. Classes were still held in a formal manner and, despite the fact that they were no longer held physically in the public school setting, they quickly became mirror images of the situations that had turned the youngsters off in the first place. Great emphasis was placed on the formal aspects of the learning situation (e.g., on problems of control and discipline, on the youngsters calling their teachers "Mister," and on reading, writing, and arithmetic in the most narrow and rigid definition of the terms) with little or no effort made to develop a program, a curriculum, or a teaching process that was in any way related to the interests or vocational aspirations of the enrollees. The youths were still reading about "Johnny and Janie going to the market" in a situation that for all intents and purposes was no different from what they had experienced in the past.

In a relatively short period of time, the youngsters, as well as many members of the staff of the NYC program, came to view what was supposed to be a single and unified program as two very different programs: there was the work crew program and there was the education program, and whatever relationship was supposed to exist between the two was very difficult to perceive. The response of the enrollees to the two programs was markedly different. Whereas the youngsters enjoyed and were learning in the work crew component of the program, they were "acting up," causing great concern, and generally disrupting whatever people were trying to teach them in their remedial education classes. Although most

people were aware of the discrepancy between the two components of the NYC program, it was very difficult to effect
any meaningful change in the general orientations, processes,
or contents of the educational component of the program.
What was most difficult for people to understand was the
fact that the situation was the way it was not because of any
"bad faith" on the part of the teachers or those who had
the primary responsibility for organizing and running the
program, but because the problem was basically one involving the history, traditions, and theories of learning that were
an integral part of the educational system. Whatever changes
in the public school system the NYC program was able to
effect were, for the most part, superficial and temporary:
the basic ideological and conceptual assumptions underlying
the school system's approach to the learning situation were
untapped and untappable by CPI.

In most cases, however, attempts at basic institutional change
have been scrupulously avoided by antipoverty programs. In
part, at least, this is because they have not defined such
change as an integral part of their own existence. Most anti-
poverty programs have settled for a course of action that
would insure their own safety and perpetuate their own
existence. This course of action has resulted in their having
become a part of the institutional establishment of their communities. That this should be the state of affairs is little
more than an indication of how most community action programs, no differently than the more established and en-
trenched "service" institutions (i.e., the schools, welfare
agencies, and mental health professions), have accepted the
assumption that as institutions they are both a part of and
apart from the community in which they are embedded.

In this chapter we have attempted to describe some of
the assumptions that either characterize or influence the
process of the creation of "helpful" settings. We have tried
to examine these assumptions from the point of view that
the importance of each assumption is at least twofold:
first, it reflects certain personal and professional values; and
second, each assumption has consequences for the present
and future development of the institution. Our overall goal
was to describe in some detail how the manner in which

one conceptualizes a problem determines in a variety of ways the means one employs and the techniques one develops to deal with the problem. We have attempted to make explicit what, at least from our point of view, have been many of the implicit and private assumptions of institution-builders. As we have already indicated, this chapter constitutes little more than a first step in the process of describing and examining the problem of how one goes about creating a setting. No attempt has been made to formulate any particular theoretical model for the development of all institutions. Our purpose was to communicate to the reader how easy it is for those of us who try to create and to innovate to become the prisoners of our own conceptions, assumptions, and ideologies.

There is little doubt that becoming aware of certain problems constitutes the first step in the process of developing more realistic and appropriate coping behaviors. But, as is the case in most clinical relationships, the fact that one is made aware of certain problems that have heretofore gone unrecognized or that have been avoided is no guarantee that better ways of dealing with these problems will automatically ensue. The problems must first be "worked through" in a process that is often painful and anxiety-provoking.

In the following chapters we will present the ways in which we tried to "work through" the problems inherent in the creation of a setting. *In this context the Residential Youth Center may be viewed as a case study of the attempt to develop a setting in such a way as to control for much of the self-defeating and goal-diluting irrationality that plagues and undermines so many of our attempts to innovate.* In the chapters that follow we shall pick up the story of the Residential Youth Center at that point in time when the journey to one mountain had been completed and a new journey had begun—the journey whereby the Residential Youth Center ceased being an idea and became a reality. In Chapter 4 we will focus our attention on the development of the RYC's social structure, the criteria used in recruiting its staff, and the assumptions underlying its relationship with its clients and the community.

Chapter 4   The RYC As a Setting
Its People, Programs, Organization,
and Relationship to the Community Action Agency

The whole difference between construction and creation
is exactly this: that a thing constructed can only be loved
after it is constructed; but a thing created is loved
before it exists.
—Gilbert Keith Chesterton

In Chapter 3 we described some of the assumptions and
decisions that influence the process by which helping settings are created. If nothing else, our analysis of the problems inherent in the creative process served to reinforce the
view that settings rarely develop under conditions that are
either simple to delineate or easy to control. In this respect
the creation of the RYC was no exception. Its own development—the manner in which it was internally organized, the
kinds of people it sought out as staff members, the approach
it took to its "clients," and the conceptions underlying the
evolution of the program as a whole—took place in a context of problems and concerns the solutions of which could
not help but have an irrevocable impact on the setting and
its goals. In the present chapter, therefore, in addition to
describing the particular assumptions that guided the setting's structure, choice of staff, and evolution of a "treatment
model," we shall focus attention on the broader "contextual
issues" as well as the more immediate "setting realities" that
influenced the thinking of those of us directly responsible
for the development of the new facility.

The Contextual Issue: The Dilemma of the "Change Agent"
Those of us involved in the War on Poverty have always
been caught on the horns of a dilemma. *The dilemma involves the following question: Should we try to change
people, or should we try to change conditions?* Needless to
say, most of us have taken the position, at least publicly,
that change should be affected both in the people currently
caught in the cycle of poverty and in the conditions that produced these people. Once we have said these things, we
have placed ourselves on the side of the angels for, being
patriotic Americans (or, if you will, "cautious crusaders"),

to have said otherwise would be akin to being against God, country, and motherhood. But siding with virtue against sin is one thing; being able to develop the kinds of vehicles that hold out the hope of dealing with the problem is quite another. *This is the major issue confronting those involved in the War on Poverty, and until this issue is dealt with directly and honestly we will be no more successful than our now-maligned predecessors in effecting any meaningful change either in the conditions of poverty or in the poor themselves.*

At the present time the War on Poverty is based on the assumption that permanent change can be achieved in the conditions of life in our society through the development and implementation of a variety of "opportunity" programs. The focus of these programs is the poor—those people caught in the self-perpetuating cycle of poverty—and the hope is that somehow, in some way, and in some determinable fashion, these programs will entice, persuade, or cajole the poor into becoming a part of the so-called mainstream of American life.

The thesis we have been advancing is that this innovative attempt, if it is to produce any real and lasting results, will not occur unless and until the focus of our concern shifts from the so-called objects of change (i.e., the poor) to the change agents themselves and to the settings being created through which this change is supposed to be effected.[1] It is one thing to want to change people and change conditions; it is quite another thing to create the kinds of organizational vehicles (delivery systems) that promise to achieve these goals in non-self-defeating ways. At this point the desire to change things and to change people is little more than the rhetoric of a guilt-ridden morality; the commitment to examine ourselves and the organizational structures we create is much more than rhetoric: it is work, the

[1] In a recent book surveying the problems that confront organizations that are "change-oriented," Marris and Rein (1967) provide an excellent analysis of the system conflicts and issues that can often undermine, dilute, or detract from the "reform" goals of many community action programs. We have enlarged on this issue previously elsewhere (Goldenberg, 1969).

kind of work most of us would rather not undertake, since it requires both the willingness to be self-critical and the ability to change traditional patterns of thinking and functioning.

The "Setting Reality":
Community Progress, Incorporated, in 1966

Some of us who had journeyed to that mountain in Maryland knew that when we returned to New Haven we would be returning to a community action agency that was far different from the one we had known in 1963. CPI in 1966 was no longer the awkward, scrambling child of its own infancy. It had grown, "matured," and, in the short period of three or four years, had emerged from an uncertain and precarious existence into a world of success and enforced adulthood. CPI in 1966 was the shining light in an otherwise rather unspectacular antipoverty crusade. It had already "proved" itself, had developed local programs (e.g., the work crews) that were now models upon which national programs (e.g., the Neighborhood Youth Corps) could be built, and was basking in the well-earned adulation of a country that was still groping with the problem of how to develop programs and services for the poor. But for some of us the same process that had gained for CPI both respect and respectability was also causing the organization to change and was beginning to rob it of that vitality—that indescribable, almost brazen adventuresomeness—that had characterized it during the early days of its life. CPI in 1966 was unmistakably an organization that had been seduced and victimized by its own success.

It is difficult to pinpoint the precise moment at which CPI began to change. At first the changes were small, subtle, almost imperceptible. But over a period of time they became more noticeable and, at least to some of us, more ominous. We mention this not because of any desire to belittle what for all intents and purposes was, and probably still is, the most successful community action program in the nation. We mention it for two reasons. First, any attempt to describe the development of the RYC would have to be predicated upon some understanding of the nature of its "mother" organization. In a sense the relationship between the RYC and CPI has as its analogue the school situation: in order to understand more fully the kinds of problems and processes that characterize a particular class-room, it is often helpful to have some "feel" for the culture of the school as a whole. Second, an awareness of the changes CPI had undergone between the years 1963 and 1966 was more than a little helpful to us in our own at-tempts to develop the RYC as an organization. Just as CPI had served others through its numerous and well-deserved successes, so, too, could its problems and difficulties be utilized as a learning experience by those of us who were to follow. It is for these reasons that we shall describe briefly the history of CPI as an organization.

CPI's Early Days: The "Undermanned Setting"
When CPI first began its work in the inner city, it was made up of little more than a group of people joined together by a common guiding fiction: they were bound by the vision of a New Haven freed, once and for all, from the inequities that separated men, and they shared in the belief that it was somehow within their power to eliminate both the sources and the consequences of the dehumanizing process that was condemning so many of their fellow citizens to a life of emptiness and hopelessness. To them poverty was not an abstraction; it was something real and concrete; it was some-thing they could smell and feel every time they walked through the ghettos of New Haven, for many of them had grown up in the inner city and had experienced all too personally that quiet desperation that defines the world of the powerless and the helpless. For them, Michael Har-rington's (1962) "Other Americans" had long since ceased being romantic figures in American literature and had already assumed their rightful place as concrete reminders of the inadequacies and inequities that still existed in a supposedly affluent society.

The people who started CPI were, in the finest sense of

the terms, innovators and explorers. There were few places they could turn to for help and guidance, and the knowledge that no one had ever been able to develop a truly effective human renewal program was of precious little comfort or consolation. Having little or nothing upon which to pattern what they were doing, they turned inward, to themselves, to their own experiences, and to their own conceptions of how to go about the task of revitalizing a city and its people. With only a small staff (30 or 40 people), CPI set out to do battle with an enemy whose forces already numbered several thousands and whose ranks had been swelled abnormally by the massive legacy of anger, apathy, and distrust that poverty bequeaths to its victims. There was very little time to worry about the question of "whose job it was to do what." Neither could they indulge themselves in the luxury of formulating any overall theoretical rationale for what they wanted to do and how they wanted to do it.[2] All they knew was that there was a problem "out there": it was called poverty—it lurked behind every door of almost every house that lined the streets of New Haven's ghettos—and they were going to "do something about it."

Under these conditions CPI, especially in its early days as an organization, was very much like the "undermanned" behavior setting so beautifully described by Barker (1960). With relatively few people to do the work, attention had to be focused not so much on the organization as a formal structure or on the "paper" credentials of its staff, but on the enormity of the task that lay before it. Each individual, regardless of his title or background (there was little time to devote to the problem of developing standards and criteria for admission into the organization), was placed in a situation in which his competence would be defined more in terms of his ability to handle new problems and varying

[2]The fact that relatively little time was taken in developing a general "blueprint" for action should not be interpreted as implying that CPI had no explicit ideas concerning the nature of its goals and processes. All we are saying is that CPI could not afford to expend the same amount of time as do, for example, most other experimentalists working in the laboratory setting, to deal with the conceptual issues with which it was confronted.

responsibilities than in whatever status he had derived in previous settings. The organization was small and relatively simple, and consequently, each individual was functionally important, had to accept great personal responsibility, had to focus his attention on a wide variety of activities, and had to deal with the insecurity and anxiety that such an existence inevitably brought with it. There was always an air of the unexpected, and the organization was in a near-constant state of movement and almost pleasurable turmoil. Errors were less important than enthusiasm, energy, and goodwill. Above all else, the people who populated the infant organization shared a dream that only their own personal commitment and collective efforts could transform into a reality. It was a time when nothing was impossible and when people, many of whom had never known what it felt like to be engaged in a human adventure that was intrinsically rewarding, proved, as John Ruskin (1819–1900) put it, that

When men are rightly occupied, their amusement grows out of their work, as the colour-petals out of a fruitful flower.

Despite the "magic" that permeated CPI, the organization also had its share of problems. They were the problems that inevitably beset any organization that is both understaffed and engulfed in a process of constantly having to improvise and create new strategies as it goes along. Things were often "sloppy" as people failed or found themselves too busy to keep neat files and do the paperwork that had to get done. With people constantly rushing around trying to do a number of different things in a limited amount of time, there was often an overlapping and duplication of functions. People seemed less impressed with the supposed limits of their particular areas of responsibility and more concerned with "getting the job done" no matter what or who it took to do it. Consequently, there was little overall interdependence, little concern with formal channels of communication, and a general tendency to be somewhat insensitive with respect to interpersonal relations.

Despite these problems—perhaps, indeed, because of them

—CPI was "making it," and it was difficult for anyone coming into contact with the organization even for a little while to remain unaffected by the sense of purpose and involvement that surrounded him. There was a certain uncomplicated beauty, a quiet and simple nobility of purpose as yet relatively uncorrupted by any undue concerns for individual safety or personal gain. CPI was much more than an amalgamation of opportunity programs: it was a spirit and a sense of meaning that had intruded itself into a city grown tired and old before its time.

Its problems notwithstanding, CPI began to compile an impressive record of successes. First its Neighborhood Employment Centers (NEC) became examples of how to run a manpower program in the inner city; then its work crew projects became the prototype of a national program for high school dropouts; and finally, the organization as a whole became living proof that local and national resources and neighborhood personnel could join and could cooperate, and that they could be molded into the kind of force that had a chance of holding its own in the struggle against poverty.

The organization grew, and with each success it grew more and more. In a relatively short period of time, CPI's group of 30 or 40 "charter members" had grown to a staff of more than 200 people as many of its experimental programs became bigger, more institutionalized, and accepted as integral parts of an expanded concept of services for the inner city. With continued growth and success there came attention. At first it was local in nature, but it soon began to assume national proportions. CPI was no longer the small, "way-out" organization hidden away in some "average-sized" city. People from other parts of the country started coming to New Haven to "find out how to do it"; greater sums of money began pouring into CPI projects (both those of the ongoing variety and those still in proposal stage); and the organization was brought to the attention of a basically appreciative and responsive nation. CPI was no longer a community action program—it was the community action program.

The Change Begins

It was probably around this time that things began to change, that CPI began to fall victim to its own success and become the prisoner of its own accomplishments.[3] An image had been created, and success brought with it not only the realization that much more could now be accomplished— that much more was now possible—but also the need to cloak this success with a certain kind of internal respectability. Although people still spoke—and probably spoke more— about the "problems out there," more and more attention began to be focused on the organization itself. In time this led CPI into becoming increasingly more specialized and professionalized as greater energy was devoted to stabilizing the organization, "cleaning it up," and developing "smoother lines of communication" and more clear-cut definitions of areas of responsibility. People were no longer rewarded for "getting the job done no matter what" but were increasingly told or found out for themselves that there was "a place for everybody and everybody in his place." There were now relatively explicit channels of communication, chains of command, and a "proper" way of getting things done. People now became much more conscious of their position in the organization, and issues of personal security and advancement within the organization became areas of great concern. The organization as a whole seemed to become much less flexible internally and much less willing to "do battle" with the established agencies and institutions that surrounded it. It appeared as if CPI, having won a place for itself, was now entering a stage during which it would strive to consolidate its gains, both internally and externally, and work toward the goal of institutionalizing itself on a long-term basis. Perhaps more than anything else, it became a time when CPI and its people, having won so many battles,

---

[3]As is the case with most changes that occur over time, it is difficult to point with certainty to any one event, much less to any single day, as signifying the beginning of the process of change. All we can try to do is describe in general terms the changes that occurred and the significance of these changes for the organization as a whole. Our own recollection—a recollection certainly open to dispute—is that it was during the very years when CPI was at or near the height of its success that change first became noticeable.

began to lose the war. What the organization had gained in the streets of New Haven's ghettos it was now beginning to lose inside itself. CPI in 1966 was not the same organization we had known three short years before: it was an organization beginning to show the symptoms of so many other institutions that start out by trying to change existing conditions only to wind up building monuments to themselves.

The Organization of the RYC: The Development of a Social Structure

If there was anything to be learned from CPI—from its successes as well as its failures—it was that there was an intimate relationship between the way in which a setting was organized and the behavior of the people who populated that setting. Consequently, although the RYC was funded to serve inner-city residents, singular attention was focused not on the clients *but on the staff*; not on the creation of another self-perpetuating institution *but on the development of a viable organization whose most important goal was to create the conditions under which human beings (i.e., the staff) could begin to fulfill themselves both as individuals and as members of a group.* In short, the decision to make the staff and the organization of the RYC the top priority of concern was itself based on an assumption: if people, regardless of their backgrounds or levels of formal preparation, were involved in what for them were meaningful, intrinsically gratifying, and growth-producing human service activities, the results could not help but be beneficial to the clients with whom they were engaged.

We have already described some of the characteristics of the ways in which most human service institutions are organized. In the preceding chapter we confined our descriptions of the pyramidal structure to some of the more observable and, in some ways, more superficial dynamics of that particular type of organization. What we did not focus on were some of the more important assumptions about man and conceptions of human potential that are both inherent in, and give rise to, the hierarchical organization of a setting. *It is important that we now describe some of these conceptions, since the organization of the RYC was based, at least in part, on an unwillingness to accept many of the basic premises underlying these assumptions and conceptions.* But what are these conceptions, and how are they related to the way in which a setting is usually organized?

The Pyramidal Organization

To begin with, most human service organizations are structured according to what Tannenbaum (1966) has called "economic ends." It is a situation in which the goals of the organization transcend the individual or collective needs of the staff. The staff is expected either to "fit" or not get in the way of the "grand design" of the organization. Under these conditions it becomes imperative that the organization have a formal order, a clear purpose, a dependable technology, and a system of authority through which people can be compensated, manipulated, replaced, and coordinated in terms of the particular needs of the organization at any point in time. More than anything else, it is a situation in which the prevailing view of man is that of his inherent and essential expendability.

But there is more to the pyramidal structure than the view of people—especially people occupying positions of low status and little power—as essentially expendable. The view of man's essential expendability is itself predicated upon a host of assumptions concerning the nature of man and a number of conceptions concerning what man is capable of and how he can change. Some of these assumptions, as McGregor (1961) has pointed out, are that man is indolent and works as little as possible; that he lacks ambition and likes to be led; that he is essentially self-centered and indifferent to the needs of the organization; that he is resistant to change; and, perhaps more than anything else, that he is gullible. The conception is one of man as a being who labors not because his work is, or need be, intrinsically gratifying or personally fulfilling but because by working he is able to obtain the extrinsic means by which he can satisfy his needs. Moreover, the conception is one of man as an essentially irrational creature, a being who cannot be trusted and who must, either through coercion, threats, or incentives, be controlled. As Schein (1965, p. 49) puts it:

The burden for organizational performance falls entirely on management. Employees are expected to do no more than the incentive and control systems encourage and allow; hence, even if an employee did not fit the assumptions made about him, it is unlikely that he could express alternative behavior. Consequently, the greatest danger for an organization operating by these assumptions is that they tend to be self-fulfilling. If employees are expected to be indifferent, hostile, motivated only by economic incentives, and the like, the managerial strategies used to deal with them are likely to train them to behave precisely in that fashion.

To be sure, the most frightening consequences of the assumptions underlying the pyramidal structure are that sooner or later people come to believe (consciously or otherwise) many of the assumptions that have been made about them and behave as if these conceptions were, indeed, both appropriate and valid. The conventional pyramidal structure could not long endure were it not for the fact that the very people about whom these assumptions have been made and for whom the organization has been so structured come to accept what has been said about them and to function in precisely the kinds of ways in which they have been presumed to function. When people are rewarded for being uncreative, when security is achieved not through the exercise of freedom or imagination but through behaviors that define one as compliant and dependent, it becomes difficult if not impossible to view one's own needs for growth or self-actualization as in any way connected with one's participation in the world of work.

Basic to the development of the RYC was the notion that its own social structure, no different from that of any other setting, irrespective of organizational philosophy, would be a reflection of the kinds of assumptions made and conceptions held about the people (the staff) who comprised the setting. If what people did or didn't do, what they felt they could or couldn't do was, at least in part, a function of the kind of setting of which they were a part, then it was incumbent upon the setting both to create the conditions and to develop the processes under which change was possible. Consequently, the development of the RYC as a social structure was predicated on the assumption that given the kind of setting in which people, both as individuals and as members of a group, could begin to explore their own potential in an atmosphere that no longer viewed them as expendable but that, rather, was dedicated to their own development and growth, they would, indeed, prove to be the kind of staff capable of working effectively with a target population (i.e., the "hard-core" poor) heretofore deemed "unreachable." In short, although, as we have already pointed out, the RYC was explicitly funded to meet the needs of chronically impoverished inner-city residents, its "real" focus was on the development of a "delivery system" designed to meet the human needs of its own members. For us, Spinoza's statement:

So long as a man imagines that he cannot do this or that, so long is he determined not to do it: and consequently, so long it is impossible to him that he should do it.

became the starting point for developing a setting in which the "impossible," could now become, if not possible, at least "imaginable."

"Horizontality": A Conceptual Alternative to the Pyramidal Organization

With this in mind, the RYC was structured along lines which, for want of a better word, we termed "horizontal." By *"horizontal structure" we meant a setting whose organization would make it possible to combine the positive characteristics of the undermanned behavior setting with the more efficient administrative aspects of other types of organizations without allowing either form of organizational philosophy to dilute the program's goals of individual and collective growth.* In its simplest form, the notion of horizontality involved the creation of conditions under which the staff could: (1) learn from one another in a situation characterized by reciprocity and mutuality; (2) develop a clinical sensitivity and perspective that was both individually and collectively helpful; (3) pursue and receive the kind of training that would facilitate the assumption and utilization of personal responsibility; and (4) work and live in an atmosphere of interpersonal openness and trust.

Clinical Aspects The horizontal structure came to mean many things. *On a clinical or service level it meant that each staff member, regardless of his position in the organization or formal "job description," would carry a case load.* Carrying a case load was defined as assuming the total responsibility for all decisions and interventions involving a resident and his family. No staff member, regardless of his status in or out of the organization, would presume to make clinical decisions involving another staff member's cases. Staff meetings were clearly to be utilized for purposes of trying to influence the decisions people made, but it was left completely up to the individual staff member to make the final determination in his case.

The rationale behind the "horizontal" sharing of clinical responsibilities was a simple one: that no one be spared the experience of dealing with a client and his family. This was undertaken in the hope that under such conditions people would begin to participate in one another's problems, could share and work through the anxiety that such responsibilities inevitably create, and would eventually come to view one another as sources of knowledge, help, and support. We wanted to make it as difficult as possible for people inhabiting positions of differential status and power to look at one another and say: "You don't understand my problems. You sit up there and tell me what to do but you don't know what I'm feeling. You haven't been through it yourself." Clinical "horizontality" was designed to put everyone "on the line" in the hope that it would enable people of different backgrounds and experiences to learn from one another in an atmosphere of mutual trust and respect.

The Sharing of Functions In addition to its clinical aspects, horizontal structure also involved a sharing of many of the specific behaviors and duties usually associated with different jobs. Although for purposes of funding it was necessary to define functions in a relatively narrow manner (i.e., Director, RYC workers, live-in counselors, Deputy Director, secretary, cook) and to submit a formal hierarchy of authority, in point of fact everyone on the staff was expected to learn and to be able to function in a variety of different jobs. Thus, for example, everyone was expected to "live in" in order both to relieve the regular live-in staff and to be able to experience what life at the RYC was like at 3 o'clock in the morning. Everyone would prepare the meals during the regular cook's days off, and know enough about different people's jobs to be able to assume their functions in the event of any emergency or unforeseen situation. *Again, the goal of this "interchangeability" (rather than "replaceability") of roles was to enable each member of the staff to have a rather direct experience of what life was like in another person's role and, hopefully, by so doing to prevent the development of the kinds of "minor kingdoms" that only separate and insulate a staff from one another.* At the RYC, at least structurally, there was to be no such thing as "my job," "my piece of the action," and "my office." The attempt was made to learn how to function as "creative generalists" rather than to encapsulate people in some real or imagined technical specialty.

Administrative Aspects   On an administrative level, horizontal structure was intended to facilitate the development of mechanisms that could inhibit the growth of an essentially unhelpful and calcifying bureaucracy. *With this in mind, the staff made a particularly important decision early in the life of the RYC: the actual administrative functions and duties of the Residential Youth Center were taken out of the exclusive hands of the Director and Deputy Director and distributed among the staff in terms of individual interests, abilities, and past experiences.* Consequently, problems relating to the budget, public relations, the setting up and chairing of meetings, in-service training, inter- and intra-agency affairs, and program coordination were delegated to, and made the responsibility of, individual members of the staff. Each staff member was expected to keep the rest of the staff abreast of his administrative duties in the hope that we would all be able to learn from one another's functions. In the process we hoped we would gain a fuller understanding of the variety of administrative issues that had to be dealt with in a project such as ours. In a very real sense we were all novices in the field of administration. No member of the staff had ever directed a program, and consequently, the distribution of administrative duties was part of an overall process of both learning the techniques and methods of management and mastering the criteria that administrators and program developers utilize in making technical decisions.

Individual Growth and Responsibility   As we have already indicated, the development of the horizontal structure was predicated upon the conception of a setting dedicated to individual and collective self-actualization. The sharing of clinical and administrative responsibilities was an essential and integral part of that process. In addition to this, however, we felt it important that the setting be structured in a manner that would both allow and encourage an individual to pursue and develop those work-related areas of his life in which he, and he alone, had an abiding and personal interest. We assumed that such personal fulfillment would result in activities that would be exciting and helpful to our clients. *This being the case, each staff member, in addition to his clinical and administrative duties, was given the opportunity of conceptualizing, developing, and coordinating an evening program, a program growing out of his own interests, training, or experiences, a program that would be available to all RYC residents and their families, and a program for which he, and he alone, would be responsible.*

In theory, the form and content of these programs could be limited only by the range of personal interests represented on the staff. In point of fact, the programs that actually emerged (e.g., music, athletics, carpentry and auto mechanics, remedial education, counseling, and a self-help project) were directly related to some aspect of the program leader's past experiences, current interests, or vocational goals. Although it was hoped that these programs would, indeed, attract and involve youngsters residing at the RYC—especially during those times (i.e., evenings and weekends) when they were not at work and had time on their hands—of equal importance to us was the notion that the programs themselves offered each and every staff member a chance to pursue some area of interest that meant something to him as an individual.

The Hiring and Departure of the Director

Figure 4.1 shows the organization of the RYC both as it could have looked were it structured in a typically "pyramidal" fashion and as it actually appeared in its "horizontal" form. In addition to the conceptual and theoretical reasons behind the manner in which the RYC was structured, there were several other, very practical concerns that made it important that the setting be organized in a horizontal fashion. One of these was the fact that it was known, from the very beginning, that the Director would be leaving the program after the first six months of the RYC's life.[4] It was also clearly understood that once he left the program no one would be brought in from the "outside" to take his place and "run" the organization (CPI had already agreed that once the Director left, the Deputy Director would "move up" and that

---

[4]It was clearly understood by all those concerned (e.g., CPI, the Department of Labor, and the Psycho-Educational Clinic) that the RYC's first Director, a member of the Yale faculty, would return to his academic responsibilities on January 1, 1967, after having spent six months with the program on a full-time basis. After January 1, 1967, he was to be involved in the RYC program as a consultant. The reason for this type of arrangement was that one of the goals of the program was to prove that you did not need a "professional" to run a program—clinically oriented though it was—like the RYC. Another consequence of this arrangement—a consequence we only became aware of with the passage of time—was that the very fact that the first director of the RYC was *not* a full-time employee of CPI and, hence, was relatively immune to the social and political pressures of the "mother" organization, was an asset in the development and implementation of the program. It provided the Director with the kind of leverage (i.e., that he did not "need" the job of directing the RYC) that enabled the RYC to function with a degree of latitude and freedom that might not have been possible were the Director totally dependent upon CPI for his livelihood.

The Horizontal (RYC) Structure

RYC Staff

		Deputy	RYC	RYC	Live-In	Live-In
Staff Titles	Director	Director	Worker	Worker	Counselor	Counselor
	Counselor	Secy	Cook			

Functions:

I Clinical Responsibilities: All staff carry case loads*

II Administrative Responsibilities: All staff carry administrative duties

III Individual Programs

The Pyramidal (Mythical RYC) Structure

Functions:

I Administrative, Fiscal,
and Clinical Policy   Director
Responsibilities

I Clinical Supervision and   Deputy
Program Coordination   Director
Responsibilities

I Service Responsi-   RYC   RYC
bilities (Clinical)   Worker   Worker

I In-house   Live-in   Live-in   Live-in
Maintenance   Counselor Counselor Counselor Secy   Cook
and Control
Responsibilities

FIGURE 4.1 THE ORGANIZATIONAL STRUCTURE OF THE RESIDENTIAL
YOUTH CENTER AS COMPARED TO ANOTHER (MYTHICAL) RYC
STRUCTURED ALONG PYRAMIDAL LINES.

*Although every member of the RYC staff (with the exception of the
secretary) carried a clinical case load, the size of the case load varied
from individual to individual depending on his other (administrative
and individual programming) responsibilities. Thus, for example, the
Director carried only two cases because of his responsibility for co-
ordinating the in-service training and research aspects of the program,
whereas the RYC workers each carried five or six cases. The RYC was
expected to deal with 20 residents and their families at any one time,
the total being cumulative to 50 during the course of the year. The
determination of the size of every individual's case load was dependent, in addition to his other programming and administrative
responsibilities, on the amount of time that was available to the individual to work closely with the residents and their families. The
live-in counselors, for example, worked during the day in CPI's
Neighborhood Youth Corps program. Consequently, they were free
to work with residents only during the evenings and on weekends. This being

he, the "new leader," would select his own Deputy Director from among the people already on staff). Under these conditions it seemed that horizontality was the most appropriate form of structure to enable people to receive the kind of training, in all areas of clinical and administrative responsibility, that could be helpful if and when they were to assume leadership roles in RYC or RYC-like programs.[5] From the point of view of training, horizontal structure made it possible, at least from our point of view much easier, for people to know and to experience in a very direct manner almost every phase of the program's operation.[6]

Of equal importance in the development of the horizontal structure was the fact that we wanted the RYC to function on the basis of "discussion not dictation": we wanted the staff to participate fully in the making of policy, and to do so through a process predicated upon people feeling that they were important to the organization and perceiving themselves as having definite stakes in its fate. But in order

---

the case, they were each assigned only one case per person, as was the cook. The secretary was not given a case load for a variety of reasons, all of which were discussed with the entire staff. It was felt that because of her status (she was a married woman with a young child of her own) and the physical limitations of the program (there were no separate facilities for a woman) it would be difficult for her both to live in, as did the rest of the staff, and to be "on call" at any and all hours of the day or night. The secretary did, however, in addition to her secretarial duties, carry administrative (research and documentation) and individual program (parent group counseling) responsibilities. Despite differences among staff members with respect to the absolute number of cases they carried, the primary goal in sharing clinical responsibilities was to give everyone the experience of working with a resident and his family.
[5]Basic to the development of the RYC was the idea that movement should come (that leadership should emerge) from "within" the organization. At the present time CPI is running two RYCs, the original one for boys and a new one for adolescent girls. The Director and one of the RYC workers of the new Center are both from the original staff of the Boys' Residential Youth Center. The man who is now running the Girls' RYC moved to that position from his position as Deputy Director of the Boys' RYC. Another member of the Boys' RYC has moved into the spot he vacated. The new RYC worker at the Girls' Center used to be the secretary of the Boys' RYC.
[6]Although the RYC was founded upon the concept of role interchangeability and the sharing of functions, people did, in point of fact, have different job titles and received different salaries. The meaning and implications of these financial inequities and job distinctions will be explored in later portions of this book.

for such a situation to exist, it seemed essential that the staff be able to talk with one another and to decide things from positions of direct experience in an atmosphere that would facilitate the sharing of ideas, suggestions, and concerns.[7] This being the case, it was important that every member of the staff be able to function in a variety of different areas and in a number of different roles. Above all, it was important, especially if we were to use our experiences to make policy decisions, that we be able to "know," in as concrete a manner as possible, something about the problems with which we were or would be confronted.

These, then, were the reasons, both conceptual and practical, behind the development of the RYC as a horizontal organization. We were concerned first and foremost with many of the organizational assumptions inherent in the pyramidal structure. We had serious reservations about many of the implications of the pyramidal organization, especially with respect to its conception of man, what he is capable of, and how he can grow and change. The social structure of the RYC was developed as an organizational alternative to these views.

The Staff: The RYC's "Inexpendables"
As we have already indicated, one of the purposes of the RYC program was to explore the question of whether or not, given appropriate conditions for learning and growth, so-called nonprofessionals could indeed assume the kinds of clinical responsibilities usually associated with mental health professionals. But, as we have tried to make clear, for us the "real" issue involved much more than the attempt to train additional mental health workers: at stake were all the

[7]The emphasis placed both on group decisions and on the development of patterns of communication that were open and direct was crucial to the development of the RYC. The importance of these concerns was reflected in the fact that "sensitivity training" was, from the very beginning, an integral part of the in-service training program at the RYC. In Chapter 5 we shall discuss what we meant by sensitivity training and provide the reader with a number of examples of how it was implemented and the kinds of issues it involved.

assumptions (see Chapter 3) concerning the criteria by which we gauge "human potential."

The development of the RYC, especially with respect to the selection of staff, was predicated on the assumption that the nature of one's formal background or training was relatively unimportant for the complex kinds of human services we wanted to provide. What we are saying is that in order to undertake the venture at all, one had to assume that people could learn, could change, and could function in ways heretofore unexpected. Under these conditions, staffing the RYC had more to do with getting certain kinds of *people* than with getting certain kinds of *credentials*. Consequently, the basic criteria for selecting staff had to do with (1) the amount of observable or inferable commitment and involvment that a candidate indicated toward the work, and (2) the amount and kind of experience the individual had in working with members of the target population.

Criteria and Processes of Staff Selection   There is little doubt that our extensive involvement in CPI during the years preceding the initiation of the RYC program was of great importance in the selection of the RYC's basic staff. It meant, on the one hand, that we already knew the work crew foremen and had some appreciation both for the ways in which they related to the youngsters with whom they worked and for the role that their own commitment and concern played in their efforts to be of help. It also meant that we were in a position to understand better some of the extraindividual (i.e., organizational) circumstances surrounding an individual's desire to become a part of the RYC staff. It was, at least to us, only natural that the search for a staff begin with the work crew foremen.

The selection of staff for the RYC was direct. No tests of any kind (e.g., aptitude, value profile, or intelligence tests) were given to any of the candidates. Anyone wanting to work at the RYC was interviewed by the program's Director and Deputy Director. The interview consisted of explaining the program to the candidate, eliciting his reactions, and discussing the problems and uncertainties of the program with him.

Our experience with the work crew program, coupled with our knowledge concerning the state of CPI as an organization, was sufficient to produce an image of the "kind" of person we hoped to involve in the RYC. *First, we wanted people who were dissatisfied—and who were willing to voice their dissatisfaction—with the limitations and restrictions imposed upon them by their current role in the community action program.* We were, in a sense, looking for people who not only were angry about what was happening to the agency but were also concerned enough to "bitch" about it, even though such behavior was almost guaranteed to keep them from "advancing" within the organization. In point of fact, several of the people who eventually were hired for the RYC staff were either seen as "troublemakers" or as individuals who were "not doing good jobs" by other, usually higher-salaried and more prestigious members of the organization. *And second, we wanted people who not only were committed and dedicated to working with the poor but were also both willing to experiment with a variety of different helping techniques (knowing well that none of them offered any guarantee of being effective) and ready to face the inevitable anxiety that such a venture would produce.*

During the period of time that candidates were being interviewed for RYC staff positions, the program's Director kept a diary of his reactions to the interviewing situation and his impressions of some of the people who applied for jobs. The following is one entry from this diary. We include it at this point because the reader might find it helpful in understanding the criteria by which candidates were evaluated. *Interview 12: May 1966.*

Today, Scotty and I interviewed Jack T. I think we both knew, even before the session was over, that we wanted Jack as one of our RYC workers. As soon as he left the office we kind of looked at each other, both of us knowing, almost without a word, that Jack was the man for the job.

So far, Jack is the only guy we want to hire who is not a work crew foreman. Although Scotty has known him for some time, I never met Jack until today. At the present time Jack is a Neighborhood Worker working out of the Newhallville area. He is a Negro, 34 years old, married, and has four children. Prior to coming to work for CPI he was a packing house worker.

Jack came a few minutes late for the interview and as soon as he came in he greeted Scotty, nodded to me, and took a seat from which he could look out of the window and onto the street.

Scotty and I began in the usual way. We told him about the job and about the RYC program as a whole. We gave him the usual spiel about it going to be a program "unlike any program ever run"; about how we wanted to work with kids and families in ways which were different and unorthodox; about how we wanted to create a program that would allow the staff to develop their own talents and would encourage and help people to assume the total responsibility for working with a client; and how, when I left in January, nobody would be brought in from the outside to run the program, but that movement would come from within the staff. It was the usual pitch.

During the whole time that we, mostly I, explained the program to Jack he never once looked at me. All he did was nod occasionally and continue to stare out of the window. I got the feeling that Jack either didn't believe what we were saying or that he just plain didn't care. But if he didn't care why was he down here in the first place? It couldn't be because of the salary that the job would carry because no one knew what it would be. And even if he knew that the job might involve an increase in pay there were still a lot of other openings in CPI and we sure didn't put on a big advertising campaign to get people to apply.

I think that my most vivid impression of Jack and of the whole situation was that I was sitting and talking to a man who acted as if he had heard all this before, had been "put on" many times by stories that stressed "growth, responsibility, and advancement," and just couldn't care less about "words." When we asked him about what he was doing at CPI, he responded by saying: "Officially or on my own?" Naturally, we said: "Both," and Jack took it from there. He told us in a somewhat bored way about his "official" duties as a Neighborhood Worker and about how he is supposed to contact and recruit people for the Employment Center but not to get "too involved with them" on a personal or counseling basis. He told us about how he drives people to and from appointments, offers them "support," and does some follow-up work after they have been placed on jobs or in training programs.

The only time he kind of lit up was when he began telling

us about his "on my own" work. With a bit of a glint in his eye (I must have imagined this because I rarely saw his eyes, what with him almost constantly staring out of the window) he told us about his nighttime activities; about how he works with "shook-up kids" from his neighborhood; how he spends all his time talking with them on street corners and in their homes; and how he tries to keep them out of trouble by involving them with him in a makeshift judo program (Jack T. is a black belt in judo).

Although he never said so, I got the feeling that one of the reasons Jack enjoyed his night work was that he was able to function in some of the very ways in which he could not work during the day. In other words, at night and informally, he could, indeed, get close to his "clients," counsel them, become deeply involved with them, and deal with their problems in a direct and unrestricted manner.

I also got the feeling that Jack was a fairly angry guy. He mentioned once or twice, always in passing, about how little he felt "the professionals" with whom he worked and who now supervised his activities knew about slum kids. He made no effort to hide the fact that he was somewhat disillusioned and unhappy about the way the War on Poverty was going. Despite what seemed to be his strong feelings he remained outwardly calm and completely self-possessed.

It was a strange interview in many ways. I guess mostly because the more Jack spoke about his concerns and reservations about all CPI programs (and, by implication, the RYC program), the more convinced I became that I wanted him on the staff.

When the interview was over, and as Jack was leaving the office, I said to him: "Jack, if we hire you as an RYC worker in our program do you think there's a chance that some day you'll look me straight in the eye and not stare out a window when you talk to me?" He almost, but not quite, smiled and said: "Maybe, we'll see."

The Original RYC Staff   Nine people made up the original staff of the RYC. Eight were males, and one (the secretary) was a female; five were white, four were black. By and large the staff could properly be called indigenous to the inner-city community; in the cases in which the people were not indigenous by birth they were certainly "indigenous" in terms of past experience, length of inner-city residence, or socio-economic background. Thus, for example, while the mean age of the staff was 29.6 years, an average of 25.4 of those years were spent in one or another inner-city neighborhood in either New Haven or New York. In terms of both educational background and previous work history, the staff was made of people who were essentially nonprofessionals. Almost all of them had neither the formal training nor the academic background in those areas (psychology, sociology, social work) generally acknowledged to be of importance in preparing people to deal effectively with troubled individuals. Of the original nine staff members, only one had a professional degree. Most of the staff had high school diplomas, one had had a year of business college, and one was a high school dropout. The staff's occupational backgrounds, prior to their joining CPI, covered a wide variety of work experiences. The continuum extended from that of being in a highly skilled profession to that of being a semiskilled or unskilled laborer. Briefly, these work experiences included being an automobile mechanic, an X-ray technician, a supermarket employee, a professional singer, a policeman, a baseball player, a book department manager, and a packing house worker. Despite the differences among them—and aside from the fact that they all seemed to share a deep commitment to and concern for the problems of poverty—they had one thing in common: they "knew" the inner city and knew it rather intimately, for their own backgrounds were not too dissimilar from the people whom they would be serving.

In addition to the nine full-time staff members, six other people completed the staff. They were all students at Yale University and became involved in the RYC through the activities of the Psycho-Educational Clinic. It will be recalled that one of the goals of the RYC program was to explore the possibility of establishing a research, training, and service relationship between the Department of Labor, CPI, and Yale University (see Chapter 1). The involvement of students, both graduate and undergraduate, at the RYC was a part of that exploration. But it was also much more than that: the use of the RYC as a setting for the clinical and research training of students and clinical psychology interns was intimately related to, and a part of, the goals and processes of the Psycho-Educational Clinic. Within the limits imposed upon them by their academic commitments and schedules, every student from the University was expected to become a part of the RYC and to function in many of the same ways as the full-time members of the staff. This meant that they would carry a case load, live in to relieve other live-in counselors, and become involved in developing a program of their own. From the point of view of the Psycho-Educational Clinic, the RYC represented the kind of setting through which there could emerge a pattern of clinical training and research that would be consistent with its own commitment to broaden the definition, scope, and relevance of clinical responsibility.

The Clients: People with Troubles and Troubled People
Thus far, we have confined our discussion of the RYC to a description of its organizational structure and personnel. In focusing attention on the setting and its staff, we have tried to illustrate how the organization as a whole, in both its conception and its development, was influenced by the notion that individual and group behavior were in large part a reflection of the dynamics and values of the settings in which people work and live. In theory, this should be as true for the RYC's clients as for its staff.

More often than not, however, helping institutions have been described as if they were populated by two very different groups of people, the staff and the clients, each with observably different needs, problems, and styles of life. In its most extreme form, the conceptual dichotomization of those who in fact coinhabit a setting has resulted in the institution being described as if its clients were tangential to the setting rather than an integral part of its social structure; as if they were there merely to receive certain kinds of services and need not be viewed as playing any meaningful role in the setting's evolution, its distinctiveness, or developing ethos. Only in the last 15 years, primarily through the work of Stanton and Schwartz (1954), Levinson and Gallagher

(1964), and others, have the helping professions begun to realize the extent to which both the givers and receivers of help are influenced by and, in turn, exert an influence upon the social structures of the settings that have brought them together.

It is for this reason that this chapter would be incomplete if it did not focus attention on those people, the clients, who helped develop the RYC. Their inclusion at this point is neither gratuitous nor accidental, for the RYC was predicated on the assumption that its staff and its clients were far more similar than they were different; that we all shared certain needs for meaning, relatedness, and a sense of competence; and that all of us, consequently, could benefit from a setting that was dedicated to meeting those needs.

It is difficult to describe the people whom the RYC was funded to serve without falling into the all-too-convenient (and possibly inappropriate) trap of referring to them as "sick." More often than not, the conditions and problems associated with poverty have been equated with and labeled as forms and symptoms of emotional disturbance. One of the consequences of this labeling process has been the tendency to hold the individual, and only the individual, responsible for his difficulties, and to view him as somehow "at fault" or "out of step" with the rest of society. At other times the problem is dealt with as if the individual had absolutely no control over his behavior or the conditions affecting his life. From this point of view, people are seen either as victims of fate or as casualties of a "system" that is essentially and unequivocally oppressive in nature. It is almost impossible, given the current values and orientations of our society, to avoid completely any conception of people, let alone people in need of help, that would be free from the pitfalls inherent in any model that speaks of or implies "illness." Perhaps the safest thing to assume is that both views of the problem are partially true and hopelessly incomplete. It is for this reason that we refer to our clients as "people with troubles and troubled people." It is for the same reason that the Department of Labor, in funding the RYC project, took deliberate pains (thankfully) to point out that one of the goals of the program was to "facilitate the individual and familial growth of poor and/or disrupted individuals." Our own orientation was to view the problem in terms of an individual's ability to develop the kinds of coping behaviors that would enable him to manipulate, influence, and negotiate the system in ways that not only fell, however broadly, within the limits of socially acceptable or tolerable behavior, but were also not self-defeating and self-humiliating.

The Original Clients The RYC was funded to work with those youngsters (boys between the ages of 16 and 21 who were both out of school and out of work) and families that fell into the so-called hard-core classification. They were, in point of fact, people on whom just about everyone had given up; and by "everyone" we mean both the traditional agencies (i.e., the schools, the Welfare Department, and the mental health professions) and the not-so-traditional agency, the community action program itself.

The first group of RYC residents (20 youngsters) came from families characterized by chronic unemployment, social disorganization, and severe interpersonal conflict; they were, for the most part, families with long histories of dependency, "welfarism," and unsuccessful contacts with the mental health professions. Most of the boys who were admitted for voluntary residency had previous records of involvement with the law, at one time or another had been incarcerated in a reformatory, institution, or mental hospital, and were failing in the most elementary job training program (CPI's prevocational work crews) administered through the community action agency. A few of the boys were on the "threshold of success" but were thought of as being held back by "bad home situations." All the boys were high school dropouts; all were involved in one or another of CPI's opportunity programs.

Of the first 20 youngsters to enter the program, 12 were Negro and 8 were white. Although their ages ranged from 16 to 20, the average age was 17.4 years. Seventy percent of the residents had been arrested one or more times prior to their entry into the RYC program, and while the number of encounters with the law ranged from 1 arrest to 12, as a group they averaged 2.9 arrests per individual. Most of those who had had contacts with the law had been arrested for offenses ranging from loitering and trespassing to crimes involving petty theft, auto theft, breaking and entering, burglary, and assault. Only 3 of the boys had never spent any time in an institution of one sort or another; 85 percent of the youngsters had been incarcerated in jail, a reformatory, an institution for the mentally retarded, a center for emotionally disturbed and homeless children, or a state facility for the mentally ill. Almost half the boys who had been institutionalized had spent more than one year at the institution. The group as a whole had spent an average of 1.61 years in one institution or another. At the time the RYC program began, only 2 of the original 20 residents were living in a two-parent home; of the remaining 90 percent, 55 percent were living in fatherless homes, while the other youngsters were residing either in foster homes, with relatives, or alone. Of the 20 original families served by the program, 80 percent were on one or another form of welfare. These included partial or complete ADC (Aid to Dependent Children) programs and welfare programs run either through the local or state governments. Only four families were self-sustaining. By and large the first group of 20 youngsters and their families seemed to come as close as possible to fulfilling the criteria currently in use for labeling people as "hard-core" or "chronically disadvantaged."

Statistics are a convenient and necessary way of summarizing and organizing data. They are helpful in providing a concise overview of the general characteristics that depict a particular population. This is as true for the statistics concerning the RYC's clients as it is for those applied to any other set of individuals. All statistics must, of necessity, sacrifice some degree of individual complexity in the quest for categorical preciseness. Consequently, any statistical summary of the population served by the RYC program must be viewed as a shorthand description of a group of individual and unique people. For example, the fact that 70 percent of the RYC's youngsters had had some contact with law enforcement agencies does not tell us much about how and why these events came to pass; nor do the statistics provide much in the way of helping us understand the circumstances, motivations, and experiences of the youngsters in that group. those youngsters (boys between the ages of 16 and 21 who The same can be said of almost any other statistical description involving the RYC's client population. There may be many reasons for dropping out of school and a host of different feelings associated with being a dropout. In each instance there is a tale to be told, and no two tales need be the same.

The Youngsters In the following pages we shall attempt to provide the reader with a more comprehensive and differentiated picture of the kind of youngster for whom the RYC was created. In each capsule portrait we attempt to supplement whatever information is known about the youngster with the impressions we have gotten of him in the different phases of the program.

Billy T.

Billy is a 17-year-old white youngster who has been in the Neighborhood Youth Corps program for a short time. He came into the program at the request of one of his friends who was already on a work crew. His friend suggested that he go down and speak with one of the neighborhood workers about the work crew program and about the chances of his eligibility to become a member. Billy saw this as a way for him to begin to "set myself on a straight line." At that time Billy was awaiting a court hearing on a charge of breaking and entering. Although he had worked "now and then" on a laundry truck, Billy was willing to take a cut in pay in the hope that he would be able to be in a situation that offered the prospect of a daily schedule. Billy spoke with the neighborhood worker and was placed on one of the work crews.

Billy is a short, skinny, good-looking boy who walks with a somewhat exaggerated spring in his step and wears elevator shoes. Because he is slightly built and wears tight continental pants, his elevator shoes only seem to accentuate his shortness.

Billy speaks as if every word he says ought to be taken as a direct challenge. When speaking with someone he rarely looks that person in the eyes, but almost invariably focuses on the other person's Adam's apple or chin. He speaks in short, clipped phrases that, no matter how quietly he is talking, sound as if they had been shot from a muted revolver.

It seems quite important to him that he be fully aware of any and all movement that takes place about him, almost as if these movements have a direct and determining effect on what his next move will be. Even when engaged in a conversation, Billy often turns his back on that person and quickly surveys the situation to check on who, if anyone, is listening or who is in the immediate area. His behavior is like that of a person who constantly finds himself in a new and potentially dangerous situation: he must be acutely aware of the placement and behavior of those who might attack and he must be ever-vigilant and ready to respond to any ominous or unpredictable movement that takes place around him.

Once Billy becomes convinced that an individual's movements do not signal the beginning of an assault, he can begin to relax and allow that person to enter his space of free movement. When this happens a metamorphosis occurs, and a shy, somewhat self-conscious 16-year-old boy emerges. He can begin to smile and laugh ever so gently about the fiction of Billy as a "hard man." He can talk about how difficult it can be constantly to feel vulnerable, small, and frightened. At these times, once Billy is sure his "confession" has not fallen on the wrong ears, he can speak about his love of the soil, the things that grow, and the wonder of a stone that "lives on and on." As Billy puts it:

You keep seeing this grass every year and you wonder where it goes and where it ends. If you put a rock in the bushes, a heavy rock, you know it's going to be there forever, no matter what happens to you."

Billy was born on the outskirts of New Haven. He lives with his mother and one of his older brothers. Billy has five brothers and one sister.

Billy has "no use" for almost all of the members of his family. According to him:

Well, my father was a wino. Him and my mother would always fight and I'm glad he's gone. Me, I always fight with my 23-year-old brother. He's an ass-hole, a brown-noser, and always taking over. I argue a lot with my mother. She always nags me about staying out of trouble. She's probably right but she never stops nagging me.

Billy also feels that he has very little status in the home and very little to say as to what should or should not happen at home:

I can't do nothing in the house. I can't play records or watch what I wanna on T.V. I gotta do what everyone else wants to do. I'm the youngest now and they never let you forget it.

Billy left school in the ninth grade for reasons that are somewhat similar to the feelings he has concerning himself and the way in which the other members of the family react to him. He did not like having to stay in classrooms for extended periods of time. He felt "penned in and cornered." He always felt imposed on by teachers and experienced school as a place where people were always trying to make him do things without consulting him. Billy got into constant arguments with his teachers because of their desire that he "do something" and his desire to be "let alone."

Billy's first contact with the law occurred in August 1964. He and a group of his friends were caught in a stolen car. Billy says he was unaware that the car had been stolen. At that time he was taken to Juvenile Court, given a talking-to, and told, "keep your nose clean from here on."

In November, Billy stole a car and took it out of town to race. As he was racing down a road he lost control of the car and it cracked into a telephone pole. Billy is not sure exactly why he took the car, but he says:

I was just walking around with a friend. I was feeling pretty disgusted. I don't know exactly why I did it. Maybe it was because I had nothing to do, or maybe it was because I had a beef with my girl.

The police arrived on the scene and Billy was taken to the hospital, where he remained for a week. He was taken to Juvenile Court but was released after being warned not to get into any more trouble.

From December 1964 to March 1965, Billy committed a series of crimes in which he broke into various restaurants in the New Haven area and stole a total of $600. In this case Billy feels he "had to" steal the money:

My mother was out of work and she was getting ready for an operation. All I heard at home was bills, bills, bills. I figured I had to finally help out and get the money to pay off the bills. After I got the $600 all the bills were paid.

Once all the outstanding bills were paid off Billy became somewhat frightened at the ease with which he had been able to obtain the money. He had broken into 17 establishments and had never been caught. He began to think that "things were getting out of hand." Billy then got in touch with a friend of his who was on the police force and arranged to meet him in a pool hall. He told his friend about the thefts he had committed and asked him for advice on how to go about extricating himself from the situation. The police officer suggested that Billy accompany him to the police station and make a complete confession. Billy agreed to do this and was told that he would receive some consideration because of the manner he had gone about "turning himself in." Billy was then allowed to go free on bail and is now awaiting a hearing.

Billy thinks that he would like to be a lawyer some day.
He puts it this way:
I like the lawyer's racket. I know what it feels like to be
in trouble. Some day I want to be a lawyer for kids.

Bob L.
Bob is a 17-year-old Negro youngster who has been in
the work crew program for almost a year. He came onto
the crew shortly after having been expelled from high school.
His expulsion was preceded by a series of suspensions, all
of which emanated from his "incorrigible" behavior in the
school setting. This behavior has variously been called
"provocative," "aggressive," and "disturbed." He came into
the program as a "self-referral" by presenting himself one
day at the NEC serving his neighborhood.

Bob is a tall, extremely handsome, and well-built youngster who is probably the best-dressed boy in the program.
He dresses in neat, conservative, Ivy League attire and
usually is meticulously groomed.

Bob prides himself on being the "coolest cat" in the program. Nothing, supposedly, ever fazes him. He acts as if
his entire being were an impenetrable shield, impervious
armor whose coat of arms is an "I don't give a damn"
smile. Bob is bright and perceptive, quick to size people up
and detect their particular sensitivities and weaknesses. He
exploits these weaknesses in a taunting and offhand manner
as if to suggest he has seized on some long-hidden secret
and understands it fully. However, his attacks, no matter
how direct and painful, are made with the ease and preci-
sion of a deft surgeon. His assaults and cuts are made neatly
and quickly, and he immediately retreats like some graceful
ballet dancer exiting from a suddenly darkened stage. Before any retaliation can come, Bob is gone or he is smiling
warmly in a completely disarming manner. No matter how
infuriating or provocative his behavior, Bob remains an engaging youngster who is well-liked by the foreman and the
other boys in the program. Bob is liked almost in spite of
himself, and he never ceases to be both amused and satisfied
with this state of affairs. As he puts it:
I'll cut you down and you'll come up thanking me.
But that's life, baby, that's life.

Bob was born in New Haven and has lived in the city his
entire life. He lives with his mother, stepfather, younger
brother, and sister. His mother's first husband, Bob's father,
lives in Washington, but Bob gets to see him periodically.

For all his apparent "coolness," Bob is a boy with problems, and his problems are easily recognized by many

people. Bob drinks, and his drinking has gotten him into difficulties both in the school setting and on the work crews. Although he has often been referred—and has gone for varying amounts of time—for psychiatric treatment, he prides himself on the fact that few doctors have "gotten anything out of" him:

It's a panic. I'd go to the shrink and snow the man so fast it wasn't funny. He'd try and ask me all kinds of questions and I'd cool it so bad he'd like to wind up with some head doctor himself. Nobody ever got anything out of me.

Bob isn't very sure of his future, and knowing Bob, his position is almost predictable. Bob will not, at least at the present time, allow anyone to feel as if he has truly committed himself to anything. For them to think this would be an insult to Bob. All his energy appears to be wrapped up in creating the impression that no one thing in the world is more salient or warrants any more personal commitment than any other thing. The world is an equivocal series of events, and Bob acts as if his role in life is to dispel anyone's illusions that this is not so. For Bob disengagement has become a way of life, and he has a stake in maintaining his stance as the work crew's herald of the "cool world."

In describing the clients whom the RYC was created to serve—especially the youth—we have tried to focus attention on the fact that one could view their needs and problems to be of such kinds as to require extensive remedial interventions, the kinds of interventions usually associated with the more traditional clinical or treatment processes. Were we to assign clinical diagnoses to the youngsters—and many of them had been assigned such diagnoses in the past—these diagnoses would likely span the entire range of emotional and psychological pathologies. The boys could be described —and, in some cases, quite appropriately so—as having schizoid personalities, psychopathic and sociopathic character disorders, organic pathologies, psychoneurotic personalities, and mental defects, and as characters in any other diagnostic category currently utilized in labeling patients. Most of them were having difficulties because their feelings and attitudes, their work habits and interpersonal relations, had combined to produce a youngster who was socially and psychologically unprepared to enter into, become part of, and succeed in the world of work. Their unemployability was both the product and the symptom of a pattern of life that had left them ill-equipped to cope with the responsibilities and obligations of the existing social order. Their feelings about themselves and others were the feelings of people who have become estranged from a world that was incomprehensible, a world with which they could not cope in any meaningful and self-satisfying manner. For them, to be alienated, isolated, and insulated in a world of multiple and endless paradoxes, a world of limited or nonexistent alternatives, was not a way of life, it was the *only* form of semiviable existence.

It would be legitimate to ask why these youngsters were not being seen or treated in clinics and by private therapists. The answers, as we have already indicated, are many and varied, and are not entirely accounted for by the lack of financial resources or the unavailability of clinical facilities. They appear to be more firmly embedded in the sociological and cultural variables that separate these youngsters from the institutions and clinical facilities available—and often not so readily available to them in a psychological sense—in the community. Part of the answer might also be sought in our traditional definitions and conceptions of what the requirements and conditions for appropriate clinical interactions are, and the nature of what constitutes clinical functioning.

The Program: Structured and Unstructured Help
From the outset, the RYC was conceived of as a program in which environmental manipulation would occur within the context of a developing and ongoing relationship among an RYC staff member, "his" youngster, and the boy's family. At no point was it the RYC's intention to allow parents to view the program as one to which they were "losing" a son or as a place that would "free" them of whatever responsibilities they had for their children. The RYC was to be a place where people, both youngsters and their families, could begin to view and experience themselves and one

another in ways that would allow them to deal with their problems in an atmosphere free from many of the self-defeating conditions under which they had been leading their lives. The RYC staff member was to be the catalytic agent, the vehicle, in this process.

As a program, the RYC was to house 20 youngsters and work with 20 families at any one time. Over the year, the program was to serve 50 residents and families. Each resident was assigned a worker. It was the worker's responsibility, using whatever means and techniques at his disposal, to get to know his youngster and family "like a book" and to use himself as a therapeutic lever in their lives.[8] The worker's "job" was to gain access into and earn the trust and respect of people who had come to fear, distrust, and, in some cases, despise "change agents" (e.g., welfare workers, social workers, school and law enforcement personnel) of one sort or another. The formal goals of the program were simple and clear enough: (1) to help the youngster and his family become employed or enter employment opportunity programs that they wanted; (2) to help them deal with some of the barriers or problems (psychological, social, or other) that stood between them and a life that was more fulfilling and satisfying; and (3) to make it possible within a relatively short period of time (6 months) for the youngster either to return home or to establish himself in his own apartment. It is important to point out and to repeat that with the exception of preparing a youngster to leave the RYC physically, the aims of the program with respect to its clients were essentially no different from its goals for its own staff. In both cases, creating the conditions for individual and collective growth were the primary purposes behind the development of the setting.

On a theoretical basis it was hoped that during the day the

---

[8]"Working with" the boys at the RYC was to come to mean being with them, fighting with them, counseling them, and experiencing and sharing their successes and failures on a 24-hour basis. The same was true of working with their families. In both cases it meant becoming involved with them in ways and through paths that most "helping" people would not or could not travel.

residents would be out of the RYC (hopefully) attending work. The worker could use this time to visit his youngster's work site, but it was also a time to work with the boy's family. During the evenings and on weekends the RYC was to be used for special programs. These programs were open to all residents (eventually, to the entire community) and their families. They were the staff's "individual interest" programs, which included programs in carpentry, automobile mechanics, music, judo, resident and family sensitivity sessions, remedial education, municipal government, and athletics.

At no time was the program to be allowed to become or to resemble an institution: there were no visiting hours, parents were encouraged to come at any time of the day or night, the residents paid rent, and the boys were free to go home any time they wanted. The program, both formally and informally, was to consist of a house in which people– not "patients" or "inmates"—could work and live with one another, could grow and begin to perceive themselves as no longer powerless to alter and influence their lives, and, perhaps more than anything else, could begin to make some sense out of the paradoxical and oftentimes contradictory world we all share.

In this chapter we have tried to describe some of the characteristics and reasons behind the development of that "delivery system" that we called the Residential Youth Center. We have also tried to describe the context, both historical and conceptual, in which the setting was developed. Most important, we wanted to provide the reader with some "feel" both for the people who were to inhabit the setting and for the ideas that shaped its evolution.

By way of introducing Chapter 5, we might point out that many of us, even in those early days of thinking and planning, were acutely aware of the fact that this unborn thing we called the RYC had already assumed a significance that went far beyond the development, however innovative, of another helping institution. We were, for better or for worse, engaged in the process of creating a community—not a therapeutic one in the narrow sense of the term, and certainly not one devoted solely or primarily to meeting the needs of its "clients," but a community that would enable *all* its members to participate in a series of extended growth experiences. Under these conditions it quickly became clear that the question of organizational structure was but one of the issues that had to be dealt with if the setting was to approach its goals. Another issue involved the need to develop a "mechanism" that would maximize people's abilities to profit from their day-to-day experiences in the setting. In Chapter 5 we shall both describe this mechanism and offer examples of how it was used.

Chapter 5 The Problem of Training

Being, lived in dialogue, receives even in extreme dereliction
a harsh and strengthening sense of reciprocity; being, lived
in monologue, will not, even in the tenderest intimacy,
grope out over the outlines of the self.
—Martin Buber

In Chapter 4 we described the organizational and interpersonal assumptions that influenced the development of the
RYC as a setting. We also described in some detail many of
the dynamics and characteristics of its formal structure. In
the concept of "horizontality" we had what we strongly believed to be the kind of organizational framework within
which the goals of the program, both its official and un-
official goals, could be fulfilled. Through the sharing of responsibilities and concerns, we hoped both to create the
conditions for increased individual and group competence
and to inhibit or prevent the development of those cancerous
and self-defeating conditions that all too often sap an organization of its vitality, rob it of its innovativeness, and
hasten its demise. But given the complexity of the RYC program and the grandiosity of its goals, coupled with the
quality of commitment that would be demanded of its staff,
we felt we needed something that could do for us on an
interpersonal level what the horizontal structure symbolized
on an organizational level. It was imperative that we develop
an internal mechanism, an interpersonal forum, that would
mediate between the organization's structure and its people.
A vehicle was needed through which the staff could learn to
communicate with one another in ways and with a freedom
rarely found in most organizations. We needed, in short, a
training process through which we could share our experiences and problems in an atmosphere characterized by mutual
trust and dedicated to our own development both as individuals and as members of a group.
    The search for an interpersonal complement to structural
horizontality was not an easy one. Few models existed, and
most of those that were available did not seem appropriate

to our particular needs. In time we turned to what for want of a better term can only be described as *sensitivity training.*[1]

The T-Group Phenomenon

Since 1947, when the first National Training Laboratory was established in Bethel, Maine, we (or at least a large and increasing number of social scientists) entered into the T-group era, the age of the "laboratory approach to reeducation."[2] To its advocates, sensitivity training represents a unique opportunity through which the resources of the behavioral sciences and the values and needs of a democratic society can be united and can form a reciprocal working relationship (Bradford et al., 1964). From this point of view, the T (Training) group becomes a setting that affords its members the opportunity of learning about themselves, improving their interpersonal skills, and joining with one another in the quest for rational solutions to group and social problems. The T-group itself is predicated upon a basic and pragmatic humanism, and it stresses the fundamental importance of growth and self-actualization both for the individual and the group. To its detractors, the T-group is a "game," a "cop-out," however intellectually rationalized and scientifically fortified it might appear. For this group of critics, sensitivity training represents little more than the cultivation of those palaverous skills which allow, indeed enable and reward, people who might otherwise seek to create real social change

[1]We will restrict our description of sensitivity training at the RYC to that group, the staff, with which we are most familiar and in whose sensitivity sessions we participated directly. It should be pointed out, however, that sensitivity training or some variant thereof was not confined to the staff of the RYC. Regular group sessions were, and continue to be, held for both the RYC's residents and their families. In addition, regular "open meetings" are held among and between the different groups (staff, residents, and families) involved in the setting.
[2]For a comprehensive review of the history, dynamics, and development of the T-group movement, the reader is referred to Bradford, Gibb, and Benne (1964). For a description of some of the problems and particular applications of sensitivity training, the works of Lippitt (1961), Bradford (1961a, 1961b), Mial and Mial (1961), and Argyris (1965, 1966) are most helpful and informative.

to live with the status quo and to accept their own impotence and powerlessness with a modicum of dignity.

Any new and potentially significant movement in the area of human affairs is bound to have its share of champions and critics, but be this as it may, sensitivity training has grown and prospered in a climate of general acceptance and, at times, even faddist enthusiasm.[3] At the present time, T-grouping (or any one of the number of guided group inter-action processes that have evolved out of the experiences of T-groupers) has made inroads into, and has been utilized by, organizations with varying histories, traditions, goals, and values. It, or some of its concepts and practices, have in a relatively short period of time become almost "standard equipment" in many large businesses, industries, universities, and even, of late, the State Department of our own govern-ment (Argyris, 1967).

Within the context of its reeducative framework, a T-group is commonly used in two ways: as a vehicle for ex-periences in personal growth and/or as a clinical tool to be employed by experienced T-group leaders (they prefer to be called "change agents") in their attempts to be of help to organizations that are having problems and experiencing difficulties. When used for purposes of personal growth, a training group has a number of characteristics. By and large the group is composed, although by no means exclusively, of professionals and/or people with administrative or super-visory functions. The group members do not know one another, have not worked together in the past, and may never again see one another once the training group experience is terminated. The group meets in a setting that is different and removed from the organizations and communities from which its members come. The T-group experience itself is usually intensive and relatively short-term in nature. The group is given a "leader," a person with experience in guid-

[3]The vehemence with which T-grouping is both attacked and de-fended, as well as the cultist quality of many of its converts, must, one supposes, be somewhat similar to the situation that surrounded the introduction of psychoanalytic thinking and practice into this country not so many years ago.

ing group interactions. The leader stays with the group for the duration of the program but, like the rest of the members of the group, usually severs his relationship with the group once the training sessions have been completed.[4] In one form or another, the participants in the group are confronted with the problem of creating a group that will meet the requirements of all its members for growth. The data, as Bradford et al. (1964) point out, "are the transactions among members, their own behavior in the group, as they struggle to create a productive and viable organization, a miniature society; and as they work to stimulate and support one another's learning within that society." The group's participants are helped to diagnose and experiment with their own behavior and relationships in this specially designed but, at least from our point of view, highly artificial environment. The role of the trainer or leader is to "help to establish processes of data collection, data analysis, and diagnosis of the changing here-and-now experiences of the group and its members" (Bradford, et al., 1964). The overall goal of the T-group is clear: that its members, through the process of experiencing themselves and others in this group problem-solving situation, emerge from the setting with a heightened awareness of themselves and of the effects of their behavior on others, be able to function more effectively in other group situations, and derive a greater appreciation of the human growth possibilities that are inherent in productive and mutually satisfying collaborative experiences.

Sensitivity Training in Relation to the RYC

There are two reasons for our having taken the time in this chapter to describe, at some length but certainly inadequately, some of the philosophy and processes of the T-group movement. First, we felt a basic identity with its goals, orientation,

[4]Our description is clearly of the so-called typical T-group. Bradford et al. (1964) point out that the population to which the T-group experience is now being made available also includes laymen, people from different cultural or national backgrounds, children, youth, and college students. Also, in some instances the membership (total or partial) of a single organization is accommodated in a single training group.

and values; we felt very strongly and took very seriously the fact that whatever results the RYC was to achieve would rest in good part on the degree to which we could support and encourage one another's growth, learn to collaborate in mutually satisfying and helpful ways, and derive a sense of personal and collective meaning from the setting of which we were all a part. We felt, in short, that what happened to us as a staff was at least as important, if not more so, as what we did for our clients; but that in any event, what we felt both as individuals and as members of a group would surely influence our transactions with the people we were supposed to serve. The second reason was that as a group, despite our acceptance of the potential value of sensitivity training, *we did not conform to the "typical" requirements of most T-groups, nor did the manner in which most T-groups are normally conducted seem to meet the particular needs of our setting or its people.*

The Inapplicability of T-Grouping
There were many reasons behind the lack of "fit" between the needs of our group and the more or less traditional conditions under which sensitivity training is carried out. To begin with, unlike most T-groups, which meet rather frequently and intensively over a short period of time, our group would be, both of necessity and by definition, an ongoing one. We were indigenous to the RYC, would be working with one another continually, and could not view the setting as a transient or temporary one, as some wooded sanctuary where one could "let his hair down," become "sensitized," and then leave. Another difference was that our sensitivity group would consist of the organization's entire membership and could not be restricted to a few people in so-called key positions of influence. We would all be in the same group and would not, as is often the case in T-grouping, send individuals off to different groups. Third, with the exception of one individual, the RYC's staff was composed entirely of nonprofessionals, a population that the T-group movement has, as yet, neither sought out nor reached to

any degree comparable to its impact on professionals, white-collar workers, and people in managerial or executive positions. As a group we were, at least in the beginning, not at all convinced that talking was the best or most appropriate way of resolving conflicts. Many of us felt uncomfortable in the world of words and had not yet learned, as Thomas Mann put it, that

Speech is civilization itself. The word, even the most contradictory word, preserves contact—it is silence which isolates.

Another important difference was that the person who was the nominal leader of the sensitivity training sessions was also the organization's "official" leader. This raised a number of theoretical and practical issues for him as well as for the rest of the staff. Because of the conditions imposed by the setting, the leader could not extricate himself from the group, could not be content with guiding "the group's" interactions. If he was to be a part of the group, then he, too, was "vulnerable"; his actions, feelings, and problems were subject to the scrutiny and help of the group. Of final but perhaps greatest importance was the fact that this group, unlike most laboratory training groups, would have to use its sensitivity sessions to deal with many of the actual problems confronting the RYC. These problems (i.e., policy decisions, intra- and interagency relations, and client service) were "real" in the most concrete sense of the term, and the ways in which they were resolved would have a direct bearing on the future of the setting and the lives (and livelihoods) of all its people. We could not luxuriate in the knowledge that what we were dealing with, however real it might appear at the moment, were, in fact, a series of artificially induced problems from which one could escape once the training sessions were at an end. In one way or another, we and the people with whom we were working would have to *live* with our decisions.

The Rationale and Goals of Sensitivity Training at the RYC
Whatever form our sensitivity training sessions finally took, they would have to address themselves to a number of specific

issues, and not the other way around. It was to be a situation in which the methods adopted would have to be appropriate to the problems encountered, not vice versa. We knew (or at least had some ideas) about the general areas in which we would encounter difficulty, and consequently, we were able to define, however tentatively, a number of reasons and uses for our sensitivity training sessions. For purposes of summary we shall list some of the reasons and areas for which we envisioned the use of staff sensitivity training.

Problems If there was anything we had learned (and learned well) from our involvement in different organizations (e.g., the public schools, the Regional Center, and CPI), it was that one could be certain of only one thing: *there would always be problems*. The problems would vary in content and intensity, but they would always be there, always pose some present or potential danger to the organization, and always threaten the goals of the setting and the welfare of its people. To say that one could always count on the existence of problems seems to be little more than a glimpse of the obvious. Our past experiences, however (see Chapter 3), had left us with a residue of unhappy examples of just how rarely this apparent truism is taken seriously enough to be translated into, or lead to the development of, the kinds of organizational vehicles that might enable a setting to deal with its problems in non-self-defeating ways. To be aware—however dimly, perhaps even unconsciously—of the inevitability of problems is one thing; to anticipate their occurrence and to plan or devise internal mechanisms for handling them is quite another. Every organization "knows" that at one time or another it will be confronted with problems involving differences in values among its staff, with interpersonal conflicts, and with different perceptions of the nature of the institution's goals and the means of achieving them; but few organizations prepare themselves to deal with these issues in anything but reflexive and crisis-oriented ways. At the RYC, for example, long before the formal advent of the program, we could be fairly certain that the very manner in which the setting was structured guaranteed the occurrence of certain problems. It was inevitable that horizontality would create problems for those of us who had always functioned in hierarchical organizations. Just as horizontality brought with it the possibility of greater freedom and the potential for individual growth, so, too, did it promise to create conflicts for people who had often been rewarded for being passive, dependent, and noncreative. There would be other issues, issues that would compound and exacerbate the "usual" personal, interpersonal, and organizational problems with which we would be faced. There was the "professional-nonprofessional" issue, the problems that would arise from a setting in which people worked and lived with one another so intimately and intensively, and always, always there was the question of race—ever present, ever influencing the course of events, and sooner or later raising its head in confrontation.

The anticipation of problems and the realization that we would have to develop a vehicle for dealing with them were only a few of the reasons for turning to sensitivity training, for wanting to "institutionalize" it, and for making it a formal and permanent part of the organization's structure. We were acutely aware of the fact that problems would never be "solved," but we hoped to be able to use these sessions to deal with our problems in a preventive, albeit tertiary preventive, manner. Institutionalized sensitivity training was to be used as a mechanism, indigenous to the setting, through which we could deal with our problems openly and regularly, and hope that by so doing they would be kept from interfering unduly with the goals of the program or the individual and collective growth of the staff.

Internal Self-Reflection and Self-Correction   One of the most sobering aspects of our previous involvement in other helping settings was the experience of seeing just how often and how quickly an organization can be robbed of its vitality and lose control over its own destiny. In time, some organizations seemed to assume a life of their own, propelled as if by some nameless internal dynamic, oblivious to the commands of those who nominally remained its owners. Eventually, a point is reached at which events become irreversible and change becomes impossible. It is at that point that the institution's builders "officially" become the prisoners of their own creation.

It was very important to us that we be able to control this "thing" we were creating before it came to control us. We did not want to see happen to us what on a much larger and more frightening scale Sorensen (1965) observed in the U.S. State Department: the "frequent sterility" and the "built-in inertia which deadened initiative." In sensitivity training we saw the possibility of developing a self-reflective and self-corrective mechanism, a process that would enable us to evaluate ourselves and the program constantly. If we used it properly (and honestly), it would allow us to look at ourselves, who we were, how we were changing, and to judge whether or not these changes—either in ourselves or in the setting—were of the enhancing or self-defeating variety.

Clinical Training   Despite the fact that very few members of the staff possessed the formal credentials, we were all— almost by definition, and certainly for all intents and pur- poses—clinicians. Our days and nights at the RYC would be replete with human encounters and interactions, and would involve us in a series of unending helping relationships. We would all be working with clients—trying to help a youngster make sense out of a conflict-ridden world, or assisting his family in their quest for a fuller, more satisfying life. Like all clinicians, our effectiveness would in large part depend on the quality of the relationships we were able to establish with the people we hoped to help. And, like all clinicians, *we could only assume that the more aware we became of our own behavior—the more "tuned in" we were to the ways in which we were "coming on" to one another—the more effective we would be in the helping situation.*

In addition, we felt that if we could extricate ourselves from the morass of clinical and personality theories, effective clinical functioning could be viewed in terms of the ap- plication of a few relatively specific principles. Of these principles the most important appeared to be the following:

1. *The Principle of Complexity:* A problem is generally more complex than it seems.
2. *The Principle of Conceptualization:* The manner in which one conceptualizes a problem influences how one tries to deal with it.
3. *The Principle of Intersubjectivity:* It is imperative, in any clinical interaction, to attempt to perceive the world through the eyes of the "other."

Over and above these "principles," however, was the fact that the clinician's own sensitivity—his ability to perceive, interpret, and respond to the experiential communalities that bind people and define the human condition—is his most powerful ally in the helping situation. Some come by this ability almost naturally and need little if any additional training; others simply "don't have it," and never will have it however intensive and prolonged their training. Most of us, however, are neither "naturals" nor "unteachables"; we possess a certain basic sensitivity and look to training as a way of developing and expanding that gift. In sensitivity training we saw the possibility of developing the kind of continuous in-service training that would sharpen and strengthen our clinical abilities. If we could learn to deal with the harsh realities of our own limitations and interpersonal problems, we hypothesized, it could only be helpful to us in our transactions with our clients.

Decision-Making and Growth As noted previously, because of the manner in which the setting was structured, all basic policy and administrative decisions were to be arrived at through group discussion rather than by executive dictation. In addition, this "community" we were building was predicated on the assumption that, given the appropriate conditions, people could learn (or relearn) that their needs for personal competence, interpersonal effectiveness, and group cohesiveness were universal in nature and could be achieved through the help and support of their co-workers. But in order for this to occur—indeed, in order for us even to begin to approach this idealized state—it was imperative that we learn to open ourselves to each other, for, as Buber (1956, p. 137) put it:

A real community need not consist of people who are perceptually together, but it must consist of people who, precisely because they are comrades, have mutual access to one another and are ready for one another.

Given these goals, we saw in sensitivity training a group process that might enable us to *discuss problems and reach decisions in an atmosphere of mutual trust and respect.* In addition, it seemed to be the kind of group situation that could foster the development of openness and interpersonal accessibility.

A System of Feedback and Research   The final reason for sensitivity training was its potential use as an instrument for research and as a source of feedback. In sensitivity training we saw a way of *providing ourselves with a continual supply of data, the kind of information we could use as a way of evaluating what was happening both to ourselves and to the organization we were trying to build.* We viewed it as a sort of "developmental chronicle" through which we could trace the evolution of the RYC and to which we could refer for information concerning how and why we arrived at any particular decision.[5] In addition, as the permanent record of an organization it could be used by researchers interested in the problem of the creation of new settings.

An organization is rarely static or unchanging. It "moves" and alters its functions and directions constantly. At certain times the particular antecedents and consequences of change are more observable than at other times. But when an organization changes—when it alters its purposes, goals, or orientations—this change usually occurs over time and is as much a reflection of what has gone before (its history and process of development) as it is a response to current conditions and future concerns. To the degree that an organization is conspicuously aware of this fact, especially of how important the past is in determining the context in which most decision-making takes place, to that degree will the organi-

[5]Early in the history of the RYC the staff decided to keep some permanent record of its sensitivity sessions. Some sessions were stenotyped, the proceedings duplicated, and the verbatim records handed out to the staff. At the remaining sessions a staff member would take "running notes" of the meeting, type them up, and enter them in the "organizational diary" of the RYC.

zation free itself of the tendency to repeat unconsciously the mistakes of the past. At the RYC the assumption was made that by studying and analyzing our own history we might avoid the fate of so many organizations that act as if they no longer control their own destinies or understand their own histories.

Sensitivity Training at the RYC: The Model Defined

Thus far, we have attempted to provide the reader with a summary of the reasons and considerations that led to the decision to incorporate some form of sensitivity training into the overall structure of the RYC. The remainder of this chapter will be devoted to explicating the specific forms this training took and, more important, describing some of its more concrete results. The fact that no staff member had ever participated in a T-group was probably a mixed blessing. It meant, on the one hand, that we could not make use of many of the specific techniques and processes that have emerged out of the T-group movement. On the other hand, however, neither were we bound by any preconceived notions of what form guided (or unguided) group interactions need necessarily assume. We could design and if need be redesign the meetings to meet our needs rather than try to fit our problems into some prearranged training model.

Prior to the time the RYC began holding sensitivity sessions on a formal basis, the staff as a whole met to discuss and design the specific form its training sessions would take. During this period the staff tried to prepare itself, as it were, for the experiences that would follow. In retrospect, these plenary meetings were sensitivity sessions in and of themselves, for they provided the staff with its first opportunity to begin to explore such issues as trust, confidentiality, and the potential (both for good and ill) of interpersonal openness. During these meetings we became acutely aware of just how varied our perceptions of sensitivity training really were, and of the different ways in which our concerns influenced our conceptions of what the sessions should look like, what issues they should involve, and how they ought to be conducted. In time the group was able to agree on a format for the sensitivity sessions that were to follow. It was decided, for example, that we would conduct our sessions three times each week. The time for each of these sessions was to be "reserved," and, barring any emergencies, nothing was to be scheduled which could interfere in any way with the group meetings. It was also decided that the meetings would be "closed," that only the full-time members of the staff and the clinical psychology interns from the Psycho-Educational Clinic could attend them, and that whatever was discussed during these sessions would "remain there" and not be discussed "on the outside." Finally, because of the different concerns on the part of various members of the staff, it was decided that there would be three types of sensitivity sessions and that, with the exception of "Individual Sensitivity," which was to be held at least once a week, the kind of session held on any particular day would be determined by the kinds of problems the group felt it wished to discuss.

In the pages that follow we shall define and give examples of the three types of sensitivity sessions that were held at the RYC between June of 1966 and January of 1967. For the most part, the examples offered are taken from the verbatim transcripts of these sessions.[6] Wherever possible we shall attempt to provide the reader with both a brief description

[6]The decision to include examples taken from the period of time between June 1966 and January 1967 was made for two reasons: first, because it was during that time that the author was a full-time member of the staff and therefore in a position both to understand and to be affected by the same problems and concerns that confronted the rest of the staff; and second, since one of the primary goals of this book is to explore the problem of the creation of settings, it seemed appropriate that attention be focused on the RYC during that period of time (i.e., the time during which the organization was conceived and the early days of its development) when many critical decisions were made.

The staff of the RYC was consulted and consented to the use of the excerpts of the sensitivity sessions included in this chapter. For purposes of publication, however, the names of all members participating in the meetings have been changed. Although the examples used have been abridged (the length of the verbatim transcripts of our sensitivity sessions—which averaged more than 80 typed pages—made their unabridged inclusion impossible), no attempts have been made to expurgate, "clean up," or in any way alter the content of the sessions.

of the background of each of the problems discussed and some indication of how each issue was "resolved."[7]

Individual Sensitivity   The first type of training session held at the RYC was called, for want of a better term, "individual sensitivity." As the name implies, individual sensitivity was perhaps the most personalized of the different kinds of training sessions held each week. Its goals were to provide a specific individual with feedback concerning how his behavior, his particular way of "coming on," was being perceived and responded to by the other members of the group. The focus was on an individual's modes of relating and the kinds of feelings and reactions he engendered in others. In addition to discussing a particular individual and sharing with him the kinds of things about him that turned people either "on" or "off," attention was directed to the question of how the group itself was discussing that person. Were we, for example, using the individual as a scapegoat, as a symbol for many of our own problems, or as a convenient target for problems that cut much deeper into the very fabric of the setting? It was, in short, a situation in which the group was asked to help a specific individual become more aware of the effect, both good and bad, of his behavior on others, while at the same time opening itself up to a critical self-examination of how the group was functioning in the here-and-now situation.

[7]As indicated previously, the question of the resolution of conflict must be viewed in relative terms. For many of the problems with which we were confronted, no absolute or enduring solutions could be reached. When people are dealing with issues (e.g., problems of race) that have long personal histories, involve a number of different emotions and motivations, and include a host of values, perceptions, and beliefs, it becomes difficult to speak in terms of absolute solutions. Consequently, our goals in the sensitivity sessions were not to "solve" problems but to bring them out into the open, place them before the group, and make them available for discussion. To the degree that we could bring ourselves to talk about issues that usually remained in the background—rarely discussed but always influencing behavior—we felt that we were engaging in conflict resolution. From the point of view of our day-to-day interactions, however, the goals of the training sessions were clear: to deal with problems in such a manner as to keep them from interfering unduly with our ability to function together as a group.

Prior to the time the RYC held its first individual sensitivity session, the group had agreed on a procedure for conducting these sessions. The procedure was rather simple, unique, and not a little anxiety-provoking. First, the names of all the members of the staff were written on pieces of paper, which were folded and thrown into a hat. A member of the group would then pick out one name.[8] Whosever name was picked out was "it" for that session. The individual whose name was selected would then remain silent for the next 30 minutes, during which time the floor was "open" to anyone who wished to share his feelings about the individual with the group. If silence ensued, we could discuss that silence, speculate on its meaning, and relate it to the feelings and concerns of the group at that particular moment. Usually, however, the session would begin when one of the members of the group would volunteer to share his experiences of the individual, proceed to describe these experiences, and open his perceptions and feelings up to the rest of the staff. The remaining time would be devoted to both a discussion of the various feelings brought up by the different members of the group and an analysis of the ways in which we seemed to be communicating to one another about the particular individual in question. After 30 minutes the floor was turned over to the person whose name had been drawn from the hat. He could then take as much time as he wished to share with the group not only his experience of what had been said about him during the previous half-hour but also his perception of the manner in which he was discussed and the kinds of problems the group seemed to have in communicating both to and about him. It was a time during which the individual could reflect on what was said about him while at the same time providing the group with an appraisal of its own modes of functioning. When the individual

[8]Approximately six months after individual sensitivity sessions had been held on a regular basis, the group decided that it was ready to try to discuss the relationships between particular members of the group. A new procedure was then adopted in which the names of "pairs" of individuals would be dropped into the hat, whatever pair was pulled out thus becoming the subject of that training session.

had completed his "rebuttal," the entire group would try to summarize what had transpired, engage one another in discussions concerning the meaning and implications of the session, and try to arrive at some tentative conclusions and suggestions for dealing with the interpersonal "data" that had been placed before it. The sessions lasted from one to three hours and would be terminated whenever the group felt that it had accomplished about as much as it could during that session.

Individual sensitivity session example No. 1: June 21, 1966. There is an enormous difference between preparation and confrontation, between planning and implementation. Without doubt the time taken by the staff to "prepare itself" for Individual Sensitivity was time well spent. This does not mean, however, that when confronted with the "real thing" any of us felt completely primed or adequately prepared for the experience. But one way or another we were in it; it had begun, and on June 21, 1966, the staff of the RYC held its first Individual Sensitivity session.

As the Fates would have it, the first name drawn out of the hat was that of the Director's. What follows is an account of that session taken from the Director's diary. Although the session was not recorded, the Director, for reasons to be made clearer in succeeding chapters of this book, kept a personal chronicle of his experiences and feelings during the early days of the RYC. To be sure, the individual sensitivity session of June 21, 1966, was of such a nature as to be both recorded in his diary and indelibly etched in his memory.

I couldn't honestly say it was fun, but it was more than a little instructive and quite possibly one of the more revealing experiences of my life.

We were all sitting around, all of us just a little bit edgy with expectation, for we knew that today we would have our first Individual Sensitivity session. We had all written our names on pieces of paper and had placed the slips in a hat. Butch stuck his hand in, pulled out one slip, and with an expression combining both amusement and relief, he announced: "It's the Chief Honcho, it's Kelly."

I can't possibly explain how or why, but somehow I almost

"knew" that mine would be the first name chosen. Call it intuition, call it coincidence, call it luck; but one way or another it "had" to be that way. It was in the cards. I remember looking around the room and thinking: "O.K., big mouth, now it begins. Sit back and listen."

Things remained quiet for what seemed like a long time. In retrospect it was probably only a minute or two. It's funny how time expands or contracts when one has to wait and wonder; when silence makes its own noises.

The guys were looking at each other, almost as if they were taking a silent vote to see who would begin, each one weighing the consequences of what he could or couldn't afford to say. One or two of the guys laughed mechanically, another shifted uncomfortably in his seat. Chip, with that ever-present sardonic look on his face, gazed from person to person, shook his head in mock sadness, and said: "Aw come on, he can't give us *all* pink slips or he won't have a staff." A few of the guys chuckled but quickly became silent again.

Finally, Lance said: "Look, what's everyone so afraid of? He's just a little guy. Besides, if he tries to make any trouble I'll just sit on him." (Note: Lance is a man who carries the weight with which to back up his words.) Butch looked at Lance, laughed, and said, "That's O.K. for you to say, buddy, you're his cousin. But I'm no kin to that man and I'm not about to take *your* word for it."

It was at this point that Scotty, bless him, really put his finger on the problem. He reflected back to the group its apparent difficulty in talking about me but shifted the focus onto the general issue of trust and to the question of whether or not people felt that they could ever "open up," regardless of how many guarantees they had been given.

The group responded to Scotty as if he had just said what was really on their minds. Staff member after staff member began to give examples, drawn from other experiences in other settings, of how often they had been "conned" by false promises of trust, openness, and confidence. Each staff member, in his own way, gave testimony to how difficult it was to level with one another, to "talk straight," and to believe that what he would say would not be held against him. Over and over again the point was made that the only way to "get ahead" or, indeed, even to survive in an organization was *not* to tell people what you really felt, and *not* to open yourself up or "stand out."

After some time, time during which the group seemed to

agree—although no one said so openly—to "chance it," Jack looked at me, then looked back to the group and said: "O.K., let's give it a shot. Maybe this'll help Kelly, maybe it won't, but there is something about the way he comes on—at least the way *I* think he comes on—that's kind of annoying. Now I don't know what kind of Director he's going to be. I don't even think he knows yet. But I wish the hell he'd cut out these daily sermons."

Now, Jack is a guy who, even at this early point in the game, seems to have earned a great deal of respect from the rest of the staff. He's usually rather quiet, but when he speaks the rest of the staff listens. Everyone now seemed to lean forward a little bit to hear what he was saying, and when he finished, Vito said: "What do you mean, Jack? I think I know but I'm not sure."

Jack then went on to describe in greater detail exactly what he meant. We went on for quite a while, and, while I'm sure I'm not quoting him perfectly, this is roughly what he said: "Well, it's like this. Every time we have a meeting, which is roughly once a day, Kelly seems to feel that he has to keep telling us how great we're gonna be, how successful we're gonna make this program, and how we're gonna be different than any other staff in CPI. Once or twice, O.K., but after a while he turns me off. I say to myself, 'Why the hell does he have to do that so damn often? Does he know he's doing it?' Then I begin to think: 'Hey man, maybe he has to tell us how great we are because deep down he doesn't believe it; because deep down what he's really trying to do is convince himself of something that even he's not sold on.' So all the while, while he's telling me how much he believes in me, I begin to think that it's phony; that he doesn't really believe it himself. And that's when I turn him off and stop listening."

There was no long silence after Jack had finished. Several of the other staff members knew *exactly* what Jack meant and, while they saw it a bit differently, they did not hesitate to make it clear that they, too, were affected by the same problem. Butch put it the following way: "I guess it's almost like he can't believe that the rest of us are as sold on this program as he is. It's like he has to keep selling us because he's afraid we don't feel as strong about it as he does."

"I think it even goes deeper than that," said Scotty. "I know how committed Kelly is to the ideas about this program. He feels about it like a father feels about a new kid. But I think that he doesn't believe that the rest of us share his amount of commitment; that this program doesn't dig at our insides the same way it's eating at his. Maybe it's hard for him to accept or really believe that we're in this just as deep and just as hard as he is. Maybe we haven't proved it to him what with the program not even really off the ground yet. But he's got to realize that either he's got a real hang-up about it and won't ever be satisfied that the rest of us feel as strong about it as he does, or it's the kind of thing where no proof needs to be given. Hell, we're in this room today, and that oughta be proof enough."

When Scotty had finished, Butch said: "Faith. It comes down to faith. Kelly talks about faith; about faith in man, faith in the program, faith in human potential, and all that crap. But that's like giving a lecture at Yale to a bunch of kids where he feels like he's got to convince them. Forget it, Kelly. Stop talking faith if you don't have it in your own guts."

"Now I think *you're* going off half-cocked just like Kelly," said Jack. "Don't start screaming and accusing him, Butch. Just let him know what he's doing, maybe why he's doing it, and how it comes across to us. Maybe if he's got enough 'faith' (there was some laughter at this point) he'll be able to understand what's being said and learn a little from it. All I know is that he's got to realize that the rest of us don't need convincing, that we don't want to be goosed all the time, and that we're in this damn thing with him all the way, sink or swim. Let him learn this and believe it, and Kelly, save that energy from the speeches so you can use it to get some work done."

I've tried to write down the way in which most the session went. I know, however, that long before Jack had finished summarizing the group's feelings, the impact of what the staff had been talking about really hit home. In point of fact, they were right. Although I was honestly unaware both that I was giving so many lectures and that maybe unconsciously I had serious doubts that the others were as committed to "my baby" as I was, the fact of the matter was that I was acting and coming across to the staff in exactly the ways they decided. It was like a mirror was being put in front of me and I was being asked to look into it. The effect was little short of dramatic. I was, indeed, acting more like a preacher trying to save souls than as the "leader" of a group of talented people. And some of the reasons for my behavior were clear, at least now that the staff had shared their feelings with me. Perhaps one of the most helpful suggestions that came out of the meeting was Richie's. He said: "Kelly, what you got

to do is give up your "baby" or at least learn that the rest
of us are as much the father as you are. If you do that then
you won't have to worry so much about the rest of us
loving it as much as you do."

I don't know what the aftermath of today's session will be
like. I don't know if the other sensitivity sessions will be as
helpful to others as this one was for me. All I know is that
today I found out something about myself, and in a way
that made me really think. But one other thing seems certain.
A part of me, I guess, will always be a preacher, but this sure
as hell is no flock of sheep I'm preaching to. They seem to
know I like to preach and will probably tolerate it. But only
out of compassion, and only for as long as the "preacher"
himself keeps the faith.

Individual sensitivity session example No. 2: August 24, 1966.
Only rarely did we have an Individual Sensitivity session in
which the group's focus remained on the person being discussed. More often than not it soon became clear that the
individual being talked about was little more than a convenient vehicle through which we could bring up problems
that concerned us all. It was much easier, at least early in
the life of the RYC, to begin by directing our attention to
what was supposedly an "individual" problem, and then to
"use" this individual as a sort of catalytic agent for the discussion of issues that had implications and ramifications for
the rest of the group. The following example is a case
in point.

With all its emphasis on helping people to succeed, one
of the least studied problems in the War on Poverty has been
the problem of success itself; and this is as true for those
people (e.g., nonprofessionals) who "succeed" and "move
up" within the poverty agency as it is for the people who
receive poverty services. The problem of success, no less than
the problem of failure, is a general one, for it involves such
basic issues as preparing and training people to deal with
their newfound success and helping them learn to handle
the inevitable conflicts that arise when roles change and their
status shifts.

The "official" subject of the August 24, 1966, sensitivity
session was Vito. But he was "it" only in the sense that his

was the name drawn from the hat that particular day. Vito's career at CPI read very much like a classic American success story, and his star was still very much on the rise when he became a member of the RYC staff. He had entered the organization in one of its lowest paying and lowest status positions (neighborhood worker). In a short period of time, however, he had "risen" to being a teacher in the remedial education component of the work crew program and, most recently, had been promoted to the job of Education Supervisor, a position that brought with it more money as well as greater responsibility and authority. At the RYC he would now be in charge of coordinating all educational programs and also would serve as a live-in counselor. Although Vito's sensitivity session began with the usual assessment of how he was "coming on" to the rest of the staff, it soon veered away from Vito as an individual and became focused on the question of success, how it affected people, and whether or not "making it" created more new problems than it solved. The issue was clearly important enough to transcend the individual, and the staff soon found itself confronted with the necessity of examining its own values and aspirations, and of focusing attention on the relationship between success and "making it," on the one hand, and complacency and "selling-out," on the other.

Scotty:
Vito, your name just got pulled. You're IT for today.
Lance:
My friend Vito. My friend Vito. I have nothing to say except that Vito will do okay if he listens to me. (Laughter)
Kelly:
Apparently the sensitivity session we had on Lance didn't make any damn difference.
Scotty:
The way I feel, Vito—did you start off as a neighborhood worker?
Vito:
Yes.
Scotty:
As a neighborhood worker, I guess you experienced quite a few different things, working really closely with people. Then when you went into teaching in the remedial educa-

tion program you were one of the best teachers, and you were more or less rewarded for your duties. Since you have been an administrator, you more or less lost some contact with the real meat of our problems. I don't know. I feel you have slightly lost something.
Butch:
He has been brainwashed by the administration.
Scotty:
Not brainwashed, but something does rub off, because I have experienced it myself. And you find after a while, you don't talk the way you did with the kids. You get sort of distant. I hope this hasn't happened to you, Vito.
Kelly:
I think Scotty has really brought up what my feeling is. I first got to know Vito when I was just a consultant to the foremen in the work crew program. Vito was the only teacher that the foremen ever talked about, and that the foremen ever said the kids talked about, as being someone that they genuinely liked and respected. He used to get close to kids. His classes were the best ones. I guess I lost touch with Vito for about a year and a half as Vito went up and up and up in CPI. I think that in some ways I feel that you sold out, is what I am saying really. I feel that at some point along the way the "goodies" got there, and when the "goodies" got there and when the prestige got there, I think in some ways you sold out.
Scotty:
I would like to explain something. I know what Vito went through, and I think I experienced it myself. I'm glad that I was chosen for the RYC, because I want to be back in the field where I functioned best. I feel I was much better as a work crew foreman than I was in any other position they promoted me to—and this is my own personal feeling.

Although I continued on after I left as a work crew fore-man to keep contact with the kids, but I mean people them-selves change their feelings about you, and it causes you to change. Because I know I have been approached by kids that I used to wrestle with and fight with on the crews. You know, now they talk to me, "Scotty is a big man now," and this and that, and they only talk to me like at a distance.

After a while you seem to get this feeling, and you begin to react in the same way, and start talking at a distance. Because I had to catch myself quite a few times, and try to pull myself back into focus. But I don't think it is all Vito's fault. People, you know, people help you to change. When you change your position, they more or less have you on a

different level, and they talk to you that way, and gradually you start fitting into the picture that you have been set in.
Kelly:
Man, what Scotty says is so true. I think Scotty said it just the way it is. We begin, I think—and this goes for all of us— we begin to act the way people expect us to act. And sometimes we may be losing ourselves in the whole process.
Jack:
This is a concern I had when I was a neighborhood worker. I thought about this, and in the evenings, you know, after working hours, I'd go home and eat and come back out and go out to the hangouts of the kids, so I wouldn't let this get ahead of me, so I wouldn't lose this kind of thing, the things that I had with the kids. I was always afraid of this. It's easy to happen. Once people start to identify you with a certain position, you know, they come on real strong with the "Mister" type of thing. It's too easy to happen.
Lance:
That might be one reason why I'm not close enough to be able to make any comments about him. I don't know. I don't really communicate with him. I have spoken to Vito a couple of times, and when I think back about it, I don't remember what that guy spoke to me about. This might be one of my hang-ups, still deep-rooted educator hang-ups.
Hoppy:
Do you still see him as an educator, as we sit here?
Lance:
Yes, I still see him as that.
Scotty:
Like I was saying before, when I first came to CPI and I met Vito—you know, to me, I have seen the change. But I think, like I said before, he's a victim of his own success. He was placed in a position where he more or less had to put people in their place. After a while, you know, he is more or less complacent in his position. It actually changes you. I know I had to do the same thing. I still went out with the kids on weekends, still kept in contact with them, so I wouldn't lose it—but I knew I had lost some of it.
Hoppy:
This suggests something to me which may sound like a really wild idea, that everybody involved in CPI, even with the people who are the administrators, as they move up, they should have a kid assigned to him, or one kid that he works with, that he befriends, and sort of becomes like an advisor, like a friend more than anything, partly to keep his own perspective, no matter how high he gets in the hierarchy.
Kelly:

I think Vito is in a very difficult position now. I really wouldn't want to trade places with him, you know. He's going to be straddling two fences, and he's going to have, in a sense, well, he's going to have to in a sense live in the two worlds that have been created for him, you know, the world of administration and the world of personal contact. And I'm concerned about it, because I think it is a lot to ask of any man.

I still get this feeling when I talk to Vito now, that somehow Vito talks to me different than he did a year and a half ago.

Jack:

What I think is happening with Vito, from what you are saying—because I know I have watched Vito when he has been talking to, well, we'll say to you—I think when he is talking to you, he's trying to make himself feel comfortable in talking to you. In a way, he is talking on so-called your level, you know. And I think he's uneasy and uncomfortable when he's talking to you, because I can see the mannerisms that he's going through, the way he's picking his conversation.

Whereas, when Vito talks to me, you know, he doesn't have this type of thing going with himself. He just talks off the head. He's more comfortable.

Chip:

I haven't been able to get a word in edgewise, but I don't see it that way at all. When I started working here, I started at Hamilton Street. Vito was doing research at Hamilton Street at that time. Then he became a neighborhood worker. During what we call our disposition conferences Vito and I tangled horns a couple of times.

Kelly:

Tangled about what?

Chip:

He was always a champion for the kids. Like if I had a kid on my crew, and I had the kid up to here, and I brought it up at a disposition meeting to drop the kid from the crew, or something similar to that, or suspending him, Vito would fight tooth and nail for this kid, not to suspend him, not to drop him.

We used to have some pretty hot sessions over there. And then the transformation came with the promotions. When he went down to the Skill Center, it was very noticeable that the shoe was on the other foot now. Vito was dishing out the discipline, and he didn't hesitate a minute. If a kid screwed up at the Skill Center, "Out, go home." And for a while it was a subject of conversation among the foremen, "Gee, what a change. Here is a guy that used to fight tooth

and nail for a kid. Now the kid doesn't stand a chance. If he does anything wrong, it's out."
Scotty:
I think it's because of the people Vito had to work with.
Chip:
That could be.
Scotty:
It probably rubbed off.
Butch:
I have seen you change. I have seen Vito change. I think a lot of times, that is what affects, the white shirt bit.
Scotty:
I remember when I went down as administrative assistant, and I came back to the Skill Center one time and I was talking to you. And you might have said I have changed, but I noticed the way you talked to me. You know, it made me feel kind of uneasy.
Butch:
That's right.
Scotty:
You weren't talking to me like a foreman anymore.
Butch:
That's right. You weren't one of us anymore.
Scotty:
But it works both ways.
Kelly:
But there's another thing too. Don't forget, we also are talking about ourselves now. Like if this Center works, my God, everybody knows that in the next Youth Centers there's a chance that a good many of the people on this staff are going to be "administrators." How do you avoid— well, maybe it is an unfair question, Butch. But you say that you now have less respect for white shirts and ties than ever before. But let's put yourself in Vito's place for a minute. Let's all of us try to put ourselves in Vito's place for a minute. How would you feel if suddenly, let's say, you are the Director or Deputy Director of the Youth Center? How do you think you will change? What are you going to do not to change?
Butch:
I don't know. I hope I never see the day, and I plan not to, if I move up, is to never overlook and understand the kids' side of it, and especially the training that I have had as foreman, the understanding that I have gotten of kids as a foreman.
Kelly:
We have been, I guess, coming around to the view that when

you move up or when you move into another position, you begin playing a role that other people expect you to play, and you change. Like I think Chip said, from being the champion of the kids, you become the guy who is quick on the trigger to kick a kid out. I don't feel that Vito or any of us have to apologize for moving up. But I also wonder about what Jack says, that moving up is one thing; but being strong enough to resist the temptation to become somebody that you are really not is another thing.

Chip:
Get the white shirt ready. One of the things that might be a very small thing, but at the Skill Center, when Vito was a "teacher" (indicating quotation marks around "teacher" with fingers), one of the things I think made him click with the kids was his mode of dress. Vito was a "hep cat," with the boots, tight pants, loud shirt and jacket. (Laughter) This is what the kids dug.

Butch:
Now he has the loud plaids and checked tie.

Chip:
They used to talk about Vito, what a dresser. Now he wears regular shoes, you know. Of course, the pants are still a little tight. Even his mode of dress has changed with the position. And the kids, they notice this.

Hoppy:
An awful lot of this has to do, all the way through, with how people—we have said this several times—look at you, too. Suddenly your job changes, so that other people who may not have looked at you before begin to look at you, and the way they look at you makes a difference to you, so you start to dress to please them, because suddenly they are paying attention to you, and they never looked at you before.

Butch:
This has always been my hang-up. I was always trying to impress guys that I had no business to impress.

Scotty:
Boy, when they told me I was being promoted to work in the main office, like a fool I ran to New York into the discount place and bought me seven suits so I could have a different suit every day. And I went up there, and after a while they started calling me "Mr. CPI" because I came in there with a different suit, vest, you know, briefcase.

Kelly:
I think we ought to turn this over to Vito now.

Vito:
I haven't bought many new clothes since those days.

Chip:

Why not? You can afford it.
Vito:
I've still got that pair of boots. I still wear them. I don't know, I remember those days back at Hamilton. You know, I kind of look back on my days as an administrator. I don't know. Maybe the whole thing did change me so much I didn't even really notice myself becoming this real tough guy. I thought I was kind of easy. I don't know. Maybe a lot of what you said is true. I don't honestly think I have lost the feeling for the kids that I had a couple of years ago when I first started. I don't think so at all. I think I was in a different kind of position, and the kind of feeling that I had wasn't as easily noticed as it would have been a couple of years ago.

The white shirt and tie kind of throws me. I always wore a shirt and tie from the day I started with CPI. I feel comfortable with a shirt and tie. I like to wear a shirt and tie. If I wore a shirt and tie twenty-four hours a day, I would be very happy. I'm very comfortable like this.
Lance:
Even sleeping?
Vito:
I dug the tie and I wore a tie all the time.
Chip:
I don't know where you dug them up, some of them.
Kelly:
I really think you're copping out, Vito. I think what people were saying, I know what I was trying to say, is that the shirt and tie must be the symbol. I think people were saying that you as a person changed.
Vito:
You know, I may have changed. Chip said something—I didn't think I had changed that much. I don't know whether I have changed that much that I don't even notice it myself. But while you guys were talking, I was looking at myself. How do I feel toward the kids? Do I feel the same way now as I did a couple of years ago? And you know, I don't know whether I am trying to defend myself to myself. I don't know. I still think that I feel the same way.

And the other thing, when I was an administrator, you know, I began to see something that bothered me. Working with the kids and building this relationship and feeling for the kids, I wondered if at times you weren't becoming blind to the kids own needs, and sometimes a kid did need somebody to say, "shut your damn mouth or you are going home." And if the kid continued and pushed, you would send him home.

I began to see, maybe this is something the kid never got, somebody to tell them what to do, straighten them out, instead of somebody being a good guy, patting them on the back and saying, "Try to do it better the next time," and the kid walking away laughing, "I got away with it again."

Jack:
What I'm reading from Vito is him saying that his feelings haven't changed with regard to the kids, but because of the position that he was put in, he wasn't in the same position where he could stand on the bandbox and whoop and holler for the defense of the kid. This is the thing that is getting the hang-up with him now, which is what he is saying.

Vito:
The other thing, let me ask a question. You know, I heard a lot today about white shirt and tie. And like Butch said, "I hate the guy with the white shirt and tie."

Chip:
I don't think he meant that.

Vito:
I know that, Chip. I don't think there's anything wrong with a white shirt and tie. I think it's the way the guy comes on to the kids.

Kelly:
I think Vito has put his finger on it. I think Vito said, "It doesn't matter. It's the kind of guy you are."

Vito:
But my role did change, and the decisions I made were different. They weren't so much toward the kid any more. My position had changed. I had to think, not only of the kid, but of the teachers and the whole program. I don't know. I guess the decisions I made were kind of hard sometimes. I was like the hatchet man at the Skill Center. When a kid did wrong and he came to see me, I didn't like that. I didn't want to be that kind of guy. And I honestly saw myself really changing.

Kelly:
Maybe from here on at the Youth Center, you don't have to be a hatchet man any more.

Vito:
I don't want to be. But one question I want to ask. I want to ask one question. Going back to the white shirt and tie, and forgetting me and feelings about the guy with the white shirt and tie, and the guy that moves up, I wonder, after listening to the conversation, if people don't automatically assume a person changes just because he does move up and just because he does wear a shirt and tie.

Scotty:
I guess some people do, maybe always will.

Group Sensitivity "Group sensitivity" sessions, the second type of training sessions held at the RYC, were conceived of as "open meetings" in which any staff member could bring up any problem that he felt was affecting the functioning of specific individuals, the group, or the RYC as a whole. Unlike the individual sensitivity sessions, there were no formal rules or procedures governing who or what could be discussed. Thus, for example, if an individual had any feelings concerning his relationship with another staff member, he did not have to wait until that individual's name was pulled out of the hat. He could use the meeting to air his feelings, initiate some sort of dialogue with that individual, and receive immediate feedback from the rest of the group. At other times the meetings were used for purposes of gaining perspective—perspective about ourselves, the program, and how both were changing over time. More often than not, when used for purposes of self-reflection, the meetings often involved such issues as the problems of horizontal functioning, the relationship between particular policies and the overall goals of the organization, and the problems confronting the organization in terms of its relations with other programs or agencies connected with CPI. But whether they were used for purposes of resolving interpersonal conflicts or gaining perspective, the underlying rationale of these meetings was basically preventive rather than remedial in orientation. The long-range goal was the development of a process, an interpersonal forum, perhaps, that would enable the staff to deal with its problems at a point in time *before* those problems erupted, *before* they seriously interfered with functioning, and *before* they assumed a magnitude that decreased the probability that they could be solved in a rational manner.

Group sensitivity session example No. 1: September 7, 1966. Problems of cooperation and competition are a continuing source of difficulty in most American institutions. To be sure, this is in part due to the almost inescapable con-

flict that confronts people—the majority of us—whose
legitimate desires for personal advancement are often dependent upon or require interpersonal and group cooperation. Perhaps the problem is so much a part of the American
mystique as to defy resolution. Nevertheless, within any
organization—the RYC is no exception—problems of competition and cooperation are always present, and unless they
are dealt with at a point when communication is still possible,
they guarantee future discontent.

The following is an illustration of how group sensitivity
sessions were utilized to begin to deal with a problem at a
point in time when the channels of communication were
still open, and when people could still turn to one another
for support and help in their efforts to avoid or diminish
future conflict. The important point here is not whether or
not the particular problem was "resolved" but that a mechanism had been created through which the problem could be
brought out into the open, discussed, and placed before the
group rather than, like some festering sore, remaining quiet,
hidden, yet inflamed.

Butch:
I want to bring something up to the group. I think that Jack
and I are heading for a possible crack-up or pitfall, or whatever you want to call it, because him and I are of two basic
natures, and I feel a lot of it is on my part, and there's a
lot also on Jack's part.

Lance:
Wait a minute. You mean you are both heading toward a
showdown more or less?

Butch:
We are becoming very competitive in nature. I see Jack
coming on as a real "Flash Gordon" or sometimes possibly
with a cocky attitude, a false attitude so to speak—"false"
would be the better word for it.

As I say, a lot of it is what I read into it. But yet, it has
to come from an understanding of both of us. I don't want to
speak for Jack. But I would probably imagine that Jack probably feels some of the same competitiveness that I am feeling. I think this is coming because we are trying to outdo
each other on the staff.

Lance:
That's your saying it.

Butch:
That's right. This is something, as I say, that I want to bring up, but Jack and I have to work it out among ourselves. But if the understanding is not made by both of us, to work with each other closer, then it does become a problem with the rest of the staff. Then two factions are not working harmoniously. We are working independent of each other.
Jack:
You know, with regard to myself, it's usually amazing, when I come to work with a group of people—and it came on this way in the past—as a matter of fact, I usually can sit down beforehand and write the opinions that everybody gets of me when they first meet me, you know.

I have been given an opinion as being a snob, or the guy that thinks he is better than everybody else, and all that type of thing around this line. And sometimes it is like what came out here.

And when it gets to this bit with Butch and myself, I would like to say, Butch, this is mainly coming from *you* and not from me. J don't feel any of these things.

The clash that you think that we are coming to has me really concerned, because I know for a fact that it is coming from you. I have been giving thought night after night on how I can get around or get Butch to see a lot of the hang-ups that he has, or hang-ups that he just believes, and they are not by and large anywhere near true.
Jean:
What I want to say is do you guys ever sit down and help one another out, you know, talk out this problem?
Scotty:
Well, I think Jack stays more or less withdrawn with some of his feelings, and I don't think it is going to help any. Maybe he hasn't really tried to talk it out with Butch.
Jack:
Now here again, when you get to what Scotty was saying about me not saying about my feelings. As I say, my thoughts are how I can say things that won't tick Butch off or make him feel I am ticking him off the wrong way or I am trying to say I know something he doesn't.

Most of my thoughts since I have been on the staff are on Butch, as to how you can do certain things without coming into some kind of conflict with him. Like every time something is said—as soon as I say something Butch seems to jump all over me.
Scotty:
As we all know, for some reason or another—maybe it's the

way Jack looks at people—but he has been pretty successful with his cases. Maybe because he is a RYC worker along with Butch, Butch thinks, "If I am not successful, or if I am successful I want to do it on my own, especially without help at all. I don't want to have to say I was successful because I used his tactics. I want to be able to say that I was a successful RYC worker because of my own ideas and because of the way I went about it, and not successful through Jack."

Jack:
How can I help this guy without making him think I am trying to tell him how to do this and that? This is the reason I don't usually say too much when it comes to Butch. I don't want him to get the idea I am trying to ride herd over him in any kind of way.

It is just that I have a thought about something that he is trying to do which may assist him in his thoughts, but it seems when I say it, or mention this to him, he gets the wrong outlook.

Chip:
I think Butch still has a few hang-ups. He still thinks people are trying to put him down. Actually I think they are not; they are trying to help him, but he still hasn't been able to get over that feeling of not being able to accept help.

Butch:
I admit that I see a lot of things in Jack that I wish to hell I saw in myself. I think the reason why it comes on in this way is because of this competitiveness. Some of the things that I see are, one, I see a lot in Jack I want to see in myself but I don't see it.

I see a man who is a natural with people. He is the easy-go-lucky guy who can communicate with people and get along in any kind of setting. This I had found I had problems in, which is another reason.

Jack:
You know, Butch, my grandmother told me years ago, when I was a little kid, regardless of the persons around you, you will find you'll be a lot better person by just being yourself. Then, you know, your good qualities will come out and you won't have to worry about being like anybody else.

Kelly:
You sound like a minister.

Jack:
Hey, my grandmother was a lovely lady.

Butch:
Well, your grandmother aside, I do see a definite competition between you and me, possibly to a point, if we con-

tinue to go on the path we are going, we won't be able to sit on the same side of the table with each other.

Jack:

Come on Butch, don't be so dramatic.

Hoppy:

I see it more as misunderstanding than anything else, really, talking to both people, and just a kind of a way—this is why I think these kinds of meetings are really important, because I think Jack comes on to Butch in a way that sort of makes Butch feel very defensive. And Jack doesn't mean to do that at all. But he is very conscious of this. One kind of criticism of him that I would have is, rather than face it sometimes, I think he keeps his mouth, you know, shut when he has something he would like to say, or else he might in order to avoid the conflict.

Scotty:

I think that Jack feels that if he did say what he wanted to say, what good would it do? This is the feeling that he has, that it won't do any good, but maybe more harm. I think this is one of the reasons why he holds back on a lot of things he wants to say, because he wants to keep harmony within the staff. But I think by you not telling him it makes him feel this way even more so. If you came out and told him, eventually he might realize that you are not trying to be a smart aleck, that you are trying to help him, and finally it will get across to him. But by holding back, that's not helping at all.

Kelly:

I agree with Scotty. You seem to be taking the point of view that if you don't do something, then someone won't think something. And I think what Scotty is suggesting is that until you do do something people are going to keep thinking whatever they want to think.

Jean:

How do you expect people to get to know your true feelings? By keeping quiet?

Jack:

No, by their being involved with me, like say with this type of program.

Kelly:

But how can anybody be involved with you unless you come out to them, too? That is what Jean is saying.

Scotty:

I guess the only way people are going to get to know you is if you come out and meet them.

Lance:

(singing) Come out, Jack, wherever you are.

Kelly:
What are the feelings of the rest of the staff?
Vito:
I don't know. I really don't know.
Chip:
I don't know them too well. Don't look at me.
Clark:
Beats me, buddy.
(prolonged silence)
Butch:
It's a nice-sounding air conditioner over there. (laughs)
Kelly:
So far, we've focused the whole discussion on Butch and
Jack. Maybe it's easy on us that way. But I get the feeling
that the problem may be bigger, may involve other things.
I'm really not sure, but that's what I feel.
Butch:
As far as me and Jack is concerned, maybe we got to settle
this by understanding each other closer. But—
Jean:
The only thing I see is that there is conflict between the both
of them (Jack and Butch) that we probably don't feel be-
cause more or less the competition sets in. They are both
out to, you know, to show each other up. I think it's more
obvious in their case but it exists, I think, in all of us.
Butch:
Maybe I'm copping out, but I don't think you would see the
competitiveness, say, between me and Kelly who are in different pay scales. But for people like me and Jack in our
position, yes, then I think you would find the competitiveness.
For this reason, Jack and I are going further off. Like if it was
Scotty or Kelly it wouldn't make that much difference because they are already above me. I don't have to worry about
sort of competing with them or anything. It couldn't happen
worse because Jack and I are cohorts, are equal, and this
is, I think, what brings it on.
Hoppy:
I have a question that has been bothering me for a while.
What is it, with this type or organization that the Director
and Assistant Director get more money than the rest of us?
We all do the same things. Right? So maybe if we all got the
same money we wouldn't compete.[9]

[9]The problem of differential salaries—especially in a "horizontal" organization—raises a host of theoretical and practical issues. Although
the issue was not pursued in this session, it was raised in subsequent
meetings; in Chapter 10 we shall offer some observations on the
problem.

(some, but not much, laughter)
Scotty:
But there is competition among the whole of the staff.
Maybe it's part of working on a horizontal level. Christ, I
hope not. Maybe it's just human nature.
Jack:
I agree that maybe it's a general sort of problem on the
whole staff.
Butch:
I think it is a staff problem, the competitiveness there. I
think instead of the staff working right now as a staff should
work, I think at least the way I see it, the individual setting
or the individual nature is still there.
Lance:
I myself would like another session on this. Especially so as
those of us who can't get a word in edgewise on all you
talkers can get to mouth off.
Clark:
Stick it to 'em, Lance.
Hoppy:
There is this basic problem, that you want people, like on
staffs like this, who are somewhat dynamic in their own
ways, and who are ambitious. Maybe a little bit of this goes
along with someone who wants to get ahead and do a good
job. It seems to me there is a real problem here, and unless
we iron it out we could be in for a lot of heartache and
trouble. Maybe Butch's just bringing it up was a good beginning, but I think it's only a beginning.

Group sensitivity session example No. 2: July 6, 1966.
Within any organization a change in leadership is almost
guaranteed to be accompanied by a certain degree of unrest,
dislocation, and anxiety. It is a time when people—the new
leader as well as the rest of the staff—must regroup, reorient themselves, and begin to adjust to a situation that will
inevitably differ, in any number of ways, from the one that
existed only a short time before. To be sure, many of the
problems created when a leader is replaced are "natural"
ones, ones that should be expected and viewed within the
framework of the normal consequences of change. But as we
have already indicated (see Chapter 3), the manner in which
an organization is prepared (or, more commonly, not prepared) for a change in leadership often determines both the
extent and the severity of the problems of succession. When,

however, as was the case at the RYC, the new leader of the organization differs from the old one in terms of certain "public credentials" (i.e., the new leader is a nonprofessional), problems of preparation and succession are compounded by a host of feelings and concerns that, while certainly related to the question of change, involve much broader issues of professional-nonprofessional attitudes and working relationships.

In July of 1966, five months before a change in leadership was scheduled to occur, the problem of preparing the staff for the change was begun. The issue was brought up during one of the staff's group sensitivity sessions by the then Deputy Director. He posed the problem in such a way as not only to enable us to deal with the question of change but also to begin to examine our feelings and concerns about being professionals or nonprofessionals. By bringing the problem out into the open, he enabled the group to begin a dialogue that is still going on to this day.

Scotty:
To start off the session, I would like to bring up something that I have discussed with some of the people on the staff. And I would like to throw it open to the whole staff and get your reaction. As we all know, Kelly is the Director of the Residential Youth Center, and he will be leaving us in January. As of January, I will be taking over as Director. And I have the feeling that once Kelly has left the RYC there may be a change of attitude on the staff because maybe they might have had more respect for Kelly because of his degrees while I'm a nonprofessional. I would like to throw this open to the staff and get some of your feelings on this.

Butch:
I will tell you one feeling I have. What is going to be the view of those on the outside or downtown with respect to this when Kelly leaves? Will they try to bring in another professional?

Scotty:
Well, as Kelly has said in the past, there will be promotions from within the RYC. We've already talked about that in other staff meetings. There will be movement from within.

Kelly:
You know, in a way, I think the question Scotty asked has been avoided. I think he was asking about our feelings both "as professionals" or "as nonprofessionals" about each other,

about ourselves in this job. Scotty laid it on the line, and I think we avoided his question by bringing up another one.
Butch:
I haven't avoided it. In fact, I am asking the very same question that he is asking. Will we accept him as a nonprofessional? Now that he has got the chance to move up, will he accept *us* as nonprofessionals and move us accordingly? Because it seems every time you turn around in the main body of CPI it is almost impossible to get a job unless you play politics or you are a professional. And this is the way I honestly feel.

I remember once there was an opening at CPI for a vocational counselor. I applied for it. I felt that two years as a work crew foreman, working and counseling kids, and trying to help them find jobs qualified me for the job. But I was told: "You're not even under consideration. You don't have the proper requirements."

Now as far as Scotty is concerned, how can you say how a person is going to work out? Everybody has seen you in action. (laughter) Scotty I know only as an individual, as a foreman that I have worked with. How can you pass judgment on a man as to how he is going to work? He may work out twice as well as you.
Vito:
Butch has a point. To prejudge whether or not in January we are going to be able to accept Scotty is something that you can't do right now.
Butch:
We all have our doubts.
Jack:
I think what Scotty is really trying to say in a roundabout way is: Are we thinking of this thing in regards to color or position or title? This is the question he is really asking. In other words, after Kelly leaves, because Scotty is, say, a Negro taking over Kelly's place, will you give him the same respect and everything that you are giving to Kelly?
Butch:
I would like to say one thing...
Jack:
Let me finish this. I say if we have anything like that on our minds we might as well forget the whole thing. We are not here on account of whether somebody is Jewish, Negro, Polish, or what.
Butch:
One thing I would like to say. You just made a remark which I think is a piss-poor remark, because nobody in here has any bias as far as race, color, or religion is.

Kelly:
Why don't we ask Scotty what he really meant?
Scotty:
What I really meant was, as far as that goes, we have
seen Kelly in action. And you know Kelly has many degrees and
he is a professional. I am a nonprofessional. You have seen
me in the role of a foreman and as a field supervisor. And
maybe you haven't had much contact with me as an ad-
ministrative assistant.
  What I wanted to know is because of the fact that I am
a nonprofessional, I was wondering if there was going to be
some resentment or some feeling about my taking over.
Butch:
Let me ask you a question. Do you have any doubt in your
mind as to whether or not you have any fears that we might
not accept you as a Negro versus white?
Scotty:
No.
Butch:
Because that is one problem that should be cleared up right
off the bat. Discrimination here just doesn't belong.[10]
Vito:
You know, one thing bothers me. Do you respect and work
for a person just because they have degrees? I wouldn't,
you know. I know a lot of people that have degrees and
I wouldn't give you two cents for them. I think it's the way
the guy functions in the job. If the guy proves himself in
the job, how can you hold him back because he doesn't
have a degree?
Clark:
That's right.
Vito:
I don't think the degree adds anything. It adds a little bit
of knowledge maybe. It gives a guy a little start on the job.
But if a guy is able enough and capable enough to run
the job on what he has, why give the guy with the degree
more credit?
Kelly:
I don't get the feeling that Scotty was asking people to pass
judgment.

[10]Although the question of race was apparently not the most important
concern in Scotty's mind at this particular time, the reader should not
conclude that the issue itself was not a source of continuing concern.
The vehemence with which the group sought to deny its existence
should be ample indication that it was, even at this point, an issue of
significant concern. The final example of sensitivity training will focus
directly on the problem of race.

Vito:
Another thing that hit me is the kind of thing that I think we are all shooting for, to make this project successful, to have it catch on so that other Centers will be opened up. We are all nonprofessionals, the majority of us. And we are all shooting for some kind of Deputy Director or Director position eventually. And if we should say to Scotty, "You are a nonprofessional, you should not have that job," in this way, we are denying *ourselves* the opportunity of ever getting this kind of a job.
Butch:
That is what brought up my question. Will CPI accept the fact that Scotty is a nonprofessional? Of course, when another Center opens up the big shots "downtown" are going to have the final say, or whoever gets the funds are going to have the final say, as to who is going to be on that staff. Are they going to turn around and accept us for our efforts devoted to making this staff work, or are they going to come back as I say, with the same old feelings that, well, this new guy has a degree while Joe Blow over there doesn't have anything outside of the fact that he has worked in the RYC? In that case, we are going to be right back down to the same old bit. Are they going to reward us for merit? Or are they going to say, "Sorry, you don't have the professional degree"? This is a big fear of mine.
Vito:
You raised a good point in the past, even though we might prove ourselves to be successful, by being nonprofessionals we still have to take a back seat when higher positions become available.
Butch:
I have almost two years with CPI. And Chip would back me up on these words to the hilt. I have heard the comment, I have seen the letters come in—"beautiful job, you are doing a terrific job." But I haven't seen any of the promotions that come as a result of doing that supposedly great job. I'm sure Scotty will be accepted. What I want to know is, will Scotty accept the fact that we are just as nonprofessional as he is? Will he depend on us?
Richie:
It seems to me there are two problems. One is—I don't want to put words in Scotty's mouth—but when I heard the question, I kind of heard two questions. One was: How am I going to do personally in this job? The other was: How am I going to do as a nonprofessional in this job? Now, how you do personally is up to you; but when we go around

making the rounds of the different parts of CPI to talk about the program we always stress that one of the unique things about this program is that the staff is made up of nonprofessionals. And we are trying to prove that this job can be done by nonprofessionals as well, if not better, than professionals. And so, in a sense, this is going to be up to the whole staff to prove whether or not nonprofessionals can do it. And I would think that the whole staff would be kind of on your side.

Kelly:

You know, there's another side to this professional-nonprofessional thing. We've been talking only about the feelings of the nonprofessional. I've also had to deal with the problem, but from the other side of the fence. And some of my experiences and feelings have also been affected by the professional-nonprofessional issue.

One of the feelings I had when I started working with the foremen and with the work group program was this very terrible feeling of almost wanting to apologize for having a degree. I didn't like the feeling. I think my feeling was not very different than the kind of feeling that Scotty was expressing. In a sense, what Scotty is saying is: "Am I going to have to apologize for being the Director *without* a degree?" whereas before I had the feeling, "Do I have to apologize to the staff for being the Director *with* a degree?" I think in both cases it is the same kind of feeling. We were both, in one way or another, uncomfortable with the situation. It works both ways.[11]

[11]There is little doubt that professionals and nonprofessionals supposedly "working together" in the War on Poverty are often separated from one another by an emotional schism predicated on feelings of mutual ambivalence. One of the many reasons for this situation appears to be related to the fact that the War on Poverty itself was, at least in part, an outgrowth of the failure of "professionals" to deal adequately with the problems of poverty in the years preceding the Kennedy administration. At this point, the fact that this "failure" was only relative in nature and in good part a function of the enormous and only dimly understood complexity of the problem is not the issue. What may be a much more important source of continuing irritation to the nonprofessional is the fact that despite his sudden prominence, the needs of most professionals to maintain some degree of status and orthodoxy have resulted in his (the nonprofessional's) being viewed and used in a clearly subordinate or ancillary capacity. The situation is further complicated when, as is often the case, the particular techniques and orientations employed by the professional (i.e., vocational counseling, case work, psychotherapy) begin to fail to impress the nonprofessional sufficiently to cause him to give up his demands for functional equality and to be content with doing the professional's "legwork" or "scut work." Be that as it may, and granting the fact that a host of other feelings and attitudes enter into the ambivalence

Jack:

The part of the question that Butch was talking about was in regards to the rest of us. He wants to know what our chances as nonprofessionals are to become a Director of other RYCs.

Vito:

But there's one thing we're forgetting. The kind of non-professional movement within this particular project is something that is different from the nonprofessional movement as I see it in the rest of CPI. In other projects, people that are nonprofessionals that move ahead are usually, you know, responsible to a professional. In other words, a professional is

---

that often defines the relationships between professionals and non-professionals, problems of mutual trust, respect, and confidence do exist and do, all too often, interfere with the process of achieving the very goals (i.e., "getting the job done") that bind both groups.

While what we have described here may be true of the situation generally, personal experiences and confrontations do bring with them a form of face validity. As indicated in the sensitivity session now being presented, the Director often felt himself in the position of wanting to "apologize" for his credentials, of wanting sometimes to plead: "Don't blame me for the sins of my fathers." Another of my colleagues who has worked extensively with nonprofessionals, Dr. Albert E. Myers, has reported similar experiences. Dr. Myers, a man of many talents, has written a poem that conveys some of the feelings we have tried to describe. His poem is entitled "My Impediment," and with his kind permission we present it here.

I tried to hide it
Oh, I tried to hide it
I tried to keep it within
But it took no wit
To see it flit
All over the bar we were in.

It made me sad
Yes, quite sad
When my defect they did discover
It was something I'd had
Since only a lad
From which I would never recover.

They were kind
Really, very kind
They pretended not to hear
Though in their mind
They could not find
A way to say, "disappear."

And so we stayed
We just stayed
Each on our separate rung
We could have played
If I weren't betrayed
By my college cultured tongue.

the person who is overall in charge. And what is happening
here is that when Kelly leaves and Scotty moves up, Scotty
is a nonprofessional. The next person that comes on the staff,
if this person, you know, does come on the staff, is going
to be a nonprofessional, and this means that the whole
project is going to be run by nonprofessionals. This is the
kind of thing that is going to happen.
Kelly:
The more we use the words, the more I wonder what we
really mean by "professional" and "nonprofessional."
Vito:
I could give you my own personal definition. First of all,
I think you have to break that up into three categories. First
of all, there are two kinds of professionals. There is a professional in the sense that a person has degrees and has been
educated. That's one kind of professional. But the real professional is a person that has degrees, but also has the working knowledge to be able to administer and to run a program,
to work effectively in the field that he has been trained in.
And I think that his education is essential in becoming this
kind of a professional.
   The nonprofessional is the person that can function in a
job, and may have the abilities to move and hold the same
type of job that a professional can, but is limited in the
amounts of education that he has.
Butch:
I think another type professional is a person who, even
though he never went to college, has been working all his life
in this type of work. I would classify him as a professional.
This is another way that I would determine a professional.
But you are still a nonprofessional because they don't leave
you any avenues to advance or to go. You are stagnant in
your position. You are typecast, which is a phrase that I have
always used as a foreman. You are typecast.
Richie:
How about the situation where someone does a task, and you
say, "He is a real pro." He could be a singer, a car salesman,
or whatever the case may be. You say, "He is a real pro."
Is that the same thing?
Butch:
Not the same thing.
Richie:
That's an abbreviation for a professional.
Butch:
All that means is that you are good in one particular job,
but you are not a professional all around, because you are,

so to speak, limited. As I say, there are no avenues for you to go outside of the position in which you do well. No one would ever recognize you.

Vito:

What you have to do when you talk about professional and nonprofessional is put some guidelines on which area you are talking about. You know, a guy can throw a baseball real good and be a pro, and he doesn't need an education. But a guy can be a real good social worker, but because he didn't have his MSW, he is going to be held back. So that, you know, if we are talking about professionals and non-professionals here, I think we should talk in terms of our own employment and the types of work that we are doing. And we should limit the definition of the nonprofessional and the professional.

Richie:

In other words, you are talking about, not according to how a person does his job, but the title of the job.

Vito:

No.

Richie:

So, in other words, when you are talking about professionals, you are talking about things over which the individual has no control.

Butch:

That's about right.

Richie:

No matter how good a job he does, he can't overcome, he can't cross the boundary between the professional and the nonprofessional. You are setting up a kind of a boundary that can't be crossed on the basis of job performance. Is that what you mean?

Butch:

Yes. There are only a few isolated exceptions. The rule says that when you come to the line, anything above the line is going to be a man of considerable knowledge and education and breeding. Below the line is not.

Kelly:

Where did that word "breeding" come from?

Butch:

I took it out of the dictionary. Everyone in this room, I think, has seen nonprofessionals do a good job, do a damn good job, if not a better job, than a professional. But that's as far as it goes.

Lance:

It's awful funny when professionals seem to come to us for

help, while at the same time they're getting twice as much money as us.

Butch:

One thing I want to say. Scotty is an exception to the rule. He is not an educated man. He started out the same as any one of us; as a foreman. But how many comparative positions are there such as his? Are there men of the same background as his filling these positions, or are the positions all being filled by men of better education and degrees?

Kelly:

I don't think the question is: Show me the guys who made it who aren't professionals. I think the question is a lot more complicated than that. Maybe the real issue, and the one that we are running away from by trying to pinpoint individuals, is how the hell do we feel—confronted as we are in this room and confronted as we will be throughout the life of the project—as professionals or nonprofessionals working with professionals and nonprofessionals? And what are the differences? This is the more important question, I think. What differences do the ways in which we feel about ourselves, and the labels that we put on ourselves, make in terms of how effectively we function in terms of this project?

Butch:

I don't think the label has any importance.

Clark:

Come off it, Butch. You're always talking labels.

Butch:

I said, I don't think the label has any importance. What the people above me think as to what I feel is where the label has got the importance.

Kelly:

You say, for example, from your point of view, labels don't make a difference; and yet you use the word "breeding" to describe differences between people. What does "breeding" mean if not that it has something to do with the way you see yourself and others.

Butch:

Look, all "breeding" means is that you won't cross any boundaries. I was brought up on the west side. The rich were on the east side. The east side is taboo. You don't cross the tracks. This is where I was born and raised. This is the way my whole life is run.

Gruen:

Haven't you crossed any tracks by being right in this room? Haven't you moved?

Butch:
I have moved, but you can't consider it any change.
Gruen:
There is no big change?
Butch:
No big change.
Jack:
Do you feel that you are still at the same level as you were when you were a child, when you lived with your parents, the same level as they were economically and socially?
Butch:
Yes, I still have a low income. I am one step out of poverty.
Chip:
Personally, I think making $100 a week is all right.
Butch:
Look, what I am really saying is, when you turn around, you have your Director, you have your Associate Director, you have your Yale interns, and the RYC worker is right back at the bottom of the totem pole. I still have in my mind that Kelly is at the top of the pyramid, I am at the bottom. Now, comes one year from the time we start, if we prove that we can work parallel, then I will have really moved, your theory has been proven, and everybody's curiosity has been satisfied.
Kelly:
Would your curiosity really be satisfied? I wonder.
Butch:
Yes, in one respect. Yes, because then I could say that I have been accepted for my job and my job alone, the work that I do.
Scotty:
You know, the feelings that Butch has. Now, a few years ago, I had the same feelings and the same experience.
When I was working at the Yale Co-op, I started there as a stock clerk at $50 a week. And I finally worked my way up to the book department and managing the paperback section of the book department. And quite a few times we had new men come in with college degrees, and I would have to train them. And they would start with a salary that I was working on after five years. Here I was with the experience in doing what they felt was a good enough job to put me in this position. Then in turn they would turn around and put someone else on the same level with me with no experience. And I would have to train them. And they would start with the same salary that I was making after five years. And they told me I couldn't go beyond this salary because

I didn't have any degrees. And another thing. I used to give suggestions to my boss. And he would decline them and say, "Oh, that's ridiculous," and so on.

So, one time I gave him a suggestion, and he told me, "No, that wouldn't work, that's ridiculous."

So, speaking with this other kid with a degree, I told him, I said, "At the next staff meeting, I want you to give this same suggestion." And he did. And it was accepted with open arms. So, after that, I got my hat.

Vito:

You know, Butch brought up this horizontal or parallel thing, and I have been thinking. You know, this is just one little project in a whole big world, with all kinds of organizational structures. And supposing we do find this kind of system works. Some day this whole program isn't going to be running. And it may happen any year. And if we are not successful in terms of the service that we provide for the kids, then we are no longer here even though our parallel structure has worked. We are going to have to go back into a real world where the pyramid is the thing.

Jack:

The question arises: Can we adjust back to the pyramid thing? Back to a situation where people with degrees are always over you and telling you what to do?

Lance:

When your kids are hungry, you adjust.

Richie:

You know, it's a funny thing. In a way, this program represents an ironic thing. We are trying to make a full circle. When CPI first started it consisted of about as many people as are sitting around this table, maybe not even that many. It was started by nonprofessionals. Most of the people who started CPI were nonprofessionals. The bigger it got, the more narrow the pyramid became. The ironic thing was that the more the program became successful, the more programs there were. And the more programs there were, the more it began to fall into the old kind of structure with professionals and nonprofessionals and whatnot. What we are trying to do now here, is to take it back in the sense to the original days, when the people for the most part who started the whole program were real nonprofessional people, real nonprofessionals by Butch's standards, too.

Vito:

He's right. You know, if you go back and look at the nonprofessionals and the way they have behaved as the organization grew, it was they who, if not directly at least

indirectly, are responsible for the limitations placed on the nonprofessional movement within the organization.
Lance:
It's crazy. The whole world is crazy. We'll never solve the professional-nonprofessional problem.
Kelly:
Sure as hell not today.
Lance:
Probably never.

In point of fact, Lance was quite right: the problem was never really "solved." In time the staff "settled," quite uneasily, on the concept of the "pro" as the most appropriate way of resolving the professional-nonprofessional issue, at least with respect to the RYC. "Pro" became the label applied to anyone, whether he had a degree or not, who seemed to be able to work effectively with the people (the residents and families) whom the RYC was funded to serve. An "amateur," by implication, was anyone who, despite his professional training (or the lack thereof), "just didn't have it" when it came to working with the target population. But even this apparent solution was never fully accepted by every staff member. Many questions were left unanswered; many feelings remained unresolved. But what was accomplished, and what the group sensitivity sessions were intended to accomplish, was that channels of communication were opened and were kept open, and we all, despite our fears and trepidations, became less and less hesitant to open ourselves up to one another.

Special Sensitivity At different times and for different reasons, the staff of the RYC would agree that it was time to "get away from things," sit down, and begin to discuss certain problems that no one person felt comfortable bringing up by himself. These "special sensitivity" sessions usually took place every six months and were used for purposes of taking a "long hard look" at ourselves, what we were doing, and where we were going. At other times, especially when a particular crisis had arisen or when some traumatic event was still fresh in our memories, the group would meet in a fashion not too dissimilar from an emergency "Cabinet"

meeting to discuss the problem with which it was confronted. Taken together, these "special" and "emergency"
meetings comprised the final type of sensitivity training sessions held at the RYC.

Special sensitivity session example: November 16, 1966.
It is all too easy, and certainly more than a little comforting
personally, to assume that when people of different races
and backgrounds unite against a common enemy (e.g.,
poverty), their newfound singleness of purpose will be strong
enough to bridge the social and personal differences that
separate them. It is an easy assumption to make because it
allows one to focus all one's attention on the problem "out
there"; it is a comforting assumption because it enables
people to delude themselves into thinking that they, unlike
all others, have been spared the fears and hatreds that
permeate our society. Reality quickly belies the assumption.
But more shattering than the reality itself is the fact that even
when confronted with the horrible emptiness of the illusion,
the effects of that illusion have already made their presence
felt, have already limited the alternatives available to deal
with the issue. The problem of race is a case in point.

The reader will recall that one of the primary purposes
behind the decision to utilize some form of sensitivity training at the RYC was the belief that it would enable us to begin
to talk about problems (e.g., race) that we "knew" were
bound, in one way or another, to influence the development of the setting and the relationships among its members. Our experiences in other helping settings (see Chapter 3)
were replete with instances in which the question of race had
become a significant factor in the situation, an issue which,
although rarely discussed or brought out into the open, was
a constant source of quiet, sometimes even "deadly" conflict.
Although, as was the case with so many other issues, we
harbored no illusions of ever being able to "solve" the problem, we did believe that by bringing the problem to the
surface we would be depriving it of some of the power it
derives from its unwitting allies—silence and avoidance.

Toward the middle of November 1966, barely two months

after it had opened its doors, the RYC was the scene of a riot. In retrospect, although some might prefer to call what happened a "disturbance" or an "incident" (and try to justify *not* calling it a riot because very few people were involved), from the point of view of those of us present it was, and will always remain, a full-fledged riot. The following is a summary of what happened that night in November.

Soon after the RYC opened its doors, the first group of residents to enter the facility formed a "House Council." The House Council had a number of functions. With its advisors (one full-time staff member and an intern from the Psycho-Educational Clinic), the House Council functioned as a governing board through which the residents could set house rules, as a forum in which staff and resident grievances could be aired, as a sensitivity group for the residents of the RYC, and as a place where the youngsters could organize, plan, and implement recreational and social activities. Late in October, using the Council for purposes of planning social activities, the residents decided to hold a series of weekend dances at the RYC. The first dance held at the Center was something less than a spectacular success. Few people showed up and the evening was a rather depressing and "dead" one for the youngsters. With the passage of time, however, the word got around the neighborhood, and each successive dance became bigger and better than the one before. Soon the boys were confronted with a somewhat different problem: too many people were showing up, many more than could be accommodated in the house. The Council members decided to limit the number of people at these dances to the residents themselves, their dates, and "invited guests." Again, the word went out around the neighborhood.

The evening of the next scheduled dance started quietly enough. The residents, their dates, and the invited guests showed up as usual. In a little while the sounds of the "Bugaloo," the "Watusi," and the "Skate," filled the air as the youngsters danced, drank (soft drinks, of course), and enjoyed themselves. Around 11:00 P.M. a number of kids from the surrounding neighborhoods appeared on the scene and wanted to get into the house and join the party. Some of the residents and staff met them at the porch and told them that they could not come in. They also tried to explain to them the reasons why it was impossible (it was actually against the law) for any more people to congregate in the house. Some of the boys in the group outside the RYC began talking of "crashing" the party. Things became tense and the youngsters inside the house began making preparations for the expected assault. The kids outside started milling around.

At this point two RYC staff members, one white and the other black, came out to the porch to try to talk to the group, a group now becoming angrier and more restless with each passing second. Most of the youngsters standing outside the RYC were black, and the black staff member began to talk with them. In a short while the kids began taunting the white staff member, cursing him, and calling him "Whitey" and "Honky." Suddenly the white staff member broke from the porch, waded into the group, and the melee was on. Other staff members came out of the house, pulled the white staff member out of the crowd, and dragged him back through the doorway and into the Center. There was a good deal of pushing and punching going on, and the police finally were summoned. By the time they arrived most of the fighting was over. The remaining youngsters ran away as the squad cars approached. The party was over—for everyone.

As soon as the police had gone and the house was "bedded down" for the night, those of us who were still there went into the office to talk about what happened. Although the discussion started out with the goal of "formulating policy" with respect to future dances, it soon became clear that what was really troubling the group and what we really had to talk about were the feelings touched off by what we all agreed was clearly a racial incident.

For the next three hours we talked about the problem of race. Whereas we had previously discussed the issue in what can only be called abstract terms, we were now dealing with it from the point of view of a concrete and shared experience. We had all been present, had witnessed, and had been deeply affected by the events just passed. It was no longer a "theoretical" problem, one to be talked about pleasantly and solved by the skillful manipulation of pious platitudes and approval-winning clichés. The problem was as real and as close as the bruises on the face of the staff member who had "blown his cool."

The session finally broke up at about 4 o'clock in the morning. We were all exhausted, both physically and emotionally. But for the first time we had really begun to level with one another and to explore our feelings about race. Before leaving the office we decided to continue the discussion the next day and to make sure that those few staff members who were not now present were there for the "special" or "emergency" sensitivity session that was to come. The following dialogue is taken from that next day's session.

Kelly:
I don't know whether we can call this a sensitivity session or not. My own feeling is that it is probably as important a sensitivity issue as any we've ever had. It involves not just the incident that happened last night. What is involved is a lot more.

It involves a lot of the kinds of feelings and ideas and attitudes we have had about the whole issue of race, and although we have talked about it on staff many times I think that what happened last night put the whole problem in a perspective it never had before.

If we make the assumption that the kids think about this problem and act on the basis of their feelings about race in a variety of different ways, I think we, too, have to be aware that we also have feelings about it.

Although it is not in the framework of our usual sensitivity meetings, I would like to start off by asking Butch to just talk about what his feelings were as he was standing out there on the porch.[12]

Butch:
Well, as we talked about it, about what happened and everything, there were a couple of things that struck me funny. I think I have learned something out of it. It was kind

[12]For purposes of identification, we should point out that Kelly, Butch, Sterns, Lance, and Chip are white; Scotty, Jack, Clark, Silver, and Jean are black.

of worth the bruises that I got out of it. I really didn't
honestly think there was as much hatred between black and
white as there is in New Haven. This past night was maybe
the first time I honestly knew what it meant to be colored.
I was white and they were crucifying me for it. All I heard
was, "Whitey, over there, you keep your goddamned mouth
shut. You don't say a word." This I think really started the
whole incident because after a while, my temper started
burning to a point where I don't know whether I wanted to
turn around and scream, "Why, you crazy bastard, what are
you trying to prove? I am working with you, you know. I
am not against you. I am with you."

I honestly didn't think they saw this. I am not denying that
I have got some racial prejudice, because I have. But I do
feel that I took too much for granted; that, you know, just
because we are open-minded and can talk and can socialize
and think nothing of going to restaurants and think nothing
of going out together, and think nothing of kidding around,
that more or less everybody was supposed to feel the same
way. I just found out that isn't so.
Kelly:
It kind of sounds like two things. First of all, you blew your
cool. The second thing was that you suddenly began to see
the world, I think, through the eyes of the Negro kids, except
you were on the other side this time.
Butch:
I used to run into a lot of cases where a bunch of kids would
be trying to bust into a place or start a rumpus, but I knew
them by sight, and we could kid around. I could walk in and
say, "Hey, baby, cool it." And one of the guys was sure to
say, "Take it easy, he's all right. He's from CPI. I know him."

What really got me this time was out of the clear blue
sky, all of a sudden, this "Whitey" bit comes in, and I
couldn't figure it out for the love of me. After a while, after
I heard it ten or fifteen times, I could have cared less about
nonviolence or anything. The same way, the other thing that
scared the living shit out of me, when I got into the fight, I
didn't have any fear of being cut or anything like that or
getting belted. I just had the greatest goddamned urge to
kill somebody up there.
Jack:
Was this before you were hit or after when you got this
opinion of wanting to kill somebody?
Butch:
During it. I think it started right after the first blow was
swung.

Jack:
That's what I mean, before or after you were hit?
Butch:
I think it started right there. Suddenly I had this kid up against the wall. All I could think of is that I wanted to really kill the kid. I think if I would have carried a gun I would have killed the kid.
Sterns:
Were you thinking in racial terms about the kid then?
Butch:
I can't honestly say. I don't know. I had such an urge. I have been born and raised in gang fights. I have been born and raised in barroom fights in the service, but I rarely ever had that urge like I did last night to kill. If anything, I would have to say it was a racial overtone.
Kelly:
We are kind of directing this at Butch. I think that Butch is bringing up something that every one of us, in one way or another, has had to face, had to feel about it, and think about it. It isn't an issue that was just born with Butch.
Jack:
I am against what you're saying about this being directed at Butch. It is not directed at Butch. I don't think it is. At this time Butch is presenting what happened. He is the only one that can give the answer.
Kelly:
You were there, Jack. What did you feel at the time? How did you feel when you saw it going on?
Jack:
To tell you the truth, I didn't really feel anything. All I knew was that Butch was a guy I was working with and if I didn't help him he would have got stomped.
Butch:
What did you think about the "Whitey" comment?
Clark:
I was standing out there. The kids were trying to egg him on and get him out there. Actually, they kept saying it until he came off the porch. Seems like they were waiting for him and they closed in on him.
Jack:
What you were saying before, if you can remember, during the time of the incident, I was doing most of the talking. Every once in a while you would come in and comment. When the kids started with the "Whitey" bit you started talking a lot more. Then I knew the real trouble was coming. They accepted me but they weren't going to accept nothing you said. All it could do was get things more excited. They didn't want to hear you or listen to you.

Butch:
But if colored kids aren't going to listen to me, to a white guy, how am I going to work with them as an RYC worker? Even though the fight was not with RYC kids, but with kids from the outside, how can I have a bona fide relationship with a colored kid if there is always that under-hidden hatred for a white versus colored.

The same way, now, maybe I will be saying, "Why that black bastard, I can't stand his guts." Do I now go and find another way of working with colored kids?
Lance:
I don't know.
Butch:
All I am saying is, how does it affect the way in which you work with a given kid? Do you work always keeping in mind there is a definite distinct racial problem, or do you turn around and say, "Well probably the kids we are working with maybe do have that problem, but are a little more liberal-minded in their thinking and are willing to at least try." I don't know whether I saw it, or read into it or what. I seemed to find some tension among even our own kids when I came back into the house.

One kid I definitely sensed it in was Bobby. I seem to find almost a new change or new attitude of dislike toward me. Maybe it's just because I went out and fought his kind.
Kelly:
Chip, you were a cop for a lot of years and you had to be involved in a lot of very tense situations involving black people and white people. What happened there? What were your feelings?
Chip:
I was neutral. I just tried to treat them all the same. I didn't care whether they were black or white. If they were doing something they weren't supposed to be doing they got treated the same way. I was too busy to think.
Jack:
What Kelly is saying, during the course of the period of time you were a police officer, you arrested Negro kids and ar- rested white kids, or both at the same time. Weren't there times when, say, you arrested a new Negro kid when he gave you a tongue-lashing as the white person arresting him?
Chip:
You get that all the time. "You're only arresting me because I'm colored." You get this bit every time you arrest one of them.
Butch:
Can I ask you this question, like, one of the things I think that upset me was what you say, you try to stay neutral and

weigh everything, judge it, how it comes out in all the evidence there. The same way there are a lot of colored people I dislike. I don't dislike them for being colored, just personally dislike them.
Chip:
As a person.
Butch:
Right. You try to say you are walking neutral, that you're trying to work with both sides and keep an open mind, but what happens—say, what are your feelings if somebody starts slandering you for being white?
Chip:
I've been called a few choice names and you're right. You know, I didn't feel good about it. I mean, you know—but it didn't make any difference in what I did. I was arresting them and they were going to be arrested regardless.
I didn't throw any extra charges on them or anything, you know.
Jack:
You hit them in the head with the stick, right?
Chip:
No, no, I didn't hit them either. I knew how the people felt.
Kelly:
How did you know how these people felt?
Chip:
Because you hear it all the time. We were practically living with them. When you're working up on Dixwell Avenue, you're living with them.
Kelly:
What do you think the Negro people feel?
Chip:
They hated—not because I was white, but because I was a cop. They hated you just because you're a cop. Whether it's white or Negro you have got that uniform on and that's it. They don't like you.
Sterns:
If you're a white cop . . .
Chip:
You've got three strikes against you then.
Scotty:
Can I speak as a Negro? (laughter) I'd like to say a few things that I felt and that I've seen, you know, through my life and growing up. Right from the beginning a Negro kid has to fight for survival. Growing up you find that because you're a Negro there are quite a few doors closed to you. Like coming up through high school, maybe you had a

counselor where you knew you were doing better than a white kid, but your counselor would gear you to just get you through school and maybe go through a trade school, while the white kid was geared to college.

Coming up, you go to an integrated school and get to make friends with some white and colored. Me as an individual, I always rated a person depending on how they treated me. Whether they were black or white didn't make any difference.

Jack:

After you grew up—

Scotty:

Let me finish. But you find you lose a lot of these feelings after junior high school and high school. You know, you can go to their homes and this and that. But then I think what turns it back is the minute that you graduate from high school all this changes.

As a kid, I can go into his house and play with him, play with his little sister or something like that, but now I'm an adult, you know, and I'm out of high school. All of a sudden the white friends that I went to school with, some of them stopped speaking to me. Some of them didn't want to associate with me.

I even know people that I graduate with, I can't get as much as a "hello" from them. So you begin saying, "Well, maybe a lot that I learned that my parents told me is true about white people." When persons turn around and you find out they are not what you think they are, this makes you twice as hard, you know, toward this race. When I found out some of the things they were doing and saying behind my back, this made me bring back all my feelings that I was taught as a kid. You know, they are reinforced twice as hard. This was my feeling, you can't trust them. Italians, you can't trust them. They befriend you and talk behind your back, stab you in the back. This is what I have experienced. I mean, I used to go into this kid's house and sit down and eat with him every day. As a friend I said to him, "Mike, if you had a sister—me and you are just like brothers now—if you had a sister and I wanted to marry her, how would you feel?" He came out and told me, he said, "I wouldn't want it. I want to be your friend. I'll tell you the truth. I'd hate your guts." he said.

Different things like that makes you change. The thing about the kids that are coming up nowadays, with a lot of things going on, like this thing about black power, they hear these words "black power." The white people hear these words "black power," but they don't know the real definition of "black power."

You could sit down and break it down to the Negro kids what black power really means, then maybe things would be different, but the way they are here, those words "black power" they see the word "black" and they think "I'm black, and power means my two fists. That means fight the white man."

You know, it does mean not only fight the white man, but it means fight for what is right. You know, I think behind black power, as far as a neighborhood; like if all of Legion Avenue the majority of people over there are Negroes. It means black power because they are Negroes, the majority; they should have the say-so over there and should have the say-so of how they want to run the community. This is one meaning of black power.

Another thing is that as far as in school, you know, when we see that a school is highly integrated with Negroes, if all the authority in school are white, that the people in the PTA within the community, they should be able to make decisions for their kids. They should be able to decide. They should be able to decide whether their kids should be geared for college or geared for a trade school. These are the meanings of black power.

You know, people get the wrong idea, especially a young kid. You can't explain these things to them. They hear "black power" and the first thing they think of is fighting and fight any white man, you know, that tries to put them down in any way, shape, or form. This is the root of a lot of our problems.
Kelly:
Jack, you looked like you wanted to stop Scotty a moment ago.
Jack:
Oh, yes. The reason why I was going to stop him was to say how Negro kids always came up under the white man some way.

When Scotty was going through his bit there, I say, most of the black kids have this, like he said, until they get out of high school. Then when they get out of high school they feel that a lot of feelings that they have had about not trusting the white man is right. Because now it comes to what Scotty left out, which is employment, and through employment he starts to get a lot more feelings about the white man as no good and as holding him down and been holding him down all his life.

Scotty:
It starts before the employment, though, because it's back
in school.
Jack:
It's through the employment that it really comes out, these
feelings.
Scotty:
I mean, I know, like I have a niece who is getting straight
"A's" and she wants to go to college. I had to personally go
up there and tell her counselor, "Look, I want her to go to
college and take the college course. She is going to college.
I don't care what you say."
He was trying to gear her to some kind of sewing or
basket-weaving crap.
Kelly:
We are talking now—the conversation looks like it has drifted
toward discussing education, discussing employment, discussing the whole problem of how we deal with the issue with
children and how it is dealt with in public schools. What
about us as a staff?
Butch:
The question I wanted to ask Scotty—not to put you on the
spot or anything—are there different sets of standards how a
white person is supposed to react to you versus a colored
person?
Scotty:
No, there is no set of standards. I take a person for what
the person is and how they treat me.
Butch:
Let me ask you a question then. By that statement, then, I
wouldn't be able to say that our kids are different than the
ones that are out on the street that we had the incident with.
Sterns:
That's right.
Butch:
Those feelings that were exhibited out there on the front
lawn are the same feelings working here now.
Jack:
Except for the fact that the kids here have seen you, where
the kids on the lawn don't or didn't.
Butch:
Sometimes I guess I agree with that.
Clark:
A lot of kids come to my room and come to me and tell me,

"I don't want a white man working with me." That's the truth.
Butch:
How come these things have never been said before?
Clark:
This has been brought up a long time ago.
Kelly:
We bring it up but we never talk about it really.
Scotty:
I think we never pinpointed it right to the definite problem.
Jack:
Lance brought it up one day when he said—which I think really is quite true—he said there are going to be certain incidents that are going to arise where he thinks that it should be a Negro—it would take one of the Negro staff members to quiet it down. This is true of the hostility type of feelings that these kids have in the back of their mind.

Whenever an incident arises with a Negro kid where the kid is angered, he is going to see that white person in front of him representing all of the things he has hostility about, where he is going to need and listen to another Negro confronting him about the problems. Otherwise, he is not going to see it that way and not going to be quieted down.
Butch:
One of the things that has happened, that I never did all of my time as a foreman or even here until just recently once, I never asked a kid how he felt about having a white worker or whether he preferred a colored worker. The only kid I ever asked that was Rudy C.

I said to him, "Do you really want me as a worker or do you prefer to have a colored worker?" He said, "It doesn't matter," I said, "What gives between you and I?" He came out with an answer, he said, "You just don't understand me." The only thing I can honestly read into it is that "You don't understand me because I'm colored and you're white and you don't understand the problems that I have got."
Kelly:
I keep asking myself the question—I say, "Scotty, Jack, Silver, how does it feel to be black?" Not only how does it feel to be black, but how do you see white people? And the only thing I can come up with, and what really sets this off is Butch really blowing his cool when suddenly he was called, maybe for the first time in his life, over and over again, "Hey, Whitey; hey, white mother f——; hey, whitey, hey, whitey."

I have a feeling that the white people, the white people on our own staff, myself, are unprepared for this turning of the

tables. We don't know how to handle it. Maybe Butch blew his cool because, unlike a Negro, he hadn't learned or experienced how to handle this kind of put-down. It wasn't a part of his usual life. Look, I remember one time, about 5 or 6 years ago, when I went on a Freedom Ride. We all had to swear to be nonviolent and all that. Well, I found it harder *not* to swing at the guys calling us names than if I could allow myself to fight. And these guys weren't even Negroes calling us names, but white guys like we were.
Butch:
But the words they used were not the same. I was getting crucified because I was white. I wanted to know why I was being crucified. It never happened to me before.
Scotty:
That's the problem, where it never happened to you. I heard it so much in my life, "nigger this and that," I'm immune to it. I got to a point where by the time I got to junior high school, I wasn't fighting no more. You call me "nigger" and I'll call you a "dirty wop" or call you "dirty sheeny" or something.
Butch:
If they sat there and said, "nigger lover" to me, all I'd have to do is laugh and say "dumb bunch of ignorant bastards out there." But they were calling me "whitey." I had no answer for them.
Lance:
Scotty, the point is you said if somebody calls you "dirty nigger" you'll call them "dirty wops." Is there actually that much difference in the two words, between the two words? These are both slang words. I'm not trying to hide my head in the sand or anything like that.

It seems to me like there is a bigger—I believe the word is "connotation" put against the word "nigger."
Scotty:
The thing about it, you'll find a lot of white people will say "nigger" before a nigger will come out and say "wop" or something like that. If you say "nigger" to a colored person, he is going to fight you. If you say "wop" to a white person, they're not going to fight you.
Silver:
I was thinking about when you said about Negroes and whites, you know, you see it goes way back to slavery when they were calling them "niggers" and what not. It goes back that far, a long way back.
Kelly:
How do we begin, even as a staff, to deal with the problem?

In a sense what I am asking is how do the Negro staff members help the white staff members to understand?

Scotty:

Okay, I'll tell you something that I felt. I know the other Negro members have felt the same ·thing on the staff and that is there have been times when I felt actually—I don't know whether it's prejudiced or what—I felt that Butch was neglecting some of his kids because they were Negroes and he was taking more interest in his white kids. I never brought it out. I felt that Butch didn't understand them and that Butch wasn't spending the time with them because he didn't understand them, and he really didn't want to get that involved, you know.

Lance:

Why didn't you say so then?

Scotty:

I did bring it up in a nicer way before.

Lance:

Why bring it up in a nicer way? You brought out a direct point. Had the direct point been brought up before that, feelings might have been hurt for a few minutes, but then we might have been able to start getting to the problem then.

Kelly:

Maybe we'll never get there, but I have a feeling if we can begin to talk like Scotty just talked about Butch, feelings and such, without being afraid of the words or afraid that we are going to fall apart, maybe then we can begin to really deal with the problem.

Scotty:

Maybe in the long run my keeping quiet was doing more harm than good. I thought I was sparing feelings and trying to keep peace in the staff.

Jack:

You presented a question before which, you know, you said how do or how can the Negro staff members assist the white staff members. I think the whites must learn to accept it, the statement of being called "Whitey" without getting violent themselves.

Scotty:

We'll call them "Whitey" every day until they get used to it. (laughter)

Jack:

What you're asking for is assistance.

Butch:

I think one of the ways you can help is to make known to

us the strong feelings of hatred and why the hatreds are there.
Jack:
I've got some books you can read, buddy.
Kelly:
Called a diary? (laughter)
Butch:
I never knew or really honestly felt there was so much hatred here. The same way like you see all these riots in Chicago and stuff, my family would talk and say, "Gee, I wonder if that's going to happen here." I'd say, "No, it would never happen here because I don't think that there is that much racial overtone here in New Haven or that much hatred here." Yet now I am starting to change my mind because last night I found out how much hatred there really is. Maybe we really don't know how a Negro feels in this country or this town.
Jack:
I've got a book I'll let you read.
Butch:
You and your books. I don't think these are feelings a lot of us really are aware of.
Sterns:
I had a similar kind of experience when I was in the Peace Corps. It's different but it can be compared in some ways. I'm trying to think how it can be relevant. I was in Africa for two years and I was in the minority, a white man in a black country. It's an entirely different set of feelings that go along with that, but there were times when I thought to myself, "Gee, you know I'll bet this is somehow like a Negro feels in the United States." All of a sudden you're the only one out there, and the only reason you are being singled out is because you're white instead of black. When it gets to you, you begin to think in racial terms. You begin to think, much against your will, like "get away you black spear-chuckers." That's what we used to call them to have some kind of defense. "I came over to help you, you know." This is one thing they don't—
Clark:
They don't like that.
Sterns:
They don't like that.
Scotty:
One thing I was going to say about what Sterns said, bringing up feelings of giving, you know, always I'm going to give you something or I'm doing something for you. This is one

of the things that I think the white staff members should be aware of. These Negro kids feel, they feel that they are being robbed of their pride. Just like the thing I brought up as far as when I was going downtown as an administrative assistant. I told the big shots and the other people, I said, "Look, I don't want a job where you can just sit me down and I'm going to be a nice little brown boy up there for people to look at or a figurehead. I want to feel that I earn something. Don't rob me of my pride. Let me do it on my own."

If you noticed, many a time you hear a Negro kid say to you, "I'm not asking you for nothing. Don't give me nothing." This is their feeling. Also a lot of times the white attitude is that, "Look, I'm doing this for you. I'm giving you this." This is the last thing you should say to a Negro kid because he doesn't want that.

Jack:
What you are saying is the Negro's feeling in general. He may not have a lot of things going for him, but he does have his pride and he gets real hurt when his pride is, you know—

Scotty:
"I'm not asking you for nothing," these kids say. You've got to present it to them in such a way—although you might be doing them a favor—you have to present it in a way that they are earning it, accomplishing it themselves. This is one of the things that I feel a lot of the staff members in CPI are not aware of.

Butch:
I don't think this is just a Negro thing. This pride thing is important to all the kids we work with.

Kelly:
Jean, you have been very quiet the whole time. I have a feeling you're not quiet because you're not thinking.

Jack:
She holds all the razor blades for the kids. (laughter)

Kelly:
You're a black woman, now, and—

Lance:
How about that.

Scotty:
She's West Indian.

Kelly:
Are you West Indian?

Scotty:
This is something that is really ridiculous. The white people have drummed it into the Negroes' heads that it is

so horrible to be Negro that they try to escape into little groups like, "I'm West Indian," but I'll be damned if they weren't the first ones to get off the boat from Africa.

You see, they put their ass up on their shoulder and talk about "I'm West Indian." That galls me to no end. Ninety percent of them are blacker than me. They talk about "I'm West Indian, not Negro." I'd rather beat the hell out of one of them than fight with a white person about something.

Lance:
Hey, take it easy, calm down. What are you trying to do? What are you picking on West Indians for? I'm the white man, I'm supposed to be your main enemy.

Scotty:
You're trying to show us you're not prejudiced.

Lance:
I am?

Scotty:
You know, I'm more leery of a white person who says, "Hi, Scotty; my best friend was a colored boy," than I am of anyone else.

Jean:
Talking about that, Scotty and I went down to an attorney for one of the kids the other day. We sat down for an hour and all we heard was Sammy Davis, Jr., Nat King Cole, Jimmy Brown, "Why, some of my best friends are Negroes." Scotty and I didn't say anything the whole time.

Scotty:
We went down there and from the time we walked into his office, the first thing he said, he started talking about all these nice colored people he knew and, "Look at Sammy Davis, Jr."

Chip:
Sammy Davis, Jr., is Jewish.

Jean:
I'm saying to myself, "Why didn't he say Frank Sinatra?" We were yawning and after a while he was quoting all these Negroes. After a while Scotty and I didn't communicate. When the man went out of the office I said, "Scotty, one of the rare times in your life, did you get the feeling you were colored?" We almost said it spontaneously. I just bit my tongue, more or less.

Kelly:
What bothers me is that it is almost as if—and maybe I'm wrong, maybe I just feel hurt—but almost no matter how close I get, say with Scotty, no matter how close we got, I might never know whether Scotty ever really trusted me.

Jack:
That is a two-way street.
Lance:
It's a feeling you get between people. You can never go up and say, "Scotty, do you really trust me?"
Kelly:
I'm talking about—
Butch:
It's true then. Is there always—then am I lying to myself in my own beliefs? Are we all lying to ourselves, putting on one big damn show?
Sterns:
It's like two different cultures.
Scotty:
I think the reason why there is doubt among races, like Jack said, it works both ways. It is because of different experiences that you have. Like people say the most liberal people you want to come in contact with are people in the entertainment business. I was an entertainer for ten years. Let me tell you one time in Silver Springs, Maryland, there was this white guy in the show I was traveling with. We got to be real good buddies. His girl friend came to town with a friend and evidently they were putting on a front for me. This girl friend of his was just playing up to me like nobody's business. She was winking at me and waving at me. I was being a friendly old dumb nigger, winking back, and this and that. You know, when I got off the stage, they had to put me in a car and run me out of town because she went and told a white policeman that I was making passes at her. They had a crowd out there ready to lynch me.

You see, when different things like this happen to you, you build up feelings of whether or not you can trust a white person.
Jack:
Get close, but not all the way close.
Clark:
I had a similar incident like that when I was in the service. I was in Georgia and a friend of mine—I thought he was a friend, anyhow—we went to town together. He was a white friend. We were walking around town and everything was going good.

He said to me, "Let's go to get a bowl of spaghetti." I said, "It's a good idea. I haven't had spaghetti in a long time." So we went down to the store to get some spaghetti and I went in with him and I sat down with him. This guy says to us, "Sorry, we don't serve niggers." I said, "That's all right, I don't eat them either." (laughter)

So I got up and I figured he would go with me. He stayed right there.

Jean:
Did he know that is why you left?

Clark:
Yes, he knew. I told him.

Lance:
He stayed there?

Clark:
He stayed there?

Chip:
He was probably hungry. (laughter)

Scotty:
Kelly is probably saying to himself, "Gee, I wonder if Clark really trusts me."

Jean:
I was going to say that a lot of this trusting of white people, you know, would you trust a Negro? I think it goes back to childhood, you know. You were hanging around with white kids and whatnot. Your mother would say, you know, "You can only go so far. One of these days if you get in a fight the first words they are going to call you is a dirty nigger. You're building yourself up to a letdown." This is more of a protective shield.

Jack:
Yes, it is. What Jean is saying, "He looks like he is for me so I will be for him. But should I allow myself to completely have faith in this kind of thing when I know from past experiences that it's going to be the same kind of thing, be a thing where I have been let down." There is always that item in mind, should I or shouldn't I, and more often it comes out to be a thing that you shouldn't because you have been burned and burned and burned before.

Jean:
How do you trust anyone, black or white? I mean, regardless of color. How do you know when to really put your trust in someone, anyone?

Lance:
Look, if you're bringing up the whole problem of "trust," forget it. I think up to now we have had enough trouble just beginning to talk to each other about race, just talking our feelings out. I mean, just our basic feelings we have had a hell of a lot of problems just getting to the point of being able to take and put the feelings on the table. Don't be greedy. Have a heart.

The session ended with the problem essentially unresolved; and despite the fact that the question of race was brought up time and time again in succeeding months, it was never "cleared up" in the sense that it ceased being an issue of great concern and potential conflict. Nevertheless, the mere fact that it *was* brought out into the open—that we could not pretend that it did not exist or that by ignoring it it would "go away"—increased the possibilities that it could be dealt with in ways and with a commitment not typical of most settings.

In this chapter we have tried to describe and give examples of the concept of sensitivity training as it was developed at the Residential Youth Center. Although it is more than likely that the philosophy of "training" employed at the RYC was generally consistent with the ethos of the "T-groupers," we have tried to point out how its particular form and content were determined by the dynamics of the setting and the needs of its people rather than by the automatic transfer and application of T-group methods and theories.

From the point of view of the creation of a setting, the importance of what came to be called "RYC sensitivity training" rests more on what it reflects about a conception of organizations than in its potential for universal application in the particular form developed at the RYC. In other words, the very decision to employ sensitivity training was itself predicated on a certain conception of organizations, a conception that accepted the idea that an organization was more than a little vulnerable so long as it did not take seriously the need to develop some form of internal mechanism that would both mediate between its structure and its people and create the conditions for trust and interpersonal accessibility. In the final analysis, however, despite the fact that its use could be amply justified in terms of research, clinical training, decision-making, and feedback, the most important function of sensitivity training at the RYC was to enable people—all of us—to talk, without fear and without regrets.

In Chapters 4 and 5 we have described the RYC both as an organization and in terms of the particular concept of training it employed to develop the kind of social structure that would be responsive to the needs and aspirations of all its inhabitants. In the next chapter we shall turn our attention to the variety of problems that confronted the setting during the days and weeks *before* it became a functional reality. In Chapter 6, therefore, we shall take up the question of the RYC's "prehistory."

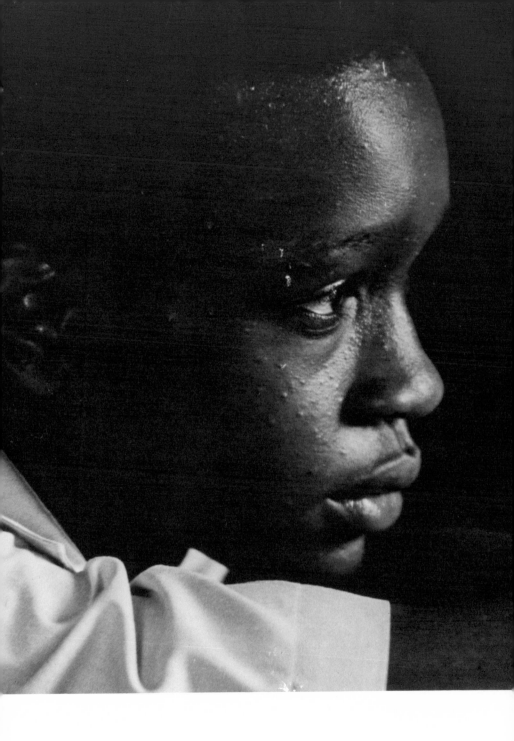

Chapter 6   The RYC's Prehistory
Problems of Preparation and Community Penetration

The "will" is posited as reflective decision in relation to certain ends. But it does not create these ends. It is rather a mode of being in relation to them. "Passion," though it may posit the same ends as will, proceeds with less deliberation in choosing the means and methods to be employed.
—Jean-Paul Sartre

There is a myth, publicly disavowed but privately protected, that an institution is born on the day it opens its doors and starts doing "business as usual." We refer to this as a myth only because, public protestations to the contrary, institution-builders often act as if the decisions they make and the actions they take before a new program becomes operational bear little relationship to and have few consequences for the eventual appearance and success of the program itself. But if there was anything to be learned from our prior involvement in the community (see Chapters 2 and 3) it was this: the fate of any new program, whether or not it survives (and even if it survives, whether or not it achieves or approaches its goals), is dependent not only on the soundness of its ideas but also on how it is introduced into the community. In short, there is an intimate relationship between the problems of conceptualization, planning, and implementation, on the one hand, and the way a program looks once it assumes an existence of its own, on the other. The two are inextricably bound to each other; and what may well signal the beginning of that self-defeating process through which new and often innovative programs create the conditions for their own destruction is the belief, the myth, that this is not really so.

In this chapter we shall describe some of the more important decisions and events that influenced the development of the RYC prior to the time it became a physical reality. Our purpose in doing this is twofold: first, to convey the importance of the actions taken during a program's preoperational period of life; and second, because we are assuming that many of the problems with which the RYC was confronted are both generalizable to and relevant for any thoroughgoing analysis of the question of how one introduces change into an ongoing social system.

The Community and the Processes of Change

Rarely, if ever, is any new program, especially one labeled either "innovative" or "experimental," welcomed into a community with outstretched arms. Most communities, particularly those with some degree of stability and continuity, are slow to accept and accommodate themselves to any new program that brings with it the specter of change. One need only review the work of Cumming and Cumming (1957) to appreciate how quickly a community can "close ranks" and mobilize its resources to undermine a program that it interprets as potentially threatening to the existing social order. And even in those instances in which a community can be described as in a state of transition or, as Levine and Levine (1968) put it, in a state of "acute social change," it is rarely the case that the question of change is taken lightly. A community consists of a complex series of interlocking (though by no means mutual) interests—interests defined over time and invested with a degree of apparent, if not actual, validity.[1] Its composition bespeaks a delicate balance of power groups, institutional relationships, and spheres of influence (even historical imbalances can be defined as forms of balance). Each segment brings with it some particular view of the world; but together they define that community, give it its uniqueness, and share in its perpetuation.

Under these conditions, *any* change, be it the addition of a new program, the loss of an old one, or the change of an existing one, must almost by definition be perceived by some as a threat, if only because it serves to upset the balance of power. It may well be that the basic conservatism of most communities is not only understandable but in the long run, even desirable; but from the point of view of those whose goal is to introduce "change," it is a situation fraught with difficulty and potential danger. In essence, it is a state of

[1] Our use of the term "community" has little to do with the size of a given area, its population, or its particular geography, although these variables play a crucial role in defining the context of a given setting. Rather, by community we are referring to an area (e.g., a neighborhood, a town, even a "block") that can be defined in terms of certain ongoing institutional processes and group relationships that, over time, have given rise to a particular pattern of enduring values and traditions.

affairs in which one's actions (what one does and how one does it) must, in one way or another, be predicated upon an understanding of just how potent a factor the "communal reality" is in both defining and setting the limits for change. This is not to say that the community necessarily dictates or possesses formal "veto power" with respect to *all* changes that occur in the setting. What it means is that the attempt to introduce change into an ongoing social system must consider the setting, its history, and its dynamics as crucial variables affecting both the development of the new program and the choice of strategies for its implementation.

Although the RYC formally came into existence on September 16, 1966, its fate, no different from the fate of most new programs, may well have been determined long before it ever opened its doors for "business." This fate, if one can call it that, was written in the decisions and actions—in the orientation—taken toward the problems of preparation, anticipation, implementation, and transition.[2] Common to all these problems was the conception that each decision was guaranteed to affect certain segments of the community differently; that each decision brought with it certain implica-

[2]What we have called "the problems of preparation, anticipation, implementation, and transition" all can be viewed as particular instances of the more general issue of means-ends relationships. If we assume that the myriad goals of the War on Poverty are basically "good" or "worthwhile" (i.e., that they seek to improve the well-being of people in general), then the means-ends issue becomes a question not of *whether* to do something but rather of *how* to do it. It is a situation not unlike the statement made by the ex-President in Gore Vidal's play *The Best Man*, who, when confronted by the self-defeating vacillation of a particularly idealistic contender for his party's presidential nomination, blurts out: "There are no ends, only means." Thus, for example, while the problem of preparation (which involves the particular issue of time perspective) can be viewed as phenotypically different from the problem of anticipation (which is concerned with such questions as "Who does the new program threaten?" "What forces must be won over?" and "What vested interests are involved?"), the two problems are genotypically related in the sense that they both involve an analysis of means-ends relationships. In the final analysis, the basic problem confronting those people concerned with introducing change into ongoing social systems is that of developing both a way of thinking and a series of strategies that will maximize the probabilities of success and minimize the resistance that inevitably accompanies attempts at innovation or social reform. The work of Marris and Rein (1967) makes this quite clear.

tions for future decisions; and that if implemented incorrectly, each decision could either lead to no results at all or, more ominously, to results quite different from those intended.

In the pages that follow we shall attempt to describe the "prehistory" of the RYC from the point of view of how its development and implementation were "shaped" by a means-ends analysis of the confluence of interests and concerns that surrounded it in the community. The process of trying to start the RYC necessarily involved us with such diverse elements in the community as its residents, the police, the traditional helping agencies, the families with whom we wished to work most directly, and, of course, CPI itself. To be sure, all these groups had much in common; but they also differed markedly in their particular goals, concerns, and fears. We could be sure that the RYC would mean different things to each of these groups; that they would perceive and interpret its goals differently; and that unless steps were taken early to initiate some meaningful and broadening contact, each group could (and probably would) react to the program in a manner predicated solely on its own view of the world. With this in mind, the "prehistory" of the RYC became an adventure in and of itself—a time during which the staff of the RYC sought to involve itself with others without sacrificing its own sense of self-determination; when it sought to influence without dominating; and when it walked that fine line between meaningful collaboration and self-defeating fusion.[3] Limitations of space and memory—par-

[3]Sarason (1968), in a paper dealing with the problems involved in the creation of new settings, has focused attention on what he terms the "beginning context." The beginning context is that period of time, always quite early in the life of an institution, when decisions are made and orientations developed that have far-reaching effects for the future of the unborn setting. One such orientation he defines as the "mine and not mine" attitude that the "leader" of an emerging setting must take toward "his" institution if he is to maximize the likelihood of its acceptance into the community. It is an attitude that requires that the leader, if he is to maintain effective control of the setting, must actually give up some of his autonomy and "ownership" and involve with him in the creative process those forces in the community which will be most affected by the new program. It is this attitude of "mine and not mine" that we are trying to describe when we speak of "that fine line between meaningful collaboration and self-defeating fusion."

ticularly memory—make it impossible to describe all the events that took place prior to the time the RYC opened its doors to its first 20 residents. Consequently, we shall restrict ourselves to a description of those events which, in retrospect, are both firmly fixed in memory and had some direct bearing on the development of the program. Some of the events to be described are humorous, others are not funny at all; some resulted in positive gains for the program, whereas others generated conflicts that have not been resolved to this day; some can broadly be defined as successful, and others must be viewed as failures. However, all the events in one way or another helped to shape the RYC as it looks today.[4]

We Were Not the First: Some Additional Background
To begin with, one thing should be made clear: we were far from being the first group of people to develop the idea for an inner-city or neighborhood-based residential facility. Long before the RYC was funded—even before its ideas were formalized into a specific proposal—the need for some sort of residential program was recognized by a number of individuals and groups living in the ghettos and slums of New Haven.[5] By and large these were poor people (people with no formal organization to represent their interests and people with little in the way of personal power or community

[4]The events to be reported are all taken from the diary that the RYC's first Director kept during the early months of the program's development. For purposes of clarity and organization, these events will be discussed in terms of the interactions that took place between the RYC and three major segments of the community: community organizations and agencies, the RYC's residents and their families, and the RYC's "mother organization," CPI.
[5]Even from a historical point of view it would be difficult, not to mention inaccurate, to refer to the RYC as a completely new, different, or singularly innovative approach to the problem of service in the inner city. One of our colleagues, Dr. Murray Levine, has pointed out to us that, if anything, the concept of the RYC represents a "throwback" to the settlement house movement that was so prevalent in this country some 80 years ago. Hull House, for example, founded in 1889, was a setting very similar to the RYC. Not only was it a neighborhood-based operation whose goal it was to develop services appropriate to the ghetto resident, but it was also a setting in which indigenous nonprofessionals assumed a variety of different responsibilities and a place where prospective members of the helping professions received a significant portion of their "practicum" training experiences.

"status"), and as the following example indicates, their efforts to start such a center were doomed to a premature death.

Example 1: July 1966.
Today Richie and I met with a group of local ministers in one of the churches on Dixwell Avenue. The meeting itself was about as uneventful as a meeting can be. We explained the program to them, outlined some of its goals, and tried to convey our desire that they become involved in the program, offer suggestions and criticisms, and view it as a program whose aims were consistent with many of their own objectives. They, in turn, communicated their interest, told us of their willingness to work with us; they were, how can I put it, about as blandly responsive as a group can be without falling asleep. What they were really telling us, I think, was that they wouldn't bug us if we didn't bother them.

But something of note did take place at the meeting, and it had nothing to do with the ministers. Even though the meeting was supposed to be between the ministers and ourselves, a woman showed up, took a seat in the back of the church, and insisted on staying. Needless to say she was allowed to stay. Although she didn't say anything during the course of the meeting she seemed more interested in what we were saying than any of those "officially" present. She often leaned forward to hear what was going on, seemed a little agitated at times, and often wrung her hands as we were talking.

As we were leaving the church, the woman ran after us and caught us on the steps of the building. It was a hot day, and the woman was perspiring profusely. Her clothes were soaked through with sweat.

After she had stopped us, with tears in her eyes, she thrust a few typewritten pages into my hand, stood back, and said: "Read this." She stood close by me as I read the document, almost as if she were afraid that I wouldn't give it back to her.

The document I read was a proposal for the establishment of a halfway house to be located in one of the inner-city low-income housing projects. Many of the ideas contained in the proposal were very similar to those in the original RYC proposal. Although the primary goal of this woman's project was to provide rehabilitative and residential services to young people (teen-agers 16 to 21 years of age) coming out of jail —her ideas were far more rehabilitative than preventive in orientation—many of the basic concepts contained in the proposal were exactly the same as ours. Both proposals, for example, called for indigenous nonprofessional personnel to carry the major responsibility for working with the Center's clients; both stressed the importance of working with both the youth and his family; and both were predicated on the assumption that the recipients of the service should.be intimately involved in the direction of the facility. What was more amazing, however, was the fact that her proposal was dated *September 1964*, a full year or more before any of us had ever even begun to think about an RYC.

It took me a while to finish reading the proposal (it was a tattered document replete with misspellings and grammatical errors), and the woman had calmed down a bit by the time I was through. We had a chance to talk with her for a while and this is what we found out.

The woman, a Negro lady in her late forties, was herself a resident in the housing project in which she wanted a halfway house to be located. She was on welfare and had a teen-aged son in jail. She, along with one or two other mothers in similar circumstances, had spent long hours painfully trying to formulate and write the proposal which I had read. Once the proposal was completed, she assumed the primary responsibility for getting the project funded. She sent copies of her proposal, together with personal letters, to almost everyone she could think of who might be in a position to help her. Copies had been sent to the mayor, CPI, local ministers, and even to R. Sargent Shriver in Washington. Only once had she received a reply from any of the people to whom she had sent her ideas (she had once received a form letter to acknowledge the receipt of her proposal). She was today no further along than she had been almost two years ago. She was still a woman with ideas and no project; the worn and tattered four-page proposal was all she had to show for two years of fruitless labor.

Oh, we said all the "right things." We tried to share her indignation, told her about many of our own frustrations in trying to get the RYC funded, and offered her suggestions as to whom to see about her proposal. Maybe the only concrete thing we did was promise to help her on condition that she become involved in the RYC and help us try to incorporate and achieve many of her own goals through our project. We shook hands on that. For the first time since we had begun talking she seemed to relax a little. I think she even smiled although I can't be sure. I came away feeling that we had offered her precious little in return for her help. It was a lousy bargain any way you look at it.

As we left, I couldn't help but wonder where the hell the

RYC would be today if I wasn't on the faculty of a prestigeful university, if I wasn't "in" with a powerful organization like CPI, and if the leader of that organization hadn't accompanied me down to Washington and used his considerable influence to get the project funded. I think that in all probability I would be very much like that woman, a nameless and faceless person eating my guts out and running around with a tattered proposal and no project—just another casualty on the road to "participatory democracy". What a waste.[6]

The RYC and the Community

As we have already indicated, it is exceedingly difficult to speak of "the community" as if it were a homogeneous "thing" composed of groups with similar and nonconflicting values, goals, and traditions. Despite the fact that different community groups may share a common concern (e.g., both the police and local action groups are concerned with the safety and well-being of a neighborhood), it does not follow that their views of the problem, its causes, and proposed remedies have any more in common than the views of two people who are complete strangers to each other. Consequently, all we could assume was that in approaching "the community" with the RYC we would be involving ourselves with particular groups, each of which would have to be dealt with individually before they could be "molded" into a helpful consensus.

Perhaps the most important thing "going for us" in our initial contacts with community groups was the fact that we could confront each group with a project that was not only far from being operational but was also, at least in proposal form, so generally worded as to allow for flexible interpretation and substantial modification. We were, in a very real sense, asking each group to participate in the creation of the

[6]It should be stressed that the situation described above is not limited to people who are poor, politically "naive," or socially powerless. Graziano (1969), in a powerful paper detailing the myriad problems confronting professionals (i.e., people whose standing in the community is supposedly buffered by accepted credentials, a sense of power, and a knowledge of social institutions) who wish to develop programs perceived as threatening by the "mental health power structure," has described experiences (and results) very similar to those encountered by the ghetto resident in our example.

setting at a point in time when merely passing judgment on the project was not a viable option unless the particular group was also willing to accept some of the responsibility for its development. We did not want to put ourselves in the position of having the RYC perceived as another *fait accompli,* as a program that was already fully developed, was about to be "imposed" on the community, and was now being presented to "interested parties" for their largely ceremonial "rubber stamp" of approval. It was equally important for us that we learn what the world looked like through each group's eyes, and that we seize the opportunity to work with them (and, we hoped, to influence them) at a point in time when whatever concerns they felt about the RYC had not been reinforced by the experience of being either unaware of the setting's existence or excluded from its planning.

The Initial Approach: Some General Characteristics and Problems With rare exceptions, our initial approach to each group had three major objectives: to inform, to interest, and to involve. Only occasionally were all these objectives reached, and only very rarely during our first meeting with any particular group. More often than not these initial meetings, if at all successful, were helpful in the sense that they succeeded in laying the foundations for a continuing dialogue between the RYC and the particular group involved.[7] Nevertheless, there were particular reasons for our viewing each meeting as a chance to inform, arouse, and involve. To begin with, we made the assumption that the more people really *knew* about the RYC, the less they would be likely to rely on fantasy or fear to "fill in the gaps" of their knowledge. Thus, for example, "informing" a group often involved us

---

[7]We learned very quickly to become somewhat suspicious of any group whose initial response to the RYC was anything more than a cautious and tentative acceptance of the program. More often than not those groups (e.g., local merchants) that seemed initially to be most responsive to the program and gave it their most immediate and resounding endorsement turned out to be the very groups that offered, at best, the least in the way of help and, at worst, the most in the way of opposition. Conversely, it was often the case that groups whose initial reaction to the RYC was highly guarded and equivocal (e.g., neighbors) turned out to be most helpful and supportive community allies.

in a process of helping certain individuals to verbalize many of their conscious (and often unconscious) concerns about the program. In some instances, through the process of providing information we became engaged in discussion concerning the differences between "kids with problems," "poor kids," psychotics, and the "hopelessly crazy." In each case, however, we found that the less we left to chance or ambiguity, the less a group tended to distort what was being proposed.

The goal of trying to "interest" a group was, in the final analysis, more "our" problem than anyone else's, and it was not until we became acutely aware of just how self-defeating our own enthusiasm could be that we were able to modify or "tone down" the definition of what we meant by trying to "interest" a group in the RYC. Let us explain. As must be quite evident to the reader, most of us were "sold" on the RYC long before it became a physical reality. To us it was much more than a project: it was a world that we were creating, a very personal world that symbolized the fulfillment of a number of heretofore unmet needs. In other words, we were "turned on" by the RYC, and, at least early in the game, we tried to generate a similar enthusiasm in all the groups with which we met. Both consciously and unconsciously we were trying to convert the world and enlist every able-bodied listener for our "noble crusade." In point of fact, the opposite was more often the result. Far from winning converts to our cause, our enthusiasm was scaring people away. We often "came on too strong," overpowered our audiences with our excitement, and perhaps even generated guilt in many of our listeners by unwittingly communicating a message that said, in effect: "There's something terribly wrong with you if you don't feel as deeply about the RYC as we do." At other times our enthusiasm was interpreted as "phony," unnecessary, and perhaps even as a "con job." In a fairly short time (and through the sensitivity sessions described in Chapter 5) we became acutely aware of how our attempt to interest people in the RYC was actually "turning them off," and we were able to redefine both what we meant by interest and how we could foster it in others. The result was that we began to deal with each group in such a manner as to convey the message that we were interested in *them*, in *their* ideas, and in *their* impressions, rather than the other way around. It was our job to extend ourselves to others, and not vice versa. In point of fact, we really needed them much more than they needed us, and it was this message that finally engendered interest in the RYC.

With this background, the final goal of our initial meetings with various groups in the community, the goal of "involvement," was approached from the point of view that the more a group felt itself to be a part of the RYC, the greater would be its support of the project in the difficult days to come. Although no formal attempt was made to have any group "commit" itself (and its resources) to the project in any concrete or particular manner, an effort was made to involve at least one person from each group in an ad hoc Community Advisory Board that would meet with the RYC's staff during the time the project was being developed. At times it was possible to capitalize on the fact that certain people from the community were, indeed, uniquely interested in the RYC in the sense that they saw it as a program through which some of their own interests could be realized. Thus, for example, it was possible in one case to "sell" the program to a particular group simply because one of its members was interested in carpentry and subsequently was given the responsibility of helping us set up the woodworking shop that would be located in the basement of the Center. In general, however, the focus in these early meetings was to communicate to each group that it could, if it so desired, have a sense of "ownership" in the prospective Center—that we were both ready and willing to take the question of reciprocity seriously.

Although we met with more than a dozen different groups during the period of time between the writing of the proposal and the day the Center became functionally operative, we shall describe in the remainder of this section our interactions with only three of these groups: the Resident Advisory Committees (RACs), the police, and the mental health professions. We have chosen these groups not because our approach to each of them was necessarily different (we have already indicated that our focus with almost every community group was to inform, to interest, and to involve that group in the RYC), but because each group's concern about, interest in, and perception of the RYC was different in the sense that it was predicated upon a particular history, set of traditions, and hierarchy of values. In describing some of the interactions between the RYC and these groups, we shall attempt to show concretely how the RYC as it finally emerged was influenced to one degree or another by the particular concerns that characterized each group.

The Resident Advisory Committees (RACs)   Long before the RYC came into existence, CPI, through its neighborhood penetration, had stimulated the development of what were called Resident Advisory Committees. These committees, composed of neighborhood residents who were elected for terms ranging from one to two years, functioned in an advisory capacity and, at least at the time the RYC was born, served as consultants to and as channels of communication between "downtown" CPI and the neighborhoods served by its programs. In 1966 there were seven such RACs (one for each of New Haven's inner-city neighborhoods), and while their formation was spurred by CPI's desire to develop some kind of grass-roots involvement in New Haven's poverty program, the RACs themselves (i.e., their lack of power and control in terms of developing, implementing, and controlling various aspects of the poverty program) were clearly a reflection of CPI's understanding of what the term "maximum feasible participation" really meant.[8] Nevertheless, CPI's RACs were generally composed of people who took their roles seriously,

[8]The Ford Foundation (1967), in an evaluation of CPI recently made available, has cited the need for investing local groups like the RACs with the power and capability to develop and administer their own programs. This emphasis on the decentralization of poverty operations even within a single city, and on turning over the power and control of these operations to neighborhood groups (i.e., the poor), represents a significant change in the meaning and interpretation of the term "maximum feasible participation." In 1966, however, CPI's RACs had no such power, capability, or control. They were, for all intents and purposes, groups whose primary function was to advocate, to advise, and all too often "to consent."

seriously enough to serve without pay and to give generously of themselves and their time in order to have some voice in the determination and development of services for the inner city. By and large these were people who "cared," and the fact that they themselves were often on the "receiving end" of poverty services did not make them a docile, compliant, or silent group. If anything, the opposite was more often the case. They wanted "in," felt that being poor did, indeed, give them the right to be heard, and they rarely hesitated or shied away from "telling it like it was."

Our meetings with the RACs were rarely quiet or "polite" affairs. Although the early sessions seemed calm enough, as soon as the RACs became aware (and convinced) that we were not asking them merely to "rubber stamp" a finished product, the RAC members became much more vocal, and at times they even appeared to be using the RYC as a convenient vehicle for expressing many long-smoldering feelings that they could not verbalize with respect to other projects in which they had played a largely ceremonial "consulting" function. In the long run, however, the RACs were among the most helpful of the many community groups with which we became involved.

If there was anything about which the RACs were adamant, it was that the RYC never be established as an "institution" or come to view itself as in any way isolated or insulated from the neighborhood in which it was located. Specifically, they were quite concerned that the RYC might easily be perceived (and eventually perceive itself) as a "correctional" institution rather than as an "opportunity program" combining residency with manpower and skill training. To avoid this situation, they suggested (and we quickly accepted) that in all our contacts with community groups we stress the fact that although the RYC would house 20 youngsters, its programs (both evening and weekend) were open to any and all teen-agers in the community. In addition, they felt it important that we make clear our feeling that the RYC be viewed as a "community center," and that we back this up by offering the RYC as a facility to any neighborhood groups in need of a place to meet.

We shared the RAC members' concerns regarding the importance of the RYC's never becoming an "asylum" in the Goffmanian sense of the term, either to itself or others. Many of us almost instinctively reacted, even overreacted, to the word "institution" by immediately (and perhaps unfairly) conjuring up the picture of a place whose impregnable walls served to perpetuate a life of oppressive regularity and depressing conformity. Consequently, in order to guarantee "movement" and accessibility, the decision was made that, unlike Job Corps, no "pass system" would be employed to restrict the mobility of residents and no "visiting hours" would be established to limit the accessibility of the RYC to "outsiders." The Center was to be "open" 24 hours a day, and both residents and nonresidents could come and go as they pleased. The attempt to "deinstitutionalize" the RYC before it ever became an institution had its lighter moments and, as the following example illustrates, was sometimes carried to extremes which, if not corrected, could have had adverse effects on the program.

Example 2: August 1966.
Well, last night we finally picked out the colors for the kids' rooms, and I'll bet my year's salary that no "institution" ever looked the way ours is going to look. Actually, I'll bet no institution ever even picked out its colors the way we picked out ours. I'd better backtrack a bit.

Last night we had a staff party out at my house. It wasn't just a party; it was a PARTY. The whole staff was there and most of the people brought their wives. We invited John, the RYC's landlord and contractor, and he also showed up. Actually, there were two reasons for inviting John. In the first place, he's been working just as hard as the rest of us and he looked like he could use an evening of relaxation. In the second place, we've really been running a little behind schedule. We had planned to have the colors for the house already picked out by this time, but, for one reason or another, we've never gotten around to deciding on what colors to paint all the rooms. John's men, on the other hand, are just about ready to start painting the place and we felt that we could take a few minutes out from partying to go through his color charts and decide on what colors to use in which rooms.

As it turned out maybe we should have taken those "few minutes" *before* the party really got going rather than when we finally decided to do it. To make a long story short, we were all pretty crocked when we finally got around to picking out the colors. Sue had made a real fine punch and some of the staff had brought along some of their own stuff to add to it whenever it looked like we were running low. By the time we all got around to selecting colors for the RYC I doubt whether any of us could have told the difference between red and blue. Well, we finally settled on a bunch of different colors, and after looking at them today (in the cruel light of the morning-after-the-night-before), I can only laugh again.

Now we've been spending a lot of time in staff meetings lately making damn sure that the RYC never becomes an "institution." As far as the colors for the house are concerned, we all agreed to stay away from the institutional grays and greens. Well, we sure as hell don't have any drab grays and dull greens. We've got "bitter-sweet orange," "lavender mist," "sunflower yellow," "Parisian blue," and "oyster-shell white." The white is fine—but the other colors are kind of weird, to say the least.

Less than two months after the RYC opened its doors to its first 20 residents, only one of the rooms retained its original colors. One youngster, after seeing for the first time the colors that had been used for the rooms, especially for "his" room, went over to his worker and said, in no uncertain terms: "Look, Jack, I'll live in a yellow room; I'll live in a blue room, I'll even live in an orange room. But I'll be goddamned if I'm ever gonna put my parts down in no purple room." The real point, however, was that in the process of satisfying our own needs (i.e., the need to keep the RYC from looking anything like an institution), we had violated one of the cardinal tenets of the setting: the principle of involving the residents in any and all decisions affecting them and the RYC. In point of fact, by excluding the residents from the decision-making process, we were doing more to make the RYC into an institution, in the most serious sense of the term, than if the Center had been painted gray or green; we were acting as autocratically as any group of "keepers."

In addition to offering suggestions concerning the overall orientation of the RYC, the RACs had a definite hand in helping us locate and decide on the building that would house the program. They, perhaps more than we, were acutely aware of the "image" or "reputation" that would inevitably precede the RYC regardless of where it finally found a home. Consequently, using their own knowledge of the "character" of different neighborhoods, they were able to facilitate the process of finding an appropriate setting by directing our attention to those neighborhoods where they felt we had a chance of "making it." Each of the neighborhoods they suggested not only was a neighborhood whose racial composition was such as to increase the probability of "accommodation" but was also a neighborhood that would fulfill our desire to locate in a setting that was both in the inner city and accessible to (within walking distance of) other inner-city neighborhoods.

After much deliberation—and not a little second-guessing —it was decided to try to locate the Center in what is known as the Dwight Street area of New Haven. During the 1920s the Dwight Street area was known as one of the more substantial middle-class neighborhoods in New Haven. Its population was overwhelmingly Jewish, and some of the city's "first families" lived there. Although some of the area's original families began leaving the neighborhood for the suburbs in the 1930s, the neighborhood remained a fairly "stable" one until the war years. Most of the people living on Dwight Street owned their own homes, and many of them worked or ran businesses in or near the neighborhood. During World War II the "character" of the area began to change. White "transients" moved into the fringe areas surrounding the neighborhood and, over time, began to take over more and more of the area and get closer and closer to what might be called the "hard-core" middle-class families that remained in the neighborhood. In the 1950s Negroes began moving into the neighborhood, and the "transient" fringe area began to become the dominant characteristic of the neighborhood. With the passage of time, more and more of the "original" families left the neighborhood and the setting was, in a sense, "turned over" to the lower- and lower-middle-class whites and blacks who remained. Today, a substantial part of the Dwight Street area is scheduled for redevelopment or rehabilitation. Of the people currently living in the neighborhood, 60 percent are white and 40 percent are black. The whites tend to live on or near the "main drag," while the blacks occupy most of the houses located on the side streets of the area. The Dwight Street area itself lies midway between two other inner-city areas called "the Hill" and "Dixwell." The Hill is an area made up largely of white (predominantly Italian) and Negro people from the lower and lower-middle classes; Dixwell is predominantly a black ghetto made up of people whose incomes are similar to those of the people living in the Hill.

As for the building that now houses the RYC, it, too, has an interesting history. The building, a large 15-room Victorian house set on a corner of two of the main streets of the area, was originally a single-dwelling home. For a long time only one family occupied its premises. When the "character" of the area first began to change, the building was converted into a boardinghouse. During the war years the building underwent a sort of elegant revival and became, at least for a short time, one of the city's better "houses of pleasure." After the war, however, the building began to fall into "disrepute" (the author should be allowed his share of poor puns) and disarray, and it became a rooming house for transients. When the RYC took over the building, it was both dilapidated and "worn-out," a house rich in history but poor in plumbing.

Once a neighborhood had been picked out and a house located, the RACs turned their attention to the problem of helping us make the transition from meeting with community groups that had little to do with the specific area in which we would be located to meeting with residents who were now living in the immediate neighborhood that housed the RYC. Since at least a few of the RAC members lived in "our" area and would now be among "our" neighbors, they were able to identify those neighbors we could count on as "friends," those who would have to be "won over," or those who had "enough skeletons in their own closets" as to cause no trouble at all regardless of what they thought about the project. Their last and perhaps most important function was to introduce us to many of the residents in the area and to use themselves and their reputations as symbolic "collateral" in order to facilitate our acceptance into the neighborhood.

Once we had been introduced into the setting and given a certain amount of tentative backing, we kept in mind what we had been told by the RAC members who knew the neighborhood and its people and began our own canvassing operation. It was still at least two months before the RYC would become operational, and the time was used for "casing the joint," making initial contacts with specific individuals, and setting up a host of meetings (not dissimilar from those already held with the RACs) with local residents. These meetings were not held in any CPI facility but were held purposely in a setting with which the local residents were familiar and in which they felt comfortable (i.e., a local church). It was important that "we" come to "them" and that the meetings be held on what was, at least at that point in time, "their turf." Because of the prior information given us by the RAC members, we rarely went into these meetings "cold": we already had some ideas concerning who would say what, the nature of some of the specific concerns that would be raised, and what we might do in order to head off or prevent certain problems. The following is an example, admittedly a successful one, of just how important some of this prior information really was.

Example 3: September 1966.

It may well be too early to say for sure, but at this point it looks as if we've just about got Mrs. B. "sewed up." If we have, indeed, succeeded in winning her over, it could be a very important victory for the program. The long-range effects of having her with us rather than against us are hard to calculate at this point, but one way or another I'd feel a lot more comfortable with Mrs. B. as an ally (or even as a neutral) than as an enemy.

(*Note:* Long before we ever became involved with Mrs. B. we had been "warned" about her by a number of people from CPI and the RAC. She was, or so we were told, a "most difficult person" to work with. There were several reasons for this. To begin with, Mrs. B. was not known for her love of CPI. She had her own conceptions and ideas about poverty and, more important, about why some people were poor and what should or should not be done about it. Still more important, however, as a long-time resident in the Dwight Street area she had been able to amass a considerable amount of power and influence among the local residents. Consequently, although she had no "official power," whenever she was confronted with something that CPI contemplated doing in her area with which she did not wholeheartedly agree, she could mobilize a good deal of public opinion and sentiment. Finally, by virtue of her years of residence in the inner city, Mrs. B. had direct access to and knew how to use those with some degree of official power (e.g., aldermen, civic and religious leaders) in order to get them to support her own particular views and complaints.)

The first time we met Mrs. B. we saw nothing, either in her behavior or her views, to contradict what had been said about her by some of the RAC members. She was, indeed, highly skeptical about the RYC (even more so when she found out that it might be located in "her neighborhood") and did little to discourage the notion that not only would she "let us know, loud and clear" what her views and concerns were, but that she would also *act* on the basis of these views. What *was* striking, however, was that in the process of letting us know where she stood, she also communicated a message, albeit indirectly, that went something like: "I'm not only threatening you, but I'm trying in the only way I can to let you know that I am 'available' if you take the time and trouble to read between the lines of what I'm saying." We, in turn, responded far more to the invitation part of her message than to its manifest content.

There then began a series of meetings with Mrs. B. At no time during these meetings was any attempt made to change Mrs. B's "public stance" about the RYC. If anything, we tried to convey to her that it was specifically *because* she was "against us" that we wanted her to "monitor" the operation, be available to criticize it, and let us know exactly what from her point of view could or could not be done. Clearly, however, in order for Mrs. B. to fulfill her functions as our "official critic" she had to be available to meet with us several evenings each week, and this, in turn, implied that she would have to commit a good deal of her spare time to the project. She accepted these conditions more than happily and never missed any of the many evening meetings that were subsequently set up.

The meetings with Mrs. B. were largely informal in nature, often involving only Mrs. B. and one or two of the staff. Over a period of time we were able to get to know Mrs. B., get to know her in a way that enabled us to begin to understand some of the reasons behind her "public stance"—reasons that had as much to do with her unmet social needs as they did with her own particular political philosophy.

To begin with, Mrs. B., a white woman in her early sixties, has lived in the neighborhood for many years. During that time she has seen many of her friends leave the area. More recently, death has taken others with whom she was close. She no longer works full time and has a lot of time on her hands. Her husband, a man several years older than she, does very little except stay at home and watch television. She is, in short, a proud person, a woman whose life (once so active and filled with people) has become increasingly empty and devoid of meaning. She wants and needs attention, and seems to fill at least some of these needs through her activities in the community. To be sure, her stance vis-à-vis CPI may indeed be based, at least in good part, on some genuine philosophical and political differences between herself and the agency, but one can't help but wonder (and marvel) at the degree of visibility and attention she receives not only because she opposes many of CPI's programs but also because of the manner (oftentimes the vehemence) with which she pursues her opposition.

Perhaps we were seducing her, cultivating her, or manipulating her; I don't know. I'd like to think that we were offering ourselves and the RYC as a vehicle through which she could begin to fulfill her needs. One way or another, the interest we showed in her and the attention she received from us fostered the development of a close and ultimately helpful relationship.

Perhaps the most important single event, the one that may very well have helped us "turn the corner" with Mrs. B., occurred when we found out that she was an ex-librarian who maintained an interest in libraries. We have offered her, and she has accepted, the responsibility of setting up an RYC library from the many books that people and agencies have donated to the Center. That's why I now think that we may have reached a point with Mrs. B. where she no longer sees us as "CPI" but rather as a program in which she has a place and through which she can derive some important personal gratification.[9]

As we have already indicated, the overall focus of our meetings with neighborhood people was not discernibly different from our approach to the RACs. In both cases the attempt was made to inform, interest, and involve people in the developing project. With specific reference, however, to our meetings with the people living in the neighborhood in which the RYC would be located, what was added to the "formula" was the attempt to share with them some of the problems that the program might create—*before* these problems ever occurred. Thus, for example, long before the RYC ever became operational, we knew (or at least believed very strongly) that once we opened our doors and took in our first 20 residents a "period of adjustment" would take place during which certain problems would inevitably occur. We could anticipate that the "noise level" in the neighborhood would rise significantly, that "strangers" (i.e., some of our youngsters' friends from other parts of the city) would begin hanging around the Center, and that the lights in the house might be burning at all hours of the night. We shared these expectations with the people, tried to help them prepare themselves for it, and in general attempted to provide them with an appropriate framework within which to view these events if and when they occurred. We knew that we could never fully anticipate or prepare people for the variety of problems that would both beset and emanate from the RYC, but we could, at least in these meetings (and through the

[9]Mrs. B. completed her work on the RYC library long before the Center was ready for occupancy. Once the residents moved in, however, we discovered that one of the youngsters was interested in books and wanted to find out how libraries were put together. We told Mrs. B. about this and introduced her to the boy. In time she became his "part-time worker," spent many evenings at the RYC with him, and used the boy's interest in books as a way of developing a rather good relationship with him. This was a youngster whose relationship with his mother left much to be desired, and at least for a time he was able to relate to Mrs. B. and to find in her many of the things he could not find in his interactions with his mother.

creation of the Community Advisory Board), begin to create a climate of trust and communication.

The Police To say that the police have a particular and uniform (no pun intended) view of the world and that the world, in turn, has an uncomplicated and clear view of the police is to make a statement that is at once both appealingly simple and hopelessly inaccurate; for whatever truth there is to the statement resides in the fact that the police, no different from the RACs or any other community group, are perceived and perceive themselves as occupying a certain position in the community and playing a certain role in the conduct of its affairs. Beyond this, however, it becomes increasingly difficult to form any useful or meaningful generalizations other than to say (at least from our experiences) that the more we became involved with the police, the more impressed we became with the diversity and complexity that characterizes this particular community group.

As was the case with respect to the RACs, our initial contacts with the police took place several months before the Center opened. One of the RYC's staff members, a man who had spent 17 years on the force, laid much of the groundwork for these meetings, and he was able to help us prepare for them by giving us a picture of how the "world" looked through the eyes of the police. He stressed (as the following example will indicate, quite correctly) that the police, perhaps more than any other group having community responsibilities, are among the last people to hear about trouble or potential trouble and the first to be condemned when it occurs. This, he felt, was one of the primary reasons for much of the mistrust and suspicion that existed between the police and a variety of different community groups. In other words, by being deprived of the possibility of acting in a preventive manner and by continually being placed in the position of having to react to crises already "in progress," police were being "helped," albeit unwittingly, to evolve the sort of image of themselves and others that made genuine cooperation and mutual trust highly unlikely. That the problem of

police-community relations is far more complex than we have indicated needs no elaboration, but from the point of view of those of us who felt we had to initiate some sort of dialogue with the police, it was a helpful point of departure.
Example 4: June 1966.
It looks more and more as if Chip was right. Today we had our second meeting with the police and I think we all came away feeling a lot more comfortable with each other. Our luncheon session with Lieutenant A. of the Juvenile Division and Lieutenant B. of the Vice Division started off cordially (if a bit guardedly) and ended in an atmosphere of, I think, genuine relaxation.

Much of the conversation that took place seemed to bear out Chip's description of the police as a group of people who, despite their individual differences, share the feeling that as a group they are rarely consulted about or involved in a problem until *after* a serious blowup has occurred. More than in any of our meetings with other groups in the community, I felt that the police genuinely appreciated our coming to them with the RYC before, as Lieutenant A. put it: "We have to meet 'downtown' rather than in a restaurant." Lieutenant A. went on to illustrate his point by telling us about the time that a man with a gun had been seen registering at the YMCA. No one bothered to call or inform the police about the situation, although a number of people were aware that something was brewing. Lieutenant A. didn't specify exactly why the police weren't informed, but he implied fairly strongly that it had something to do with the way most people view the police and the role they play in the community. At any rate, it was only after the man had started shooting up the place that the police were called and came into the situation. He was livid; it concerned him that people were more willing to risk injury to persons and property than they were to call the police at a point in time early enough for them to prevent the development of a serious, even fatal situation.

I guess the only really sticky part of the meeting came up after Lieutenant B., testing (I think) our willingness to "cooperate" with the police, asked us if we would allow him to place an informer at the Center if he felt that such action would help him keep tabs on the teen-age narcotics traffic in the city. We tried to explain to him that were we to consent to his request we could not in all honesty run the house the way we wanted; that such an act on our part would be both antithetical to the goals of the setting and injurious to the relationships we hoped to establish with the residents. I'm not at all sure he was happy with our response, but he didn't press the issue.

One of the concrete results of the meeting was the spelling out of the "basic rules" of the RYC. Residents coming into the house will be told that there are four rules. They are: (1) No drinking on the premises; (2) No narcotics, drugs, or glue sniffing; (3) No guns, knives, or other "hardware" in the house; and (4) No girls allowed above the first floor. We tried, although I think unsuccessfully, to make the point that we hoped the residents themselves (through the development of their own House Council) would take the primary responsibility for making most of the rules that govern the house, and that consequently we would not confront them with too many rules (most of which we were sure they would interpret as arbitrary and unfair) so early in the game. The police were more than mildly dubious about the wisdom or effectiveness of this arrangement, but they went along with it as an "interesting experiment."

Over a period of time, and given this chance to meet in a "non-crisis-oriented" fashion, we were able to present the RYC and discuss its problems in an atmosphere that could facilitate, if not guarantee, accommodation. Under these conditions the police, now somewhat more relaxed and less defensive (as we were), proved to be very helpful. To begin with, given what they felt was the potentially "explosive" nature of the setting, they were able to suggest certain strategies for avoiding premature publicity. Thus, for example, they suggested that we "go slow" and "soft-sell" the RYC with respect to the news media. From their point of view, any kind of premature or unnecessary public visibility could only hurt the program both by putting increased pressure on the residents and by creating an essentially unhelpful "fishbowl" atmosphere for the setting as a whole. In addition to helping us with our "public relations," the police, especially those in the Juvenile Division, helped us gather much of our necessary research data by opening their records to us and by allowing us to use their files in compiling the histories of many of our youngsters.

More than anything else, however, our contacts with the police served to create the conditions under which we could begin to appreciate the complexities as well as the ambiguities of each other's world. Archaic and mutually held stereotypes were no longer the only basis for a relationship: the police were no more the unthinking and insensitive extension of the "system" than we were the "mollycoddling" and liberal extension of academia.

The Mental Health Professions   The story of the relationship between the RYC and the mental health professions is an example of a situation in which the gulf between people with common sympathies but divergent philosophies can be greater and, in the long run, more difficult to bridge than the gulf between people (e.g., the RYC and the police) who initially perceive themselves to have both divergent sympathies *and* divergent philosophies. Unlike our meetings with the RACs and the police (meetings that, as we have already indicated, were often characterized by a good deal of initial suspicion and mistrust), our encounters with members of the mental health professions were always cordial and harmonious. But also, unlike our meetings with other groups in the community, very little was ever accomplished and no substantial or meaningful collaboration ever grew out of these meetings. We ended as we began: united in our goals but divided by our conceptions of how to achieve them; a classic case of two people with a similar view of heaven but very different conceptions of how to get there.

The initial reception accorded the RYC by members of the mental health professions was very much like the welcome of an embattled and overburdened warrior for a new and obvious ally. We were both fighting the "good fight," and initially, at least, this was enough to guarantee some sort of immediate kinship. That this kinship did not last or, more important, that it did not develop into anything resembling a "united front" is symptomatic of just how far any of us in the helping professions are from having defined or evolved a community role for ourselves that is at once both consistent with our traditions and responsive to the needs of a changing society. This is neither an indictment of nor a rationalization for the failure of the RYC and the mental health professions to develop a mutually satisfying relationship; rather, it is, as the following example illustrates, a statement of the situation as it currently exists.

Example 5: September 1966.
We met today with a number of psychiatrists, psychologists, and social workers from the New Haven area. Unlike our meetings with other groups in the community, it was they (the people from the mental health professions) who extended the initial invitation rather than the other way around. It was quite a change to feel "wanted" as opposed to having to present ourselves in such a manner as to be "accepted." Unfortunately, we came away from the meeting with the feeling that either we, or they, or both of us, were "successful" in changing the atmosphere from one of "being wanted" to one of "being tolerated." The reasons for this state of affairs are probably many and varied, but I can't help but feel that the way I handled the situation had a lot to do with it.

To begin with, I should point out that most of the people who attended the meeting were themselves already involved in one or another aspect of "community psychology and psychiatry." In other words, we were among "friends," among people who had already accepted the fact that the mental health professions, if they were to meet their social responsibilities, would have to begin to reorganize and reorient their ways of functioning. Many of the people in the room were already engaged in the development or implementation of new programs of service for the inner city. Consequently, our initial reception was not unlike the reception one "soul brother" might extend to another. They were interested, receptive, and supportive before we ever said one word about the RYC. Maybe I should have stopped right there and quit while we were still ahead.

Anyway, after the preliminary introductions had been made, I began by describing the RYC (i.e., its basic philosophy, orientation, and structure) in as much detail as possible. I told them about our "horizontal structure" (contrasting it, most unfortunately, with the "team approach"), described sensitivity training, gave them a rundown of the backgrounds of some of the youngsters we would be working with, and ended by sharing with them our intention of giving nonprofessionals the complete responsibility of working with a youngster and his family.

Before I could even finish the presentation, I began to feel a distinct change in the "climate" of the room. Questions (or more precisely, arguments) were raised regarding almost every point I had raised. The concept of horizontal structure was ripped apart as "inappropriate" for a setting whose staff was composed of people with different amounts of formal training; serious questions were raised about the advisability of entrusting nonprofessionals with the responsibility of making clinical decisions; concerns were voiced about an "institution" whose leader seemed so determined to share his power with people knowing so little about the intricacies of personality theory; and doubts were voiced concerning the kind of "treatment" that would be provided to youngsters having such long-term problems (and whose diagnoses were so serious) as our youngsters had.

For my own part, I responded to these questions and concerns by becoming more and more defensive, challenging assumptions, prodding people to produce "hard data" to back up their points, and generally assuming the role of an angry advocate. It was not only a poor performance but also one, I think, that kept adding fuel to the fire.

The meeting ended, thank heavens, soon thereafter. The chairman made a few summary remarks and gave us the usual "God be with you" blessing. We left as quickly and as gracefully as possible.

The months that followed showed a gradual but by no means total rapprochement between the RYC and the mental health professions. Thus, for example, we accepted their offer to make their treatment services available to any RYC residents who wanted to see someone on a one-to-one basis.[10] At times it was possible for individuals from both the RYC and the more established helping agencies to work closely with one another, but this was always done on an individual basis and it never became an integral part of either setting's program. In general, however, the feeling that prevailed was that there was enough work for everyone, and, since we could not agree on any common strategies or processes of help, it was best that we go our own ways.

It is difficult, even at this point in time, to assess what part

[10]One of our original hopes was to explore the possibility of an RYC worker and a professional clinician collaborating in the treatment of an individual; but fears raised by professionals concerning "confidentiality" made this impossible. We had also hoped that the RYC might become a training facility for psychiatrists and social workers entering the field of community psychology and psychiatry, but this, too, never materialized.

"personality factors" played in the development of the events just described. To be sure, our initial response to the concerns raised about the RYC by members of the mental health professions must have contributed some "noise" to the system. At the very least it served to create an unhelpful polarity between the views of the RYC and those of the other helping agencies. But to focus solely on questions of individual personality would, we believe, be directing attention to only a small part of the total variance. Any attempt to understand the situation completely would, as we have already indicated, necessitate a much more thoroughgoing analysis of the theoretical and historical conflicts that grip a profession when it begins, even ever so slightly, to change.

The RYC and Its Residents and Families

Pride! If they had little else, if poverty and despair and alienation had deprived them of most other things, it had not robbed them of their pride; and it was to this lingering sense of pride (this inherent and universal need for respect) that the RYC would have to direct its efforts if it was to develop any meaningful relationships with its potential residents and families. The decision to orient the program in this particular manner was not an accidental one, nor was it predicated on any naïve, idealistic, or ivory-towered view of man: it was a decision based on the feelings and recollections of people (i.e., the staff), many of whom had already experienced and knew only too well what it was like to be poor, what it was like to be treated as if self-respect, pride, and hope were no longer essential parts of one's being. The reader will recall (see Chapter 5) that Scotty put it in such a way as to make us all more acutely aware of how our attempts to offer help might be viewed by our youngsters. He said:

"Don't do something *for* me; do it *with* me. Don't *give* me anything; let me *earn* it. I've got *Pride*, baby, don't take that away from me."

As was the case with most of the decisions made during the period of time before the RYC was ready to open, the "pride decision" had a number of consequences for the development of the program. The most important of these was that the RYC, instead of being developed as an "assistance," "support," or "therapeutic" program, was defined as a "self-help" program and was presented to potential residents and families on that basis and that basis alone.

The Focus on Self-Help Without doubt the concept of self-help can and does mean different things to different people. For the RYC it came to mean that the criteria usually employed in defining a relationship (i.e., what am I offering and what can I expect to receive?) were no longer either viable or relevant dimensions when applied to the problems of individual growth. It meant, for example, that growth takes place in the context of a series of transactions between people, and that under these conditions self-help was little more than a reciprocal process in which at least two people (the "helper" and the "helped") could, and should, expect to change as a function of their having "been" with each other.

Concretely, however, the initial decision to develop the RYC as a self-help program led to a number of subsequent decisions, all of which sought to define (sometimes even in operational terms) what self-help really meant. To begin with, it meant that the RYC was a voluntary program;[11] that a youngster could leave the program whenever he wished and would not be bound by any formal contract or, as is the case in the Job Corps, by any financial inducements, subtle or otherwise.[12] It also meant, however, that the RYC was not a program of "handouts"; that a youngster was expected from the very beginning, to "pay his way" in the form of weekly

[11]The "voluntary" nature of the program has become a continuing source of concern to the RYC's staff. Is it, for example, a truly voluntary program when, as is now so often the case, a youngster in trouble (i.e., picked up by the police) is given the "choice" between the RYC and a state correctional institution?

[12]Every youngster, even after his entrance (physically) into the Center, was told that coming into the RYC did not commit him to staying, even temporarily. A procedure was worked out whereby a new boy was not formally placed on the RYC roster until one week after he was already living at the Center. That first week was set aside or "reserved" as the period of time during which the youngster could "try the setting on for size," sample its programs, meet the other boys, and decide whether or not he wanted to give the RYC a "full shot."

rent.[13] And finally, it meant that a youngster (together with his worker, hopefully) would set his own goals, that these goals need not be the same as anyone else's, and that they were not immutable or "forever goals."[14]

Contrary to the way in which it was usually presented to different segments of the community, the RYC was never presented initially to its potential residents and families in a "group" setting. Rather, it was left up to the individual worker (i.e., the staff member who had decided to work with a given youngster and family) to make the initial "connection" with a family, involve himself with them, and use his relationship with them to "prepare" them for the group situation in which they would meet and begin to work with other families involved in the program.[15] The rationale behind this

[13]It was, of course, the staff's hope that a youngster's rent would be paid out of wages received from some job or job-training program. In the beginning, however, we often found it to be the case that a boy would "make his rent" not by working but by conning or gambling other boys out of their money. Needless to say, whoever youngster was making his rent *that* way would hear about it from those members of the staff whose boys were being fleeced. This "hearing about it" from other staff members often provided the particular worker with the "extra motivation" (i.e., "The next time your kid cons my kid into a card game and gets all his money, I'm gonna take it out of *your* check") to get his boy into an "honest" work situation.

[14]A procedure was developed whereby every youngster, after he had decided to stay at the RYC, sat down with his worker to set certain specific goals for himself. These goals included a discussion of such issues as the youngster's estimate of how long he might be at the Center, what kinds of vocational plans he had for himself, and where, in general, he saw himself going after he left the RYC. Although these goals were understood to be only "exploratory" or "tentative" in nature (they were almost always revised in one way or another during the youngster's stay at the RYC), they did help a youngster and his worker by providing them with a common frame of reference to use as a "jumping-off point" during the youngster's RYC career.

[15]A rather simple procedure was developed through which cases were "assigned" to workers. Whenever the RYC became aware of a potential client, the staff would hold a disposition meeting. At this meeting the client's file, usually obtained from the referring agency (e.g., the Welfare Department, CPI, or the police), was read, examined, and discussed. Then, rather than finding out who had an opening and could take another case, the question was asked: "Who is 'turned on' by this case? Who either knows this kid or sees something in the situation that makes him want to work with the case?" Invariably, at least one staff member would find something in the situation to excite him and make him want to work with the youngster and his family. It was on this basis that a case was "assigned." The assignment, however, was understood to be a temporary one, and, as sometimes happened, a

procedure was a simple one: given what we assumed would be the initial distrust with which many potential clients might greet the program, it was felt that one person (presumably someone already committed, in one way or another, to that family) would have a better chance and be more effective both in presenting the program to a particular family and in handling whatever problems arose in relation to it. Only after a family already knew about the program and had begun to build a relationship with their worker were they asked to meet with other families in order that they might get to know one another and help in the development of the program.

Since, as we have already indicated, the RYC's definition of self-help was predicated on the assumption that people could share their concerns as well as their aspirations, it was possible to approach residents and families from the point of view that unless they were willing to participate with us in the development of the setting, unless they were willing to share *our* problems, the program would, indeed, be little more than another "welfare program" disguised as self-help. This message itself had both symbolic and concrete implications. On a symbolic level it meant that not only for moral but for very practical reasons, we could not and would not relate to our "clients" in terms of the stereotypes that all too often had come to characterize the relationships between the "haves" and the "have nots," between those offering help and those receiving it. Neither would we, for example, "buy" or perpetuate the image of our clients as a group of people who were dull, dependent, or deranged. Similarly, we would not present ourselves as people who were always sure of what we were doing or, indeed, convinced that we even knew exactly what had to be done. On a concrete level it meant that our clients, if they agreed to participate in the development of the RYC, would not only have to have a stake in its future but would also have to accept the responsibility

---

youngster and his worker could decide that due to any number of reasons (e.g., personality conflicts) a "switch" could be made. The overall goal, however, was to assign cases not on the basis of openings in a worker's case load but on the basis of a particular individual's interest in a youngster and his problems.

that inheres in a sense of ownership. Thus, for example, if they were to participate in the decision-making process, they would also have to involve themselves in the everyday or more "nitty gritty" problems confronting the RYC. The following is an example of what direct involvement by staff and clients meant during the days before the Center became operational.

Example 6: August 1966.
If nothing we ever do from here on turns out "right," we'll have last night to remember as a time when all the pieces suddenly fitted together and all the ideas finally made sense. It was a beautiful evening, just beautiful; but before I go off on another one of my adjectival rhapsodies, let me back up a bit and tell the story as it happened.

Even though the RYC is still a long way from being ready to begin formal operations, we have been working with our kids and families as if we already had a program. Our major goal has been to try to involve them directly in the development of the Center and by so doing to convince them that the program is indeed as much "theirs" as it is "ours," that it needs their ideas, and that its success depends on how they see the program and what they are willing to put into it. But up until last night it was mostly words—ours and theirs; now I think we've gotten beyond the words.

For a long time now we had been looking for a way in which we could demonstrate, in a very concrete manner, at least two things: first, that we are not another "handout" program; and second, that we both want and need the people with whom we will be working to develop a stake in the Center as a whole. Well, oddly enough, the fact that our budget is a relatively small one made it possible for us to begin to accomplish both things. It happened in the following way.

When we began to order furniture for the RYC, we all soon became aware of the fact that our "furniture budget" was really pretty small and that unless we were willing to buy a lot of secondhand stuff we would soon use up all the money in that category. The staff was opposed to buying secondhand stuff, so we had to sit down and figure out another way of furnishing the house. Well, to make a long story short, somebody (I think it was Lance) came up with the idea that if we built or made some of our own furniture we could save enough money to make sure that one way or another everything in the building would be new (furniture that we built was defined as "new"). A quick look at the budget confirmed Lance's estimate, and after only a little discussion it was decided to do it the way Lance had suggested. Someone else (I don't remember who) then came up with the idea that this making of furniture was tailor-made for involving the parents and youngsters in the program; that it was a concrete and specific activity that would enable them to feel a part of the RYC. Again, the idea met with almost immediate approval. All that remained was for us to figure out what furniture could be built in a relatively short time and how to present the idea to our youngsters and their families.

Both problems were relatively simple ones to deal with. As far as the furniture was concerned, we called Frank ("our" architect) and he quickly came up with a design for a homemade bed. He showed us how, by using different sized pieces of wood and only 16 screws, we could, in almost no time at all, build a bed frame. Then he volunteered to help our youngsters make these beds—so that was that. Then one of the people who has been volunteering time with us came up with the idea that she could get curtain and drape material donated by a local merchant and that the mothers of our boys, along with some of the wives of the staff, could probably make the curtains for the whole Center. The idea quickly took shape: the boys could build their own beds and their mothers could help make the curtains for the Center. It sounded right.

We then had a meeting with the boys and their families and told them both about our problem (the limited budget) and about the idea (that the boys build their beds while their mothers made the curtains). Their reaction was mixed. The boys were gung-ho for the idea, but their mothers were somewhat less than enthusiastic. The more we talked about it, however, the clearer it became that the lack of enthusiasm on the part of some of the mothers had nothing to do with their acceptance of the idea, but was related to the fact that many of them did not know how to use an electric sewing machine and, consequently, felt that they could not help in the project. Some of our wives came to the rescue. They described how easy it was to learn to use a machine, related some of their own experiences in learning how to sew, and gradually convinced the mothers to give it a shot with the clear understanding that if worse came to worse they could all do the sewing by hand. All that remained was for us to arrange to use CPI's Skill Center (a facility developed by CPI for training and remedial education), a place that had both the sewing machines we needed and the woodworking shop in which we could cut and fit the pieces for the beds. This was quickly done, and last night we had our first session of bed-making and curtain-sewing.

As I said before, it was just great. The kids were in one room learning how to make beds, while their families (mostly mothers and sisters) worked in an adjacent room making the curtains. Even a few fathers showed up to lend a hand. A number of the staff's wives were there and they brought coffee, soda, and doughnuts to keep us going.

It's difficult to describe the atmosphere at the Skill Center last night. People were laughing, kidding each other, and the air was filled with a kind of joyous informality. Oh, there were a few problems. We had to take a couple of kids out of the room because they started fighting over who was going to use a certain screwdriver first. One mother got a bit dis-couraged over not being able to learn to use the sewing ma-chine as quickly as she had hoped. In both cases, however, we were able to avoid any real problems. In general, every-one (especially, I think, the staff and their wives) seemed to feel relaxed and involved in something that was both fun and satisfying. More important, however, was the obvious delight that *everyone* took in being able to work on something to-gether, in being a part of something, and in beginning to ex-perience a sense of competence and participation. To be sure, it's only a beginning, but at least last night was an important first step. Mostly, I think, because our youngsters and their families are beginning to trust us and believe us when we say that we want to work *with* them and not *for* them.

The Decision-Making Process In addition to the kind of direct staff-client participation described in the previous sec-tion, the attempt was made to develop a vehicle through which both residents and families could become involved in the RYC's decision-making process. Thus, for example, long before the RYC ever became operational, the parents of our youngsters were approached in terms of the formation of a Parent Group, a group that would meet every week at the RYC.[16] We hoped that these meetings could serve both as a

[16]As indicated elsewhere in this and other chapters, the youngsters living at the RYC were all members of what came to be called the House Council. This council, it was hoped, would provide the residents with the mechanism through which they could begin to participate in the actual running (i.e., developing policies and programs, setting rules) of the Center. In time, the House Council and its members also became interested in and established their own sensitivity sessions in addition to participating in the discussion of house problems and RYC

vehicle through which the parents could be continually informed as to the progress and problems of the Center (and, we hoped, could make suggestions and initiate programs to aid the RYC) and as a setting in which they could get to know one another, perhaps discuss their common concerns, and explore one another's problems. Basically, however, the particular form the Parent Group finally took and the role it would play in the affairs of the RYC was left up to the parents. All we hoped to communicate at this early point in time was that the RYC was not interested in separating parents from their children, in isolating parents from the setting, or in assuming the position of having taken over the parents' legal or moral responsibilities for their youngsters.

In general, however, and as will become clearer in the experiences to be described in Chapter 7, the most important single element in our early relationships with residents and families was just that: that they occurred early, *before* the program was ready to begin; that they began at a point in time when people could share in the development of a setting, and when relationships could be evolved in the context of solving problems that were both concrete and of mutual concern. Under these conditions the program could develop more "naturally" or more organically (maybe even more honestly) than would otherwise be the case. Moreover, and as the following example illustrates, the problems of transition that inevitably confront any new program could be dealt with much more openly.

Example 7: September 1966.

Last night's meeting with our kids and families turned out to be a much more complex and, hopefully, productive affair than I think any of us anticipated. Naturally, as is the case with most of the things that have been happening, it's much

---

"business." It should be pointed out, however, that the resident House Council was not established until after the RYC was already a physical reality. This decision and the reasons for it represented a calculated risk on the part of the staff and, as events turned out, a bad one. In Chapter 7 we shall describe some of the problems that beset the RYC when it finally became functional. In retrospect, it appears as if some of these problems might have been avoided (or at least handled more quickly and effectively) had the House Council been in full operation prior to the day the RYC opened.

too early to tell what kinds of long-term effects last night's meeting will produce; but for the time being, at least, I think we all have a much deeper appreciation of how much further we have to go before we achieve the kind of staff-client trust that we all want.

The meeting was called because of all the problems we've been running into trying to get the Center started. Originally, the RYC was supposed to be renovated and ready to open on August 1. Then it was supposed to open on August 15, then August 21, and on and on. Now here it is, almost the middle of September and the damn place still isn't ready to take in its first residents. With every delay, with every pushed-back opening date, we've been put in the position of going back to parents and saying: "Sorry, next week. Next week for sure." After a while it began to look like some kind of pathetic comedy: we'd show up and before we could even say anything the parents would nod their heads, give us the "what-is-it-this-time?" look, and tune us out.

I guess part of the problem has to be traced back to our own naïveté and lack of experience with this sort of business. Up until now I think we've all lived in a world in which when someone says he'll have something ready on the first of the month, we expect it to be so. But I guess we've learned that the world of renovations and contractors just doesn't always work that way. It seems as though new problems, something to cause another postponement, crop every day.

Anyway, it got to a point where we were actually embarrassed to face the kids and parents. Furthermore, it became almost impossible to have a staff meeting without one of the staff bringing up the feelings of the kids and parents he was working with with respect to the effects of all of these delays on his relationships with them.

About a week ago, after the fourth or fifth postponement, we (the staff) sat down to try to figure our way out of the mess that our own enthusiasm (coupled with the delays in renovations) had created. After some discussion and after a number of suggestions had been turned down (e.g., threaten not to pay the contractor unless and until he was able to finish his work on the building by a certain date), Chip was able to put the problem into the kind of perspective from which we could evolve some way of dealing with the situation.

Chip's overall approach to the situation was to view it as another opportunity for involving our clients in a problem, for leveling with them and asking their help, rather than as a situation calling for any further camouflaging behavior on

our part. Once he had defined the problem in these terms—
in terms that were more consistent with our overall orientation with respect to our clients—it became relatively clear
what should be done.

The decision was made that we would show our youngsters and parents what was going on; that we would bring
them to the unfinished house, go through it with them, and
discuss with them the kinds of problems (e.g., plumbing,
painting) that were holding us up. We also decided that since
it was already clear that a number of our kids and parents
had a host of feelings about the situation, it would be a good
idea if, after taking everyone on a tour of the house, we all
got together in the living room and discussed whatever feelings people had on the subject.

Well, last night we did just that. We all picked up "our
case loads" and brought them over to the RYC. Each one of
us took our kids and families on a tour of the house, pointed
out the problems, shared with them our own disappointment
and feelings about the situation, and finally returned to the
large downstairs living room.

Once we were all assembled, I, together with some of the
other staff members, began a discussion of the problem by
reiterating our own feelings about the situation, especially
those having to do with how we must have appeared to the
kids and parents when, as had already happened several times,
we kept putting them off and promising that "next week for
sure" we would all be in the building. With only this as a
point of departure, the parents and youngsters, most of whom
it appears had been sitting on their feelings for some time,
really opened up and told us some of the things that had
been going through their minds.

The discussion soon became something like a chorus of
feelings. They told us how the situation had led them to doubt
our sincerity, how it had made them begin to feel that the
program was little more than another empty promise, and
how, as was so often the case in the past with respect to other
programs, they had begun to question the very purposes and
goals of the program. Several parents took turns, sometimes
even cutting one another off or interrupting one another, to
relate their past experiences with what they termed "so-called
help programs." Over and over again the same picture
emerged: that they had been misled, misinformed, or treated
as if every bit of help was like some gift from heaven, a gift
not to be questioned and one that could be withdrawn whenever it was decided that they were no longer sufficiently co-
operative to suit the "gift giver's" purposes.

For most of us the experience was more than a little moving. Despite what might be called the overly dramatic and totally one-sided picture that we were getting, several things were quite clear. To begin with, as a group it appeared that our parents shared a certain view of themselves, especially in relation to helping or assistance programs. They saw themselves as numbers rather than as people, as pawns who could be manipulated and moved in accordance with some prearranged design over which they had no control and little if any choice. By virtue of being poor they felt themselves to be at the mercy of people. But most of all they were furious that this type of relationship was rarely if ever defined for what they felt it really was. As one mother put it: "It wouldn't be so bad if people came right out and said you're no good and never will be. But they keep smiling at me, keep giving me my check, and keep acting as if that's the way it really is. But they never say it, leastways never to my face. But you get to know it, you get to feel it just the same."

What had begun as an attempt on our part to level with our kids and their parents, to share with them some of the problems we were having in getting the RYC ready, had become a situation whose history extended much further back in time than any of us (at least any of us on the staff) had realized. The feelings that were being brought up went back a long time, probably as far back as the time when the people first began their histories of involvement with public assistance agencies. To be sure, and this bears repeating, what we were hearing were the voices of anger and despair, voices that may or may not have been reflecting the world as it really is. But that's the way they see it and at least at this point in time, no "hard data" are going to suffice to convince them otherwsie. For us the situation signified a number of things. First, that we were (and probably still are) defined as enemies until we prove ourselves to be otherwise. Second, that we took a major step in that direction by having the kind of meeting we had tonight. And third, that we sure as hell better not forget what we learned tonight. We either go all the way with this orientation of involvement and participation or we cut bait and stop trying to fool ourselves and others.

The RYC and CPI

Although funded by the Department of Labor, the fact that the RYC was to be administered through New Haven's community action agency meant that the program would, for all intents and purposes, be joined to and become a formal part of the organizational structure of CPI. It was to be another program in CPI's "umbrella" of inner-city services, and, as such, it not only would be expected to coordinate its particular functions with other CPI programs (e.g., Neighborhood Youth Corps, Neighborhood Services) but also would be responsible, both administratively and in terms of basic policy, to what had by that time already come to be called "Downtown CPI." From the very beginning, then, the RYC was confronted with the reality (indeed, the necessity) of developing its program in such a manner that it remained true to its own objectives while at the same time responsive to the needs of its "mother organization." It was a situation in which the RYC (as is the case with any program that either develops within or is grafted onto an existing or established agency) would have to deal with the problems of independence and autonomy, on the one hand, and accommodation and coordination, on the other.

The point we wish to emphasize is that the situation was in no way atypical with respect to the RYC. It was an entirely "normal" situation, one that every new program must face if it wishes to use its preoperational period of life as a time in which to develop effective mechanisms for intra- and inter-agency cooperation. With specific reference to the RYC and CPI, however, what complicated the situation was the fact that the organization of which the RYC was to be an integral part was one whose general understanding of itself as an organization—whose basic "life style" as it were—was no longer consistent either with its own early history or with the goals of the RYC.[17] As pointed out previously (see Chapter 4), CPI in 1966 was in many important respects a very

[17]Without trying to belabor a point, we wish to stress the fact that our description of CPI (its orientation, processes, and patterns of help) should by no means be interpreted as implying that as an organization CPI had changed its basic commitments to the poor or to the development of innovative helping services for the inner city. What we are describing is a situation in which these basic and genuine commitments had become encapsulated in a host of organizational concerns and bureaucratic problems, problems whose effects were both undermining the goals of the program and sapping the staff of the strength and will it needed to pursue them.

different organization from the one we had known three or four short years before, and rather than describe in repetitive detail how or why the organization had changed, we shall list what were, at least from our point of view, some of its major characteristics as well as some of the areas in which difficulties between the RYC and CPI might be expected to occur.[18]

The Horizontal Setting in a Pyramidal System By 1966, CPI was, in both the best and worst sense of the term, a relatively well-established organization. Its organizational chart had become fairly complex and it was replete with clearly demarcated lines of communication, well-specified areas of responsibility, and highly defined limits and ranges of authority. People knew what they were expected to do; their roles were neatly spelled out; and patterns of communication and interaction had become highly routinized. On the one hand, things were less sloppy: there was less overlapping and duplication of functions and less wasted effort. On the other hand, things were less exciting: there was less individual freedom in the definition and performance of one's job, and people, especially those occupying positions toward the base of the pyramid, felt increasingly removed from the decision-making process. By and large, there was an ever-increasing gulf between administrators and "front-line troops," a greater reliance on memos as mechanisms of communication, and a diminution of personal contact between people occupying different positions of status and responsibility in the organization.

Under these conditions, it was clear that the RYC, especially

[18]As was the case with respect to the term "community," it should be clear that in referring to "CPI" we are not implying that the organization as a whole or everyone in it formed a single and homogeneous unit. Although the organization, in general, had undergone a distinct change over the three- or four-year period of time during which we were affiliated with it, many individuals and even some parts of the agency itself were both aware of these changes and actively involved in trying to "right" the organization from within. Thus, no differently than was the case in our description of the community, CPI even in 1966 was not composed of individuals all of whom either shared in or had accepted the changes that had beset the organization. There was not, in short, the kind of consensus that one would need to feel comfortable in referring to CPI "as a whole."

with its horizontal structure, might be perceived as a setting whose ways of doing things were out of step with the rest of the organization. Its emphasis on the sharing of administrative and clinical functions, the deliberate effort to blur both role and job distinctions, and the orientation toward the development of interpersonal accessibility and openness were in many ways antithetical to CPI's view of itself and how it could best fulfill its service responsibilities. In short, over and above the kind of temporary dislocation that any new program creates for its mother organization, the existence of a horizontal subsystem within a pyramidal superstructure was bound to create certain difficulties and exacerbate others.

The Professional-Nonprofessional Issue CPI in 1966 was an organization which, while not dominated by "professionals" (i.e., people with "proper" credentials in the fields of human service), had certainly adopted or been forced to adopt attitudes toward service that were characteristic of most treatment institutions. Thus, for example, most clients were "cut up" in the sense that a variety of different people, each one presumably with a particular and circumscribed area of competence, had a "piece of the action" and a portion of the responsibility for what happened to the client. Any youngster in the work crew (Neighborhood Youth Corps) program, for example, might have a foreman, a neighborhood worker, a vocational counselor, and a social service worker, each of whom was responsible for his "piece of the action"; and each in turn was responsible to "his" particular supervisor. In most cases, even with respect to a particular youngster, "treatment decisions" were generally made not by those who "knew" or had extensive contact with the individual but by people who either occupied higher status positions in the organization or had superior professional credentials. The functions of the nonprofessional, though continually exalted and pointed to with pride by administrators, had been severely limited and curtailed, especially when compared to the role they had played four short years before.

By contrast, the RYC was predicated on two assumptions, the first of which was that more effective service was based not on cutting up the client but on providing him with one person (a "creative generalist," if you will) to whom he could relate, someone who would be able to assume the total responsibility for working out with the client a particular course of "treatment." The second assumption was that the most appropriate person to assume this clinical responsibility was the nonprofessional. Under these conditions, the program's focus would have to be on the development of people (i.e., the staff) rather than on the development of special or ancillary services.

The Consequences of CPI's Success Finally, CPI in 1966 was an organization whose success had begun to be translated into a need to perpetuate the agency and its people. Although it was an understandable and, in some ways, inevitable consequence of success, this need to perpetuate its own existence had resulted in the organization's becoming, on the one hand, increasingly isolated and insulated from the community and from criticism, and on the other, less pliable and changeable from within. The need for personal advancement and security had to some degree replaced the collective pursuit of excellence, and the development of "minor kingdoms" had in some measure siphoned off much of the energy that in previous years had been directed toward "changing the world," however impractical and impossible that might have been.

The RYC, by contrast, was conceived of as an organization which, if successful, would be in a state of continual though (hopefully) controlled change. Given its commitment to self-reflection and self-correction (see Chapter 5), the RYC was founded not on the principle of self-perpetuation in the narrow sense of the term but on the premise that basic organizational change in the service of human development (even the kind of change that would eventually and inevitably put an organization "out of business" or transfer its control to others) was a preferred way of life. Furthermore, as was the case during CPI's earlier years, one of the RYC's primary goals was to use itself and its own setting as a vehicle for changing other community agencies. The grandiosity of its goals notwithstanding, the RYC in 1966 was much more like the CPI of 1962 than any of us were aware. Yet this very similarity between the RYC and the CPI of a bygone era could, unless handled effectively, create more problems than it solved; for it could confront the mother organization both with a picture of itself as it had once been and, by extrapolation, with an image of what it had become.

As might be surmised from this, our approach to CPI during the RYC's preoperational period of life differed from our approach to other community groups in at least one important respect: we knew more about the organization and had had more firsthand experience with the agency than was the case with other segments of the community. CPI was no stranger to us and, even in the beginning, we were no strangers to CPI; and although familiarity offers no guarantee of acceptance (witness our experiences with groups representing the mental health professions), it does insure a reasonable degree of initial contact. The following example summarizes the nature of those initial contacts and describes some of the ways in which our prior knowledge of the organization was helpful during the early days of the RYC.

Example 8: October 1966.
In going over my notes I found that nowhere have I kept as good an account of our early meetings with people from CPI as I did, for example, with respect to other groups in the community, like the police or the RACs. I don't know why this should be the case, but it is. So now, while I have the time, I'll try to summarize what these meetings were like, at least in terms of my memory of them.

To begin with, I think almost everyone in CPI "knew" about the RYC long before we ever presented the program in any formal, meeting-type way. News travels fast at CPI, and, like any organization, the grapevine picks things up almost as soon as they happen. Besides which, people must have known about the program, even if they didn't know exactly what it would be like, simply because they knew I was interviewing people for the staff.

At any rate, our first formal meeting about the RYC took place at the semiannual CPI Manpower Conference. Twice each year the Manpower Division (the Division in which the RYC is located) of CPI meets to review programs and to keep "the troops" informed as to what's happening. CPI's Director of Manpower felt that this meeting would be an appropriate time for us to present the soon-to-be RYC.

Our presentation went off fairly well. We described the RYC in as much detail as possible, considering the limitations of time and the size of the gathering. It was clear from the very beginning, however, that the sheer number of people present (about 150) would make it difficult to present the program in a way that would enable or encourage people either to discuss their feelings about the program or make suggestions as to how it might be developed. What I do recall, however, was that even at this first and obviously preliminary meeting there seemed to be a greater immediate acceptance of the program and its concepts (e.g., horizontal structure, sensitivity training) by people who might be labeled as the rank and file, as opposed to those occupying administrative or supervisory positions within the organization. Because of this, as well as some of our feelings concerning the future of the program within CPI, we tried to do only two things at this Manpower Conference: to inform people in at least general terms about the RYC's overall content and structure; and to make it quite clear that we viewed this meeting only as a start, and that we would be following it up with further meetings to be held with smaller groups or subdivisions within the organization.

From that point on, Scotty and I made it our business to visit each and every subdivision within CPI. Although I couldn't swear to this, I think we probably visited about a dozen CPI settings within the next three weeks. Thus, for example, we visited each of the five Neighborhood Employment Centers, two sections of Unified Social Services, the work crew and remedial education programs, the Community Action Institute, and so on.

It was, indeed, at these smaller, more "intimate" meetings (there were rarely more than 15 people present) that we could get down to brass tacks. I'm sure that the fact that we (certainly Scotty and I, at least) felt more comfortable with a smaller group had a lot to do with it. At any rate, it was at these meetings that we were able really to go into detail about the program, invite people to participate in its development, and seek to involve people in its problems. What became increasingly clear to us was that to some people the RYC was a threat, while to others it was something of a hope.

Perhaps the most important aspect of our early contacts with the various subdivisions of CPI was the extent to which

some of our prior experiences in the organization were helpful to us in the sense of making us acutely aware of some
of the prevailing attitudes and sentiments within the agency.
For example, we knew that given the current status of the
organization, few people would perceive our calls for "cooperation and communication" as genuine unless we provided them with a viable mechanism within which this might
take place. Consequently, we went into each of our meetings
with a CPI subdivision with a concrete proposal. We invited,
sometimes almost insisted, that each group elect or appoint
one of its members (independent of his or her status within
the particular subgroup) to be on a special or ad hoc RYC-
CPI Advisory Board. This Board would work closely with the
staff of the Center and could function both as a vehicle for
the sharing of information and as a source of ideas for and
criticisms of the RYC. This advisory Board was formed and
proved to be more than a little helpful to the RYC, especially
during the hectic and tension-ridden days that followed the
formal opening of the Center.

The decision to follow up our initial presentation of the
RYC at the Manpower Conference with this series of smaller
meetings was also based on the assumption that we had no
guarantee that we would be understood simply because we
had described the program one time. Being able to go over
the program more than once with a group of people enabled
us to deal with some of the distortions and misinterpretations
that were generated by our initial description of the program.

In addition to using our "CPI meetings" for purposes of
explaining, describing, and interpreting the program, these
early contacts helped us develop specific referral processes.
Rather than bypassing existing "flow" processes and developing new ones (an act that would certainly and with great
justification be interpreted as threatening to existing procedures), it was decided that the RYC would depend on other
programs within CPI (e.g., Neighborhood Youth Corps, the
Neighborhood Employment Centers) as its major referral
sources. It was also decided that a member of the referring
agency within CPI would always be present at, and would
participate in, the disposition meeting held at the RYC at
which the decision concerning the new referral would be
made. At no time, except in an emergency (i.e., if a youngster were thrown out of his house or if a boy were found
sleeping in a hallway) would the RYC make a decision concerning a new referral without having the benefit of additional counsel from someone within CPI who knew the particular youngster.

In summary, our goals with respect to CPI were no different from any other community group or agency. In all cases we hoped to use this preoperational period of time to involve people in the RYC. With CPI, however, the pursuit of these goals had to take place in the context of what we "knew" rather than assumed about the organization. And what we "knew" was not only that people would perceive and react to the program differently but that their particular perceptions and reactions would have predictable consequences for the development of the program. This, coupled with the fact that we had a fairly good idea as to who would or would not support the program, enabled us to focus our attention and direct our efforts at certain people and in certain ways. Now, with the Center open and functioning, we can look back and see a number of ways in which we could have used those sessions more profitably. But still, those meetings were important, and if they didn't solve all of our problems with CPI, at least they didn't leave us totally unprepared for what was to come.

In this chapter we have tried to describe some of the more important events and decisions that influenced the development of the RYC prior to the time it became a physical reality. Our primary purpose was to convey to the reader just how significant a program's preoperational period of life is in determining the present and future history of a setting. And since, as we have already indicated, the problems that confronted the RYC during its early phases of development were, in principle, no different from those that might confront any newly emerging setting, one might assume that the problems described have some significance for any thoroughgoing analysis of the question of how one introduces change into an ongoing social system. In this respect the present chapter should be viewed as a preliminary attempt to define and describe some of the basic issues confronting those of us who are engaged in the problem of the creation of settings.

Despite the importance of what we have called a program's preoperational period of life, it should be clear that no amount of preparation or planning is ever enough to guarantee that a program will run smoothly once it actually opens its doors for business. In the final analysis, however, it is during the period of time before a new setting becomes operational that its creators have the opportunity (and a rather unique one at that) to begin to appreciate and to experience rather directly the enormous complexity of their undertaking. And to the degree that this experience is a sobering one, to the degree that it enables one to surrender the myths concerning a program's "real" date of birth, to that degree it cannot help but prepare one for the days that lie ahead. In our next chapter we shall describe those days.

Chapter 7 The Doors Open

War talk by men who have been in a war is always interesting; whereas moon talk by a poet who has not been on the moon is likely to be dull.

—Mark Twain

It was mid-September and a late summer sun hung limply, covering the afternoon sky with a warmth as yet unchallenged by the chill of approaching night. After what had seemed like innumerable delays—some justified, others not—the RYC was ready to receive its first group of residents. In Chapter 6 we explored some of the issues that confront a setting *before* the day it becomes "officially" operational; in this chapter we shall describe the problems and conflicts, both administrative and personal, that beset a program *after* it has become a functional reality.

If, as we have tried to indicate, it is a myth to assume that a setting is born on the day it opens its doors, so, too, is it a myth to presume that there is anything like being "adequately prepared" for the moment a program finally ceases being "preoperational" and begins that phase of its life in which it assumes a "public" existence. It is a situation not unlike the one confronting a couple on the day before and the day after the birth of their first child. Life is drastically and irrevocably changed once the child emerges from the womb and declares its being with its first shrill breath of greeting. In both instances no amount of preparation ever seems "adequate" or sufficient to enable one to cope with the myriad problems presented by the new arrival.

Once again, as was the case in previous chapters, we shall focus attention on the opening days of the RYC for a variety of related reasons. To begin with, these days were, in and of themselves, important ones—important in the sense that they held a deeply personal significance and meaning for those of us who had been a party to the development of an idea, had witnessed its gradual evolution and transformation, and were now presiding over its emergence as a reality. Moreover, the crises that occurred during those early days, how they were handled, and the effects they had both on the program in

general and on its people (the staff) in particular merit some
kind of public awareness. In addition, as we have already indicated, the creation of a setting is a complex human process,
a process involving motives, values, ideas, and emotions, and
a process about which we know very little. This being the
case, the present chapter (no different from the last) is an
attempt to provide some of the descriptive data that might
facilitate the kind of theory construction through which the
problem of the creation of settings can be understood and
approached from something other than a purely "individual-
artistic" frame of reference. Finally, it is during the early days
of a new setting, during the days when almost everything
that can possibly go wrong usually does, that one finds oneself in the rather unique position of asking the kinds of questions (and, at times, even coming up with what seem like
reasonable answers) that have relevance in terms of future
research. In the case of the RYC, this meant becoming
acutely aware of the more general implications of such problems as action, leadership, and bureaucracies.

For purposes of clarity, this chapter has been organized
into two parts. The first involves a detailed description of life
at the RYC from the day it opened its doors to the time, some
two weeks later, when most of its staff felt that the setting
might "survive."[1] The data for these descriptions are all taken
from the Director's diary of events covering that period of
time.[2] The second part of the chapter draws upon these data

[1]We shall be describing the RYC during that period of time in which
its existence was most precarious and when its days were filled with
intense conflict and constant turmoil. It should not be assumed, however, that because our description ends on a note of having survived
this "period of adjustment," the succeeding days and months were free
of problems. As we have already tried to indicate, if there is one thing
that can and should be taken for granted, it is that a setting, so long
as it is truly viable (and sometimes even when it is not), will never
be conflict- or problem-free. In Chapter 10, therefore, we shall review
some of the problems and concerns that continue to confront the RYC
even now, some 18 months after its birth.
[2]After some soul searching and with more than a few reservations, it
was decided that if we were to use as data the Director's diary of
events, this material should be presented in its original form. As is the
case with all such data, names and places have been changed. We
should point out, however, that as is true of most personal documents,
this diary constitutes but one individual's perception and interpretation

and uses them as the basis for a preliminary and retrospective analysis of some of the issues (e.g., leadership, action, and organizational structure) inherent in the problem of the creation of new settings.

The Opening Days

Day 1: 9/16/66.
Well, now it begins; and if the weather (sunny and mild) is any kind of omen—one looks for omens at a time like this—then the RYC will prosper. Danny (the Supervisor of the work crew program) has promised to light a candle for us in church this evening. We thanked him and told him that while he was at it he might as well light two of them just to make sure.

The process of moving into the Center did not, thank goodness, go according to "plan." We had originally hoped to have all the kids move into the house as a group. As it turned out, however, because of the fact that each staff member had to work out a different schedule of picking up his kids, the kids (almost all of whom were accompanied by either a relative or a friend) moved in at different times of the day. Consequently, moving in went much more smoothly and took place in a much more leisurely way than we had anticipated. Each boy had a chance to move in with his worker and with the help (and attention) of someone close and familiar to him.

For most of the kids moving in involved much more than just toting a few suitcases into the Center. For example, each kid had to work out some kind of arrangement with his roommates and worker to make sure that his bed got into the house. Since all the boys built their own beds at the Skill Center, the beds had to be lugged over to the house and brought up to the rooms. The same was true of the lamps they built. Consequently, the process of moving in was a fairly complex and time-consuming one. There were at least two reasons for our wanting this to be the case. In the first place we're hoping that if moving in involves work, hard and tiring work, then the kids will be pretty pooped by nightfall and won't have too much energy available for raising the kind of hell they've "promised" (or threatened) to raise to-

---

of reality as he experienced it. As data of an autobiographical nature, they suffer from the same limitations (e.g., lack of psychological distance, limited perspective) as do most intensely personal documents. They do, nevertheless, convey a rather detailed picture of the RYC during its most stressful period of time.

night. In the second place, simply because there's a lot of heavy work involved in moving the furniture into the RYC, we thought it might "force" the kids to begin to work together, especially to cooperate with and begin to know their particular roommates. It was really something to see the way Jack had Cliff and Wayne working together to move in their stuff. Here are two kids who, unlike most of the other kids, really "know" each other, and this knowing each other hasn't (at least up until now) resulted in any undue feelings of warmth between the two of them. Maybe it's because of the ways or the conditions under which they've gotten to know each other: in psychiatric centers, jails, and mental institutions. At any rate, Jack really had them hopping, and whenever it even began to look as if they were going to start something, there was Jack standing between them, just as calm, cool, and collected as ever, with a little smile on his face as if to say: "Now come on fellas, you're not gonna spoil a nice day like this with that silly-ass stuff." They didn't.

The RYC stands on a big corner lot, and there's lots of grass surrounding the house. But today you could hardly see the grass for all the wooden beds scattered around the grounds. Turns out that most of the kids didn't feel their beds were really finished or had enough of a "personal" touch to them. Consequently, most of the kids brought some paint or stain with them today and decided it would be a good idea to finish off their beds before taking them into the house. What a scene! Twelve beds, no two of them in the same position, being painted or drying, and scattered all around the house. Looked like some psychedelic wooden quilt being sewn together by a dozen tailors, none of whom wanted anything to do with the others.

When it began to get dark, and after most of the kids were about as "settled" as you could expect for a day of moving, Chip managed, I don't know how, to prepare (I think with some help from a few of the mothers) a really nice buffet. There were trays of cold cuts, some deviled eggs, sliced bread, pastries, Kool-Aid, and hot coffee. It really went well and we all gorged ourselves, especially the kids. I'm beginning to believe all those stories about the "drinking problem" that a number of our kids are supposed to have. Except that in this case what they were drinking was as "American as apple pie"—tons and tons of milk. It got so bad that we had to run out twice to buy more of the stuff.

As soon as dinner was over the kids took off, leaving the rest of us with the job of cleaning up what had begun to look like a disaster area. The dining room was really a mess, and it took us about an hour to get it cleaned up enough to suit Chip. I can't say we really minded, though. It was good to get rid of the kids for a while; it had been a long day, a day of apprehension as well as anticipation, and it felt good to be able to relax, even if relaxing involved clearing tables and cleaning up the dining room. It also gave us a chance to have a relatively quiet cup of coffee with some of the parents before taking them home.

After the parents had been taken home, we (the staff) all kind of sat around not saying very much. I think we were all thinking our own private thoughts because it was just that kind of time—a time for personal musing, reflection, and fantasy.

On my part I know I was thinking a helluva lot about what we'd already been through and what the future might be holding in store for us. For example, we're all pretty sure that the next few days (maybe weeks or months, I don't know) are going to be pretty rough on all of us. We've already discussed the possibility of the kids really blowing off steam, what it would mean, and how we might handle it. The new setting, the unspoken impact and meaning that it holds for each kid, the phenomenon of strangeness that's bound to affect each kid somewhat differently—all these things, complicated as ever by the reality of "individual differences," promise to make life "interesting" at the very least. But in addition to all this, I fear that this "period of adjustment" will be even more stressful than expected because of the numerous delays that have forced us to keep changing the opening date of the RYC. We, as well as the kids, have had continually to stop, start, and stop again: hopes have been raised only to be dashed as the RYC was not ready for occupancy. I guess we could say, if pressed, that these delays were used well (i.e., to increase the involvement of the kids and the parents in the developmental problems of the Center), but one way or another I have the feeling that these disappointments may well have created the kinds of feelings that will come back to haunt us. Even now, the very day we're moving into the Center, the RYC isn't really finished. The outside painting isn't done, the bathrooms aren't all finished, even some of the kids' rooms need work done on them. But we felt that we couldn't wait any longer; and for the record let it be clear that the decision to move in today was not a unanimous one. Some of the staff still feel strongly that we should have waited until the facility was really completed and ready for occupancy.

We also know that we're probably in for a period of rather

intense "testing," a period of time during which the kids will undoubtedly test each staff member as well as each other. A "pecking order" will be established, people will be maneuvering for position, and everyone, each in his own way, will seek to impose some sense of personal order on this as yet rather unstructured setting. It will probably be more than a little interesting and at times even frightening to see the particular form of testing that each kid uses. For some, maybe like Sam, Cliff, Leland, Wayne, and Bucky, this testing will undoubtedly involve some kind of physical violence or challenge. They've almost "promised" us as much and may very well feel honor-bound to follow through with these promises. For others, like Tim, Ev, Marty, and Shorty, those who are weaker and more "immature" than the rest of the kids, it will probably involve some kind of mischief or patience-testing behavior. But one way or another the kids are going to test us, and it will be in our response to that testing that we all begin to define ourselves to each other. The fact that at the present time the house has very little, if any, formal structure (i.e., rules, restrictions, etc.) to it is guaranteed to play into, and in some ways exacerbate, this period of testing.[3]

[3]As indicated in Chapter 6, with the exception of the "four basic rules" (i.e., no drinking in the house, no dope, no guns, knives, or other weapons, and no girls above the first floor), the RYC opened without any other prearranged restrictions. The decision to allow the RYC to open in such an unstructured manner was deliberate and was based on the following assumptions and observations. It was felt that to open the setting with a fairly rigid and extensive set of rules (e.g., curfews, in-house penalties for rule violations) would be at best meaningless and at worst self-defeating. We reasoned that for us to have imposed this kind of structure too early or without involving the kids in the decision-making process almost would have guaranteed that the youngsters would experience it as another dictum, another set of arbitrary laws, handed down from above and, at least from their point of view, without any basis in experience. Consequently, these rules would *have* to be broken simply because they were there and because the process by which they got there was one from which they were excluded. We were gambling that sooner or later the boys would experience the need for additional limits and a greater degree of structure. They were, after all, adolescents, and despite the categories in which they had been placed and through which they had usually been reacted to, they were basically teen-aged kids, adolescents whose manifest desires for freedom are almost invariably accompanied by complementary needs for structure. This being the case, we were hoping that in time the residents would "ask" for this additional structure, either behaviorally or symbolically; and once this occurred we believed that they would either help (through their own governing body, the House Council) to develop and implement these limits or, if the staff imposed these limits, "go along" with them because the additional structure that was imposed would now have some sort of foundation in their own experiences.

And finally, I'm sure that we're in for a time during which we'll begin to be able to evaluate the effects (or the lack thereof) of our preparatory group sensitivity and clinical training.

Interestingly enough, even though all the kids promised when leaving the Center after supper to "stay out all night and not come back," they were all back in the house by 11:00 p.m. They sauntered in very casually and none of us reminded them of their "promise."

Tonight Scotty will stay on duty to help out the "regular" live-in counselors (Vito, Lance, and Clark). Tomorrow night, I'll take it.

Day 2: 9/17/66.
All hell broke loose last night. Came in this morning at 8:00 a.m. to find a bleary-eyed and haggard-looking Scotty. Never realized how bad Scotty could look after a night of no sleep and pandemonium. Lance also looked horrible. But for some reason both Vito and Clark (God bless them) slept through it all.

When I came in, I found Scotty slumped over a cup of coffee and looking down at the table in front of him as if it held some strange attraction that only he could appreciate. When he looked up at me I wasn't sure for a second whether he was going to smile, cry, or belt me in the mouth. Well, he didn't smile or cry, and thank God he didn't smack me in the mouth. He just kind of stared right past me so I figured it was safe to sit down. After ignoring me for about three minutes, he told me what had happened.

Seems that the kids decided that the RYC would make a good 24-hour playground, and they devoted their first evening in the house to testing that assumption. They were up and down the stairs almost all night, laughing, screaming, fighting, playing their record players at ear-shattering volume, and generally trying as hard as possible to topple the RYC through their frenzied activity. Scotty and Lance were like firemen trying to deal with a dozen different fires at the same time. No sooner would it seem as if they had controlled one fire when another would break out somewhere else in the house. It was a losing battle to begin with, and the fact that Vito and Clark were able to sleep through it all didn't help things one bit. Both Scotty and Lance were really pretty pissed-off about the situation but didn't want to make an issue out of it.

Besides the general hell-raising that went on, the night was punctuated by a few specific problems. To begin with, Tim (who Scotty swears he'll kill some day) had the bright idea of lugging the pool table up from the basement and setting it up in the living room. Even though Scotty told him not to bring the table up, and explained to him the reasons why, Tim waited until Scotty was off putting out another "fire" somewhere in the house and then calmly proceeded to get a few of the kids to help him bring the pool table up from the cellar and set it up on the first floor. Tim is like that, a real Dennis the Menace type of kid. He's small, cute and, at least from Scotty's point of view, a big pain in the ass. Well, Scotty almost went through the roof. But just at the point when Scotty was about to do something "drastic," Tim looked up at him, gave him his most angelic "little-boy" look, and completely disarmed Scotty with a thoroughly appealing visage of childhood innocence-prankishness. So, Scotty just threw up his arms, cursed under his breath, and stalked off muttering to himself something about what a crazy job this was going to be.

The kids pulled one other thing that we really didn't expect. It seems that the roof here at the RYC holds some particularly great fascination for a lot of the boys. By climbing out of their windows and straddling the ledge they were able to go sit on the roof and stare into the windows of some of the people who live across the way. The fascination is clear: there's a good-looking girl living across the way and the kids were hoping to get a look at her while she was undressing for bed. Tonight, at least, their quest was in vain. Still, this climbing on the roof is going to be a problem. Not only could it lead to trouble with the neighbors (the kind of trouble we sure as hell don't need), but it's also dangerous, and one false step by a kid up on the roof could be disastrous.

Since the kids were up virtually the whole night, very few of them were able to get up and get out of the house in time to make it to their jobs. We wound up today with about ten kids sitting around the house or lying in their rooms sleeping. One of the staff (Chip, I think) remarked that it seemed as if they were sleeping during the day in order to be fully awake for their evening "activities." Seeing them lying around the house was particularly galling for Scotty. Here he was dog tired after a sleepless night, and there they were, the causes of his sleeplessness, sleeping like little babies while he had to be working his tail off.

At today's staff meeting Scotty and Lance reviewed all the

gory details of last night. We all kind of sat silently, almost transfixed by the catalog of horrors they reported. When they finished, we all kind of looked at each other and tried to play it cool. We reviewed the situation and went over the fact that we "knew" this was going to happen, that we "knew" we were taking a chance by not having more rigid rules, and that we "fully anticipated" the troubles we were now facing. I think that only a part of us really believed what we were saying; that part of us which needed reassurance and looked to the group for that reassurance. At any rate, we succeeded in convincing ourselves that what we were doing (or not doing) was right and that in the long run it would pay off. Despite this, however, I think most of us were more than a little uneasy with the way the meeting went, and I fear this uneasiness will get worse and worse the longer the chaos persists.

Tonight I get to try my luck with the kids.

Day 3: 9/18/66.
It was murder, just plain murder. No matter how much I try I can't find anything even remotely amusing (not to mention hopeful) to write about what went on last night.

The kids decided to stay up all night, and they all damn near did it. From the time most of the staff left for the night until early this morning (around 5:45 a.m.), the RYC was the scene of some of the wildest and, at times, some of the most frightening things I've ever seen. It was like some bizarre circus concocted by a demented ringmaster.

To begin with, as has become almost expected, the kids were all in the house by midnight after threatening to stay away all night (sometimes I wish they *had* stayed out all night). But from the time they hit the Center until early this morning they seemed to dig into their bag of tricks and continually came up with something new, something just a little more bizarre, a little more infuriating, a little more dangerous than whatever had gone on before. For example, Cliff swinging from the light fixtures at 2:00 a.m., in the morning; back and forth, a diabolical gleam all over his face as he threw light bulbs against the living-room walls, laughing as each bulb went crashing into the wall, shattering all those around him with a thin stream of pouring glass. For example, Wayne sitting in the dining room, staring at a piece of buttered bread in his hand, and finally throwing it against the wall to the accompaniment of his own blood-curdling shriek. And later, Wayne again, sitting on the couch,

his head bent low to the ground, spitting all over his bare
toes and giggling some far away giggle. For example, Shorty,
Monty, and Bucky doing a high-wire act on the roof at 3:00 in
the morning. Or Sam, Walt, and Leland surrounding Ev and
taunting him about being "retarded" (I sometimes wonder
at the degree of cruelty, the capacity to hurt needlessly, that
we humans are capable of).

At times tonight it really looked as if at least a few of the
kids (Shorty, Monty, Tim, Marty, Norris, and maybe Walt)
really wanted to go to sleep. But I'll be damned if any one
of them wanted to be the first to break the pattern, the first
to admit his "cowardice" in front of the rest of the kids. Consequently, they too stayed up with the rest of the boys and
outdid themselves in proving their "right" to be considered
one of the gang.

Oh yes, I am now the proud owner of a new name. Today
Shorty let it be known that from now on my name is Golden-
bones or Goldenstones, or just plain Bones for short. Right
now I don't know how to feel about this "singular honor."
Maybe if things were different I'd be kind of proud of this
new name of mine. After all, they call Scotty, "Nose," and
Jack is called "Judo Jack." But somehow, what with all the
trouble going on, I can't get overly excited about suddenly
being "included in" in this fashion. Sometimes, especially like
last night, I'd rather not be around at all . . . ever.

At the present time it seems as if Cliff is emerging as the
kid who instigates most of the more bizarre things going on.
He's really a pretty sick kid with a host of strange behaviors.
For example, it's almost impossible to understand him when
he speaks to you. His speech has an explosive quality to it:
it literally shoots out at you and envelops you in a cloud of
incomprehensible mutterings. Only Jack, his worker, seems
to be able to understand him or make sense out of what he's
saying. For another thing, he's always wearing this crazy white
hat; won't take it off and gets furious if anyone even suggests
that he remove it. He starts waving his arms around, cursing,
and seems to be about to have some sort of seizure. It's a
very frightening thing to see, but Jack tells us to just ignore
this behavior and to literally outscream him when he begins
to have this kind of episode.

Besides Cliff, Sam looks like he's going to be a particularly
difficult kid. At the present time he seems to be emerging as
the "bully-boy" of the RYC. Sam's a big kid with a lot of
meat to him. He's also a kid who seems to expend an awful
lot of energy trying to frighten people with his scowling,

ever-menacing glances. But according to Scotty (his worker), who's known him for a long time, Sam's just a big overgrown bully, a kid who's really a coward at heart. Right now I'll go along with what Scotty says, but to tell the truth I'm not really convinced that Sam's just "a lot of talk." Scotty tells us that the best way to handle Sam is to stand right up to him, challenge him, and make him back away. Maybe that's O.K. for Scotty (Scotty's about 6' 1" and weighs somewhere around 200 pounds), but as far as I'm concerned (me being all of 5' 6 1/2" and weighing 155 pounds), every time I look at Sam I get this picture of him picking me up and breaking me in two. I don't know. I just don't know.

Today's staff meeting was similar to yesterday's except for the fact that everyone seemed much less confident and much more on edge. In trying to describe the events of last night I used the word "exuberant" to explain what some of the behavior was like. It was a poor choice of a word, but it did seem to relax a few people. The staff picked it up, and whenever I detailed another of the things that happened last night the guys looked at each other, smiled, and replied chorus-like: "Oh well, just some more of that youthful exuberance." I have a sneaky feeling that I shall come to regret ever having used that word at all.

Day 4: 9/19/66.
It doesn't look as if the end is in sight. Last night was a repetition of what has now been going on ever since we opened the Center. Butch was on duty to help Lance, Vito, and Clark. I just can't stand going into details so I'll just list what went on.
1. A sink was torn out of the bathroom wall on the third floor. Most of the staff believe it was Wayne's doing but, naturally, nobody's talking.
2. Somebody broke Marty's mirror.
3. During the night Wayne was taken to the hospital with a cut over his eye.
4. We suspect that Tim has been sniffing glue.
5. Someone has been urinating in Ev and Marty's room and defecating in their closet.
6. The kids stayed up just about the whole night again.

It's pretty clear by now that the "in-group" of hell raisers consists of Wayne, Sam, Cliff, Monty, and Shorty. They seem to be the kids who do most of the "organizing" for whatever goes on at night. It's a curious group (three "strong" kids and one "weak" one), but together they seem to be able to keep things at fever pitch for a long time.

Perhaps more than anything else we're beginning to get a "feel" for what each kid is like. So, rather than space this out, I'll try to give a very short capsule description of each kid as I see him.

Tim: A small, tow-headed kid who looks (and acts) very much like Dennis the Menace. Cute, stubborn, mischieveous, and loud. A kid who acts as if he has studied (and mastered) every nonviolent method of irritation as yet devised by man.

Robbie: Quiet, self-contained, and strong. Clearly a follower, but a kid that no one (I think including the staff) wants to mess with unduly.

Curt: A loner. Wears his hair very long, stays out of the house a good deal, and acts as if he wants nothing to do with any of the kids living there. Plays drums, wears hippie clothes, and acts the part of the unconcerned and amused observer of all that goes on around him.

Sam: Big, mean-looking, flamboyant, and menacing. Not a leader but certainly a kid whose participation is sought in any and all goings-on at the RYC. Does not seem to command much respect from the other kids but does seem to be in the middle of everything.

Walt: Comes on like he wants to "succeed" in the worst way but gives most of us the feeling that he's conning. Talks a good game but always seems to come up with some alibi for his involvement in what seem like self-defeating behaviors.

Cliff: A strange, unpredictable, and frightening kid. Difficult to relax with and hard to understand. Violent, upsetting, and bizarre when angry; charming, handsome, and delightful when calm. A boy of rapidly undulating moods, moods that change with no apparent external stimuli.

Ev: Shy, self-deprecating, and painfully targeted for abuse. Acts the role of the incompetent loser, the kid whose only way of being close to people is through self-mocking.

Marty: Another loner. Self-conscious (because of his poor eyesight among other things) and withdrawn. Loves to talk but is rarely listened to. Wants to be with people but seems content with feeling spurned.

Norris: Above it all. A good-looking kid who wants nothing to do with the other boys, but a kid who seems to inspire their respect. Self-confident, arrogant, talented, and independent.

Shorty: Mr. Hollywood. Funny, annoying, and scared. A kid who's "on stage" 24 hours each day; a kid with a talent for discovering everyone's weakness and exploiting it in comical but often painfully accurate ways. A boy who acts as

everyone's mirror in order to avoid looking at himself.
Monty: Big, Stubborn, and moody. A kid who's used to having things his way, and doesn't know how to take no for an answer. Seems to like the Center and uses it as his own personal club.
Leland: Small but probably the most feared kid in the house. Tremendous build and a violent temper. Has great leadership potential but cannot see beyond his own personal well-being. Relates to the staff as another staff member but commands a great deal of respect from the rest of the kids.
Wayne: Perhaps the most bizarre and "sickest" kid in the house. Is alternately violent and charming, out of it and very much with it. Seems to hallucinate actively, especially when his mother comes to see him (she comes every day).
Heinz: Wild-eyed and moody. A kid who seems very frightened of the other boys but almost equally afraid of himself. Talks a great deal about death, almost as if it were a personal friend of his.
Bucky: Big, boastful, and loud. A kid with a big "rep" in town. Seems under pressure to make a rep for himself here. A kid with great talent but even greater self-doubt. Alternately a winner, a loser, and a rationalizer.

Today's staff meeting was perhaps the most disorganized and discordant one to date. Everyone seems to be getting more and more jumpy and less willing to view what's happening in terms of its overall context or long-term goals. We all seem to be searching, sometimes wildly, for some way of dealing with what's going on. At the present time it seems as if we (the staff) have divided up into our own version of "hawks" and "doves." The hawks feel that we have to do something drastic and dramatic (and immediately) to put a halt to the present situation and reaffirm our control of the setting. Some of their suggestions include suspending or terminating the core group of troublemakers, applying immediately a host of "hard" rules and curfews, levying heavy fines on all the kids in order to pay for the furniture and fixtures that have been broken, and organizing a "patrol" to police the house during the night. The doves, on the other hand, have taken the position that the time is not yet ripe for either the introduction of staff-originated limits or the development of a competent resident-initiated set of rules and regulations. Luckily (at least from my point of view), the doves have been able to point to a number of factors that lend support to their thesis that the kids are beginning (but just *beginning*) to realize the consequences of their own behavior and are starting to show signs of almost "asking," at least symbolically, that limits be set. For example, Sam has lost two full-time jobs during the past three days because of his inability to get up in time to get to work. Shorty and Tim have both been sent home from their jobs because they fell asleep at work. Heinz, Bucky, Leland, and Monty have begun to complain bitterly about not being able to get breakfast because of their inability to get down in time in the morning. And Norris has begun to raise questions about wanting to remain in a house "with a bunch of nuts and babies." All these things lead us to believe that while the kids won't come right out and ask for additional structure, they are at least letting us know that they are getting to the point where such structure, if applied by the staff, would not be interpreted solely as a unilateral and repressive act. For the present, at least, the doves have won out.

Today's staff meeting did result in a few decisions that might be helpful. Everyone felt that the live-ins were under even greater pressure than the rest of the staff. Consequently, in addition to the staff member who joins the live-ins on duty each night, it was decided that the rest of us would be considered on duty regardless of the time of day or night. Thus, for example, if Cliff is acting up (as he always seems to be), and if the people on staff do not feel that they can handle him, Jack (his worker) would be called into the situation regardless of whether or not he was "officially" on duty. I use Cliff as an example simply because he seems to be the kid who presents everyone (except Jack) with the greatest number of problems. Although Jack thought the decision was a good one, he made it clear that in the long run he expected each and everyone of us to learn to be able to handle Cliff as well as he can. He felt that if we began to rely solely on a kid's worker to handle a particular kid, we would be creating a situation in which the kids were both denied the opportunity of interacting with a variety of different people and placed in the position of viewing themselves as dependent on a particular person for help. We all agreed with Jack's cautioning remarks, but I for one, perhaps because I find Cliff such a frightening and unpredictable kid, felt relieved to know that Jack was now "officially" on duty all the time.

Even now, when things are so patently chaotic and so seemingly disorganized, one can begin to detect the advantages of having begun to work with the kids long before the RYC ever became a reality. Some of the relationships between kids and their workers are almost things of beauty. For example, Cliff, sitting wild-eyed and furious, "demanding" to see "his worker." Or Sam and Norris pacing up and down the living room waiting for Scotty to come down to the Center. It's clear that most of the kids are "hooked" on their workers, and this being hooked must be seen as the most important single accomplishment to date.

The situation here is, I think, no different from the one usually found in most clinical facilities: not all workers are equally effective with all kinds of kids. Clearly, certain workers seem to work better and to prefer working with certain "kinds" of kids. Thus, for example, Butch seems to do best with kids like Tim and Ev, who are somewhat younger, less mature, and more mischieveous than the other boys. Jack, on the other hand, seems to enjoy working with kids like Cliff, Bucky, and Wayne, who, despite their individual differences, all tend to act out their problems in rather frightening and violent ways. Scotty does best with those kids (e.g., Norris, Sam) who've never really had a father and seem to need a strong and competent male to relate to. I think the same is true of Chip's relationship with Curt. Is it because of "personality," "similar past experiences," or particular "knowledge"? I don't know. Me, I seem to work best with "sociopaths" like Shorty. I wonder what the hell that means? On second thought, maybe I'd better stop my speculating while I'm ahead and before I start getting into questions of personal motivation and personal pathology, which might best be left to another time and another place.

Day 5: 9/20/66.
Another night of the same; maybe a little tougher, maybe not. I was on duty again, and although I try to compare last night with the other night I was here (try, I think, to find some evidence that things are getting better), I can't honestly say that I'm able to discern any differences worth noting. Most of the kids were up the whole night. I don't know how they do it, but they seem to dig deep down and find some package of energy that they still haven't used. And Christ, do they then use it.

Last night the kids decided to give the pool table a real workout. About six of them shot pool from about 7:00 p.m. until the wee hours of the morning. The pool table is down in the basement, but the shouting could be heard all over the house. In addition to playing pool, however, some of the guys (mostly Tim, Leland, and Bucky) decided that the pipes in the basement could be used as chinning bars and they almost ripped the pipes down from the basement ceiling. Also, since we do not as yet have any chalk for the pool sticks, they began using the ceiling of the basement (the plaster) as their source of chalk. The result was that they almost punched a dozen holes in the ceiling. By the time we finally stopped them, the basement floor was covered with pieces of fallen plaster.

In addition to what went on in the basement "pool hall," the rest of the night was pretty "ordinary"; ordinary in the sense that the kids raised hell all night. The hell-raising took its usual form: kids running and screaming through the house; Shorty, Sam, and Monty making it up to the roof to peek in at the girl living across the way; Wayne spitting all over himself and anyone near him; and Norris, Robbie, and Walt coming in at 4:00 a.m. to join the "fun."

I want to take a second to mention two things that happened last night. I think that the reason I want to pause and write about them is because they seemed, at least to me, to be in such marked contrast to the usual activities that now fill the nights here at the RYC.

1. At about 1:00 a.m. Cliff came busting into the Center. He had left the RYC about an hour before to go down to the Toddle House (a local luncheonette) to get a hamburger. When he came back, he was screaming, cursing, and looked about as angry as I'd ever seen him. When he came into the house he was carrying a lead pipe and he began swinging it wildly as he went running around the first floor. When I caught up with him, he seemed almost beside himself with rage. I noticed that he wasn't wearing his white hat and asked him what happened. He exploded into a monologue that went on for about ten minutes. Between his cursing and raving it was almost impossible to understand what he was trying to say, but after a while we were able to piece the story together.

It seems that on his way down to the Toddle House, Cliff had a run-in with a couple of guys on the street. One of them finally took Cliff's hat and ran away with it while the others pushed him around a bit. Cliff then ran back to the RYC, where he dug up a lead pipe that he had buried on the grounds. He took off after them but stopped halfway to the Toddle House and returned to the Center. He was now standing before me waving the pipe and screaming about the incident.

We stood like this for about 20 minutes, with Cliff alternately berating himself for not continuing to go after the guys and cursing me and everyone else who now stood around him. After a while Cliff began to calm down just enough to listen to me. I asked him to give me the pipe and told him that I wanted to know why he came back to the RYC rather than continue on after the guys who stole his precious (and it is for Cliff a very precious) hat. With what almost looked like tears in his eyes he literally screamed: "I'm back because that's my problem; I fight too much and get in trouble. Jack told me to try to cool it, to try to walk away from trouble or come to the Center when I'm gonna blow. Well, I'm back, I'm back. And you tell that motherfucker Jack that I did it, that I came back, that I didn't get in trouble." And with that he threw the pipe at my feet, took a huge gulp of air, and walked away.

2. At about 4:30 a.m. I was sitting in the living room trying to keep from falling asleep. While for most of us it was late at night, a few of the kids were still acting as if it were early afternoon, and they were running in and out of each other's rooms, playing their records at ear-shattering pitch, and making sure that those of us who were on duty didn't forget that they were still up and around. But I guess I was just about too tired really to give a damn any more, and so I just sat in a corner of the living room trying both to remain awake and get some rest.

For some reason it got pretty quiet for a few minutes, almost as if the kids had decided to become a part of the night for a little while. I heard footsteps outside the living room and looked up. There was Leland, barefoot and in pajamas, quietly walking up and down the hall. He was singing very softly to himself:

Born free, as free as the wind blows
As free as the grass grows,
Free to follow your dream . . .

I'm not sure exactly why, but for some reason I got to feeling all tight in the throat and kind of clutched up. Maybe it was because Leland is a black kid and because the words he was singing put it the way it really has to be; maybe because it was quiet for a change and the whole scene appeared so unreal and out of step with things as they usually happen; and maybe it was just because he seemed so totally oblivious of my presence, so much like any other teen-ager who finds himself alone and uses that aloneness in a very private and personal way. I don't really know why, but seeing Leland that way, and listening to him singing "Born Free," well, for a few moments everything made sense, everything seemed right.

The kids had their first House Council meeting today, but things got chaotic and although a few of them raised the issue of setting some rules for the house, the meeting broke up without any attempt to do so. It was somewhat disheartening to those of us who had hoped they would be able to organize themselves.

Our staff meeting today began and ended with the question of when and how to take some action concerning the problem of curfew and the night situation. The doves continue to prevail, but our margin of support gets smaller and smaller each day.

Two more kids have now experienced the consequences of sleeplessness. Leland and Heinz were both sent home from their work sites for failing to pay attention to their jobs. By now more than half of the kids in the house have been affected directly (i.e., have lost money) by the nighttime goings on. Sam is setting the pace: he's now lost three jobs in less than a week because he can't get his butt to work on time.

Maybe the only way to explain how I feel is to say that I'm just plain *scared*; scared that maybe the whole notion of the RYC is wrong, scared that I'm not the right kind of person to be involved in this kind of work, scared that maybe we've all bitten off much more than we can chew. But it's not only that I'm scared. Hell, everyone's scared. It's that I'm scared but go around pretending both to myself and the staff that I'm really *not* scared. That's the really frightening part of it—the loneliness of being scared and not being able or willing to share this fear with the rest of the staff. It's my first (and I hope last) act of deceit. I look around me and see everyone looking scared. Everyone's nervous, and so I say to myself: "You're the Director, so for God's sake don't look scared, don't get panicky and, above all, don't act as if you're unsure about what's happening." It's an act, a lie, and worst of all, it violates all we've tried to accomplish through our sensitivity sessions. Here I am, the Director, the "professional," the guy who spoke so much about openness and trust and sharing. And yet, here I am afraid to level with the rest of the guys, afraid to open up and share with them my own feelings of doubt and insecurity.[4]

[4]Some weeks later, when the RYC seemed to be functioning on a relatively even keel, the Director "confessed" his duplicity to the staff. The staff, rather than getting angry or bitter, accepted his confession and confronted him with the fact that not only were they fully aware of his attempted deception but that they, too, were engaging in a bit of duplicitous behavior of their own. Laughingly, Scotty put it the following way: "Hell, Kelly, what do you think we are, a bunch of dummies? We all knew *exactly* what you were doing. We even had a private staff meeting about it. We knew you were only acting, trying

Day 6: 9/21/66.
Another tough night. By now I'm sure that anyone reading this diary knows that a "tough night" simply means a night that's no different from the ones that preceded it. Besides the "usual" problems, last night "distinguished" itself in the following ways:

1. Another sink was pulled out of the wall. This time it was a sink on the second floor and it caused a mild flood.

2. Shorty, in a burst of "exuberance" (there's that word again), threw a quarter-pound piece of butter through one of the windows of the house standing next to ours. Luckily we got to our neighbor before he called the police and reminded him of all the things we told him about what he might expect to happen during this period of time. He simmered down and wished us well. He's really a very nice guy and sympathizes with what we're trying to do.

3. Wayne got himself thrown out of Gogie's (a restaurant down the street from the Center), and the owner told us in no uncertain terms that the next time Wayne showed his face around the place the cops would be called. I should add that, by and large, shop owners in the neighborhood have been most accepting and understanding of the RYC. They know we're having problems, but many of them were at the meetings we held in the area long before the RYC came into existence and so seem to be extending themselves to us at this point. Despite all the preparation, however, it's interesting to see the distortions and the different ways in which some people in the neighborhood view the Center. For example, I was in one of the local grocery stores the other day when the owner said to me: "Hey, you're connected with that new place up the street aren't you?" After I told him that I was, he said, "Must be tough working with retarded children!"

Even though I'm not officially on duty, I've been coming in almost every night. The reasons are many and varied, but primarily it's because it's so much more anxiety-arousing to be sitting around at home waiting for the phone to ring or wondering about what's happening down here at the Cen-

---

to look so damn calm and cool because you thought that if we saw you acting nervous—like we'd get even more nervous than we already were. Shoot, you couldn't hide it; we know you too well. But we decided that if it made you feel better to think that way, hell, we'd let you go on believing it. We figured that sooner or later you wouldn't be able to stand it any more and, like now, you'd have to come out and talk about it. Welcome home, brother. Now I figure we better have a sensitivity session about the whole damn thing."

ter. At least if I'm down here I can try to do something; sitting at home, waiting, jumping every time the phone rings, or having to imagine what's going on—that's just too much. But I've found out that everyone's that way. This is really quite a staff. You walk in here at 1:00 in the morning and there's Jack shooting pool with the kids in the basement. I say to Jack, "Hey man, what're you doing down here? You're not on tonight, why don't you go home and look in on the wife?" Jack looks up, smiles, and says, "Oh, I just felt like shooting a game of pool with Wayne and Cliff so I came down." Or get ready to leave about 10:00 p.m., and as you're walking out of the RYC you see Butch and Chip drive up. You go over and ask them what they're doing around the Center at this time of night and they say, ever so nonchalantly: "Well, we were just driving by and we figured we'd stop in for a few minutes." And you walk away knowing that Butch and Chip are there for the night even though they're supposed to be off duty. That's the way this staff is, and it's probably one of the few things that keeps us going. I don't know how to explain it, and maybe I shouldn't even try. All I know is that while we've never talked about it, it seems as though everyone has made the same silent decision: "This is *my* place and it's more than a place to work. It's the place I want to be, the place I helped to build, and the place I'm going to make damn sure 'makes it.' " What more can I say? I don't know what the future's going to be like— don't even know if we have a future—but right now I look around me and feel that come what may, this is one very special group of people I work with.

The toll is beginning to tell on more and more kids. Almost two-thirds of the boys are missing breakfast on a fairly regular basis. Tim, Shorty, and Monty are the biggest complainers, insisting that breakfast be served later in the day or at least when they can get down to have some. Naturally, you can imagine the answer Chip gave them. Ev was sent home again for falling asleep at work and wasn't a bit happy about that. I think we all kind of feel sorry about Ev, mostly because it seems as if he would really like to go to sleep earlier but is in a constant state of conflict between what he'd like to do and what he thinks the other kids expect him to do. It's a situation which, I think, is shared by a number of the boys at the Center. But no one wants to be the first to chicken out publicly. One of the boys (Marty) even spoke to his worker about the situation. He seemed almost to be pleading with his worker that he (the worker) take him "off the hook" by legislating a curfew so that he could finally get some sleep, be sure of getting his breakfast, and not lose any money by falling asleep at work and being sent back to the Center.

Today's staff meeting was a reasonably quiet one, and I'm not sure why. Maybe it's because we're all tired. I don't know. I do know that I caught hell from Butch for coming to the meeting late.

Day 7: 9/22/66.
Happy Birthday diary. Today we're one week old, and although the RYC hasn't burned down, there isn't very much to celebrate about. Celebrate, shit! Today was by far the worst day I've ever had since getting mixed up with this whole crazy, stupid, ridiculous thing. Maybe it's a good thing that I write this damn diary at night, at a time when I can let off steam without having to put up with any abuse in return.

To begin with, I was up almost all night at the Center. Scotty and I were there together, and between the two of us the best we could do was help each other survive another night without coming apart at the seams. Actually, it wasn't such a bad night when you come right down to it. Oh, we were up until about 5:30 this morning, but nothing really bad (e.g., more sinks being pulled out of the bathroom walls) happened. The kids just stayed up, howled as usual, and had their customary 4:00 a.m. rampage.

At about 9:00 this morning I left the RYC and went over to the Clinic (the Psycho-Educational Clinic) for the weekly meeting. The first two hours were devoted to hearing some outside speaker (I don't even remember his name any more) talk to us about his work in the public schools. Maybe it's because I was just dead tired, or maybe because I just couldn't get excited about what he was talking about, but I found myself falling asleep. To keep from dozing off I started doodling on a pad and tried to look as if I were deeply immersed in thoughts that had sprung from the speaker's presentation. In point of fact, I was just really trying to stay awake. More than once, I had to nudge myself and look around the room to make sure that nobody was looking at me (paranoid much?). All I could think of was "stay awake, look interested, and try to get through the meeting." Well, I made it—or at least I thought I did. Right after the meeting broke up, the staff of the Clinic reassembled for its usual staff meeting. Again I found myself trying to stay awake and began doodling on the pad of paper in front of me. Suddenly, like out of nowhere, I heard Seymour (the

Director of the Psycho-Educational Clinic) say, "Kelly, will you please stop that doodling! You've been doing it all morning, I find it extremely irritating, and I'm sick and tired of it." He went on really to let me have it with both barrels. Talked about my apparent unconcern with matters pertaining to the Clinic, my seeming lack of interest in the activities of my colleagues, and my increasing and apparently cynical withdrawal from the rest of the staff. Man, like if I had had a hole beneath me I would have jumped into it and covered myself up. First of all, I was terribly embarrassed. I felt myself redden as the rest of the staff looked at me, nobody saying anything, everyone just turning toward me. But most of all, I guess, I was really hurt. Not so much by what Seymour said (hell, most of what he said is probably true) but by the manner in which he said it and the occasion he took for saying it. I think I tried to make some sort of feeble reply (something like "It's not true; I was really attending to everything going on"), some crappy copout to extricate myself from the whole damn situation, but it was all in vain. Happily, Seymour stalked out of the room, the meeting ended, and I got out of there as quickly as possible.

It was only after I had gone back up to my office that I really began getting mad. The longer I thought about the incident, the angrier I got about the whole situation. Sure I was tired; sure I was disinterested in what my colleagues were doing; sure I had been withdrawing more and more from things related to the Clinic. But why not? Why shouldn't I? The more I thought about it, the angrier I got about my trying to squirm out of the situation rather than confronting Seymour and the rest of the staff with what I've been going through. I should have told them exactly what was on my mind. I should have told them about sleepless nights; about what it was like to try to be the full-time Director of the RYC while carrying a full academic load at Yale; about trying to get a place together while still working in an elementary school, teaching a course, supervising graduate students, and attending meetings at the Clinic. Hell, they expect me to care about the Clinic and my colleagues, but who the hell from the Clinic really cares about me, about the RYC, and about what we're all going through?

It's a terrible thing this RYC. It's affecting me and those really close to me (like Seymour) in ways that I never anticipated. It's becoming like some kind of albatross that won't let go.

And as if the incident at the Clinic wasn't enough, today's

staff meeting at the RYC really capped the day. I was late again (had to finish a supervision session with one of the clinical psychology interns at the Clinic), and no sooner did I walk into the room when Butch really let me have it. First, he berated me for being late two days in a row and made a point of stressing how this kind of behavior was sympto- matic of just how disorganized things have been at the RYC. "Hell," he said, "if the Director's late, if Kelly can't get to meetings on time, how are the kids ever going to feel that there's any organization or control around here." A number of other staff members picked up on this theme and began talking about just how loosely everything was being run, how little structure there was to what we were doing, and how easily the kids can spot this disorganization and exploit it. It was brutal. I really felt quite alone, totally without support, and hopelessly inadequate. I kind of sat there and listened, not knowing exactly what to say and almost not caring any more. Once or twice, I think, I tried to have us focus on the question of just why we were letting the kids do the things they were doing, but I soon gave up even trying. The meet- ing seemed to drag on interminably, and I was more than a little grateful when Scotty shifted the discussion away from me and toward the question of how or when the Resident House Council would have its next meeting.

I left the RYC around 9:00 p.m. more depressed than I've ever been since we started this project.

Happy Birthday diary!

Day 8: 9/23/66.
Before going on to describe what happened last night and today, I want to write a few words about what it's like *not* being at the RYC. It's really quite a phenomenon. Like last night, for example. You come home feeling ugly, tired, and wanting nothing more to do with the Center. You're home, and all you really want to do is forget about the place, put it out of your mind and begin, at least for a little while, to lead the kind of life you imagine "normal" people lead. But it's impossible. Every time the phone rings you jump, your heart sinks deeper into your stomach, and you wait, es- pecially if your wife has answered the phone, to find out if it's someone calling from the RYC; if someone is calling to tell you about another crisis, another emergency, or another problem that needs immediate attention. And even if the phone *doesn't* ring for a little while, it's really not much better. You sit around and wonder. You conjure up all sorts

of pictures, all kinds of fantasies. You try to relax, but peace is somewhere else.

I should point out that what I have described is a situation not peculiar to myself. I've spoken about it to almost all the staff, and they have reported similar experiences. Butch put it best when he said, "Well, I go home, but I know that I'm really not at home. A part of me is still down at the RYC, and sooner or later that part of me wins out and I find myself going back to the place which only a little while before I swore I'd stop thinking about for at least one whole night."

Well, last night was a night almost like every other night at the RYC. The kids were up pretty much the whole night doing the kinds of things they have learned how to do so well: making sure that no one, especially those staff members on duty, makes the mistake of equating nighttime with sleeptime. While the situation as a whole was not noticeably different than its been ever since we opened the place (it seems as if it's been about ten years since we first opened up), Jack, who was on duty, reported his feeling that there had been a slight change in the quality of the nighttime chaos. Last night he got the distinct impression that the kids were beginning to tire, both physically and emotionally, of their nightly commitment to "exuberance" (Jack broke up when he used the word). It's his feeling that the kids are just about ready, indeed almost begging, for us to say "that's it" and put an end to the madness. Almost everyone at the staff meeting agreed with his analysis, but we decided to let the kids have at least one more crack at instituting their own curfew through the House Council before we stepped into the situation.

Well, the kids did have another House Council meeting earlier this evening. They succeeded in electing temporary officers, but the meeting broke up as soon as someone suggested that they turn their immediate attention to the problem of devising ways of dealing with the night problems. Most of the staff feels that their refusal or inability to want to deal with this problem is a reflection of their desire that we ourselves deal with it. We all feel that the kids do not as yet want to take on the responsibility for regulating themselves and would literally "appreciate" it if we extricated them from the dilemma by providing the initial structure. Clearly, we may be fooling ourselves into believing this, but at the present time it does look as if the kids are asking us, at least symbolically, to get them off the hook. Our belief that such may indeed be the case is strengthened when we take a look at who they elected as their House Council officers. To begin with, they elected Norris as their President, and everyone knows that Norris, despite his apparent maturity, has little intention of pushing for any kind of "reforms." Although he seems to want some kind of structure, he is not the kind of guy who will openly push for it. The same could be said for Marty (Vice-President) and Walt (Secretary). And the fact that Wayne was elected Treasurer adds nothing to the hope that this Council will actively pursue a policy of trying to limit the behavior of other boys. What is most interesting, however, is the fact that although guys like Sam, Shorty, and Bucky had been openly campaigning to be elected (these three guys represent a group that is openly against *any* kind of restrictions, the rest of the kids made sure, at least as far as the Council was concerned, that they would not be given any "official" power. All these things taken together make us feel more confident that the time may be ripe for the staff to introduce the first set of formal restrictions. We talked it over at our staff meeting today and decided that we would give the kids one more night to see if they could begin to institute some form of control over their own behavior. If they cannot, and none of us really believes that one more night will result in any magical transformations, then we will get the kids together and present them with the staff's decisions regarding a house curfew.

When I went back to the RYC earlier this evening, I walked into the living room to find myself in the middle of what looked like a really bad scene. Monty was lunging at Heinz, fists closed and cursing wildly, while about six of the other boys were just standing around and watching. As I jumped between them Monty swung. His fist swept by me, about two inches away from my head (I think if he'd connected I'd have been laid out deader than a doornail). At about the same time Heinz, who is much smaller than Monty (Heinz is even smaller than I am), picked up a chair and was getting ready to crack Monty over the head. Just then (thank God) Clark ran into the room and grabbed Monty while I pushed Heinz down on the couch. They were both still yelling and cursing at each other but were at least on opposite sides of the room.

When things simmered down a bit, we were able to piece together the following story. Monty, it seems, felt that Heinz had urinated in his bed and was not going to put up with "any white motherfucker pissing on my pillow." Heinz, on the other hand, staunchly maintained his innocence and insisted that it was Wayne (a Negro) that everyone "knew was pissing and shitting in everyone's bedroom." Although both Heinz and Monty kept screaming and cursing at each other, it soon became clear that whether or not Heinz was "guilty" (I personally feel that Heinz *has* been urinating in people's rooms, but I won't go into my reasons for feeling this way), the underlying problem was certainly one in which the question of race was a predominant factor (e.g., Monty himself once told me that he "knew" that Wayne had defecated in Ev and Marty's room but did not feel that any action should be taken because "Wayne's a sick boy"). Consequently, it was fairly clear that the circumstances notwithstanding, at least a part of Monty's reaction had some racial overtones to it. When we confronted Monty with this, he completely denied it and would not even admit having used the word "white" before his favorite word ("motherfucker") when yelling at Heinz. Even after some of the other kids who had been standing around volunteered that Monty had so addressed Heinz, Monty would hear none of it and maintained that "race got nothing to do with this at all."

Eventually we got Monty to back off, and I took all the kids with me into the large living room (being very careful to keep Monty and Heinz on opposite sides of me) to sit down and talk about what had happened. To my great surprise it turned out to be one of the greatest discussions I've ever had with a group of kids. After the initial "public statements" (e.g., "I'm not prejudiced against anyone.," "Prejudice is stupid," I treat everyone alike") were gotten out of the way, some of the kids really began to talk about their feelings about race. The black kids at the meeting were Monty, Walt, Shorty, Leland, and Ev. The white kids present were Tim, Marty, and Heinz.

Walt really started things off by telling the group about some of his experiences in New York. Walt lived in New York before coming to New Haven, and he talked about some of the things that happened to him both in "Black Brooklyn" and in other, nonblack areas of the city. He spoke of growing up ashamed of his color, ashamed of his "big lips," and always feeling as if white people, whether they said so or not, were always laughing at him. He also spoke of how he once decided that he'd literally "shit all over white people" whether he knew them or not. He then related how he and a few of his friends once grabbed a white boy, took him down to a cellar, and urinated all over him making sure that "we pissed straight in his eye." Some of the other kids howled with apparent glee as Walt told the story, and Walt responded by making sure that the story was told both slowly and dramatically. Some of the other kids (the white boys, mostly) thought that Walt was crazy and said as much. Ev then began to talk about some of his experiences with white people, especially in connection with a situation in which he was going out with a white girl. He spoke of his feelings of not belonging and of how he was constantly made to feel like an outsider. A few of the white kids then began to relate some of their experiences with respect to black people: of how scared they used to feel when walking through a predominantly black neighborhood; of how they, too, felt excluded, even in the house, from activities in which black kids were involved. Finally, after more than an hour, Monty joined in the discussion. He related the many times (in school, at work, and elsewhere) he felt that people were using his color as an "excuse" for not according him the kind of treatment he felt he had a right to expect. He went on and on until one of the kids (a black kid) said something like: "Hey baby, for a guy who says he got no prejudice you sure talk a good game." Monty looked a little embarrassed and finally admitted that perhaps he had used the word "white" before his "favorite word" when referring to Heinz earlier in the evening.

Although it's difficult to say exactly what the discussion accomplished, two things stand out. First, the kids were able to sit down, albeit in the context of a crisis, and talk about a problem that concerned each and every one of them. And second, when the meeting broke up we were fairly sure that Monty and Heinz would not be going at each other the way they had earlier in the evening. At this point let's be grateful for little things.

Day 9: 9/24/66.
Well, today was C-Day (Curfew Day). Last night was no different from every other night (i.e., the kids were up most of the night and didn't get to bed until the wee hours of the morning), and so today we got them all together to go over the situation and to let them know of our decision to impose a curfew. I think most of the kids knew what was coming, and although I may be kidding myself, I really believe that some of the kids were really relieved when it finally happened.

At our staff meeting this morning we spent a lot of time "rehearsing" how we would present the curfew to the kids. I think we all agreed that how we imposed this curfew was crucial not only in terms of the success of the curfew itself

but also because it would set a pattern for how future decisions were to be communicated to the kids. What finally
happened was the following:

When the kids came back to the house today after work,
we told them that we were going to have a joint "good and
welfare" meeting after supper. The time for the meeting was
set for 7:00 p.m., and the kids were told that evening plans
notwithstanding, we expected all of them to attend the meeting. There was some ritualistic grumbling of the halfhearted
variety, but all of the kids said they would show up. They did.

The meeting began with Scotty reviewing the evening situation in all its "splendor." Scotty has a way of describing
things in such a manner that one's immediate impression is
that while he may be relating "awful things" he is *not* condemning or pointing the finger at certain individuals to the
exclusion of others (including the staff). At any rate, Scotty
went over what's been happening, reviewed our initial hopes
that the kids themselves would have been able to control the
situation, and concluded by summarizing the staff's reasons
for feeling that the time had come for us to take the initial
step toward the imposition of additional structure.

When he finished, Scotty, still not having mentioned the
specific curfew decided upon by the staff, threw the question
out on the floor and asked for the kids' comments and reactions. Despite some grumbling and squirming, the kids, I
think somewhat taken aback by the apparent lack of anger
in the way Scotty presented the problem, remained relatively
quiet.

At this point the rest of us (the staff) joined the conversation. Each of us, in turn, recounted the effects of the evening
chaos on "our own" kids. Jack, for example, was able to review the problems that lack of sleep had created for Cliff,
Wayne, and Bucky. Butch followed with his own problems
regarding Tim, Ev, and Robbie. I, and then Lance and Chip,
reviewed what had been happening to Shorty, Heinz, and
Curt. And so on. In a way I guess we were confronting the
kids, en masse, with the "catalog of horrors" that the nighttime chaos has been causing for ourselves, the kids, and the
RYC in general. Most of us were pretty graphic in our descriptions, and we made no attempt to avoid communicating
our own feelings about the situation and how it has been
affecting us as individuals.

When this was over, I summarized quickly what had been
said and once again asked the kids for any of their feelings
and ideas about the situation. Again there was no response.

It really looked like the kids were just biding their time, just sitting back and waiting to hear the actual "punishment" before striking back.

Well, at this point Scotty and Jack began to provide the kids with a "nonpunishment" rationale for the staff's decision to impose a curfew. They spoke, Jack in particular, about the fact that we did not feel we were really helping the kids to help themselves by allowing them to stay up all night and lose money (as well as jobs and job training opportunities). Scotty talked about the self-help character of the RYC and made it clear that we, the staff, were only helping to defeat the goals of the program by allowing kids, especially those who "deep down really want to go to sleep," to sabotage their own efforts to "make it." And finally, both Scotty and Jack made it clear that the curfews to be imposed were temporary ones, the hope being that once the House Council became organized, it would take over the responsibility for developing and implementing whatever restrictions the kids felt were necessary for the "good and welfare" of the house. In other words, the kids were told that once they began to want to accept the responsibility of governing themselves, they could then review the staff-imposed curfew and either change it or develop alternatives to it.

By this time the kids had sunk deep down into their chairs and were just waiting to hear what the curfew would be. I then told them that the staff had decided that during the work week (Sunday night through Thursday night) they had to be in bed by 1:00 a.m., and that on Friday and Saturday nights the curfew was 3:00 a.m. Man, like you should have seen the looks on their faces. The kids were floored. They were expecting a curfew, maybe something like 9:00 or 10:00 p.m., that was not only restricting but also repressive, and here we were saying that we had no intention of punishing the kids but only wanted to provide a curfew that would enable them to get enough sleep so that they could make it to work in the morning.[5] The response was unbelievable. No response at all. They kind of looked at each other, at the staff, and again at each other. I think what happened was that they were really thrown off balance. I

[5]Some weeks later, when the House Council had become established and was functioning on a regular basis, the residents confirmed what much of the research on adolescents has shown; namely, that teenagers, when given the opportunity of establishing their own rules and regulations, are usually more severe on themselves than are adults. They *reduced* the staff's work-week curfew for themselves from 1:00 a.m. to midnight.

think they were prepared to fight the staff's "expected" decision but were now in the uncomfortable position of having much of the fight (i.e., the anticipated nature of the "punishment") begin to look unreasonable by virtue of the curfew we were now imposing. How the hell can you really get mad about something that makes sense, isn't "way out," and isn't imposed in an atmosphere of vengeance?

Anyway, after a few minutes the kids recovered their cool and quickly discovered that a 1:00 a.m. curfew would mean that they couldn't finish watching the Late Show on TV. (the late movie is not generally over until about 1:20 a.m.). With the issue of being able to watch the completion of the Late Show their new "cause" (and a face-saving one at that), the kids quickly banded together to present the staff with a united front for purposes of bargaining. From the point of view of the staff, the kids were presenting an eminently reasonable request, and after only a few minutes of negotiation it was decided that the 1:00 a.m. curfew would "really" mean the time that the Late Show was over, but that if there was any abuse of this "concession," the curfew would revert back to 1:00 a.m., regardless of what was happening on the boob tube.

After the meeting was over, each worker made it a point to sit down with "his" kids to go over the curfew and make sure that there were no misunderstandings or misinterpretations. When I left the RYC earlier this evening, I saw Jack engaged in heated debate with Bucky and Cliff over the new curfew. It's still too early to tell, but I think that the meeting went as well if not better than any of us had hoped. We didn't get mad, gave the kids a chance to understand the whys and wherefores behind the curfew, and wound up by making the kind of concession that allowed the kids to view the situation as something more than a cut-and-dried affair between "jailers" and "jailed." I guess we'll just have to wait now and see what happens. Lord knows I don't know what we'll do (I don't even want to think about it at this point) if this doesn't work.

Want to say a word about Sterns. Sterns is a first-year graduate student here at Yale. He's a kid from Columbia, Missouri (where's Columbia, Missouri?), and aside from an abundance of motivation and some prior experience in the Peace Corps, he lacks all the "necessary credentials" for working at the RYC. In other words, Sterns is a white, middle-class young man from a nonurban (not to mention non-ghetto) background who is both quiet and well-mannered. I mention all of this for a couple of reasons. First, because he is doing one helluva job. When Sterns arrived at Old Eli, he had no place to stay (had not as yet gotten himself an apartment), and since he had been "assigned" to me (I'm his first-year faculty advisor and supposedly the person whose research interests are closest to his), I got him involved in the RYC and asked him if he'd like to live at the Center until he found a place of his own. He agreed (I think for reasons that had little to do with his initial desire to live at the RYC) and has been living at the Center since the day we started. Despite his lack of experience, he has been doing yeoman-like work. He's become a part of this place and its staff in a way that's rather difficult to describe. The second reason for my focusing attention on Sterns is because he is "living proof" (as if we really needed any) that one need not come from a background of poverty or be a member of some despised or oppressed minority group in order to "qualify" as one capable of working in a setting like the RYC. I fear that just as "professionalism" is overstressed, so, too, could the virtues of being a so-called indigenous nonprofessional become a vehicle for excluding people from active participation in this damn War on Poverty. What we really need are certain kinds of people, "naturals" if you will, people who are able to open themselves up to others and to learn, people who are willing to commit themselves to the arena of human and social action. Give us those kinds of people and the specific skills they need to acquire will follow as the night follows the day. Sterns is "those kinds of people." 'Nuff editorializing. I must admit, however, that as far as Sterns is concerned I do feel a little guilty. Here he was coming to *Yale*, one of the citadels of academia, a place where "scholarly research" (usually done in tradition-reeking and antiseptic laboratories) is *King* with a capital *K*, and a place where the measure of a man is usually gauged in very specific (and very non-RYC) ways; and what does he find? He finds himself being introduced to the Ivy League through a rather non-Ivy League setting. Poor Sterns. What a way to be introduced to graduate school, to clinical psychology . . . and to Yale.

Got a call at about 11:30 p.m. Lance called from the RYC to let me know that things were still pretty quiet. He seemed hopeful, but I had to remind him that the "night" rarely started before 2:00 a.m.

Day 10: 9/25/66.
God is not dead; he's alive and well at the RYC!
Last night we had our first quiet night at the RYC. Every-

one was in the house by 11:00 p.m. and, believe it or not, all the kids were either in bed or asleep by 1:30 a.m. A few of the kids (Tim, Robbie, Curt, and Marty) didn't even wait until curfew time before going to bed. Lance tells us that they were in their rooms before 10:30 p.m. and weren't heard from until this morning. Some of the other kids, especially Shorty, Sam, and Walt, tried to stay up until curfew time but fell asleep on the couches in the TV room and quietly went up to their rooms once Vito asked them to. Most of the guys did stay up to watch the Late Show but dutifully went up to bed as soon as it was over and Lance had turned off the TV set. A couple of kids (Leland and Bucky) looked as if they were going to "test" Lance and said that they weren't going to go to sleep, but when they found no support from the other kids, they too dragged their tails up to bed.

The tone of today's staff meeting was about as different from what it's been as one could imagine. It was as if a great question had been answered to almost everyone's personal satisfaction. We kidded each other, made Lance repeat how last night went about four times more so that we could savor it over and over again, and in general congratulated ourselves for our wisdom and perseverance. It was really a funny scene. We didn't get any work done to speak of, but none of us seemed to mind one little bit.

Only Butch seemed almost oddly quiet and apart from it all. When we finished patting each other on the back, he really tore into us all, especially me. Said he didn't understand what the whole celebration was about, that the house was no better off than it had been a day ago, that the place was still filthy as hell, that the kids were still not getting off to work on time, and that there was still no leadership or organization either in the house or on the staff. Whereas Butch directed most of his attack at the staff as a whole, his last salvo was pointed straight at me. Now, in retrospect, I think Butch was more than a little right about most of the things he said. The house *is* filthy, and maybe things aren't as organized as they should be. But at the time Butch was making his attack I was in no mood to be confronted with that kind of assault. We had just come to a point where we had begun to deal with the most pressing problem confronting us (the curfew), and here he was blasting away at all the other problems that existed in the house. And it wasn't only what he was saying, it was the way in which he was putting things. I guess that's what bothered me most of all. He spoke as if no one, especially me, had any awareness of the extent of work that still has to be done; as if he was the only one who had an acute appreciation of the myriad problems confronting the Center. Well, I could feel myself redden and begin to blow so I just kind of stopped, caught myself, and said something like: "Butch, I think you're shooting from the hip again" (for the life of me I don't know why I used the term "shooting from the hip" except that maybe unconsciously I felt that Butch, like Goldwater, was making some rather reckless statements that went beyond the situation). At any rate, while Butch's attack did take some of the joy out of the occasion, it also served to bring us all back to earth and to a consideration of the problems that still face us. It also led to a rather good discussion of how all of us, not just Butch, tend to perpetuate a state of anxiety by failing to see things in any kind of meaningful perspective because of our feeling constantly "under the gun." Thus, for example, whereas we all agreed that the curfew was the most pressing problem, once it appeared as if we were beginning to get a handle on it, our attention shifted to the next problem in the hierarchy of problems (e.g., the filthy condition of the house) and the tendency then became one of not viewing that problem in its appropriate context but as symptomatic of a general and total state of disorganization and chaos.

Have added two new words to my vocabulary. The words "bogart" and "boss." The kids use these words all the time, and they have now become a part of almost everyone's repertoire. Of the two words, the word "bogart" is, at least for me, the easier to understand. It's derived from the actor Humphrey Bogart (most of the kids really love his movies) and is used whenever one sees someone trying to get his way by means other than peaceful ones. This doesn't mean that the only way a person "bogarts" another is by fighting with him. Oh no, it's merely the threat of violence that's enough to define "bogarting." As for the term "boss," that one is a lot harder for me to pin down as far as its origin is concerned. The term is used whenever someone has something that people think is sharp or especially nifty. Thus, for example, a kid might show off a new shirt and be told: "That's boss." The interesting thing about the word "boss" is that unlike the term "bogart," which all the kids use, the word "boss" is primarily used by the black kids. My own free associations lead me to think that the term has something to do with the relationship between supposed "bosses" and "slaves," but I may well be reading more into the word than there really is. Anyway, I kind of like both words; they ex-

press a certain kind of feeling better than many other phrases
—and in a lot less time.

Tonight I'm on duty at the Center.

Day 11: 9/26/66.

Will wonders never cease: another quiet night at the RYC.
That's two in a row. Maybe, just maybe, we're home free.

There's nothing like a relatively quiet night at the Center.
That's not to say that problems don't come up (e.g., an argument around the pool table, the volume on some of the kids'
record players up too high and the neighbors complaining,
Wayne still acting crazy and muttering bizarre things to himself), but the whole feeling-tone of the RYC is different. I'm
sure it's got something to do with the fact that you now have
the *time* to begin to appreciate all the *good* things that are
happening. Things like the kids staying at the Center for
evening activities rather than running out, or the workers
invariably dropping by to talk with their kids or shoot some
pool, or the kids beginning to sit around in small groups to
talk about things and about their "plans" for the house.

Thus far, the most successful evening program is the judo
program run by "Judo Jack." Jack has set up a small practice
area in the basement and has borrowed some mats from the
Y to cushion the falls. He's even been able to scrounge up
a few gias (judo uniforms) for the kids. They're buggy about
the program and go down to the cellar even when Jack's
not around to practice. The way Jack teaches judo he's got
the kids talking Japanese, and some of them (especially
Robbie, Monty, and Walt) strut around the house in their
uniforms, bowing and saying something in Japanese to everyone who happens to pass them in the halls or the living
room. None of this "Ah so" business, but something really
Japanese.

With only the smallest amount of prodding, all the kids
were up in their rooms by 1:30 a.m. It was strange as hell;
no problems. I sat around bulling with Lance for a while and
actually got to stretch out on the sofa for some sleep at
about 2:30 a.m. The only reason that I wasn't able to get a
good night's sleep was because of the following two events:
1. The phone rang at about 4:00 a.m. As soon as I picked
up the receiver, a voice on the other end said: "This is the
police." My stomach began to fall, and my immediate reaction was one of thinking whether or not one of our kids had
sneaked out of the house and had been picked up for something (talk about stereotypes). The voice then said: "I'm call-

ing to let you know that the lights have gone out at Chapel and High Streets." I then said something brilliant like "Oh yeah," at which point the voice on the other end of the line said: "Isn't this the United Illuminating Company?" I said: "No, this is the Residential Youth Center." The voice then said: "Sorry, guess I got the wrong number. I was trying to call the electric company." He hung up, I sighed, and that was that.

2. At about 6:00 this morning there was a knock at the front door. I dragged myself out of bed, opened the door, and found myself looking at an elderly, well-dressed Negro man. He excused himself for "coming so early" and said: "I'd like to enroll my child in your club." I asked him how old his child was and he said: "Ten years old." I told him that his son was a bit too young for the program and he said: "Well, I was told that you're running a club for children and I thought you'd like to have my boy." With that he turned and sauntered away.

Today's staff meeting was devoted to working out ways of beginning to deal with the RYC's "cleanliness" problem; and it really *is* a problem. The problem has several aspects to it. To begin with, most of the kids are not cleaning their rooms, and the accumulation of junk, dirt, and soiled clothes is making it very difficult to walk by, let alone into, some of the rooms. Another part of the problem has to do with the question of personal cleanliness. A lot of the kids are not showering regularly (most of them never have) and simply stink. Consequently, the combination of dirty rooms and smelly kids is making the RYC's odor something less than thoroughly appealing. At today's meeting it was decided to begin by relying on the individual workers to broach the subject with their kids in a private and personal manner. It was also decided to call a meeting of each floor, present the problem to the kids, and assign temporary clean-up duties. Butch suggested a daily room inspection, but while most of the staff felt it was a good idea, it was thought to be a bit premature and the decision was made to hold off on such inspections until the workers and kids had a chance to discuss the problem. Again, the thinking was that we would first like to give the kids the chance to act on their own before "laying down the law." Butch agreed that it was easier to begin softly rather than by trying to, as he put it, "make an 'instant institution' of this place."

When the meeting ended and we all left the room to go downstairs, I had what I must consider to be my strangest and, in retrospect, most gratifying RYC experience to date. But in order to try to describe what happened I have to backtrack a bit.

For the past few days, Bucky, the kid with a "rep," seemed to be purposely going out of his way to give me a "hard time." This is not to say that he hadn't been trying to make life difficult for almost everyone on the staff, but he seemed to single me out as the person to whom he would direct most of his "attention." What I mean is that whenever I'd ask him to do something, regardless of what it was, he'd always make some kind of remark that inevitably sounded like the traditional "Make me!" In addition to this, for the past few days he'd taken to making sure that whenever we'd pass each other in the house he'd always be in a position to shove or push me. It was pretty clear, both to him, to me, and to the staff, that Bucky had singled me out for his own brand of "testing" behavior.

Well, this afternoon, while we were all going down the stairs from the office, Bucky brushed by me and in the process pushed me off the final two steps of the stairway. As I stumbled to catch my balance he stood in the middle of the corridor, his hands on his hips, and laughed in what was about as clear a challenge as you'd ever want to see. Now Bucky is a pretty strong kid, certainly a lot stronger and bigger than I am, and here he was calling me in front of a number of people.

I quickly looked around me (I'm a very, very cautious "hero") and noted that all my "big guns" (Jack, Scotty, Butch, and Clark) were nearby and watching. A number of the kids were also present and watching. Well, I figured so long as Jack, Scotty, Butch, and Clark are around at least he won't kill me (the assumption being that if Bucky was really messing me up badly the staff would step in and stop it), so why not give it a shot and get it over with.

I then lunged at Bucky and the fight was on. No sooner had we made contact than we began wrestling all over the living room floor. We rolled over and over, me fighting as hard as I possibly could and finding, much to my amazement, that I was able to hold my own against Bucky. Not once did we ever lose hold of each other as we wrestled and wrenched each other from one side of the room to the other. I lost all track of time and I remember thinking to myself something like "hang with the kid, don't let him wedge you into a corner and get on top of you." After a while I began to realize that for some reason Bucky was backing up, was losing the grip he had on my head, and was beginning to breath real heavylike. I figured it was now or never (I was getting tired as hell and my arms were beginning to feel like someone had been standing on them), and giving it all I had left I found myself lifting Bucky off the floor, pushing him against the sofa, shoving my knee into his groin and, wonder of wonders, being able to keep it there. I looked down at Bucky. He was panting audibly, but much to my surprise, unlike me (I was sweating like a pig), he had hardly even raised a sweat. I couldn't believe it. Sweat was running off my nose like rain; he wasn't even sweating, and yet I had him . . . I really had him in trouble. Although it was hard for me to talk without sounding out of breath, I managed to say something like: "Had enough- Call it quits?" With little more than a gasp Bucky said: "O.K. Get the hell off me. It's over." I looked around the room. The staff was still there. The kids were there. It was fine, just fine, and so I took my knee out of Bucky's groin, stood up, and trying harder than ever not to look too winded, I began sucking in air as quickly as I could.

The fight was over. The kids who had been watching it left the room. A few of them were shaking their heads. As the rest of us began to leave, I looked over my shoulder at Bucky who was not sitting on the sofa. Bucky looked up at me, and with a slight smile on his face he gave me a curious, almost devious wink. It was only then that I finally realized what had really happened: Bucky had *let* me win the "fight," had actually "arranged" the whole affair in order to make me look good, and had allowed himself to be beaten so that he could now follow my "orders" without it being said that he gave up without a fight. You've got to really understand Bucky to dig what I'm saying. He's a very smart and observant kid, a kid with a rep, and a kid who can only maintain his status in the house and still do what the staff wants him to do by making it seem, both to the staff and the other kids, that he "went down fighting." That's what the wink was all about; that's why he waited until the staff was around; and that's why he made sure that at least a few of the other kids saw what happened. Bucky had set me up for the whole thing, had "written" the scenario, and had "directed" the entire drama. *Of course*, he wasn't breathing hard when the "fight" was over. He wasn't even winded. He could have broken me in two without half trying. But he didn't. He let me win because only my winning would allow him to begin to do the kinds of things (e.g., take suggestions and direction) that he really wants to do without his "rep" being questioned. A helluva kid that Bucky!

It's really been quite a day.

Day 12: 9/27/66.
Another quiet night; the third in a row without any incidents. Didn't even get any phone calls from the RYC last night.

At this morning's staff meeting we reviewed the cleanliness problem and tried to see whether or not the way we've been handling the situation has begun to yield any results. Before the meeting we all walked through the house, made our own assessments, and then compared them with those made by the rest of the staff. In point of fact, there has been some improvement in the situation. The kids on the second floor met with Vito and set up their own clean-up schedule. With the exception of Tim, all the kids did their jobs (Cliff took care of the bathroom, Marty and Walt swept out the hall, and Ev and Robbie did a halfway decent job on their own room), and the floor, while far from being spotless, was in much better shape than the day before. The same could not be said of the third floor. Although the guys met with Clark and Lance, they were not able to agree on a system of individual duties. They will meet again later tonight. As far as the downstairs is concerned (the dining and living room areas), the situation seems to be a bit better than it has been. Butch organized some of the kids, and they decided to police the area, clean and arrange the furniture, and look after the dining room on a rotating basis. In short, although the situation is far from perfect there has been some change for the better. The most important thing, however, is that the problem is being approached *with* the kids rather than in opposition to them. We are banking on the fact that most of the kids are beginning to feel a real sense of ownership in the RYC, and it is within the framework of that kind of feeling that we believe the problem of cleanliness, both personal and housewise, can best be approached and eventually solved.

Scotty and Clark contributed a very important piece of information at this morning's meeting. They found out that for some of the kids the reason that they don't make their beds in the morning has nothing to do with their unwillingness to take the time and make the effort to do so. Rather, it seems that a lot of the kids really don't know how to make a bed. Scotty suggested that each worker approach the issue with his kid privately, and that if he found out that the boy really doesn't know how to make a bed, he begin to help the kid with the problem in a way no different from what he would do with any other problem affecting a kid.

About four hours after our staff meeting, we were visited, rather suddenly, by one of CPI's "downtown directors." He came into the building much like an inspector, toured the premises, and immediately proceeded to berate us for the "filthy, sloppy condition of the house." He was really livid, called the place a pigsty, and told us in no uncertain terms that things were going to change, "and quick."

We tried to tell him that we shared his concerns about the condition of the house, that we were working on the problem, and that we felt that in the long run we would be more successful in dealing with the problem in the way that we were approaching it (we explained our approach to him) rather than in the way he suggested (i.e., by setting up specific rules and regulations concerning cleanliness, by developing punishments for noncompliance, and by implying very strongly that those kids who could not follow the rules could "pack up and get out").

It was no use. Although I think he tried to see our point of view, it soon became clear that we were communicating on very different wavelengths. Our concerns were very different, and the ways in which we conceptualized the problem had almost nothing in common. His concerns were basically "administrative" and "political" (i.e., "What if CPI's Executive Director walks in?" "What would visitors think?" and "What if the people from Washington come down?"). Our concerns were more "clinical" or "program"-oriented (i.e., "The problem of cleanliness has to be approached from the point of view of the setting," "One of the reasons the kids are here is because they've had difficulties in just this area," and "You can't effectively legislate cleanliness until the kids experience the need for such legislation"). But it was useless.

I guess what really pissed me off about the "inspection visit" was that "the man" thought nothing of berating me in front of the staff, treating me almost as if I were a little boy who had to be disciplined by his boss. I tried to cool it but found myself getting close to exploding after "the man," apparently not satisfied with his previous assault, started anew, this time implying very, very strongly that things would go a lot more smoothly if I'd only stop subverting the staff with my "psychological ideas about permissiveness." The implication (as well as the warning) was clear: that somehow things would be better if the RYC were run in a way that conformed with "downtown's" ideas about what a residential center should or should not be like; and these "ideas" were invariably more administrative than program-oriented (this is my inference).

Suddenly, I found myself feeling much less angry and much more sad. I actually began to feel sad about what I was hearing this man say; sad that this organization, this CPI, once so dynamic and innovative, was now itself becoming just another agency, fat with power, intolerant of deviance, insensitive to the particular goals (and problems) of its member programs. There was now a "book" on how to run an action program, and the book was no longer filled with ideas and ideals but with blanket rules and regulations, with administrative processes and bureaucratic norms.

Well, I didn't blow up. I tried to explain again what we were doing and why we were doing it. Things quieted down, and he finally left the Center. When he had gone, Scotty (bless him) really put his finger on the problem. He said: "Well, I guess that's the way downtown sees the problem: if you can't get 'em out of poverty, at least clean 'em up."

In retrospect, however, I think there's more to the problem than I've reported. Take the downtown director, for example. He's not a bad guy, really quite a decent man, and a guy who deeply believes in the War on Poverty. But he's also an administrator, and, as such, he has to view and respond to the RYC from a point of view very different from ours, very different from those of us who eat and breathe RYC 24 hours a day. To him the RYC is only one of a number of programs for which he is administratively responsible. Although he doesn't "know" the program the way we do, and although it wasn't his ideas that went into shaping it, he is still the man who must account for its behavior—and account for it to people (e.g., CPI's Executive Director) who, because of their distance from the program, know even less about it than he does. Under these conditions, uniformity becomes one of the few ways of insuring control. It's a very complex problem, this question of organizational structure and its effects on individual behavior. Much too complex for a diary that's being written too late at night.

Day 13: 9/28/66.
Although this entry reads "Day 13," it is being written well into the fourteenth day of the RYC. The reason for the lateness of this entry is very simple: I was really in no condition

last night to do any writing. To be more specific, I was drunk; but even my having tied one on is part of the story of the RYC, so I'll tell about it.

The thirteenth day of the RYC was a pretty good one. All the kids went to work, the house became a little cleaner (Clark was able to help the kids on the third floor organize their own clean-up squad), and outside of the everyday, "normal" problems, things went quite well. This being the case, I decided that come what may I was going to take a night off, get away from the Center, and begin to find out what the "outside world" looked like.

Up until now I've been using this diary to describe *my* experiences, *my* perceptions, and *my* interpretations of what's been happening at the Center. It's been a selfish diary, but that's what diaries are like: they give one person's view of the world, and that's it. But whoever reads this should know that each and every member of this staff has shared in the things I've written, and not only them but their wives. The wives! Oh, these poor, precious wives of ours. They, too, are a part of the RYC and always will be. And whereas some, like myself, can use a diary to describe what's been happening, the wives, for the most part, have chosen to suffer in silence, have supported and put up with what's been going on with a dignity bordering on the absurd. I know that I have a tendency to go overboard in my description of things, but as far as the wives are concerned (mine in particular), no description, however flowery and "romantic," could ever suffice to convey just how important they've been to this whole project.

Take my wife, for example. Sue's in her seventh month now and at a point when I know she'd like to have me around and available. It's our first child that's coming, and we're both just counting the days until the baby's due. It's a time filled with anticipation and anxiety, and my involvement in the RYC certainly isn't making things any easier for Sue. I'm away most evenings, sometimes all night, and even when I'm home, I'm not much comfort to her. I walk around trying to "be" with her but always waiting for the phone to ring, always thinking about what's going on down at the Center. And Sue knows this, and regardless of how she might want things to be different, she's been little short of amazing throughout this period of time. She's always there, always "knowing" what I'm feeling, always the person to whom I turn. We talk about the RYC and the baby and Sue says that we're both giving birth to something. But she's wrong. I tell her: "Baby, you'll go down in medical history. You're the only woman who'll ever bring a child and an RYC into the world during the same year." In short, she's great, and I sometimes doubt whether or not the whole thing would be worthwhile without her. And the other wives, Jack's, and Chip's, and Butch's. They're all too much. Oh, they kid us about all the time we spend away from home, down at the Center. Winnie, Jack's wife, says she thinks the RYC has become our clubhouse and that we spend so much time there because it's the only place in town where we don't have to spend any money to shoot pool. But with all the kidding and joking, it's a problem, and a real one. I sometimes wonder just how long the wives will put up with the situation. It's not a good one. Not good at all. I now believe that one of our greatest mistakes in planning and preparing the RYC was our underestimation of the effect the Center would have on our home lives in general, and on our wives in particular. We should have spent much more time either involving our wives more directly in the operation of the Center or in preparing them for the problems that such an operation would present. We failed to do either, and I only hope it's not too late to do something about the situation.

At any rate, as I started to say, I decided that come what may, Sue and I were going to get away from it all, even if only for a little while. We hadn't been out together in ages, so last night I made reservations for us at a charming little restaurant just out of town. I still remember us getting ready to go out, me feeling almost like a guy going out on a date with his own wife. Even when we were getting dressed, I found myself wondering whether or not to take the phone off the hook just to make sure it wouldn't ring.

Well, we finally took off and arrived at the inn. Even before we sat down I thought about calling the Center, looked at the telephone booth, and decided not to. But Sue knew what I was thinking, and she said: "Why don't you call the RYC and let them know where you are just in case they want you." Like I said, I've got one helluva wife. Well, I called the Center, was told to "stop bothering everybody," and returned to Sue.

The evening was beautiful. It's early autumn now and the evenings are filled with the sweet smell of fading flowers and approaching frost. The inn we went to is set deep in the woods and borders a small lake. When the weather is warm, you can sit at tables that have been placed outside the inn and near the water. Ducks and swans swim about you, their quiet paths only accentuating the stillness of the evening.

Well, to make a long story short, I really tied one on. (It

really doesn't take very much for me to get high: two martinis on an empty stomach does the trick just fine.) We had cocktails, a bottle of B&G Saint-Emilion with the meal, and some after-dinner liqueur. We talked and talked: talked about life, love, the baby, love, the RYC and . . . love. It was just too beautiful to describe. After all this time (it seems like years), to just be able to open up, let it all out, just *BE* again.

Day 14: 9/29/66.
It's pretty clear by now that the worst is probably over.
You can almost "feel" it both in the staff and among the kids.
Last night was our fourth quiet night in a row. But it's not only that it was quiet. Hell, cemeteries are *always* quiet. It's that the kids are getting more involved in the house, beginning to attend the evening programs regularly, and beginning to act as if they really have a stake in the success of the program.

We, too, have changed. Today's staff meeting was almost lighthearted in nature. We've begun to laugh again. What more can I say?

I look around me and I see all the unfinished business. I know we've got problems, and serious ones at that. The house is still a mess; kids are still not attending work regularly; we continue to have problems with "downtown CPI"; and we've nothing tangible (statistically or otherwise) to point to as evidence of any kind of success. But you get this feeling that things are beginning to work themselves out; that we're not going to collapse; that the program is going to "make it." I don't know how, but I just know it. And I think the rest of the staff knows it. There's a quiet, almost serene confidence now. We don't talk about it, but it's there nevertheless. Maybe we should talk about it, but it seems as if we rarely talk about the *good* things that have happened. It's the problems that always dominate our discussions; and maybe that's the way it'll always be.

I think I'm also just beginning to realize how hard it's going to be for me to leave this place in January. But there's a time and a place for everyone. My time is now. Later it'll be someone else's turn. All I know is that regardless of who Scotty picks as his Deputy in January, he'll be picking from among one helluva group of people. You start with Scotty and go right down the line and all you find are people, "real people" ("menschen" is what we call it in Yiddish). Just a few examples:

Scotty: How can you write about Scotty? Scotty is Scotty; a pillar of strength, always there, always confronting you with yourself, always making you think about what you're doing and why you're doing it. He never lets up, never lets you forget that you've not only got talent but the obligation to use it. Maybe the best way of describing Scotty is to say that he's our bridge between the present and the future, the man who makes tomorrow look like it's only a minute away.

Jack: Like this judo creed, Jack is "The fire within, the serenity without." Undoubtedly the best "clinician" on the staff, Jack has a way of becoming a part of the kid, a part of his world, his problems, and his dreams. You listen to Jack talk about a kid and you suddenly feel, maybe for the first time, that you really understand a kid. For the rest of us Jack is the "Rock," the man who never panics, and the man we all look to when we're getting "up tight."

Butch: Big, vocal, uncompromising in his quest for excellence, be it for a kid or for the rest of the staff. Perhaps more than anyone else Butch makes our sensitivity sessions "go"; and by "go" I mean that he will not allow us to avoid or evade any issues, no matter how sensitive or personally involving, that he feels are important to our functioning as a group.

Chip: As hard as nails, as soft as butter. Our "elder statesman." The man who's forever berating us for "mollycoddling the kids," but also the man who always manages to find something worth saving, something redemptive, about a kid on whom just about everyone has given up. When things get tough, look around. There's Chip . . . always "by accident," of course.

Lance: If you're looking for kudos, don't look to Lance. The only "positive" recognition you'll get from him is a grunt that says: "Is that the best you can do?" Lance is the man who keeps us "honest," forever exploding our myths and exposing our attempts to deceive ourselves. More than anyone else, the man who keeps reminding us that perfection is the only road to heaven . . . and a bumpy one at that.

I could go on and on and still never finish. Each day adds a new dimension to the RYC and its people. We'll take each day as it comes along.

Tonight I share duty with Jack.

We shall end our diary with this entry made some two weeks after the day the RYC opened its doors. Despite the obviously "hopeful" note on which the diary is concluded, it should be clear that the setting's problems were nowhere near to being solved on September 29, 1966. Perhaps the only thing we could be sure of at that point in time was the fact that the RYC had "survived" its period of adjustment; that it had managed to emerge, relatively intact, from a period of time during which the setting and its people had been subjected to a series of intense and continual pressures both from within the setting and from sources external to it.

The Clinician, the System, and Action: A Preliminary Analysis
In the pages that follow we shall attempt a very preliminary analysis of some of the pressures mentioned in the preceding section, recognizing all the while that our descriptions are highly tentative in nature and that they constitute little more than an inexhaustive survey of some of the problems inherent in the creation of settings. From our own point of view, however, the importance of these descriptions inheres in the fact that they are drawn from concrete experiences in the setting itself. As such, their implications, in terms of both theory construction and future research, are of a kind as to petition for the increased involvement of clinicians and other mental health workers in the problems of "action" settings, the assumption being that "direct participation" not only facilitates but may very well be a *sine qua non* for the development of the kinds of theoretical conceptions and research methodologies that will lead to a new and more appropriate definition of the role of the mental health professional in times of accelerated social change.

Action and the Clinician Any analysis of the problem of "action and the clinician" must begin with the observation, admittedly overgeneralized, that there exists a persistent and as yet unresolved conflict between the traditional conception of what constitutes relevant and appropriate "clinical" behavior, on the one hand, and the demand characteristics of "action" settings, on the other. The "conflict" we speak of takes many forms and has been argued on many different levels, but it invariably involves such questions as whether or not it is appropriate that clinicians become directly involved in "action" settings (i.e., in settings not typically "clinical" in orientation and design); whether or not our training or traditions have prepared us for such involvement; and, in the final analysis, whose "agent" we really are—the troubled individual's or the troubled society's.

Let us begin by assuming that the conflict is no longer a "real" one, that the relentless press of historical imperatives has taken the decision out of our hands, and that the question is no longer one of whether or not we wish to become involved but rather how we might begin to "retool" our profession so that it can meet its new and shifting responsibilities in a society undergoing acute social change. We begin, then, with the assumption, as Krasner (1965) puts it, that the clinician has "no place to hide" and that he can no longer perpetuate those "professional myths behind which he can take refuge in denying role responsibility."[6]

Perhaps the best way of approaching the problem would be to admit the fact that in trying to relate traditional conceptions of "clinical behavior" to the demand characteristics of "action," we are really trying to forge an alliance between two phenomenologically different "stances in the world." In other words, any structural analysis of the worlds of the clinician and the social activist would reveal differences in attitudes, in orientations, and, perhaps most important, in the modes and conceptions of relatedness deemed necessary for the attainment of certain ends. "Action," for example, is above everything else a particular mode of being in relation to the world, a stance one assumes with respect to the exigencies of change. Phenomenologically, the world of action is the world of personal visibility, public risk, and unselfconscious partisanship—the kind of partisanship that is both

[6]While Krasner's "no place to hide" thesis is primarily concerned with problems of behavior modification and the relationship between behavior therapy and other models of intervention, his discussion of the moral, ethical, and social implications of contemporary clinical practice are more than a little relevant to the present discussion. His analysis of such problems as responsibility, influence, and decision-making is critical to any discussion of the question of what constitutes an appropriate form of clinical behavior once the locus of involvement begins to shift from more traditional helping settings to the arenas of social action. In discussing the problem from the point of view of the responsibilities of the behavioral scientist, Benne (1965) has similarly concluded that "the larger crisis of valuation has been admitted into the internal choices of behavioral scientists."

scornful of neutrality and suspicious of compromise. It is a "right now!" world, forever restless, often chaotic; a world whose basic dimensions are those of commitment, direct impact, and the unequivocal acceptance of responsibility. It is, in short, a condition of being in which there is an identity between one's own sense of incompleteness and the imperfections that define the human condition.

By contrast, the professional world of the clinician is a relatively "quiet" world, almost a tender one; a world in which two people meet, the silent agreement being that one will nourish the other's growth. The clinician does not seek, he is found; he does not impose, he enables; he does not dictate, he perseveres. It is a world unbounded by time and uncluttered by social history; a world in which catastrophe is individualized and in which man, no longer mythified as "Everyman," reveals himself in all his subtlety and complexity. Under these conditions, in which the "nightmare" is but a suicide away, "movements" become intrusions and "causes" become absurd.[7] The clinician's world, in short, is a world of personalized concern and self-conscious neutrality; a world in which confrontation, precisely because of its implications, is handled with infinite care and practiced caution. When a single life is the object of concern, one does not deal with humanity in the abstract.

The consequences of living in two phenomenologically different worlds are amply reflected in the behavior of the social scientist. The clinician, for example, makes a clear distinction between his role as a "professional" and his role as a "private citizen": as a professional he is committed to helping an individual lead a fuller, more self-enhancing life independent of the shifting political and social realities that define the human condition; as a private citizen he may be-

---

[7] It is difficult to examine, however briefly, the world of the clinician without making reference to what Camus (1959) has called the "one truly serious philosophical problem," the problem of suicide. It may well be this concern for the problem of suicide, coupled with clinical psychology's roots in the values and traditions of science, that has produced a profession that can still encourage, even demand, detachment and passivity in the midst of a relationship replete with the most personal and private of dynamisms.

come engaged in causes or movements that seek to change those realities independent of the individuals involved.[8] By so compartmentalizing his life, he is able to participate in what are, for all intents and purposes, two different worlds, and to participate in them without allowing the demand characteristics of one to alter the life style required by the other. It is a situation not unlike most human situations: a single human being lives in multiple worlds, worlds that often coexist in intention but are rarely fused in experience.

Given these premises, and making the assumption that the problems of contemporary American society are of such a kind as to make it increasingly difficult for the behavioral scientist to avoid "role responsibility," the important question becomes one of choosing the most appropriate "dynamic" for forging a new and more effective union between one's clinical and action orientations. Our own experiences would indicate that the problems inherent in the creation of new settings may well provide one of the dynamics for such a synthesis. These problems can be summarized, as Kaplan (1965) puts it, around one basic and general question: "Can men evolve new institutions that enlarge our capacity to solve today's convulsive human problems? Indeed, whether in education or elsewhere, the challenge of the creation of more efficient adaptive institutions is one of the essential problems at this point in the 20th century." From our own point

[8] In a recent article, Ridgeway (1967) has gone so far as to suggest that the most appropriate way for mental health professionals to fulfill their public responsibilities would be for them to withdraw from the arena of traditional helping practices and focus all their attention on becoming a part of movements of social change. Scheff (1967), writing from a sociological point of view, has offered the thesis that clinicians, by the very act of doing what they know best (e.g., psychotherapy), may unwittingly be helping to perpetuate a view of mental illness that is both socially outmoded and culturally antiquated. Amplifying on this position, Levine and Levine (1968, p. 28) have stated: ". . . to the degree the mental health professional sets himself up as the arbiter of psychopathology, and is inclined to view problems in living as the individual's difficulty, to that degree is the mental health professional contributing to the maintenance of cultural lag. By defining the problem as the individual's problem, by accepting the assumption of intrapsychic supremacy, the mental health professional is confirming those norms of society against which one judges human behavior. The psychopathologically oriented practitioner, necessary though he may be, is of necessity conservative, and is of necessity 'counter-revolutionary.' "

of view, and with particular reference to our experiences at the RYC, the process by which a new setting is created is one which, almost by definition, requires a synthesis of one's clinical and action orientations.

Accepting what we have just said as constituting little more than a preliminary analysis of the problem, several things remain clear. First, participation in the creation of new and "helping" settings provides the behavioral scientist with a means of resolving the age-old dilemma of whether his primary professional responsibility is to the distressed individual or to the social sources of his victimization. The very act of "creation" brings with it both the mandate and the opportunity for combining one's remedial and preventive orientations. Second, in the process of creating a new setting, one is inevitably confronted both with the limitations of one's professional training and with the awareness of the kinds of "extraclinical" skills one needs to acquire. For the clinician this may well involve, as Miller (1967) has pointed out, "an appreciation of the complexities of the political process— and how to use it".[9] And finally, in creating the conditions under which the worlds of the clinician and the activist become joined, we may, in reality, be facilitating the development of a new dimension of thought and behavior, a mode of relatedness that Kobler (1961) has called "the contemplative in action."

On the Problem of Leadership It is perhaps in the nature of things that only after one has been in a position to lead does one begin to appreciate just how potent a force the *setting* is in defining the limits (i.e., the possibilities and constraints) of leadership. However seductive it might be, the tendency

[9]It is little short of astonishing to see the degree to which clinicians are discovering the need to develop "extraclinical" skills once they leave their offices, move into the community, and become engaged in the creation of new settings. Frank (1968), for example, in developing a program for training nonprofessionals (inner-city mothers on welfare) and then placing them as counselors in neighborhood walk-in clinics, has found himself having to function as a "fund-raiser, politician, public relations man and community organizer" in order to win community acceptance for his program. It goes without saying that none of these "skills" were a part of Dr. Frank's formal clinical training or background.

to equate leadership with the charismatic machinations of the proverbial "free agent" does more to obscure than illuminate the problem: in the final analysis both the "leader" and the "led" are prisoners of the same historical process, and only to the degree that they begin to understand the dynamics of their mutual captivity can they begin to act as free agents.

From the vantage point of time, it would appear that one of the most important consequences of our experiences at the RYC was the realization of just how meaningless the concept of leadership really is until it is coupled with, and embedded in, an understanding of the history, goals, and stage of development of an organization as a whole. This is not to say that questions of personal charisma and individual differences do not enter into the situation. Rarely is it the case that an organization does not in some important ways reflect the particular values and style of its leader. What it means is that the problem of leadership, if approached solely from the point of view of the personality of the leader, offers little hope of increasing our understanding either of the role of the leader or of how the dynamics of the setting define that role and give it meaning. Indeed, perhaps the essence of that elusive quality we call charisma has less to do with the manner in which one exercises one's role as leader than it does with the effectiveness with which one changes the very dynamic that defines that role in the first place. Given this orientation to the problem of leadership, the question becomes one of understanding the degree to which leaders are aware both of the situational and organizational dynamics that define their position and of the relationship between that definition and the developmental stage of an organization at a particular point in time.[10]

[10]Although our discussion of the problem of leadership is based on our experiences at the RYC, it should be clear that the major influences on any leader often have little to do with the particular setting he leads. More often than not, the leader's range of free movement (i.e., what he can or cannot do) is defined by sources external to the situation and is defined in ways that may have little if anything to do with the goals or dynamics of the setting itself. Thus, for example, the source of one's funds, the amount of funds made available to a program, the

As an organization the RYC was founded on the assumption that only when people were a part of a setting dedicated to their own growth and development—a setting hopefully and finally free of the barriers that separate and isolate people from each other—could they develop the kinds of skills and competencies that could be used in helping others begin the long-overdue journey from poverty and despair to self-determination. With this as its basic premise, and with the subsequent development of organizational processes (e.g., horizontal structure, the sharing of administrative and clinical responsibilities, sensitivity training) consistent with this assumption, the guidelines for what constituted appropriate leadership had already begun to be set. It was, for example, both "unthinkable" and inconsistent with the goals of the program for the RYC to fall prey to what might be called the Simple Simon theory of leadership. The Simple Simon theory of leadership, predicated as it is on a conception of man as dependent, security-oriented, and uncreative, views the leader as someone who because of his superior intelligence, vision, or knowledge can and should assume the position of the unquestioned arbiter of an organization's existence. This type of leadership was now inappropriate for a setting which saw itself, its own needs, and its own aspirations as not too dissimilar from those of its clients.

A second variable affecting the conception of leadership in an organization has to do with the fact that leadership is a "time-bound" phenomenon. The development of most organizations (the RYC was no exception) is rarely linear in nature. More often than not, their life cycles and courses of development involve a series of changes: changes in conceptions, goals, and processes; changes which in pattern are probably similar to those produced by most self-renewing cultures. At the RYC, for example, an organization hardly two years of age, one can already discern at least four phases

---

underlying philosophy of the funding agent, and the quality of the relationship between the funding agent and the newly created setting have as much, if not more, to do with defining the leader's role and position as anything else.

or cycles of change. To begin with, there was the period of "innovation," a period of time during which the organization was developing that particular ethos which came to define the setting. This was closely followed by a period of "implementation," a time (and a period of upheaval) during which its basic philosophy was being translated into specific internal processes and patterns of conflict resolution. With the onset of comparative stability, the setting entered that phase of its life, the period of "consolidation," during which the very regularities that had been established could begin to be questioned and reassessed. And finally, with the increased awareness that often results from a period of intense reevaluation, one can begin to discern a period of "renewal," a time during which it appears as if the conditions are being created for the entire process to begin all over again. Given this conception of the history and development of an organization, it appears reasonable to assume that no one person need necessarily be the organization's "man for all seasons," its leader for all time. The kind of leader an organization needs—the kind of person who can best facilitate the setting's development at a particular point in time—will vary from period to period, and it may well be that the recognition and anticipation of change (rather than nonchange) is what ensures a setting's creative continuity.

Given these conditions, the conception of leadership at the RYC, at least in terms of the setting's first leader, had little to do with helping the setting achieve its more "official" or "public" goals (i.e., providing supportive and rehabilitative services to disadvantaged youths and their families). Rather, his "mandate," as it were, his most important function as a leader, was to help create the conditions under which it became possible for people (i.e., the staff) to begin to view and relate to one another as sources of help, support, and growth. Put another way, the most appropriate definition of leadership during the RYC's formative period of life was one that had to be predicated on a certain conception of organizations, the assumption being that only after an organization had developed a certain sustaining image of itself as a setting could it devote itself to the tasks for which it was funded. The priorities were clear; the conditions under which the setting was created had seen to that.

The second function of the RYC's first leader was equally clear and equally related to the goals and values of the setting: to create the conditions for his own replacement. It will be recalled (see Chapter 4) that one of the questions the RYC was funded to explore was whether or not a "helping setting" had to be controlled or administered by a professional. Under these conditions, any attempt by the RYC's first Director to perpetuate or ensure his own tenure would have violated the goals of the program. More important, however, for the RYC's first leader to have acted in any way other than to try to create the conditions for his own replacement would have broken faith with one of the basic assumptions underlying the setting: the assumption that given appropriate conditions for growth, people, often regardless of their particular backgrounds or levels of formal preparation, would be both able and willing to assume responsibilities heretofore either denied them or presumed to lie beyond their "competence." This being the case, leadership had to be defined in terms of "replacement" and "transition," in terms consistent with the values and goals of the setting.[11]

[11]It should be pointed out that most organizations are so structured that the concept of "self-replacement" cannot become an inherent and integral part of the definition and role of leadership. Put another way, the attainment of the position of leadership in an organization usually carries with it the implication that one has reached the highest point of one's development, both professionally and organizationally. Rarely is it the case that the social system has built into it any systematic progression beyond the point of "leadership." Consequently, given the power, status, and money inherent in the leadership role, it becomes difficult if not impossible for leaders either to view themselves as anything but "men for all seasons" or to conceive of the training of their own replacements as a meaningful and rewarding aspect of their own tenures of office. So long as this remains the case, so long as the social system views the attainment of leadership as the culmination rather than the continuation of individual development, so long will we have to rely on old age, death, failure, or organizational upheaval for the primary causes of changes in leadership. In many ways, the fate of the RYC might have been very different had not its first leader had "somewhere to go" (i.e., back to the University) after completing his six months as Director. It is more than likely that had he remained as the RYC's Director, he would have done little to

Final Diary Entry: 1/2/67.
Today was my last day as Director of the RYC. Tomorrow,
Sue, the baby, and I leave on vacation. For me it's over, but
for Scotty, Jack (Scotty's choice as Deputy Director), and the
rest of the guys it's just beginning.

It was a good last day, especially in light of all the place
has meant to me these many months. We cut short our staff
meeting and broke one of our own "house rules": we all went
out, bought some beer, and took it up to the office, where
we drank it. And don't think the kids don't know we broke
a rule. They put it to us right away, promised to bring it up
at their next meeting, and will surely press for some kind of
staff punishment.

At any rate, we sat around for a while, drank some beer,
reminisced, and told some dirty stories. Then the guys gave
me a wallet with an inscription that just broke me up. It
reads: "Kelly, From your exuberant RYC staff."

Tonight I was thinking about how lucky it was that my
"agreement" with the RYC was that I'd only be its Director
for the first six months of the program. My (and the staff's)
knowing, from the very beginning, that I'd only be here for
six months made things a lot easier, if not more possible.
I didn't have to pace myself as much as I would have otherwise—I could afford to "shoot everything"; and Scotty and
I could take the time to develop the kind of relationship
that would make the period of transition an easier one for
both of us.

I think it would be bad, both for me and for the program,
if I were to stay on as Director. To put it concretely, I'm
"finished," "used up," and just plain tired. Now it's Scotty's
turn. The RYC is off the ground, but it needs new ideas, ideas
that come from someone who isn't used up the way I am,
ideas more in tune with the way the RYC is today and will
be tomorrow, rather than the way it was yesterday.

At any rate, it's over. I'll stay on as a consultant and help
out with the in-service training sessions and in any other
way Scotty wants, but it'll never be the same. And maybe
that's best. All I can think of now (and this will probably
change after I've been away from the RYC for a few days) is
no more regular 4:00 a.m. calls, no more sitting in the RYC

---

help the setting in terms of its continuing development. He was, as his
final diary entry indicates, "used up" and "finished," and had he been
"forced" either by personal or "system-wide" considerations to perpetuate his tenure of office, it is quite conceivable that neither he nor the
program would have benefited from this prolongation of his "tour
of duty."

living room and wondering whether or not the RYC was really "my bag." It *was* my bag, now it's Scotty's.

Right now I'm thinking: Thank God I've got someplace to go, even if it is a place like the University, a place which, after the RYC, is bound to seem so terribly quiet and dull . . . maybe for a long, long time.

Although our brief discussion of the problem of leadership has, of necessity, been restricted to the RYC, it should be clear that we view some of our experiences as relevant to the problem of leadership in other helping settings, especially those in the process of being created. In the final analysis, however, the problem of leadership, like any other problem involving the confluence of human values and organizational goals, is embedded in the assumptions one makes about oneself and others. This being the case, its eventual understanding will, of necessity, have to await a more systematic analysis of the question of how man's conceptions about himself and others determine his behavior.

On the Question of Bureaucracies One of the more dramatic of the not altogether happy consequences of our experiences at the RYC was the realization of just how easy (and self-defeating) it can be for a program to view itself and to act as if it were a truly independent and autonomous setting, a setting completely free from external control or influence. From the very beginning the RYC was a part of New Haven's community action agency (CPI), and, as such, all decisions concerning "what to do and how to do it" always had to be made with the full realization that there would always be "forces" outside the setting, in the central administrative body of CPI, to contend with. The RYC was, in short, but one of many programs administered by and answerable to an "umbrella" agency, and this situation made it inevitable that the RYC would have to cope with a bureaucracy not of its own making.

It is extremely difficult, even at this point in time, to offer any final (or necessarily valid) judgment concerning the overall effect on a program of always having to "answer to," and often being under the control of, people and processes whose concerns are sometimes different and removed from the setting itself. Any large organization—and CPI in 1966 was a large organization—must, of necessity, develop those kinds of internal controls through which it can monitor the progress and problems of programs (subsystems) for which it is responsible. An organization's bureaucracy is, after all, an attempt to re-create in organization form the governmental pattern of "checks and balances." In theory, its major function is to provide the kind of administrative support and feedback that will enable a program to realize its goals with a minimal amount of conflict and chaos. In actuality, whether a bureaucracy facilitates or impedes a program's progress has less to do with theory or intent than it does with the bureaucracy's own conception of its role and function in those programs for which it bears administrative responsibility. This conception, in turn, is more than a little dependent on the stage of development, level of awareness, and value system of the "mother organization" itself. Thus, for example, when an organization as a whole is at that point in its life when its thrust is basically "innovative" (e.g., CPI in the years between 1963 and 1965), it will tend to develop the kind of bureaucracy that will tolerate and support "deviance" within its subsystems or member programs. When, on the other hand, an organization reaches that stage in its development when its primary concerns are those having to do with internal stability, consolidation, and self-perpetuation (e.g., CPI in the years between 1966 and 1968), it will tend to develop a bureaucracy that reflects these concerns, a bureaucracy that discourages deviance, inhibits innovation in its member programs, and rewards the kind of conformity that facilitates administrative "manageability." It is at this point that "coordination" becomes a bureaucratic euphemism for subsystem subjugation.

The reader will recall that one of the entries in the diary presented in this chapter (see *Day 12*) dealt with a visit to the RYC by "the man from downtown." It might be helpful at this point to study that "visit" from the point of view of what it offers by way of illustrating not only the overall impact on a program of having to contend with a bureaucracy but, more important, what it tells us about the predicament of those people who are a part of and must represent that bureaucracy. The following, then, is an attempt, admittedly incomplete, to describe the "world of the bureaucrat." Before proceeding, however, we would hasten to point out that, as was the case with respect to our descriptions of the "worlds" of the clinician, the social activist, and the leader, our primary concern is *not* with problems of personality dynamics, although they invariably enter into the situation. Rather, our interest is in exploring the ways in which our behavior is shaped by the social systems of which we are a part.

We might begin our analysis by stressing what was, at least from our point of view, one of the most salient features of our encounter with the "downtown" supervisor: the realization that he (perhaps more than most people) was, at least in terms of his relationship to the RYC, not free to act as his own agent. We say this for a number of reasons, not the least of which has to do with the fact that his behavior that day in 1966 (i.e., the stress he placed on the RYC "shaping up" and doing things the "right way") was at variance with both his previous behavior at CPI (during the period of time between 1963 and 1965, when CPI as a whole was a "deviant" organization) and his own history prior to the time he joined CPI (he had been an aggressive labor leader who, after coming up through the ranks, had been instrumental in organizing and leading strikes to help workers win greater freedom, dignity, and job security). In other words, despite the fact that he was a man whose own history was replete with examples of "establishment-busting," he was now no longer in a position to support the very kind of behavior that had enabled him to innovate, to succeed, and to grow. He was now the representative of an "establishment," and regardless of his own personal sentiments, he was no longer free (at least in the technical or organizational sense of the term) to encourage and support behavior that was at variance with the overall expectations of the larger system.

Given this background, it would be relatively easy to conclude that the world of the "middle-level" bureaucrat is founded upon a narrow and self-seeking compromise, the kind of compromise in which freedom and independence are sacrificed on the alter of self-interest and security. That the situation is far more complex than that becomes clear once we review the history of the RYC and consider the question of how its development could do little but exacerbate the "Catch 22"-like binds in which the middle-level administrators who would eventually "monitor" its operations were already caught. But what were these binds? How were they affected by the development of the RYC? And what do they tell us about the world of the bureaucrats?

To begin with, it would be important to recall that the RYC, no different from many other experimental poverty programs, was developed outside of CPI, was conceived of by people who were not employees of the organization, and only became a part of CPI for purposes of funding. This is not to say that CPI had nothing to do with the drafting of the original RYC proposal; rather, what we are saying is that by and large the basic ideas and concepts that went into the formation of the RYC came from people who were not an integral part of the community action agency. We mention this for no other reason than to point out what seems to be one of the basic binds that define the world of the bureaucrat: he is often, usually through no "fault" of his own, administratively in charge of programs that were developed without his active participation and involvement. It is a situation in which the man who assumes the greatest administrative "liability" for a program has the least to do with the process through which it was created. Under these conditions, it should come as no great surprise that many bureaucrats tend to view programs for which they are administratively responsible from a perspective that is predominantly "nuts and bolts" rather than "process"-oriented. When one cannot find anything of "oneself" (i.e., one's own ideas, values, or sense of direction) in a program—when, in fact, one has been excluded from the creative process itself—it is more than a little difficult to identify with that program in anything more than "administrative" ways.[12]

A related but somewhat different "bind" that defines the world of the middle-level bureaucrat is one which, for want of a better term, we might call the "authority-responsibility split." It is the kind of bind that is created whenever a person is placed in a position in which there is an inverse relationship between the degree of responsibility he must assume in a situation and the amount of authority he has to alter or influence the course of events. In the case of the RYC, for example, it was a situation in which the "downtown" administrator was *always* held directly responsible for whatever happened to the RYC but *never* really had the authority to do anything more than reinforce the kinds of policy decisions that had already been made by those above him in the organizational hierarchy. He was always in the position of being highly accountable and highly powerless at the same time, a position that rarely lends itself to anything more than feelings of ambivalence and impotence and a pattern of behavior that is oriented toward insuring a "safe" conformity at the expense of a "risky" creativity. It is not surprising, therefore, that the "man from downtown" should have responded to the RYC in the ways described in the *Day 12* entry of our diary. The bureaucrat lives in a world of endless vulnerability. But unlike those who are intimately

[12]The situation described here is of course not peculiar to middle-level administrators in large organizations; it is only more obvious in their case. More generally, it is a situation that often occurs whenever new and innovative ideas are introduced into an ongoing social system. It is a problem that has less to do with the inherent worth or merit of the new ideas than it does with the way in which these new ideas are introduced into the setting. All too often the process is as follows: the ideas are developed outside the setting, are presented to the setting's members as a *fait accompli*, and are presented with the expectation that the very people who have *not* been involved in the development of the new program will now implement it with as much enthusiasm, commitment, and concern as its creators. Rarely does this turn out to be the case. More often than not, if those who are called upon to implement a program do not feel any prior commitment to or involvement in that program, the results are at best halfhearted support and at worst hostility or apathy. It is a situation not unlike the one described as characteristic of the plight of the middle-level administrator.

involved in the day-to-day trials and tribulations of a program, his is a vulnerability that is rarely complemented by opportunities for direct participation in either the creative or ongoing aspects of the very program for which he is usually administratively liable. His is truly a "marginal" existence, for he lives in a world in which his own feelings of success or failure are always (and almost completely) dependent on the efforts of others.[13]

In this chapter we have tried to describe, in as much detail as possible, the opening days of the Residential Youth Center. Our reasons for doing so were many and varied, but primarily we hoped to be able to share with the reader many of the problems and conflicts that confronted the new setting once it ceased being "preoperational" and began that phase of its life in which it assumed a "public" existence. Beyond this, we would expect that the value of such in-depth descriptions lies in what they can provide future researchers and theory builders in the way of helpful raw data, the kinds of data that may facilitate the development of a more

[13]During one of our recent trips to Washington, D.C., a trip undertaken in the course of seeking new funds for a program that would enable us to open Residential Youth Centers in a number of different cities in the eastern or mid-Atlantic regions of the country, we had occasion to find ourselves once again in the offices of the Job Corps. Because of the nature of our negotiations, and because the proposal we had submitted was again of the experimental or demonstration variety, we found ourselves in the office of an official whose status within the Job Corps hierarchy was roughly similar to the one occupied by our own "man from downtown." At one point in the course of our exploratory conversations, we happened to glance at a poem that this official had pinned to one of the bulletin boards that hung in his office. The words of that poem aptly and succinctly summarize all that we have tried to convey in the preceding pages. In a word, the poem "tells it the way it is"—at least the way it is from the point of view of the world of the bureaucrat.

It's not my job to run the train.
The whistle I can't blow.
It's not for me to say how far,
The train's allowed to go.
It's not my place to shoot off steam.
Nor even clang the bell.
But let the damn thing jump the track,
And see who catches hell.

comprehensive frame of reference for understanding the problem of the creation of new settings.

In addition to describing the early days of the RYC, we have tried to deal with at least a few of the major issues that invariably affect the course of development of most new settings. In focusing attention on such problems as the meaning of action, the role of leadership, and the question of bureaucracies, we have attempted to analyze, however briefly and incompletely, some of the issues which, while often in the background of events, nevertheless exert a determining influence on the development and viability of most institutions. All settings, particularly those with a "helping" or "action" orientation, must deal with these issues, and we can only assume that to the degree that they are brought out into the open, subjected to critical analysis, and discussed from a point of view other than raw emotionality, to that degree can we begin to achieve the kind of perspective that will enable future builders of institutions to create settings that are less self-defeating of their goals and aspirations.

In the next two chapters we shall turn to the problem of how one goes about trying to evaluate the effectiveness of a program like the Residential Youth Center. As the reader can already surmise, the problem of researching a setting like the RYC is more than a little complex and is fraught with most of the difficulties inherent in all action research. Nevertheless, the attempt must be made to assess and measure results, and the following chapters will concern themselves with this attempt.

Chapter 8 Research
The Descriptive Approach

Some circumstantial evidence is very strong as when
you find a trout in the milk.
—Henry David Thoreau.

Given the present level of our knowledge and sophistication,
only a fool would try to claim that there is anything "scientific," in the narrow or traditional sense of the term, about
most current attempts to evaluate the effectiveness of community action programs. Social scientists by the score (all too
often, unfortunately, those with virtually no experience outside the world of academia or the comparatively antiseptic
atmosphere of the laboratory setting) have been quick to
point out the shortcomings and limitations of most research
in the area of the War on Poverty. Their lack of "credentials"
notwithstanding, however, the fact remains that from the
point of view of traditional research there is much to be said
for the cautions and criticisms they have raised about action
research. Given the frame of reference of its critics, one
would be hard pressed to try to justify the existence of action
research on the basis of the criteria (i.e., objectivity, control,
and replication) usually associated with the process of scientific inquiry.

Problems of Action Research
All too often, those involved in the area of action research
have been placed in the position of first apologizing for and
then defending what has come to be labeled parochially as
an "inferior" (rather than a "different") approach to the
problems of assessing highly volatile and complex settings.
With such a prevailing climate, only rarely does it become
possible to initiate any sort of meaningful dialogue. More
often than not, the result is the increased estrangement between those whose commitment to a particular conception
of science leads them to view the efforts of the action researcher in little more than pejorative terms and those whose
commitment to research as an instrument for social change
causes them to view the "basic researcher" as a rigid and
dogmatic empiricist who spends the major portion of his time

researching problems of questionable import. Brooks (1965, pp. 37–39), in a paper dealing with the problems inherent in action research, has focused attention on this and other issues, and has concluded:

Mention should be made of some of the constraints which operate to hinder or frustrate effective evaluation of community action programs.

The first is the long-standing tension between the realms of action and research. Certainly the actors in these two realms have tended to view each other with a large measure of suspicion and, on occasion, even hostility. The action-oriented professional has regularly lambasted the ivory tower, whose inhabitants supposedly spend all their time gathering data aimed not at solving concrete human problems, but at building bigger and better theories to be discussed at stuffy conferences and debated in unreadable journals. The researcher, for his part, is often heard belittling the action-oriented practitioner for his failure to conceptualize clearly; for his inability to think in terms of systems; for his tendency to act on the basis of subjective whims or impressions, ignoring existing empirical data which might suggest altogether different actions; for his failure to realize that the actions which he takes in the future could be made more rational and effective if only he would engage in (or support) a little follow-up research on the actions he is taking today; and for his apparent fear of evaluation on the grounds that it might call his own actions into question.

A second constraint is that imposed by the disciplinary boundaries which separate the various social sciences from one another. Poverty is an interdisciplinary problem; to approach it with only the concepts of sociology, or psychology, or economics, or political science, or anthropology, etc., is to omit a broad range of variables which must ultimately be taken into account.

A third constraint is the ethical necessity for continuous feedback of research findings into community action programs, thereby producing adjustments or improvements in their operation. While this is the correct procedure from the action—and indeed, the ethical—point of view, it has the unfortunate effect of tossing a monkey-wrench into the research design constructed at the program's outset. The person interested solely in the research implications of a program might prefer that it be carried through to completion without alteration, whether successful or not, so as to yield unsullied findings of maximal generalizability (and perhaps publishability as well). Fourth is the constraint imposed by the time dimension. Since in the United States social action programs are typically sponsored either by foundations or by political administrations with relatively short life-expectancies, the pressure for immediate results is always strong. The objectives of the community action programs are, however, long-range in nature; their attainment can become apparent only with the emergence of a new generation, hopefully, one freed from the chains of poverty and ignorance. At the end of, say, two or three years, the community action programs may have produced some detectable reorientations of attitudes and aspirations, perhaps some minute but encouraging changes in the statistics which document the plight of the poor, but to expect much more is unrealistic. Our evaluation procedures, then, must be extremely sensitive to social change in its incipient stages.

Finally, a fifth constraint is the openness of the system which the human community comprises. The community is not a laboratory in which all the variables can be carefully controlled and manipulated at will. All the diversity and unpredictability which characterizes human beings conspire to plague the researcher's attempts to construct a "pure" design for community action research.

In this chapter we shall present some of the research that was carried out at the RYC during the first two years of the program's existence. Unlike many War on Poverty programs, the RYC was funded as an E&D (experimental and demonstration) project. This meant that the question of research was, from the very beginning, of central concern to the program, and was not, as is often the case in most service-oriented projects, tacked on seemingly as an afterthought. It also meant—and this is most important—that while we acknowledged (but did not necessarily apologize for) the myriad problems, both methodological and theoretical, inherent in all attempts to evaluate the effectiveness of action programs, the RYC would become a setting within which both service and research goals would be joined.[1]

[1]For a comprehensive review of the problems of evaluative research, particularly with respect to programs of action and social change, the reader is referred to the work of Suchman (1967), Freeman and Sherwood (1965), and Beiser (1965).

The Descriptive Approach: Some Background

During one of the RYC's regular sensitivity sessions specifically devoted to a discussion of the research staff's problems in documenting the Center's development, the following interaction took place:[2]

Butch:

I've been sitting here and listening to you guys talk about
research for about a half-hour now, and frankly the more I
hear the more pissed-off I'm getting about all this research
bullshit! Right now I don't give a good god-damn if I never
hear another word about research or statistics for the rest of
my life. Now, you guys can call this a sensitivity issue or
anything you want, but all I know is that I've had it up to
here with this research crap.

(A hush falls over the room and Butch, after looking around
to make sure that his "explosion" has registered, continues.)

I'm sick and tired of sitting here and being told that now,

---

[2]It should be pointed out that when we refer to the "research staff"
we are referring to two Yale University students, both of whom were
essentially unpaid, full-time members of the staff, without whom the
job of documenting and assessing the RYC would have been impossible. We wish to thank these students, Mr. David Hoffman and Mr.
Frank Neisser, for their help in the organization of this chapter and
for all they contributed to the RYC.

It should also be pointed out that being a member of the research
staff at the RYC did not mean that the researchers' only "job" was to
gather and evaluate data for purposes of documentation and evaluation. The researchers, no different from the rest of the staff, "lived in,"
had administrative duties, often carried a case load, and participated
in the evening programs. There were two reasons for their "total"
rather than singular "research" involvement in the Center. First, it was
felt that experiencing the problems of the setting as fully as possible
would be an aid in terms of the kinds of research questions and problems that would be brought to the attention of the staff. And second,
it was felt that the researchers, no different from anyone else, should
share in the day-to-day life of the Center. From a purely research-
oriented point of view, the involvement of the researchers in the program as a whole was helpful in the sense that it enabled them to
establish rapport with the RYC's youngsters and their families, people
who very rarely make "good subjects" for research studies utilizing
interviewing and attitudinal assessment techniques. Finally, we should
also mention that the research staff, partly because of their own involvement in the program, was able to engage the help of the rest
of the staff in the evaluation of data and in the writing of governmental
reports. In a very real sense, their willingness to participate in aspects
of the program that were not directly related to the problems of research made it possible for the rest of the staff, some of whom had a
number of feelings about "things academic," to venture into areas in
which they might not normally have wanted to get involved.

after being in the Center for about five months, my kid is going to work 38 percent more of the time than before he came into the RYC. Big fucking deal! What the hell does that tell me? And what's more, what the hell does that tell people who don't know about the RYC, about the guts of this operation? Nothing. Nothing at all. It's a lot of bullshit.
Kelly:
Butch, I think you're going overboard on this.
Butch:
The hell I am. I put my blood and guts into working with Ev and his crazy mother and all I come away with is that Ev is going to work 38 percent more of the time. Big god-damn deal. Where's Ev in all this? Where am I? Where's there anything that tells about what goes on between us day in and day out?
Scotty:
I think I know what's bugging you, Butch, but you know as well as I do that Washington wants these statistics. And you also know as well as I do that whether or not we get re-funded depends a helluva lot on what these statistics show after a year.
Butch:
Look Scotty, you don't have to remind me about that. I know all about it. Washington wants statistics; CPI wants statistics; the whole world wants statistics. I know all that shit, and I know it's important. All I'm saying is that, whether or not we're re-funded, if the research doesn't tell it like it really is —you know, what it feels like to work in a place like this, what it's like to pour your whole self into a kid—then from my point of view it isn't worth a shit.

Following this confrontation, the staff decided that in addition to the "usual" research an attempt should be made to describe the program along the lines outlined by Butch. Consequently, the succeeding pages will be devoted to chronicling both the nature of the program and its effect on one person currently participating in it. Butch, we have a feeling, will not be totally satisfied with what follows (as we pointed out in the previous chapter, Butch is something of a perfectionist), but we hope he understands that at least we tried.

A Day in the Life of Will K., RYC Worker: An Observational Record

For purposes of presenting as full a commentary as possible, we have adopted an observational technique not too dissimilar from the one utilized by Barker (1951) in *One Boy's Day*. One worker was selected as the subject for the observation. We followed him for one complete day and recorded, as faithfully as possible, everything he did and said. Our focus invariably shifted from microscopic to macroscopic levels of description, depending on the nature of the activity and the amount of time available to describe the worker's behavior. We allowed ourselves a degree of inferential freedom with respect to the worker's motives, emotions, and experiences at any given point in the observation. We felt it was important and appropriate that we record in as direct a manner as possible our immediate perceptions of what the worker was feeling and experiencing at any particular time. We also felt it necessary to describe things in everyday language and not to resort to the utilization of theoretical jargon that went beyond the descriptive data. What we are most interested in is providing the reader with a full and rich account of the events and settings comprising one day in the life of an RYC worker.

The Subject: Will K. Will is a 34-year-old Negro, a tall, thin man who is married and has two children (a boy of 8 and a girl 7 years old). He became a member of the RYC's staff in 1967 when, as a consequence of the Director's leaving and the reorganization that followed (the Deputy Director assuming the Director's position and an RYC worker moving up to take the role of Deputy Director), an opening became available on the staff. Immediately prior to joining the staff of the RYC, Will was employed as a neighborhood worker in one of CPI's inner-city operations.

With the exception of five years spent in the Air Force, Will has lived his entire life in New Haven. The second youngest of eight children, he was born in what is now called "the Hill" section of the city, a part of town which, as Will puts it: "Was torn up and demolished when I was twenty-one. Now it's called 'rehabilitated.' "

Will never finished high school, leaving in the eighth grade when he was 16 years of age. School for Will was an almost interminable series of boring and meaningless experiences;

days devoid of excitement, lacking in fulfillment, and "tailor-made for devilment":

Deep inside me I think I knew, maybe after about five years, that I'd been "had." In a way I guess I really left school way before I was sixteen. It was all such a bore.

Oh, some of it was O.K., like when I felt I was really learning something that made sense. Even a few of the teachers were fine, real fine. But most of it was a bore.

Sooner or later I'd get to kidding around, like when people started taking things too serious. It was kind of like sitting there and listening to a bunch of mumbo-jumbo and eating it up like it was something real. Well, at that point I'd start to joke around or I'd take out my lunch and begin to eat it right there in class. That'd stop 'em for a while. Well, then I'd start to staying away from school and getting into a few fights with teachers whenever I did show up. I guess you could say that everyone was happy when I hit sixteen. School and I parted company by "mutual consent."

It was only after leaving school that Will began reading voraciously, a "habit" that he has maintained to the present day:

I'd pick up any book that was around and read it. Didn't matter what it was about. Law, bookkeeping, football, machinery. I'd just pick it up and read it. Now it was *me* doing it. Now it made sense.

Once out of school Will entered the "world of work," and in a period of less than two years he worked as a stock boy, a furniture lifter, a laborer on a banana truck, and a "would-be prize fighter." None of these jobs meant very much to Will. Sooner or later they all became "boring with no future."

In 1951, after taking a long, hard look at what he was doing, Will decided to join the Air Force:

I wasn't going anywhere or doing myself any good. Both my older brothers were in the service, so I decided to join up.

Besides which I was getting involved with guys who were doing more than just petty stealing or snaking around. So I wanted to get away from it all, from everything.

Will doesn't talk very much about the years he spent in the Air Force (years that took him to California, Illinois, Massachusetts, Japan, and finally, Korea) except to say that it was time "for looking, for listening, and for learning about people."

For Will, returning to New Haven after spending five years

in the Air Force meant little more than returning to the
kinds of jobs and a way of life that was his before he entered the service. Over a period of time he worked as a
cook ("Pretty good pay but lousy hours; and no time to live.")
and a bartender ("The only job where you can make some
money, meet people, and still collect your unemployment
check—all at the same time."). But regardless of the job,
something was missing, something was always missing:

Maybe it was "meaning." You know, like you're a man; and
you got to do something that makes a difference, something
that "means" something.

After getting married, Will continued to look for work, only
this time not only for jobs that paid well but for jobs that
had "a future." He tried the dry cleaning business, and were
it not for a series of demoralizing experiences, he probably
would have continued in that area of work:

I started as a helper and worked my way up to being a manager, but it didn't work out. I learned everything there is to
know about the dry cleaning business—accounting, bookkeeping, advertising, machines, the whole works—but somehow whenever there was an opening for a partner or a
chance to really move up I kept hearing things like "Will,
you're too important to me in the job you're in right now,
so I can't spare you." It got so that one time the man I was
working for wanted to sell his business, but the buyer
wouldn't buy unless I was part of the deal. Well, I wasn't
going to be nobody's boy to buy and sell, so I finally got
out for good.

Having turned his back on an area in which his performance
might have "paid off"—paid off in terms of advancement for
himself and security for his family—Will was once again a
man on the move, searching, looking, listening and, finally,
finding:

I guess you could say it's got a lot to do with Malcolm X.
I started hearing about him and then I began to read the man
himself. He said it for me and a lot of other guys.

Oh, I never went in for conking my hair or getting a
process, but I was ashamed to be black. I used to tell people
I was part Indian or some crap like that. And then I heard
the man; I read what he said; and I began to take a good
look at Will, at what was important to him, what was real,
and what had to be done.

While he knew he'd have a hard time earning the kind of

money he could make in the dry cleaning business, Will went to work for CPI as a neighborhood worker. After a while, although he was considered to be one of the better indigenous workers on the staff, Will became somewhat disillusioned with CPI, especially with some of the black people employed by the organization:

Shit, CPI after a while just wasn't what I thought it would be. I found myself with a bunch of niggers, some of them sitting around and wanting nothing more than to wear white shirts and ties and carry clipboards and attaché cases. The people "downtown" would say "Be creative," but they'd never do what you suggested. They didn't know what the people wanted, and after a while they really didn't seem to want to work with them or help them get organized.

Will is quick to admit that he "pulled strings" to become a part of the RYC.

I heard about the program and I knew that Scotty would be running it once Kelly left. I knew there'd be an opening on the staff, and I got to Scotty as soon as I could. Scotty and I have been close ever since I can remember. We came up together and to this day he's my best friend. We talked about the possibilities of me joining the staff and we talked about the problems that it would involve. You know, problems like favoritism, problems of working together and what that could do to our friendship, things like that. Anyway here I am; and I've been here for more than a year and a half so things must have worked out O.K.

There is really very little that can be added to what Will has said about himself. He is a restless man, a man whose easy smile never completely obscures his dark, sometimes-sad, often-brooding eyes. Perhaps the best way of describing Will is to say that there is an almost indefinable "presence" about him, a feeling of strength and tenderness, passion and loneliness—all these things together, sometimes muted and mingled, often stark and alone. Will's world is in many ways his alone to know, but to those of us who work with him it is a world that is rarely serene: it is a world that offers its possibilities painfully and bestows its guarantees begrudgingly:

I don't really know what I want for myself any more than I really know what I want for a kid that I work with. All I know is that when a kid's finished with me he's got to be a man and have pride. He's got to be able to say "Look at me; I'm worth something, I'm alive, brother, and I matter."

Will's Day Before proceeding with the chronicle of Will's day, we should make mention of the fact that whether or not the day to be described was a "typical" one is very much an open question. It was a typical day in the sense that it was filled with the kinds of activities (e.g., interactions with youngsters, a home visit, a trip to a boy's work site, meetings) that have become an integral part of an RYC worker's job. It was not typical, however, in a number of other respects. To begin with, the observation was not done on a day when Will's evening program was scheduled to take place.[3] In addition, the chronicle does not "catch" Will during the many times when he has been called into the Center late at night or early in the morning when one of his youngsters was in trouble, had a problem, or just wanted to talk. Finally, the chronicle does not describe Will during the times when he is either on "live-in" duty (i.e., when he spends the night at the Center to relieve a "regular" live-in counselor) or when it is his turn to spend an entire weekend at the RYC. Having thus qualified (or, perhaps, further confused) the term "typical," we now turn to the chronicle of Will's Day.

7:45–9:00 a.m.

It is Monday, July 8, 1968, and a dull, gray heat hangs over the city. It is one of those oppressive summer days, the kind of day that makes each movement an effort.

Will comes into the RYC. He moves quickly through the hall and begins to climb the stairs, two at a time, that lead from the main floor to the kids' rooms. He is wearing dungarees and a striped yellow shirt. A small wooden African figurine dangles from a plastic string around his neck. It sways from side to side as he bounds up the stairs.

Will pauses at the top of the landing and looks into a room whose door is slightly ajar. Inside the room a kid is lying, seemingly only half-asleep, in his bed. The covers are strewn on the floor and the sheet is bunched up at the foot of the bed. Will stops, looks into the room, and flings the door open so that it makes a loud thud as it slaps against the wall.

[3]Will is one of the staff members who functions as a group leader for the Residents' House Council. The House Council meets two evenings a week from 7:00 to 9:00 p.m. The House Council program, a program that provides the residents with the dual opportunity of discussing house policy and conducting their own sensitivity sessions, is one of Will's "regular" RYC activities.

Will:
Godammit Sam, don't you know you're supposed to be at work at 9? Get your butt outta bed. Jesus Christ you're ugly in the morning. Now get your ass outta bed.

(*Note*: Sam, one of Will's kids, has recently been appointed the supervisor of a teen-age employment center located in one of New Haven's Negro ghettos. The employment center's function is to help teen-agers find summer employment in any one of a number of business concerns that have made an effort to create summer openings for inner-city adolescents within their organizations. Sam has also recently been awarded a half-scholarship to a rather prestigious prep school and will be attending it in the fall if he can raise another $450 scholar-ship money on his own.)

Will:
Another thing, Ugly, did you ask Mr. Bowles about that other 450 dollars yet?
Sam:
Yeah, I asked him. He said "No can do."
Will:
Well, that means you're gonna have to scrounge around some more on your own. You got to do that yourself. Nobody's gonna do that for you. I'll be talking to Hugh Price today and find out where he thinks we can get the money. But right now get your big fat ass out of bed and out to work.
Sam:
O.K. O.K. O.K. Now get your ugly face outta here.

Will smiles and leaves the room. He walks down the cor-ridor and pauses to nod at a boy who has set up an ironing board in his room and is ironing a pair of chinos. He con-tinues on and stops before the next to last room on the floor. He looks in.
Will:
Hey Sligo, when you get back to the Center? (The boy he is talking to is sitting up in his bed and points to his throat.) Still got a sore throat? O.K., see you later. Take care now.

Will goes on to the last room on the floor. He pauses for a moment and then, with a broad smile on his face, kicks open the door.
Will:
Hold it, Nean, it's the police!
Nean:
Cut the shit, Will, it's too early in the morning.
                    (Will almost doubles up from laughing)

Will:

Nean, what you doing running around naked and with a
hard-on?

(Both he and Nean are laughing now)

Nean:

Hard-on my ass. This ain't no hard-on. Even so it's biggern
yours'll ever be.

Will:

And uglier too!

Both Will and Nean continue to laugh and "sound" on
each other. Finally, Nean slams the door in mock anger and
Will turns away.

Will makes his way back downstairs and into the kitchen.
He goes over to a large coffee urn that stands on a long
table and pours himself a cup of coffee. (The cup he uses is
Will's alone, his "personal" cup, the only square-shaped cup
in the house.) He carefully adds a lot of milk and sugar,
stirs it, and take his first sip:

Will:

Hey Chip, the coffee's weak.

Chip:

How would you know with all that crap you put in it.

Will:

Never mind how I know. It's weak as a baby's piss.

Chip:

Well don't blame me. Blame Sterns, he made it this morning.

Will:

Wait'll I see Sterns.

Will turns and goes into the office. As he does so, he lights
up his first cigarette of the day.

Once in the office Will goes over to one of the desks with
a telephone on it and sits down. It's now 8:25 and Scotty
is sitting at a desk that faces the one Will is seated behind:

Will:

Scotty, we got to do something about that plaster on the
second floor. It's falling worse than in my old house on
Spruce Street.

Scotty looks up from the stack of memos he is reading,
scowls, and looks down again.

Will:

Don't look away, man, I'm telling you it's getting real bad
up there. Plaster all over the place.

Scotty:

Think I don't know it? I also know what the hell we got to

go through to get something fixed in here, so don't go rappin'
to me so early on a Monday morning.

They both look at each other for a moment and Scotty
looks down again. Will smiles.

Will:

Mr. Director, somebody put splinters in your toilet paper
this morning.

Scotty looks up again, shakes his head, and smiles weakly.

Will sits back, pulls out a small notebook from his pocket
and begins to make out his itinerary for the day. As he writes
he mutters to himself: "Shoot, I'll be lucky to get half of
this done today." Will's itinerary is somewhat cryptic but
reads as follows:

Today
1. Call or see Steve Moore on Girls court 15 & Zampini.
2. Work Site: Gambrell, Daley, Sam.
3. Hugh Price on scholarship for Sam.
4. Call Welfare Title XIX on Daley.
5. See Mrs. Montrose on Larry.
6. Check with Mr. Williams on Larry.
7. Consent for Gambrell.
8. Pay Bills.
9. Call Walhimer.
10. Check High School for Sam's class ring.
11. Call Schultze on Daley.
12. Frank Moore job and Frank to Doctors.
13. Letter to John Kelly.
14. See Doc in jail and bring his check.
15. Work on statistics of region poverty programs.
16. Travel Log.
17. Reports for Bob Smith on 2 boys.

As he finishes making out his schedule for the day, Will
looks up and sees Frank walking through the door and into
the Center (Frank was a student at Yale University who became a staff member at the RYC upon graduating).

Will:

Hey Frank, I did some work last night on the binomial stuff.

(*Note:* Will is in the process of trying to prepare for his
high school equivalency exam. Frank has been working with
him in the areas of English and mathematics.)

Will:

I also got this book of sample equivalency exams.

Frank:

Is it a blue book?

Will:
Yeah, and there's science stuff in it, but the only thing we really got to work on is the spelling and math.
Frank:
O.K. As long as you've got the book there's no problem.
Will:
O.K., later then.

Will looks back down at the itinerary he has before him. He points his finger at the first item on the list and picks up the phone. He dials a number, sighs as he hears the number ringing, and finally begins to speak.
Will:
Hey Steve, what's happening?
Ya, it's me, Will. Look, Steve, I think we got some business. I got a kid here who walked into the RYC all by himself. Says he's wanted somewhere out of town under an alias.

(Long pause as Will listens)

Yeah, I'm gonna see him anyway.

(Another long pause. Will's eyes scan the room as he waits for the person on the other end of the line to finish.)

O.K. I'll call the Hill office on that. Bye.

Will hangs up obviously disgusted with the conversation. As he turns back to his desk he mutters: "Shit, LAA [Note: LAA is the local legal assistance agency] won't take anyone from outside the area." He continues, talking louder now.
Will:
I was gonna call Cardella but I know that him and the judge what's bound to see the kid just don't get along. Maybe I oughtta try Waxman.

Will turns back to the phone on his desk and dials another number. He cradles the phone between his chin and his left shoulder so that he can take out another cigarette and light it. After a little while he replaces the phone.
Will:
No answer. I'll try later.

Will looks up at a clock hanging near the desk at which Scotty is seated:
Will:
Hey, it's five of nine. I better get some more coffee before the meeting starts.

Will gets up and leaves the office for the kitchen. Most of the other staff members are already in the room, having entered individually or in pairs during the past 15 minutes.

Will returns with another cup of coffee. He nods to a number of the other staff members and sits down at his desk. It's not quite 9 a.m. yet, and Will grabs the morning newspaper off another desk and spreads it out before him. He begins to scan an article about the chairman of New Haven's Black Coalition being replaced after a prolonged weekend meeting. He shakes his head slowly, almost unhappily, as he reads.

(*Note*: The Black Coalition is an attempt being made by various Negro groups to unite and pool their resources for the purpose of attaining common goals. It is a recent development in New Haven, an attempt to mobilize and unite black people of varying points of view into a "united front." Will is a member of the Black Coalition and attended the weekend conference described in the article.)

9:00–10:00 a.m.:

The meeting begins with Frank, who was on live-in duty the previous night, giving the staff a rundown on what happened.

(*Note*: Because of the number of people present, the variety of topics discussed, and the complexity of the interactions that occurred, it was impossible to record everything that took place at the staff meeting. Consequently, in order to provide the reader with a sense of what transpired and still maintain our focus on Will, the topics discussed will be summarized and Will's comments will be reported as they occurred and in the context of what was going on at the time.)

Frank tells the group that after "a really fine evening" the kids started kidding around, and after a while "the kidding got a little out of hand."

He goes on to explain that around 1:00 a.m., after some horsing around, one of the residents apparently took a fire extinguisher off the wall on the second floor and sprayed it into another boy's room. In retaliation the second boy, a kid named Cal, grabbed the extinguisher that had been left outside his room and sprayed it into the room of the boy he believed responsible for having doused his room. Because the RYC is housed in an old, rickety building (i.e., because the fire hazard is so great), a rule had been passed stating that anyone caught playing with the fire extinguisher would be faced with "immediate termination." Under this ruling Cal, the boy Frank "caught" with the extinguisher, is the one who may have to be terminated from the Center. The situation is further complicated by the fact that Cal, according to both his worker and the rest of the staff, has "really been doing quite well, really trying to 'make it.'" No one on staff wants to "lose" Cal. In addition, most of the staff feel that Cal's action, while not justified, was understandable in terms of the situation as a whole and "Cal's problem" (Cal loses his temper very easily). Cal contends that "it was Bobo who shot into my room," but there were no witnesses and, as usual, "nobody's talking."

Frank finishes his report.

Frank:

I personally feel horrible about the whole thing. I know we've said that playing with the fire extinguisher leads to immediate termination, but I feel partly responsible for the trouble Cal's in. It was partly my fault. I should have been up there at the time, but I was in the office making out the nightly report. I should have been up there and maybe this wouldn't have happened to Cal. I don't know. I think we have to develop some alternatives. We can't let this happen like this to Cal.

The staff looks on intently as Frank finishes. Will drags deeply on his cigarette and looks down.

Will:

You can't blame yourself, Frank. It could have happened to any one of us.

Frank:

No, I should have been up there.

Will:

It's the same old problem of rules. We got a bunch of new guys in here now and very few of the old kids are left to break 'em in, kind of tell 'em *why* we got certain rules, kind of carry on the tradition.

Frank:

I think most of us agree with you, Will, but we still have right now to think about. Cal still stands to lose a great deal if he's kicked out.

Will leans heavily on his left arm and begins to doodle with his right hand.

Will:

You know it's always like this. Every time we make a rule it seems like the first kid who tests the rule is a kid we all love, a kid who's really trying to help himself.

Will sighs deeply, a heavy kind of sigh. A few of the other staff members smile or laugh quietly as if they know what Will is talking about.

After much more discussion, the staff makes its decision:

1. An emergency "health and welfare" meeting will be called for after supper this evening.

2. The staff will use the meeting to explain their dilemma regarding Cal to all the residents.

3. The meeting will also be used to tell the new residents the "whys and wherefores" concerning the rule about the fire extinguisher as well as the other "house rules."

4. The kids will be given a chance, without the staff's being

present, to discuss the situation with the "really guilty party" and, hopefully, to have him "come forth."

5. If no one "comes forth" or "owns up," a punishment other than termination will be developed for Cal.

There is some grumbling on the staff about "not following through with the original rule," but the decision stands.

Will squirms a bit in his seat, looks around at the rest of the staff for a moment, and finally focuses his eyes on one of the people sitting near him on his left.

Will:

I'm sorry, Tinker, but I got to bring this up. I know I spoke to you about it once before but now I think the staff has to know about this if we're gonna keep you from screwing yourself up. Now last week when I was on duty you showed up with one of the kids after taking him out partying with you.

Now I told you once before you can't go doing that with the kids. You can't get that tight with a kid. You go partying and you do a little drinking, O.K. But when you got an underage kid with you it's only trouble. Now you did it again and I'm telling you that's no good, just no good.

You got too much going for you to throw it away like that. Tinker, if you wanna party, tell me. I'll party with you. But you can't get that close with a kid, not that close.

Will finishes and the staff talks with Tinker about the problem of getting too involved with a resident, especially when that involvement jeopardizes a kid's relationship with his worker. Tinker briefly defends his actions but soon acknowledges that he might have been wrong. Will laughs.

Will:

Hell, I'll party with you anytime. I love to party.

He reaches over and slaps Tinker's hand and on this note the issue is ended and the staff moves on to a discussion of individual kids.

Butch begins to report on his kids. Will bends down for a moment and clasps his hands around his right ankle. Then he straightens up in his seat, picks up a pencil, and begins to sharpen it with his fingernail. After a while he puts the pencil down, rips a match from his matchbook and begins to clean his ears with it.

Butch describes each of his kids in great detail. The staff listens and occasionally they interrupt him. They either seek clarification, amplify on what Butch is saying by relating their own experiences with the particular kid, or offer suggestions as to how Butch might handle a certain problem involving the boy.

The last boy Butch discusses is Ronnie Collins, a particularly "tough" kid about whom Butch is very concerned. Butch describes his work with Ronnie as "so far, so good" and goes on to tell the staff that he had Ronnie's NYC (Neighborhood Youth Corps) work site switched so that Ronnie, "a kid who just can't take orders," could be with a less authoritarian foreman. He tells the staff that he thinks "the kid is really scared now and the family finally understands what we're trying to do with him." The reason for the kid's being "really scared" has to do with him having to stand trial on July 25. (Note: Prior to coming into the RYC, Ronnie was arrested and charged with conspiracy to commit theft, auto theft, perjury, and driving without a license.)

Butch continues by describing the overcrowded conditions under which Ronnie's family is currently living. He tells of "eight kids, little kids, sleeping in two rooms."

Will sinks deeper into his chair as Butch continues to detail the family's living conditions. He folds his arms across his stomach, looks down, and begins to chew on his lower lip.

10:00–11:00 a.m.:

Butch ends by turning to Will. (Note: Will is the RYC's "expert" on problems of housing.)

Butch:
I need help on relocation.

Will:
What you have to do is get a letter over to the redevelopment man on State Street. Have them send a D&I [development and improvement] man out to inspect the house. If he finds it bad enough, he'll get them on the waiting list. But make sure you call Ray McDermott, no one else down there, to make sure the notice gets sent out. Then call relocation to see if they got the notice. You say they need four bedrooms?

Butch:
Yeah.

Will:
Shoot, best redevelopment'll do is get the family on the rent certificate program. There's probably 2,000 people ahead of them on the redevelopment list.

Butch:
But they got eight kids sleepin' in two rooms.

Will:
Butch, you got to get the family to start makin' some noise. Get them to start screaming. Welfare doesn't give a damn so long as they're saving money on the deal. Help the family

to start screamin'. Right now that's the only thing'll get Welfare and the rest of 'em off their asses.

Butch ends his presentation by telling the staff that he has "copied Will's technique" for developing "a sort of 'we feeling' among the kids I work with." Butch goes on.
Butch:
What I did was take a page from Will's book. Now my kids are known as Butch R.'s Ragged Ruffians just like Will K.'s kids call themselves K.'s Kool Kids. It gives my kids a real feeling of belonging. Besides which, I kind of like it myself.

(Note: The observer felt at this point that one of the reasons behind Butch's talking about having copied something from Will was related to the fact that Butch knew that the observer was doing "A Day in the Life of Will K." Butch is not "known" for throwing kudos at staff members, and the observer believes that Butch was doing it now to make Will "look good.")

The staff laughs and kids Butch about being an "egomaniac just like Will."

The next few minutes of the staff meeting are devoted to Frank. In addition to his other duties, Frank is in charge of preparing the quarterly RYC research reports for Washington. He now fills in the staff on the status of the upcoming report and tells them that he would like each staff member to write a short "case study," in his own words, about each of the kids he is working with.

Will seems to be chuckling a bit as Frank details the kinds of things he'd like each of the staff members to write—things like "feelings, impressions, and strategies of working with a kid." Will smiles and looks at Frank.
Will:
Frank, I'll write up the kids and you correct my grammar and spelling.

Without pausing, Will suddenly jumps out of his seat and makes an exaggerated bow before the staff. As he straightens up, and just before he sits back down, he smiles broadly and looks around the room.
Will:
And to all of you who're bugging me about my high school equivalency, I want you to know that I take my exams the first week in September. Frank here is tutoring me. So now get off my back and start buggin' Chip. He's next in line to get his high school diploma. Bug Chip, he's next.

Chip leans over and turns on the fan. (Note: It is unclear as to whether Chip has chosen this moment to turn on the fan because of what Will has said, or because the room is, indeed, beginning to get increasingly hot and heavy with smoke.) Will smiles and leans back in his chair. His eyes begin to wander around the room. He gazes vacantly at the walls and finally focuses on a list that hangs on the wall directly across from him. It is a list of the names of the 120 kids who have been through the Center since it opened some 20-odd months ago. Will's eyes wander over the names, up one column and down another.

With the "business" part of the meeting over, the staff turns to the Individual Sensitivity portion of the meeting. Scotty's name is picked out of a box, and the room falls silent for a moment.

Will leans forward, carefully lights another cigarette, and looks around the room. Everyone is still very quiet.

It is finally Frank who starts things off.
Frank:
Can it be that nobody has any feelings about our Director? We must be becoming a pretty bland group here.
Will:
Well, lemme put it this way. I think Scotty's tired, tired an' maybe getting a little depressed. Some years ago I remember I went to him crying about feeling depressed and he told me to get involved with other people and not keep it to myself. Now he's got to take some of his own medicine. (Will looks directly at Scotty) Right doc?

After these opening remarks by Frank and Will, the group launches into a discussion of Scotty, his feelings, the staff's perceptions of his problems and behavior, and the causes and possible consequences of the situation as a whole. (Note: Once again it was impossible to record, however briefly, every interchange. Consequently, we shall summarize the interactions that took place and focus attention on Will's contributions to Scotty's sensitivity session.)

Each staff member, sometimes in turn, sometimes interrupting one another, offers his assessment of Scotty's recent behavior. One staff member talks of Scotty's becoming "unapproachable when he gets this way." Another volunteers the opinion that a particular kid with whom Scotty had been working "took a lot out of him, made him kill himself with the kid." Butch agrees that Scotty has become depressed of late and feels that "a lot of this, maybe 51 percent, has to do with the job." He goes on to talk about the constant frustration and the fact that "the whole staff is tired, Scotty maybe more than the rest of us." Will nods his head in agreement.
Will:
We all get run-down and start draggin' ass. But it's usually

Scotty who picks up, Scotty that it all falls on. Now I think
he's tired and it's getting harder for him to try to pick up
the whole staff.

Butch interrupts to add that he believes "it's getting harder
for him to face the staff than the kids." Will now interrupts
Butch.

Will:

One of the troubles with Scotty is maybe that he's never
really satisfied. Not with himself, with his kids, with the whole
staff. Until he himself feels satisfied, he's gonna brood. He
wants to see things move but now he seems frustrated.
Another thing I know is hurtin' Scotty. It's a thing about
the Black Coalition. I know Scotty wants to become really
involved in the Coalition. He's dying to. But he can't chop
himself up in pieces or really find the time it takes to get
involved. I think he feels guilty about not helping out people
enough, about not being able to get involved in the Black
Coalition the way he really wants.

The discussion continues. Butch ends it by turning to the
rest of the staff and saying: "Maybe the best thing is to let
Scotty talk and tell the way he feels."

Scotty, after a few moments during which he seems to be
trying to gather his thoughts, takes over and begins to speak.

Scotty:

I guess you're all really right about me being in a bad mood
and feeling depressed. I've been tired, fed up, and disgusted.
I feel like I've had it, like I'm tired and drained.
I guess I've also been feeling very guilty. Mostly cause I
know that when I get to feeling this way, I begin to pull
back. I pull back from people, from the kids, from the whole
program. I've been dumping things on everyone else, mostly
the Deputy Director, and that only makes me feel worse.
Then I become more far away, more "unapproachable," the
way one of you guys said. I guess one of the things I really
want to do now is thank Ralph here for understanding and
for taking so much off my shoulders lately while I've been
feeling this way. (Scotty smiles now for the first time.) I say
this because I think you all know I didn't think I could trust
Ralph in the beginning, what with being both white *and*
Italian. (Ralph smiles and a few of the other staff members
snicker.)

11:00 a.m.–12:00 Noon

Scotty continues.

Scotty:

Anyway, I also feel like I'm becoming hard and more rigid,
not weighing my decisions well, and coming on like to make

the rest of you afraid of wanting to approach me.
Will's also right. I do feel very guilty about not getting
more involved with my people. You know, I went up to the
Black Coalition conference over this past weekend. There was
this guy there, a really sharp guy, and he looked at all of us
and he said: "I want you all to know that there's only three
kinds of black people and each and every one of you is one
of them kinds. There's Black Men, there's Uncle Toms, and
there's Yard Niggers. Now which one are you?" Well I been
acting like a Yard Nigger and I just can't be that way. No
sir! As far as the rest of it goes, I think I got to learn not to
hold so much inside me all the time. Maybe I just got to
learn to get mad a little at a time and not let things stew
inside me until it busts me open all at once or gets me so
depressed I just cop out. I don't know but that's how I really
feel now.

Quiet ensues as everyone seems to be trying to sort out
for himself what Scotty has just said. It is Ralph who finally
breaks the silence.

Ralph:
O.K. O.K., but I want to know what can be done here and
now.

Butch:
You can't do it with words.

Will:
You got to understand that this is especially hard for Scotty.
Scotty never had nobody to turn to and to open up to. I
know. Believe me I know.

Butch:
So what do you do about it?

Scotty:
I think too often a Director is seen as a different kind of
animal. (Note: Scotty has shifted the discussion away from
him as an individual and onto the problems inherent in the
leadership role.) I don't know what it is, but it seems like
people aren't as genuine with me as with the others here.

Butch:
Maybe people are afraid to approach you because of the way
you set yourself up, the way you kind of run away from help.

Scotty:
I don't know. Maybe you're right. Maybe I do bring some of
this on myself with my own problems, my own attitude.
But I still feel like a different kind of animal.

Will:
It's probably a little of both, the job and Scotty himself.
Maybe we can't change Scotty, but I know it's also got some-

thing to do with the position. Maybe we got to look to ourselves in all this. You know, how do we help or hurt Scotty define his own self in this place?
Scotty:
I'd like that. I'd really like that; to talk about me and you in this place. It might help. It might just help.

It is now almost noon, and the staff has been meeting for almost three hours. The meeting ends with the staff agreeing to start off their next meeting where this one ended. People begin to stretch. A few start to leave the room.

Will gets up. He, too, looks a little tired. He glances over toward Scotty for a moment and their eyes meet. Neither smiles but both nod to each other. Will starts out of the office. He goes through the kitchen door and out toward the small parking lot behind the RYC. As he walks toward his car he sighs deeply, almost as if he is relieved and glad to be out of the office.

Before getting into his car, Will pauses and points to a sticker he has pasted onto his rear bumper: "Ever see the Black American Flag? Well we got one now, Charley, and that's it right there."

Will points to the flag again. Two of the four corners of the flag (the upper right and lower left corners) are red. The rest is black. In the center of the flag is a bright-orange sword, its tip pointed straight up, almost surrounded by a semicircle of orange leaves. Will explains the flag's meaning:
Will:
The black stands for black consciousness and the red is for the blood spilled by black people in this country ever since we were brought here. The sword stands for strength and perseverance, and the leaves for peace and prosperity. Kind-a grabs you, doesn't it?

Will gets into his car and leans across to unlock the door on the passenger's side of the car. The car is a powder-blue 1966 Mustang. It is steaming hot inside. Will apparently forgot to leave any windows open after parking it outside the RYC.

Will turns on the ignition and pauses for a moment before taking off. He pulls out his itinerary for the day and scans the list of things he has down to do. He crosses out one or two of them and mutters: "Shoot, I'll be lucky to get half of all this done today. But I'll tell you one thing: if I can't get any-thing good done with at least one kid during the day, I don't feel as if I've done shit."

The car takes off. Will coasts out of the RYC parking lot and into the traffic on George Street. The light at the corner of Dwight and George Streets begins to turn yellow as Will approaches it and he guns the motor to make the light before it changes to red. As the car crosses the intersection, Will quickly looks all around him as if to make sure that no one, especially a cruising police car, has seen him jump the light. Once past the intersection he leans back, arches his neck, and continues on.

Will says nothing now as he drives. (*Note:* It is somewhat unusual for Will to be silent, especially when he's with another person.) He makes a left onto Whalley Avenue, one of the main drags in New Haven, and speeds up a bit as the traffic clears.

12:00 Noon–1:00 p.m.

After driving only a few blocks, Will turns off Whalley Avenue and onto County Street. The car comes to a halt outside the New Haven State Jail. Will parks the car and gets out.

Will walks briskly onto the jail grounds and toward the visitor's entrance. The grounds of the jail are in beautiful shape. Shrubs, beds of flowers, and well-kept bushes dot the huge lawn. In the middle of the lawn, perhaps some 30 yards before the visitor's entrance, there is a large, gold-colored sign. It reads:

Any who asks you to do the wrong thing,
He is never your friend.

Will continues up the path to the jail's entrance. He climbs the stairs and enters the combination office and waiting area. Inside, two policemen are standing and talking. Two other men in prison clothes (they seem to be trusties) sit behind typewriters on either side of the long room. They look up and glance at Will as he enters. The policemen's backs are to Will, and they aren't aware that someone has entered the office. It would be difficult to hear anyone entering: two huge fans are blowing in the office and they make noise, noise enough to drown out approaching footsteps.

Will pauses a moment before going up to the two policemen. When he's almost upon them one of the cops turns around to face Will. Will smiles and exchanges greetings with the policeman:

Will:

Lieutenant, I've got a check here for one of our boys who's staying with you for a while. It's Doc's.

(*Note:* The youngster referred to, the boy named Doc, came into the RYC about 10 months ago. Prior to coming into the

Center he had spent a number of years in institutions of one
sort or another (the two state juvenile reformatories, Meriden
and Cheshire, and a state mental institution in Middletown,
Connecticut). Doc became one of Will's kids and Will worked
with him for much of the time that Doc was at the RYC. Doc
left the RYC approximately two months ago, had gotten a
full-time job, and had returned home to live with his mother.
He was arrested very recently for fighting and has been
charged with assault with a deadly weapon. Will considers
Doc one of the most difficult youngsters he's ever worked
with, a youngster with whom he "never felt quite right," and
a boy about whom he is still second-guessing himself with
respect to "what went wrong.")

Lieutenant:
A check for what?
Will:
It's a check from the Welfare Department.
Lieutenant:
We don't usually cash checks for guys that are here. Couldn't
you people cash the check for him and bring the money here?
Will:
Ya, I guess we could cash it over at the Center.
Lieutenant:
Well, just to be on the safe side, why don't you guys take
care of it.
Will:
O.K., I'll take the check on over to the Welfare people and
tell them that we'll cash it for him.
Lieutenant:
I think it'll be easier that way. You know, no complications.
Will:
No sweat. Do me a favor will you? Tell Doc I was by and
that I'll see him next visiting hours.
Lieutenant:
Sure thing, sure thing.

   Will turns to leave. He walks slowly out of the office and
down the path that leads away from the jail. He makes his
way back to the car, gets in, and quickly guns the motor.
The car takes off and Will circles the block in order to get
back on Whalley Avenue.
Will:
Those cops. Man, they won't do nothing without authoriza-
tion.

   Will falls silent again. The streets pass quickly. It's hot now,
really hot. Will rubs his arm across his mouth and runs his
hand over the back of his neck.

Will:

We're going out to the Yale Bowl to see Ron Gambrell on his work site. There's something I got to talk with the kid about.

(*Note*: Ron Gambrell is a recent arrival to both New Haven and the RYC. Originally from North Carolina, Ron came to the RYC from a reformatory where he had been for most of the 17 months since coming to Connecticut. Will became his worker approximately two weeks prior to the time this chronicle was recorded.)

Will stops the car in front of the Yale Bowl and walks up to the steel gate that serves as one of the entrances to the large stadium. It is locked. Will returns to the car and begins to drive around the stadium looking for another entrance-way. He finds an opening on the other side of the Bowl, drives through, and parks the car near one of the tunnels that lead from the ticket area into the stadium itself.

Will gets out and begins to amble through the tunnel toward the field. Three black kids are coming through the other way and one exchanges handslaps with Will as he passes him:

Kid:

Hey brother, what's happening?

Will:

Nothin' good. Nothin' good.

The kids continue on their way, and Will comes out of the tunnel and scans the playing field.

Will:

Lord make me young again. Look at that field will ya. Look at the sun hit that green. Oh, Lord, how I'd love to be young again and play on that field.

Will rests for a moment. A slight smile plays across his lips as he stands, almost transfixed, gazing across the field. He turns, looks around the rest of the stadium, and begins to walk through the stands.

(*Note*: The Yale Bowl is being used as a work site for teen-agers during the summer. The youngsters, some from CPI's Neighborhood Youth Corps program and others who are not involved in the agency, are paid to refurbish the field and get the Bowl ready for the football season.)

Will looks all around him as he continues walking. Some 30 or 40 boys are all over the stands. Most of them are scraping or painting the long benches that are used as seats. More than half the stadium seats have been repainted a bright deep blue. They stand in marked contrast to the dull grey areas that have not as yet met with the paint brush. The boys who are working dot the huge stadium like so many pebbles on a beach.

Will cannot seem to find Ron, and after shielding his eyes from the sun so that he can scan the stands, he turns and heads back out the same tunnel he used to come in. Two more kids, white kids this time, come toward him as he is going back through the tunnel. One of them stops him.

Kid:

Hey, you're Will. Remember me? Phil? You coached me in Little League Football.

Will:

Well I'll be. Sure I remember. You were on the Lions. What you doin' now?

Kid:

I go to Yale now. I'm just working here for the summer. I'm a Junior.

Will:

How about that. Still play any ball?

Kid:

Not really. Not any more. Well, good to see you again. Take care of yourself.

Will:

Yeah, and good luck Phil.

The boys leave and Will continues on his way.

Will:

Damn, but that kid was a good quarterback. He was only 13 then but smart as hell. And was he ever cool in a game. Never let anything phase him. Good kid . . . and smart as hell.

Once through the tunnel, Will pauses for a moment and then walks over to a man, perhaps he is a supervisor, and speaks to him briefly.

Will:

Say, I'm lookin' for Ron. Know where he is?

Supervisor:

Prob'ly hiding in one of the portals.

Will walks away and goes back through the tunnel once again. This time, instead of walking around the stadium, he goes straight to the field, turns around, cups his hand to his mouth and screams: "Ron. Ron Gambrell." The sound of Will's voice echoes through the stands. It becomes quiet for a moment and a voice comes booming back from the top of the stadium: "Yeah?" There is another pause, and then the same voice continues: "Will, what the hell you doin' here again?" Will looks up, locates the voice and screams back: "I come to see the kinda work you're not doing."

The figure at the top of the stadium begins to descend toward Will. Will, in turn, begins to climb the concrete stairs toward the kid. They meet somewhere in between.
Ron:
Hey man, what's happenin'?
Will:
How's it goin' Ronnie? From the looks of ya it sure don't look like you're putting out too hard.
Ron:
Later for that, man. I'm bustin' myself here.

(*Note*: Ron, a tall, well-built Negro kid, is literally covered with sweat. His pants are splattered with paint and he does, indeed, look as if he has been working hard. A black band is wound tightly around his head and it is soaked through with perspiration. Ron, about 6' 1" tall (almost as tall as Will), is much heavier than Will and seems to tower above him.)

Will:
I hear we had a little problem last night.
Ron:
No problem.
Will:
Shoot, no problem. When you're making like to kill people, that's a problem. What happened?
Ron:
Well look, man, I had this ring, see? Nice ring. Cost me five hours work to get the money to buy it. Well, last night I go to take a shower. I puts the ring on my bureau. O.K.? O.K. When I get back the ring is gone.
(Ron tells the story very dramatically and with much "gusto.")
Well, at first I says the hell with it. Then I says to myself: "Shit, I worked five hours for that ring; ain't nobody gonna take it!" So then I guess I begin to blow my cool. I lines up all the guys on the third floor and tell 'em: "I'm goin' out, and when I come back I'm gonna shoot every mother one of you if my ring isn't sittin' on my dresser. I'm goin' out to get a gun now and that ring better be back up there or so help me I'll shoot everyone up here."
(Ron laughs now as he tells the story. Will just stares at him.)
Well, I goes out to Legion Avenue to see my friends. None of them got a gun to give me so I come back to the Center with my hand in my pocket like this.
(Ron demonstrates how he faked a gun. Again Ron laughs, obviously enjoying his telling of the incident. Even Will begins to smile now.)

Well, I goes back upstairs and lines the guys up again.
Then I go back into my room and what do I see? There's
my li'l old ring sittin' as pretty as ever on the dresser. Now
what'ya think about that?
Will:
Good thing your friends on Legion didn't give you a gun.
Ron:
I tell ya, Will, I'd a shot all them guys.
Will:
Well, they can only fry you once.
Ron:
Hell, I know that. But it wasn't the money, it was the prin-
ciple.
Will:
Would it be worth getting fried for ten dollars?
Ron:
Hell no, but God love me I was hot, Will. Really hot.
Will:
I know you was hot. You think I don't know that? But you'd
be a helluva lot hotter if they fried you.
Ron:
I tell you honest, Will. I don't really think I'd a shot anyone.
That's not my style. You know that.
Will:
I don't know shit. All I know is that I don't care how hot
you get. That gun shit is out. Dig? Out!
Ron:
It sure as hell was funny, though, the way that ring showed
up so quick.
Will:
Shoot. Knowin' you, you probably left it there all the time.
Ron:
Bullshit, Will. I really looked for it before I got mad. I
really did.
Will:
All right. Now, I hear you paid 17 dollars on your rent. That's
not bad.
Ron:
I still owe you a bean, but I figured you wouldn't mind
waitin' a while so long as I made a try.
Will:
That's O.K. You figured right. Now look, there's a health and
welfare meeting tonight after supper.
Ron:
What time?
Will:
Around six.

Ron:
I'll be there. Don't worry your old bones.
Will:
O.K. Later now. Don't work too hard.
Ron:
Never do, never do.

Ron turns and bounds back up the stairs toward the top
of the stadium. Will watches him for a moment, then turns
and begins to walk back out the tunnel again. He seems a bit
preoccupied as he walks, doesn't turn to look at the field
anymore, just walks out.

Will returns to his car and gets in. He starts the motor but
pulls out his itinerary and checks off "Work Site: Gambrell"
before getting the car rolling again.

Will eases the car out of the stadium parking area.
Will:
Now we'll go see how big Sam's doing at the Teen Employ-
ment Center over on Dixwell.

The car moves through a nicely lawned residential area
and on past Southern Connecticut State College, one of the
several colleges and universities located within the New
Haven area. The drive is a pretty one: the campus of Southern Connecticut State College is a lush green that sparkles in
the sun; a huge pond sits calmly between gently rolling hills;
and the campus is dotted with shrubs and finely tended
lawns. A little farther on—no more than a minute's drive—
the scenery begins to change. The pond and the greenery
vanish and are abruptly replaced by tenements and dilapidated single-family dwellings. There is little transition between the two. All too quickly the car has "crossed over the
line" and is now entering one of New Haven's black ghettos,
the Dixwell Avenue area. The serene has been displaced by
the frazzled.

Will turns up Henry Street, a street lined with renovated
brownstones, and crosses Dixwell Avenue. He eases the car
into a parking spot alongside a modern-looking church, turns
off the ignition, and gets out. On the opposite side of the
street there stands another church, a worn-out Greek Ortho-
dox Church with a sign reading "Soul Station" hanging on
its door. Will begins walking toward it.

Will walks up the rickety stairs leading to the church, goes
through the already opened door, and looks around. The inside of the church is deserted and has the musty smell of a
room whose doors and windows have been closed too long.
The church is no longer a church: it has been turned into a
teen-age lounge and meeting area. Along one side there
stands an old pool table covered with a single sheet of

wrinkled and dust-laden plastic. The other side of the room is lined with old patent-leather couches. Most of the couches are torn, and cotton fluff hangs from the open slits.

Will stands near the middle of the large room and looks around. Suddenly a voice rings out from a small balcony set high above the back end of the old church. A teen-aged boy stands in the balcony and looks down.

Boy:

What you want?

Will:

Is Virgil around?

Boy:

No.

Will:

If you see him tell him Will was lookin' for him. O.K.?

Will turns to leave. As he begins to walk toward the door-way, another black man enters the church.

Will:

Hey Joe, how you doin'?

Joe:

Hey brother, what's happening?

Will:

Look, Joe, I'm gonna be late for the Coalition meeting to-night. I got something going over to the RYC and then I got to meet with a bunch of kids from the project where I live. When I'm finished I'll get over to the meeting.

Joe nods and then looks at the observer. His look is only partly menacing but certainly very suspicious.

Joe:

Who's the white man?

Will proceeds to explain the observer's presence and ends by saying something like: "He's O.K." Joe seems totally un-convinced by Will's explanation, grunts, and walks away. Will looks after him for a moment, takes a step as if to catch up with him, but then stops and shrugs his shoulders.

1:00–2:00 p.m.

After a moment, Will leaves the church and crosses the street to a building that can only be described as a makeshift shanty. A sign reading "Dixwell Teen-age Employment Cen-ter" hangs loosely from the front door. Will goes through the door and into the employment office.

Inside, two Negro girls, about 15 or 16 years of age, sit behind desks. Each is helping another teen-ager fill out a brief application form. Behind them, at a desk cluttered with papers, sits Sam (the boy Will roused out of bed earlier to-day). He is talking to another black teen-ager who is stand-

ing near his desk. Sam looks up as Will makes his way across
the office to where he is sitting.
Will:
Hey, Mr. Sam.
Sam:
Well, well. Good to see you, Mr. K. Need a job?
Will:
Don't give me that jive-talk Sam.

Sam is obviously enjoying the situation. He leans back,
smiles smugly and a bit condescendingly—clearly mocking
Will, albeit good-naturedly—and clears his throat.
Sam:
Excuse me, sir, but I must get back to work.

Sam turns away from Will and faces the kid standing in
front of his desk. He suddenly turns serious and tells the
youngster about "a job I can get for you down to Malley's
Department Store if you want it." The youngster nods his
head affirmatively and Sam picks up the phone and calls the
store. After a short conversation he hangs up, writes the
kid's name down on a piece of paper, hands the paper to
the kid and tells him to "get going." The kid leaves the office
and Sam swivels his chair, slowly and in an exaggerated
fashion, to face Will once again.
Sam:
I tell you that's all I ever do around here. Work, work, work.
(Sam sighs the "sigh of the unappreciated") Now what can
I do for you, sonny?
Will:
Well, I see there's no talkin' to the likes of you today.
Sam:
Ah well, Mr. K. Next time you come please make an appoint-
ment to see me first.

Both Sam and Will break up laughing and they slap hands.
Will:
O.K. jive-time, see you back at the Center.
Sam:
Later, man.

Will turns and leaves the employment center. Once outside he stops for a moment as if thinking what to do next.
He looks up at the sky and mops his brow with his palm.
Then he quickly crosses the street to another small building
whose sign reads "Dixwell Legal Rights Association."

Will mounts the stairs, again two at a time, and enters a
cramped-looking office on the second floor. Inside the office
two secretaries sit behind desks. One types; the other is sort-
ing a bunch of mimeographed papers. Will goes and stands

very quietly behind the woman who is typing. The woman is Will's wife, and after a moment or so, almost as if suddenly startled by a strange presence, she quickly turns her head in his direction.

(Note: Will's wife works as a part-time secretary for the Dixwell Legal Rights Association. She began her work as a result of Will's urging that she "get involved in what's going on." At the present time, although she is supposedly working only part-time, Will reports that "she brings home almost as much work to do at night as she does during the day." Will is beginning to question the wisdom of his having goaded her into "getting involved.")

Will and his wife speak quietly for a few minutes. Then she hands him what looks like a pile of bills that need to be paid. He smiles weakly, shoves the bills in his pocket, and turns to leave. As he goes through the door, he turns and waves to his wife. She waves back and returns to her typing as Will heads down the stairs.

Once he hits the street, Will moves quickly back across the avenue to where he has parked his car. He gets in and starts the car again. Rather than make a U-turn or go all the way around the block to get back on Dixwell Avenue, Will pulls away from the curb and cuts across a vacant lot halfway up the block. As he merges from the lot onto the connecting street he sees a police car sitting about ten feet from where he has exited. He quickly turns onto the block and glances sideways at the parked car as he passes it. Two policemen sit inside, but they apparently did not see Will illegally cross the empty lot. Will smiles as he passes the parked car and nears Dixwell Avenue again.

Will:

Shoot, first time I cut through this lot in six months and there's a cop car. Isn't that just too much?

Will turns left onto Dixwell Avenue and drives for about four blocks. Then he pulls up to the curb and parks. The car is now standing in front of a building called "The Dixwell Community Center." In addition to providing the usual community services (i.e., recreation, education, etc.) the building serves as the headquarters and offices of the newly formed Black Coalition. Will leaves the car, enters the building, and walks up to the second floor. The second floor consists of a few small offices and an even smaller reception area.

Will enters the reception area, nods to the secretary, and proceeds to poke his head into the office nearest him. It is the office of the Black Coalition's Executive Director, Hugh Price.

Hugh:
Hey Will.
Will:
Hey man, howrya doin'?
Hugh:
Good, real good.
Will:
Listen, Hugh, what're you doin' tomorrow night at 6 p.m.?
Hugh:
Nothing, but I don't know if I'll be back from Waterbury
by then. Why?
Will:
We got a ball game between the RYC and the people over
to the Children's Center.
Hugh:
I'll try to make it.
Will:
Good. Listen, has Joe spoken to you yet about the scholarship
money for Sam?
Hugh:
No, but I remember you mentioning something about Sam
having a chance to go to prep school in Milford.
Will:
Right, but Sam still needs to raise 450 dollars before he can
get to go. Is there any way the Coalition can get the money?
Hugh:
Not directly, but there's people down at the Metro Action
Center that can help.
Will:
Should I give them a call right away?
Hugh:
Ya, and tell 'em that I told you to call. They have access to
different groups that finally want to do something. If they
can't get up 450 dollars, I'd be very surprised. Just tell them
I told you to call and that I'd like to know exactly what
happens. O.K.?
Will:
Fine. I'll call 'em as soon as I get back to the office.

Will and Hugh go on to talk about "Coalition business"
and the observer, feeling very much as if this is one interaction at which his presence is both unwanted and intrusive,
leaves to wait for Will in the reception area. (*Note:* Will later
confirmed the observer's belief that his (the observer's) continued presence would have inhibited the ensuing conversation between himself and the leader of the Black Coalition.
The Black Coalition, while it works with and has the support
of many white people, is an all-black organization, and

within that framework the observer's presence at what Will termed his "strategy and sum-up conversation with Hugh Price" was both unnecessary and inappropriate.)

After about ten minutes Will emerges from Hugh Price's office. He heads directly for the door and goes back down the stairs. He has a rather concerned look on his face, almost a grim, tight-lipped expression. This "look" disappears almost as soon as Will hits the street. He pauses for a moment, looks up and down the block, and begins to head for the car again. He gets in, starts the car up, and after a moment of running his palm over the back of his neck, takes off once more.

Will heads down Dixwell Avenue toward the center of New Haven. He cuts across the center of town and steers on toward CPI's Skill Center. (Note: The Skill Center houses a number of CPI's ongoing programs, such as Neighborhood Youth Corps, Remedial and Adult Education, and Operation Headstart. The building itself is located in "the Hill" section of New Haven and is the site for a variety of counseling and skill-training programs.) Will speaks as he drives: "We got to check to see if the people in the NYC program took those two girls over to the legal assistance people."

(Note: The two girls Will is referring to are currently enrolled in the CPI's Neighborhood Youth Corps program. They were picked up by the police on suspicion of shoplifting in one of New Haven's bigger department stores. Claiming to be innocent, they contacted Will and asked for his help. Will was now in the process of trying to secure legal representation for them prior to their scheduled appearance in court.)

The car passes the Yale Medical School complex on its way toward the Skill Center. Again one is struck by a sense of "change without transition": the Medical School and its training facilities stand in stark contrast to the slums and near slums that surround them, a fleeting moment of comparative academic splendor amidst the sameness and squalor of the inner city.

As Will approaches the Skill Center, he notices that the street closest to it (Cedar Street) has been roped off and is closed to traffic. Fire hydrants have been turned on and the street has been converted, at least temporarily, into an "instant recreation area." Sprinklers have been set up, and children run in and out of the water as it sprays above and around them. They laugh and wrestle in the gutter to the accompaniment of their parents' admonitions to "watch out and don't slip." The adults ringing the area seem envious, hot, happy— all at the same time.

Will parks the car on a side street and gets out. He walks

quickly toward the Skill Center, taking care to walk at such
an angle as to be sure to be hit by the spraying water. The
water cascades above him in finely gossamer droplets. He
looks happy and closes his eyes and turns his face upward
toward the falling water as he walks on by.

Will enters the Skill Center. A few drops of water are still
on his face and he shivers.
Will:
First damned air-conditioned building we been in all day and
I got to go into it wet. Prob'ly catch my death.

The Skill Center is a large, boxlike, two-story structure. The
top floor is used for the Adult Education program; the basement houses the NYC Remedial Education program and the
Community Action Institute (a CPI-run project whose goals
are to help other communities, usually those outside the New
Haven area, to organize, develop, and implement their own
community action programs).

Will goes downstairs and heads toward the section of the
building that houses the NYC program. He waves or says
hello to a number of people along the way and goes directly
to the "foremen's room," a room that has been set aside for
meetings involving foremen and foreladies from the NYC pro-
gram. The door to the foremen's room is open and Will goes
in. One of the foreladies, apparently the one he is supposed
to meet, is already there:
Will:
How's it goin', June?
June:
Oh, fair, and yourself?
Will:
Can't complain, can't complain.
June:
Well, Will, what do you think we ought to do about the girls?
Will:
Did you get the girls over to legal assistance yet?
June:
Not yet. I didn't get the chance.
Will:
Have Hortense go with you. She's new right now and it
might help her understand some of the hang-ups if she's
with you to see the kinds of things that have to be done.
June:
That's fine with me. Now who do you think we should con-
tact with this one.
Will:
Try either Tom Weiss, Waxman at Legion, or Lessler in the

Hill. Let me get in touch with Hortense to make sure she can make it. O.K.?
June:
O.K., now when will I hear from you?
Will:
I'll call Hortense tonight and be back to you early in the morning.

Will and June continue to talk for a few minutes before Will turns to leave. When he does he moves quickly, almost as if he is late for an appointment and eager to leave the Skill Center.

Once outside, Will stops suddenly. The heat is oppressive, especially after coming out of an air-conditioned building. He pauses briefly and takes a deep breath before starting for the car.

2:00–3:00 p.m.

Once inside the car, Will announces very matter-of-factly: "I'm goin to see Mrs. Montrose about Larry!"

(Note: Larry Montrose, one of Will's boys, recently left the RYC and went to live in his own apartment in one of the small towns outside New Haven. Will viewed Larry's departure with mixed feelings. On the one hand, Larry, after completing a course in food preparation and cooking, had gotten a job as an assistant cook in a restaurant located in the town to which he moved. This being the case, Larry's leaving the Center was understandable from the point of view of his having begun to "make it," make it in the sense that he now had a steady job and was going to live in his own apartment, an apartment closer to his place of employment. On the other hand, Larry's leaving the RYC was also termed the only "reasonable solution" to an increasingly serious situation. The problem involved Larry's relationships with other RYC residents. Larry is a homosexual and had, at least of late, begun approaching other residents and propositioning them. His "acting out" had resulted in a number of fights, and he himself had recently been beaten up by a resident whom he had approached while he (the resident) was sleeping. Feeling in the house was running very high, and Will, after trying unsuccessfully to deal with the problem through group meetings with the residents, felt that Larry's leaving, at least temporarily, would be the most "reasonable solution" for both Larry and the other residents. Will continued, however, to work with Larry, and his visit to Larry's mother, Mrs. Montrose, was part of his ongoing relationship with the boy and the Montrose family.)

Will starts the car and drives away from the Skill Center. The car heads up Cedar Street and turns into a small alleyway about six blocks from where we started.

Will:
I hope Mrs. Montrose still lives at this house we're going to. Larry's mother really lives like a gypsy. Moves around a lot from place to place. Hope she's still here from last week.

The car slows down as it nears the end of the alleyway. Will looks straight ahead.

Will:
Well, I'll be damned. There she is on the front porch, and she's got Larry's younger brother with her.

Will glides the car up alongside the house and leans out the window. As he stops the car he waves to the woman on the porch.

Will:
Hi, Mrs. Montrose. How you doin' this fine day?

Mrs. M.:
Well, well, hello there, Mr. K. Nice to see you again. How's my boy Larry doing?

Will:
That's what I come to see you about. Do you have a few minutes?

Mrs. M.:
Surely, surely, now you come right on up here. We'll go in out the sun where it's cooler.

Will gets out of the car and climbs the few concrete stairs that go from the sidewalk to Mrs. Montrose's porch. Mrs. Montrose greets him at the top of the stairs and leads him into the house.

Mrs. Montrose's "house" (it is actually one of several apartments that have been created out of what once seems to have been a single-family dwelling) is a small, compact, three-room affair with the kitchen being the largest of the rooms. Mrs. Montrose, a tall, slim, light-complexioned Negro woman about 35 years of age, leads the way into the living room and stands in the center of the room for a moment, almost as if she were showing the apartment to a potential tenant.

The living room itself is extremely tiny and heavily over-loaded with furniture. Two couches, a number of chairs of varying sizes, and several end tables are crowded together, leaving very little space in the middle of the room. Each piece of furniture stands as if it had been carefully placed in a spot reserved for it and it alone. The room is immaculately clean and smells as if it has been doused with a floral-scented room freshener. The walls seem to be almost weighted down with paintings (almost all of them depicting rural life), imitation mass-produced Chinese figurines, and small hand-sewn tapestries. A large picture of Christ looms high above the couch nearest the door. It is a room that conveys an air of frenzied and hard-pressed stability: it is only partially successful.

Will takes a seat near the far end of one of the couches. Mrs. Montrose sits down opposite him in a large overstuffed chair that has been covered with frayed and faded material. Will and Mrs. Montrose begin to talk, but before they go very far, Larry's younger brother, a boy about 14 years old, enters the living room to tell his mother that he is going down the block to see a friend. He leaves the room before Mrs. Montrose has a chance to answer him. Will and Mrs. Montrose turn toward each other and continue their conversation.

(Note: As was the case with the staff meeting earlier in the morning, Will's conversation with Mrs. Montrose was far too complicated and quick-paced to record with any semblance of acceptable accuracy. Consequently, their conversation will, for the most part, be summarized, and only those interchanges that seemed particularly relevant will be reported "word for word.")

Will begins by recounting the reasons, both "good" and "bad," behind Larry's leaving the RYC. Although he discusses "Larry's problem" (i.e., his homosexual tendencies), he seems to place much greater emphasis on "Larry's being ready to 'make it'" in telling Mrs. Montrose about Larry's decision to get an apartment outside of New Haven. Mrs. Montrose, on the other hand, while acknowledging the "good things" that Larry is doing, seems more intent on discussing Larry's homosexual behavior. She succeeds in riveting the conversation on this issue:
Mrs. M.:
I tell you, Will, it's just hard to understand. Larry's a good-looking boy. The young ladies just love the way he looks and acts. Why's he want to play with boys?
Will:
I don't know, Mrs. M. It's like something he has a hard time controlling. Mostly like when he's nervous or anxious about something.
Mrs. M.:
It's his nerves. Larry's always been a nervous boy. Even when he was small he was nervous. I remember the first time he

done something bad was Christmastime when he was 7 years old. Never any problem till then. Then on Christmas Eve he just up and set fire to the curtains. No reason t'all. Just up and set fire to the curtains. Maybe he's just goin' through a stage now like he did then.

Will:

Could be. Could be.

Mrs. Montrose continues talking about Larry's "nerves" but soon returns to the "how cute he is, just like his father used to be." (*Note:* Larry's father, an alcoholic, deserted the family when Larry was about 5 years of age.) She then gets up and begins rummaging through some cartons that have been stacked in the living room closet. After a few minutes she come up with an old, plastic-covered photograph album and brings it over to Will. She opens it up and shows it to Will.

Mrs. M.:

See? See what I mean? That's Larry's father. Now wasn't he a fine-looking man? Look at that hair. Just like Larry's. Larry looks just like his daddy did.

Will:

A good-looking man, Larry's father.

Mrs. M.:

Now you see what I mean? No reason for a boy what looks like Larry to go playin' with boys.

Will:

I guess it's something he got to learn to control. He tries y'know. Tries hard. It just seems that sometimes he can't control it.

Mrs. M.:

Maybe it's only a stage he's goin' through, like with his lyin' and settin' fires. Right, Will?

Will:

That's right. That's right.

Mrs. M.:

You gonna help him get over this. Right, Will? You gonna help him.

Will:

Sure thing. But you gotta help, too.

Mrs. M.:

How's that?

Will:

Like if I tell you Larry hasn't been calling me or if he comes home to see you and tells you he's been doin' things to get him in trouble, you gotta let me know so's I can get to see him quick and maybe talk to him.

Will and Mrs. M. continue to discuss Larry and what Mrs. Montrose can do to help Will work with the boy. During the course of the conversation, Mrs. M. tells Will that the last time she saw Larry was "Friday night when he came here with a few of his 'funny friends." Will's eyes seem to light up momentarily and he asks her if these were "the same guys he used to live with over at Bassett Street." She nods affirmatively. Will shakes his head slowly, maybe even a bit sadly, before he continues his conversation with Mrs. M. He goes on to tell her that he hopes to talk with Larry about Larry's "weekend problems," especially his coming into town and staying with his homosexual friends. He finishes by letting her know that he'll be back to visit her later in the week. Will gets up from the sofa.
Will:
Well, I won't be keeping you any more, Mrs. M. I got to be goin' now.
Mrs. M.:
O.K. now, Will, but you keep in touch with me, hear?
Will:
Sure thing. I'll be back in a few days. Now if you see Larry before I do, you tell him I'm looking for him and for him to call me. O.K.?
Mrs. M.:
I be sure to do that; don't you worry about that.
Will:
O.K. then, be seein' ya.

Mrs. M. accompanies Will back through the kitchen and as far as the porch. Will walks quickly down the steps leading from the porch to the street. He pauses for a moment, turns and waves to Mrs. M., and then makes his way back to the car. Once inside he starts it up and quickly pulls away from the curb.

As he heads the car into heavier traffic Will begins to talk.
Will:
Damn. I knew he was coming back into town to shack up with those guys on Bassett Street. I was hopin' he wouldn't be doing it now that he was finally working and settled out at Guilford. But what the hell can you expect? Mrs. M. talks about Larry's "nerves." Nerves, shit! That boy never had a real man around the house. All he ever had was his mama. That's the problem right there. He don't even know what it is to be a man. Shit!

Will drives on. He has stopped talking and stares straight ahead. The streets go by, and in a little while Will eases the car back into the RYC's parking lot. He gets out slowly and walks into the Center. He looks a little down, maybe even a bit angry.

3:00–4:00 p.m.

Once inside the RYC, Will goes directly into the office and sits down in a seat behind one of the four desks scattered around the room. Only one other staff member is in the office. He nods to Will but Will does not return the greeting. Instead he glares down, pulls his "itinerary" from his pocket, and begins scanning his list of "things to do." He shakes his head sadly.

A kid comes into the office. In his hand he holds a rumpled bunch of dollar bills. He walks directly over to Will's desk, sits down in a chair nearby, and extends the money, still tightly clutched in his hand, toward Will:

Kid:

Money. Money for you.

(*Note*: The youngster is Puerto Rican. He is both new to the RYC and new to New Haven, having arrived in town just a few weeks ago. He cannot speak English very well yet.)

Will:

This for me?

Kid:

Yes. My rent. Mi alquila.

Will:

Good. Good. You have a job and now you can pay rent.

Will takes the kid's money, counts out 12 dollars, and returns the rest. He then gets up and walks over to a small safe that stands in the far corner of the office. He kneels down, opens the safe, puts the money away, and takes out a large ledger book. He then closes the safe and returns to his desk. He places the book in front of the youngster and begins to make out the boy's receipt. After writing it out, he shows it to the resident and slowly goes over it with him. The boy looks on intently as Will explains its meaning and tries to spell out a few of the words for him. Will then rips out the receipt and hands it to the resident. The youngster takes it, smiles, and carefully folds it before placing it in his back pocket. He then turns around and goes out of the office.

Will closes the receipt book and leans back in his chair. He shifts in his seat uneasily, almost as if he has suddenly become very uncomfortable, and then stands up very abruptly:

Will:

I'm gonna try to track that place down on Bassett once and for all. Can't go way the hell out to Guilford now, but I sure can try to find that place on Bassett Street. Shoot, leastways I'll put my own mind at ease.

Will almost darts out of the Center and over to his car. He gets in, revs up the engine, and takes off down George Street. The car moves quickly across town, up Dixwell Avenue again, and on toward a semiresidential area bordering the Dixwell ghetto. Will talks incessantly as he drives, the words coming out like gunfire—short, staccatolike, angry. He jumps from one topic to the next. It is an ongoing monologue, the kind of monologue that never invites comments. In rapid succession he talks about the future of the Black Coalition, the problems of grass-roots organizations, Larry's mother, and how "the white man has killed off the black males so that a kid like Larry could never have a real stable man at home to teach him what it is to be a man." The talk goes on and on, almost as if the things Will is saying have been brewing in him for a long, long time.

Soon the car turns up Bassett Street. Will slows down now and begins to peer intently at the numbers of the houses on each side of the treelined street. He finally parks the car in front of a white house near the corner: "I'm sure that's the house Larry's friends live in."

Will gets out and walks slowly up the stairs and onto the porch. The house has been divided into two apartments, each with its own entrance. Will stands for a moment and then rings the bell of the apartment on the right-hand side of the house. After a few moments the curtains part and a girl peers out from what appears to be the living room. A moment later she opens the door about six inches and looks out at Will.

Will:

Could you tell me if Larry Montrose lives here or comes to visit? (The girl shakes her head negatively. She looks somewhat apprehensive.)

Girl:

Not here. Try next door. (She no sooner finishes speaking than she closes the door quickly and scurries away.)

Will stands for a moment watching her through the living room curtains.

Will:

Bet she thought I was a cop. Can you beat that?

He then turns and presses the bell of the apartment next door. There is no answer. He waits a moment and then presses the bell again, making sure that it is ringing inside the house. Again there is no answer. After a third try Will turns

away and heads back down the stairs to the car. Will gets in and starts the car up almost immediately. The car heads back into the traffic on Dixwell Avenue.
Will:
I'm gonna take a run out to Eli Whitney School where Larry goes to night school.

(*Note:* Eli Whitney is a technical and vocational training school in New Haven. Larry is enrolled in an "advanced cooking" course, a course that meets one night each week.)

Will seems much less angry now. While he continues to talk a blue streak, his conversation is now filled with "everyday" kinds of events rather than with the type of material that dominated his monologue only a short while ago. Even the quality of his speech is different. He no longer "shoots" his words out as if attacking the listener. Rather, he talks the talk of a man who finds pleasure in musing about life's "little" or "ordinary" happenings. Thus, for example, he continually points out stores along Dixwell Avenue that are owned by friends or acquaintances, talks about people who live in the neighborhood, and makes fleeting remarks about long-gone parties and social functions that occurred in the Dixwell area. One gets the feeling that Will must know half the people who live in New Haven, and he speaks of them almost as if the listener, regardless of who he is or where he comes from, is on intimate terms with the people being referred to.

The car heads out into the suburbs again and after a short while Will pulls to a halt outside a long, rectangular-shaped, red brick building. He gets out and quickly goes inside.

Once inside the school he walks down a long, deserted corridor toward an office located at the far end of the hall. The office is lit up and a card reading "Mr. Williams, MDTA Instructor" is taped to the door. Will knocks on the door, and after a voice calls "Come in," he enters.

It is hot inside the office. A small fan located near the window blows a warm stream of air toward the man sitting behind the single desk in the office. As Will approaches the desk the man looks up.
Mr. W.:
Hello, Will, good to see you again.
Will:
How's it going, Mr. Williams?
Mr. W.:
Not too bad. It's just too hot, that's all.

Will:
You know it.
Mr. W.:
I guess you're here about Larry, right?
Will:
You know that too.
Mr. W.:
Well, he's doing very well. Hasn't missed a night yet. Talks a lot about this new job of his up in Guilford. Seems to really like it.
Will:
I hope so. I was kind of worried that he might not be making classes.
Mr. W.:
Oh no, not at all. In fact, I was going to call you tomorrow to let you know that he's been doing quite well with me. He seems to like the MDTA program.

(Note: MDTA are the call letters for the vocational training and education programs developed under the Manpower Development and Training Act of 1962.)

Will and Mr. Williams continue to talk about Larry, his performance, and his attitude in class. During the course of the conversation, Will, without going into specifics, talks about Larry having a "weekend problem" and asks Mr. Williams to "keep an eye" on him on Monday nights. Mr. Williams looks a bit puzzled but agrees to make sure that whatever Larry is involved in "doesn't affect his work with me."

The conversation comes to an end and Will stands up to leave. He and Mr. Williams shake hands and Will turns to go back out into the hallway. As he leaves Mr. Williams calls to him.

Mr. W.:
You know, I keep meaning to get down to see the RYC, but I always seem to get tied up.
Will:
Come down any time you can. Come after school, there's always something jumping.
Mr. W.:
I'll try, Will, I mean it.
Will:
Good. I'll look to see you. S'long now.
Mr. W.:
Bye, Will.

Will walks down the corridor and back out to the car. He seems to be walking a bit more slowly now than earlier in the day. Before getting into the car he stretches a long groping stretch.

Will:
Well, looks like all Will got to worry about is Larry's weekends.

Will gets back into the car and starts it up. He pulls away from the curb and heads back toward Dixwell Avenue. He is silent now, very silent, almost as if he has suddenly grown very tired of talking. The car moves along briskly, its speed bringing cool air through the open windows and vents.

The car turns right onto Dixwell Avenue and begins to head toward town. There isn't very much traffic now, and Will seems to gauge the car's speed so that he can make most of the lights without stopping. About halfway toward town he suddenly veers off the avenue and pulls into a Carvel stand (an ice cream stand) on the opposite side of the street. Will pulls up and parks the car behind the serving booth. He gets out quickly and goes to stand in line before one of the serving windows.

Will returns carrying a cup filled with ice cream and gets back into the car. Leaving the door open, he leans back in his seat and extends his feet outside the door. He sits in what looks like an almost painful "L" position, his body "folded" around the steering wheel and his feet dangling out the door. After a few moments he pulls his legs back into the car and, still holding the ice cream cup and spoon in his hand, he tilts back and lets his head come to rest "draped" over the back of his seat. He closes his eyes for a moment, hunches his shoulders, and seems about to fall asleep. In a moment, however, his eyes open wide and he leans forward again to finish his ice cream in two or three swift gulps. He then gets out of the car, throws the empty cup in a garbage can, and returns, slamming the door after him.

Will starts the car up once again, pulls into Dixwell Avenue, and crosses over to the side of the street from which he had pulled into the Carvel stand.

4:00–5:00 p.m.

Will heads back down Dixwell Avenue toward the RYC. The car cuts across town and turns left on George Street, one of the streets that run by the Center. A group of boys who look to be about 13 or 14 years old are walking on the right-hand side of the street. Will slows down and "sneaks" the car up alongside the kids. He smiles as the car inches in front of them:

Will:
That's Jeff and a bunch of kids in the summer work program.

Will looks straight ahead as the car slowly passes the boys.

He pretends not to see them. Suddenly one of the boys, the one Will recognized as Jeff, screams out:

Jeff:

Hey Will, Will, wait a minute. Give us a ride.

Will:

Give you a ride? All 12 of you in my Mustang? (Will smiles as he banters with the boy.)

Jeff:

No. Just me. Just you and me, Will.

Will:

Hell no. You guys need the walk. Got to lose some of that weight.

Jeff:

Aw c'mon, Will. Just me.

Will:

Nope. Just keep walkin'.

Suddenly Will laughs out loud and speeds up, leaving the boys far behind. Jeff screams after him (curses) as Will drives away laughing.

Once again Will pulls into the RYC's parking lot. He guns the motor before killing it and climbs out. He walks slowly up the stairs leading to the kitchen and goes into the Center.

Will goes into the office and slumps into a seat behind one of the desks. He looks tired now and sighs audibly before picking up the telephone:

Will:

Better try the people over to the Metro Action Center.

Will cradles the telephone under his chin and lights up a cigarette. Then he dials the number Hugh Price gave him and waits.

Will:

Hello? This is Will K. over at the Residential Youth Center. I was talking with Hugh Price today and he said you might be able to help me. (Pause)

Oh, you know about the Center? Well fine. (Pause)

Ya. Well I got a kid here who's gotten himself a 450 dollar scholarship to Milford Prep school. Now, he can go to school there in the fall if he can raise another 450 dollars on his own. (Pause)

No, not 400. 450 dollars. Yes, that's right. (Long pause)

Ya, now Hugh Price he thought you'd wanna help out. (Pause)

No. Sam, that's the kid, he don't need the money right away. We need it about a week before Milford goes into session. (Short pause)

September. That's right. Early September. (Long pause. Will's
eyes begin to light up.)
Now you sure about that. I don't wanna go raisin' the kid's
hopes for nothing. (Pause)
Great. That's great. I'll tell him. My number is 787-6571,
Extension 378. (Pause).
O.K., now. That's fine. Thanks a lot. So long.
    Will slams the phone down and jumps out of his seat. He
laughs and does a little jig in the center of the room:
Will:
That's it. I can go home now. Day's finished now. We got a
commitment for Sam. A real live commitment.
    Will struts around the office slapping the hands of the three
other staff members who are present. They smile and slap
him back, obviously enjoying his "performance." Will laughs
again and leaps back to the center of the room.
Will:
Now all I got to do is make that big-assed fool put his mind
to school. And he'll do it, too, or you'll all see one skinny-
assed nigger smack one big fat-assed nigger kid all over
New Haven.
    Will laughs again and goes back to his seat. Just then an-
other kid comes walking into the office and goes directly
over to where Will is sitting. Silently, he takes out his wallet,
carefully counts out 15 dollars, and hands them over to Will.
Will pulls out his ledger book and makes out another rent
receipt form. He gives it to the kid, smacks the resident
playfully on the head, and leans back. The kid walks slowly
out of the office.
    Will pulls out another cigarette and lights up. He takes a
long drag and lets his eyes wander around the room. Now
he gets up and walks quietly around the room, stopping only
to look briefly at the list of names of kids served by the
Center since its inception. After taking another deep drag,
he returns to his seat. Will no longer looks jubilant. Instead,
he looks weary and uncomfortable. He sits for a moment and
stares straight ahead as if suddenly engrossed in thoughts that
are very complicated and very personal. His eyes look a bit
glassy. The hand holding his cigarette shakes.
    Almost as if catching himself Will suddenly sits up. Then
he reaches down, opens one of the lower drawers of his
desk, and pulls out some writing paper. He places the paper
before him, picks up a pen, and begins to write what looks
like a report on one of his kids.
    Will remains in a hunched-over position for a long time.

He writes slowly, often pausing as if searching for a particularly elusive word or phrase. At these times his face screws up into a grimace and he taps his nose with the eraser of his pencil. The writing goes slowly, very slowly.

Will looks up from his work as another kid comes walking into the office. The youngster, a Negro kid who considers himself to be one of the RYC's black militants, is carrying a bunch of paperback books under his arm. Will calls out to him.
Will:
Hey, c'mere. Let's see what books you got there.

The kid walks over to Will and spreads his books out before him. The books are: *The Negro Pilgrimage in America* by C. Eric Lincoln; *The Man* by Irving Wallace; *Invisible Man* by Ralph Ellison; *Killers of the Dream* by Lillian Smith; and *The Puerto Ricans* by Clarence Senior. Will looks the books over.
Will:
That's some pretty heavy reading for a dummy like you.
Resident:
Shit on that, Will. I read better'n you'll ever be able.
Will:
Think so?
Resident:
I *know* so!

Will and the kid begin to banter about who needs more help with reading. In a little while, however, they begin to talk about some of the contents of the books before them, particularly Lincoln's books about the Negro in American history. They both become bogged down in trying to remember the names of two black men, both from Massachusetts, who fought in the Revolutionary War. They agree that the men they are both thinking about had the same or similar names and they finally open Lincoln's book and begin searching through it. After a while Will stops.
Will:
Salem! That's the name, Salem.
Resident:
That's right, I remember now. The name was Salem.

They stop arguing now and begin to search the book more carefully. Finally, after slowly scrutinizing a number of pages in succession, they come to what they have been looking for.
Resident:
Here it is. Right here. It was Salem Poor and Peter Salem. Right?
Will:
Right. See, what'd I tell ya? They got the same name. Salem

Poor and Peter Salem. I knew they had somethin' in their names that was the same.

It is now a few minutes after 5:00 p.m., and a voice comes boming out of the kitchen.

Chip:

Chow! Come on now. Suppertime.

Will and the kid stop and look at each other for a moment. The kid picks up his books and tucks them under his arm again. They both get up and go into the dining room adjacent to the office.

5:00–6:00 p.m.

Will ambles into the dining room, looks around for a moment, and goes to stand in the line that has formed in front of Chip's serving table. The line moves fairly quickly and Will moves along with it. He stops along the way to pick up some silverware from a tray that stands near the serving table. The room is alive with noise. Some of the kids and staff are already eating, and their conversations, coupled with the clank of plates and silverware, fill the room from corner to corner. Only occasionally can a single word be made out. The overall sound is that of muffled but excited and noisy chatter.

Will stops in front of the serving area. He watches closely as Chip (and a couple of the residents who have been assigned to help him prepare dinner) loads his plate with macaroni and meat sauce. When Chip finishes, or thinks he has finished, Will leans over and pushes his serving spoon back into the macaroni. Chip looks up, shakes his head in frustration, and dips his spoon back into the serving plate to hoist another serving of macaroni and sauce onto Will's plate. Only then does Will walk away from the serving table.

Will pauses for a moment and scans the room. He then walks over to a table at which four of the other residents are already seated and eating. He puts his plate down and walks over to a soda machine located near the back of the dining room. Will gets his soda, returns to the table, and sits down. The kids seated with him are Curt, Cal, Jim, and Donny.

Will begins to eat, but before he has taken his first bite, Curt places his hand on Will's arm in such a manner as to prevent Will from placing the food in his mouth:

Curt:

Will, you gonna buy me a soda?

Will:

You best take your hand away, Curt, lessen you wanna lose it.

Curt:

You gonna buy me a soda, right?

Will:

Shoot, you makin' more money than me now. You ought'a be buyin' me one.
Curt:
Later for that man. Everyone know you don't do shit all day but bother a bunch of folks.
Will:
That's right. That's right. Now get your nasty hand away anyway.

Curt takes his hand off Will's arm and Will begins to eat. After a few mouthfuls of food, Will turns to his right, toward Cal.
Will:
Hey Snickit, how's the new job?
Cal:
Tough man, real tough. I got me my own office with a telephone and everything.
Will:
Do you wear a tie?
Cal:
Hell man, you better believe I do.
Will:
Well shoot, then, now you're a real TIE-COON!

Everyone at the table, including Will, breaks up with laughter as they get the meaning of Will's words. Cal laughs harder than anyone as Will's successful "put on" finally gets to him. Will leans back and, while still almost convulsed with laughter, pats Cal on the back of the shoulders.

Will returns to his food. In a little while Curt and Calvin get up and leave the table, carrying their plates with them. Only Will, Donny, and Jim remain.

Will finishes his food, leans back, and lights up another cigarette. He seems relaxed now and tilts his chair so that its front two legs are off the ground. He takes a deep drag on his cigarette and turns toward Jim.
Will:
You working?
Jim:
No. Tomorrow I go put in an application at Yale-New Haven Hospital.
Will:
What do you wanna do?
Jim:
Work in maintenance.
Will:
Let me know how it turns out.

Jim:
Yeah.
Will:
Now lemme get these here dishes in before Chip has a fit.

Will gets up, places his silverware in his empty plate, and walks into the kitchen. He goes over to the sink and dumps his dishes and utensils in the soapy water. Now he turns, strolls back out to the dining room, and goes back to his seat. Once again he leans back in his chair.

One of the kids, Nean, walks into the dining room with Ron, the boy whose work site Will visited earlier in the day. Nean approaches Will.
Nean:
Hey Lincoln, gimme a smoke.
Will:
You pay your back rent yet?
Nean:
Paid it all up.
Will:
(Laughs) You lying little nigger. I saw your brother yesterday and he told me you had change a-jingling in your pocket and spent it all.
Nean:
(only half-embarrassed) No, I didn't.
Will:
Yes you did, you little neanderthal man.
Nean:
O.K., Lincoln, you bigot, but gimme a cigarette anyway.

Nean leans over Will's shoulder and Will allows the kid to take a cigarette from his pocket. Nean lights it up and turns to Ron, who is standing right next to him.
Nean:
Hey Ron, tell Will about the mosque.
Ron:
Yeah, lemme tell ya. Last night we made it down to Mo-hammed's Mosque. You know, the one on Dixwell Avenue. Well let me tell you, it was somethin' else.

Ron and Nean take seats at Will's table. Ron continues, telling his story with great enthusiasm and more than a little theatrics.
Ron:
Well, first off let me tell you they got an answer for every-thing. I mean everything. But first, listen here. I go to the door and this guy greets me, see? And he says: "Brother, is this your first time here?" I says yeah and then he says: "Well

brother, then I gots to search you." Real polite he is. So I says O.K., and whap, in no time a'tall, he comes up with my razor, my headband, everything. He even finds a dime I got in my back pocket. Just like that. Whap. Fastest frisk you ever seen, and all so politelike. Well, then he lets me in and asks me if I got any questions. So I says yeah and I asks him if he really thinks the Honorable Elijah Mohammed is smarter than Moses and Jesus. And he says "Sure" and then he *proves* it. He says: "Well brother, you see when Moses was alive wasn't nobody who know anything, so he gots to be the smartest man around. Then when Jesus come, he came after Moses, so he knew everything what Moses knew plus his own stuff. Now, when Elijah Mohammed come he knows what Moses and Jesus know PLUS. So, therefore, Elijah is smarter than both of 'em. Dig?"

Ron goes on and on. He describes the meeting, the people, even the mosque itself. His descriptions are vivid and very elaborate, very much like his description of his "gun threat" earlier in the day.

The discussion continues with both Nean and Will joining in. At one point Ron begins to tell the others about the Muslim Bible and how "it tells it different than the others." Will interrupts.
Will:
Now I believe some of the things they talk about, things like keeping yourself clean, and pride, and that kind of thing. But some of it is crazy, just plain crazy.
Ron:
Well now, I'm not sayin' I believe it all either. Even if I did, like I couldn't really join 'em cause it wouldn't be honest. Like that stuff about partyin'. I mean you know me. Man, I just love to party and I couldn't just give that up like that. I mean I don't believe all of what they say, but some of that Bible stuff sure make sense.
Will:
Ya know, Ron, you can find justification for almost *anything* in the Bible. Not to turn you off or anything, but you know the KKK used the Bible to justify lynchin' Negroes. I mean like the Bible can make you feel right about anything you want.
Ron:
Maybe so, but I sure like a lot I heard. It's just too bad about the partyin' business.

Ron continues to describe his visit to the mosque. He tells about the "sermon" and how it ended.

Ron:
Well, like at the end of all this preachin' 'bout pureness and
everything, that preacher he looks straight down at me . . .
Will:
No wonder. You was prob'ly the only cat sittin' there with
a process upside his head. (Everyone laughs heartily)
Ron:
Damn straight! There's all these people—the ladies all in
white and the men just a sittin' and diggin'—all lookin' so
fine and quiet. (Laughs) And there's me. (Laughs) Like to
blow your mind, right?
Will:
You all know where the Honorable Elijah Mohammed got
his start?
Ron:
From where?
Will:
From Marcus Garvey.
Nean:
Marcus who?
Will:
Marcus Garvey, that's who!
   Will shakes his head from side to side in mocking despair.
He sighs very deeply.
Will:
Lord, Lord. Looks like I'm gonna have to give you guys a
little lesson in black history. Man, Mohammed ain't nothin'
new. We been here before. You just don't know it.
   Before Will can continue, Butch sticks his head into the
dining room to let everyone know that the "health and wel-
fare" meeting has started. Will looks up.
Will:
O.K. C'mon you guys. Time for "health and welfare." We'll
just have to pick this up later some time.
   Will and the two residents get up and push their chairs
back under the table. They all saunter out, walk down the
hall, and turn into the large living room on the left-hand side
of the corridor.
6:00–7:00 p.m.
   Most of the RYC's residents and staff are already in the
room and seated. The chairs and couches have been arranged in a large circle. Kids and staff members sit in what
does not appear to be any prearranged manner: neither the
kids nor staff, as a group, occupy any particular seats.
   Will takes a seat near the entrance to the living room. He

sits in a chair that sags markedly under his weight. Will takes out a cigarette, lights it, and places an ashtray on the floor near his right foot.

The meeting begins with Frank explaining the problem and the staff's "dilemma" (as he puts it) to the residents. He reviews the incident concerning the fire extinguisher with the residents, details his recollection of the problem (how it began, its development, and its consequences), and finishes by telling the kids that "Calvin will have to be terminated unless whoever first took the fire extinguisher off the wall comes forward."

A murmur runs through the room as he finishes. A few of the kids look at each other but quickly turn away and let their gazes fall back on Frank. Will sits quietly and looks around the room. He looks very tired now, almost as if the energy has suddenly been drained out of him. He looks tired, tired and weary.

After a few minutes of what seems like deathly silence, Scotty brings the conversation back to the general question of the rationale behind the rules and penalties concerning the fire extinguisher and "walking up on the roof ledge." After reviewing the "history" behind each of the rules, he throws the issue back to the kids and asks for their feelings on the matter.

A heated discussion follows, a discussion having nothing to do with the issue as Scotty has presented it. Rather, the residents turn their wrath on the staff for putting them in the kind of position where "if we wanna save Cal we gotta sound on someone else." A number of the kids, each in turn and with hardly any interruptions from the other residents, make their position more than crystal clear.

Nean:

The whole thing stinks. The staff is tryin' to make us all into stoolies.

Bobo:

I don't know nothin'. All I know is that if Cal says I took the extinguisher off the wall he's lyin'.

Curt:

Throw out all the guys on the second floor. I'm sick of bein' kept up at night 'cause of their shittin' around.

Jim:

We didn't know about the fire extinguisher stuff. I didn't know the rule anyway.

Sam:

I don't need no staff telling me how to handle the problem. I'll take care of it myself, in my own way.

Will's eyes shift from kid to kid as each one tells the group his feelings. His face is about as expressionless as it's been all day. He sits very much like a man whose physical presence belies the fact that he has been emotionally turned off by the entire affair.

The arguing and hassling goes on and on. No sooner does it appear as if the kids are about to return to the issue Scotty has posed than they launch into another denunciation of the staff, rules in general, and the house as a whole. Nothing seems to be getting accomplished, nothing changes. The entire issue has been converted into a "we vs. them" situation with the staff and the residents being pushed into assuming polarized positions.

Finally, almost as if by some minor miracle, the residents themselves come up with a "solution" which, at least temporarily, takes both the staff and the kids "off the hook." They propose that the staff leave the room and allow the residents to discuss the situation privately. Scotty, after making it clear that the staff would be willing to meet with the residents after they (the residents) have had a chance to talk things over among themselves, looks around the room and asks if anyone else has anything to add before the staff leaves the room. No one does, and the staff rises to leave.

Will is slow getting out of his chair. He moves very much like someone suddenly too tired to care very much anymore. Finally, along with the rest of the staff, he leaves the room and walks across the hall to the office.

Once back in the office, Will walks over to the desk nearest the door and leans up against it. A few of the staff members are already engaged in a quiet discussion of the meeting just concluded. Will listens in on their conversation but does not join it.

After a few minutes, one of the kids comes into the office. He announces to the group that the residents will need more than a few minutes to finish their "private" meeting. He then asks the staff if their next joint meeting can be postponed until the morning. He also assures the staff that the residents will not take any action of any kind until after the next staff-resident meeting. Scotty accepts the residents' "terms," and the kid leaves the office. He then turns to the other staff members remaining in the office:

Scotty:
Well, I guess we sit on this till tomorrow.
Will:
It's probably best this way. Nothing ever got accomplished in there. Too much goin' on all at once. Best let the kids mull it over.

Some of the staff begin to leave the office to go home.

Will walks away from the desk he has been leaning on, crosses the room, and sits down in the chair behind the desk he used during those times of the day when he was in the office. He slumps into the seat, extends his legs, and lights up another cigarette. He takes a long drag as the last of the staff members leave the room.

7:00–7:15 p.m.

The office is empty now. The only sound is that of the fan.

Will sits very quietly. Periodically he takes a drag on his cigarette or flicks an ash into the ashtray that rests on his desk. Sounds of argument suddenly come from the large living room across the hall. The residents are still having their meeting, and from the sound of things it looks like it may go on for quite a while. Will sits as if oblivious to the noise now streaming into the office.

Will takes a final drag on his cigarette and grinds out the butt in the ashtray on his desk. He sits for a moment, then looks down at the unfinished report in front of him. He picks up his pen but then lets it fall back to the desk. Now he rises. Will:

Game time! Wrap it up, brother, ol' Will's goin' home.

Will moves quickly to the office door. He opens it and goes down the corridor leading to the front door. He pauses for a moment, almost as if he thinks he may have forgotten something, but then he leaves quickly. Once outside the Center he heads immediately for his car in the parking lot. He gets in and starts it up.

Will eases the car out of the parking lot and onto George Street. He guns the motor and heads down toward the corner. The light turns yellow as Will crosses the intersection and drives back into the bowels of the city.

Thus ended Will's day at the RYC. True to his prediction, he had completed or attended to fewer than half the items on his list of "things to do." And yet, how does one go about evaluating the meaning or effectiveness of his work? How does one gauge the "impact," if any, of his almost countless interactions with the RYC's residents, their families, and other staff members? All we really "know," indeed all an observational record is meant to convey, is *what* Will did during the course of one day's work, not *why* he did certain things or *how* they eventually turned out. From this point of view, we now know at least something about the world of an RYC worker, something of its complexity, its minor triumphs, and its minor tragedies. But we also know more than that: We know that if Will's behavior is somehow characteristic of how a staff functions as a whole, then the question of "effectiveness" might well be approached from the point of view of "outcome research." In the next chapter, therefore, we will focus attention on some of the more formal research results of the first 18 months of the RYC program.

Chapter 9 Research
Results and Interpretation

The aim of science is to seek the simplest explanation of complex facts. We are apt, however, to fall into the error of thinking that the facts are simple because simplicity is the goal of our quest.
—Alfred North Whitehead

As indicated in Chapter 8, any attempt to evaluate the effectiveness of a setting as volatile and complex as an RYC is "destined," almost from the very beginning, to be fraught with difficulties; difficulties which are certainly and appropriately inherent in the nature of the problem, but which are also compounded by both the particular "research interests" of forces external to the setting (i.e., the funding agent) and the comparative lack of conceptual and methodological sophistication in the area of action research in general.[1] In the final analysis, the researcher is "bound" in at

[1] By the particular "research interests" of the funding agent (in the case of the RYC, of course, it was the Department of Labor), we are referring to an orientation which, while entirely understandable from the point of view of the funding agent, may not necessarily be either appropriate to the complexity of the problem under consideration or consistent with the scientific interests of the researcher. Thus, for example, while the researcher's main concern may revolve around questions of individual change, change of a subtle or attitudinal nature, the funding agent's concerns may be replete with considerations of overall "cost-effectiveness" and with the kinds of behavioral changes which, while politically dramatic and observable, may be short-term or even illusory in nature. As far as the "comparative lack of conceptual and methodological sophistication in the area of action research" is concerned, here we are referring to the problem confronting anyone who wishes to investigate complex human behavior anywhere but in the laboratory setting. While it may be somewhat tangential to the problem currently being discussed, it would be important to point out that the basic "inferiority" experienced by the action researcher has its roots in the history of psychology's conscious attempt to wrench itself free from the breast of philosophy and to achieve some sort of status within the scientific community. Thus, for example, the clinician (no different from the action researcher) who attempts to investigate problems of complex human behavior (problems which, almost by definition, make "control," "replication," and the manipulation of experimental interventions more than a little difficult) is constantly reminded of the quasi-scientific character of his research. What complicates the situation even further is the fact that his own research training is a kind that expects him, reinforces him, and leads him (eventually) to expect himself to evaluate his "clinical" interventions along nonclinical (i.e., experimental) dimensions independent of the appropriateness of the experimental model for problems of a clinical nature. The result, all too often, is a hypersensitive and academically oriented researcher who eventually sacrifices meaning for method and complexity

least two important ways: first, by the necessity of having to rely on existing techniques, none of which seems entirely adequate to do the job; and second, by his own awareness that the criteria usually associated with "success" in action programs may be inappropriate to the particular phenomena under investigation. It is a situation in which research must "walk the tightrope" and yet still serve many "harsh masters." These limitations notwithstanding, we now turn to an analysis of the RYC as a setting for individual change.

Research Design

When the Residential Youth Center first opened, it took in 20 youngsters, those youths with the greatest number of problems and the longest histories of social, vocational, educational, and personal failure.[2] An additional 20 boys with similar problems were placed in a control group. Both groups were tested, assessed, and interviewed on a host of variables involving both behavioral and attitudinal functioning. On the behavioral level, we were most concerned with work attendance records, average weekly income, and community behavior (i.e., involvement with the law). With respect to attitudinal functioning, the attempt was made to measure a youngster's perceptions about himself in society, his feelings of alienation and trust, and the degree to which he felt he could manipulate the social world. In other words, the research design—a rather simple pre-post attitudinal and behavioral index-of-functioning design with residence at the RYC as the intervening experimental treatment—was geared

---

for control, a "scientist" who limits himself to studying those problems for which there is the greatest relative academic acceptance, social status and reinforcement, and professional support. Only recently, primarily through the work of Lord (1967) and Levine (1968), has the self-defeating and self-deceiving character of our traditional assumptions regarding research—especially research of the "clinical" or "action" variety—been called into question.

[2] It should be pointed out that although the RYC, as a facility, "formally" opened its doors on September 16, 1966, the staff already had been working with its residents for approximately 12 weeks prior to the time the house was ready for occupancy. The "preresidency" staff-client involvement becomes important in the light of subsequent data and in the interpretation of the research results to be reported.

to assess not only what the youngsters were doing but also how they felt about it and how they perceived themselves as people in a complex, changing, sometimes incomprehensible, but often demanding world.[3] Retesting of both groups was done between 6 and 12 months after the program began. Finally, follow-up research was done on those youths who left the RYC during its first year of existence. In the pages that follow we shall describe in greater detail the procedure by which youngsters were selected for inclusion in the program (as well as how the control group was selected), the rationale behind the development of the particular attitudinal and behavioral assessment techniques utilized in the study, and the research results themselves. Finally, we shall review the research from the point of view of some of its theoretical implications and methodological limitations.

Subjects and Procedures

Approximately four months prior to the RYC's formal inception—at a point in time after initial contacts had been established between the RYC and different groups in the community (see Chapter 6)—the process of selecting potential residents was begun. The procedure employed was a relatively simple one. After the initial meetings between the RYC and the relevant community agencies were over (meetings, it will be recalled, during which the program was presented and explained), each group was asked to assist in the process of selecting potential residents. The agencies included CPI's four Neighborhood Employment Centers, the police, and the community action agency's vocational counselors, work crew foremen, and remedial education teachers. Each group was asked to submit a list of 50 youths (males between the ages of 16 and 21) who, from its particular point of view, came closest to fulfilling whatever they thought was meant by the term "hard-core." Each group was told that we wanted the names of youngsters whom they felt to be the "most difficult to reach," with whom they had had the greatest amount of

[3]The problems associated with using as gross a variable as "residence at the RYC" as the "intervening experimental treatment" will be discussed later in this chapter.

difficulty, and with whom they had experienced the greatest degree of failure in terms of the youths' benefiting from the kinds of services each group had to offer. Each group was also told that while we hoped, eventually, to serve all disadvantaged youth, the RYC could only serve 20 youths at a given time; the youths eventually selected for the demonstration project would be chosen on the basis of "agreed-upon need" after a review of all the names submitted by all the agencies. Finally, the agencies were asked to keep both their selection procedures and their final list of names confidential so that there would be no unnecessary "raising of a youngster's hopes" or any undue or premature publicity for the program.

Once all the agencies had forwarded their lists of names to the RYC, a "selection meeting" was held to make a final determination on which youths would be placed in the experimental (RYC) group and which youths would be assigned to a control group. Again, a rather simple procedure was developed for assigning youngsters to the RYC or control groups. All the youths who had been mentioned on the lists were ranked according to the number of times their names appeared on each of the agencies' lists.[4] Thus, for example, a youth whose name appeared on the "50 Most Difficult" list of seven different groups was given a higher rank than a boy whose name appeared on only one agency's list.

Once the rankings were completed, we were left with a final list of 50 names. Of these names, and after matchings for age and race, the "top" 25 were placed in the RYC group, while the "bottom" 25 were assigned to the control group.[5]

[4]All the different groups participating in the selection procedure had one thing in common: they all devoted a major portion of their time and resources to working with inner-city, disadvantaged, and/or poverty youths. Consequently, we could be relatively sure of a great deal of overlapping; that is to say, more than one agency would have had prior contact with any particular youngster—especially if that youngster, as is so often the case with inner-city youths who are out of school, out of work, and "in trouble," had "bounced around" from agency to agency.
[5]Although, as we shall soon indicate, there were essentially no statistically significant "pre-RYC" differences between the attitudes and behaviors of the youngsters assigned to the RYC and control groups, the fact remains that the youngsters were not assigned to their groups

Although the research design was based on a total of 40 youths (20 in the RYC and 20 in the control group), an additional 5 names in each group were kept for replacement purposes. Thus, for example, since entrance into the RYC was both voluntary and predicated upon parental consent, if one of the youngsters selected for the program did not wish to enter (or if his parents, as was the case in one instance, did not wish to "lose" him to the RYC), it was important to have a list of "alternates" of comparable need with which to replace him. Similarly, although the names submitted were "up to date" (i.e., youths currently known to each of the agencies), there was no guarantee that all the youths selected would still be in New Haven by the time the program began. Consequently, for both RYC and control groups, it was felt that having 5 additional names for replacement purposes would provide us with a safeguard against a youth's suddenly leaving the New Haven area.

Thus, when the selection process was completed, we were left with the names of 50 youths (25 in the experimental

---

in a purely random manner. In other words, the 25 youths who were deemed the "most difficult" were placed in the RYC or experimental group, whereas the next 25 "most difficult" were assigned to the control group. In a very real sense the final groupings were a concrete example of how the project's research commitments were in one way or another influenced by its service responsibilities. One could say that the potential effectiveness of the program was being tested much more severely by limiting the experimental group to those youths with the greatest number of problems. From this point of view one might make a good case for the fact that by taking the most difficult youngsters into the RYC we were actually "stacking the cards" against the RYC, a procedure well within the framework of "tough-minded" empirical research. On the other hand, however, as has been pointed out to us by some of our colleagues, by placing the most difficult of our youngsters in the RYC group, we were commiting ourselves to working with those youths who had "no where to go but up." It has also been pointed out to us—and we believe relevantly and helpfully—that, contrary to most people's assumptions, "a kid must have something on the ball to be so bad." In other words, it is entirely possible that those youths who exhibit the greatest degree of antisocial behavior may very well be the youngsters with the greatest potential. At this point, all we can say is that the question is an entirely open one and one to which future research will have to address itself. We repeat, however, that with the exception of work attendance, there were no statistically significant differences between the RYC-bound and control groups on any of the attitudinal or behavioral measures that were administered before the program began.

group and 25 in the control group); these names had been drawn from the original 178 names that had appeared on the lists of the eight groups which, independent of each other, had assisted in the selection process.

Measures and Assessment Techniques

Previous research has shown that attitudes, especially attitudes toward oneself, are a major determinant of behavior. In addition, it has been found that the development of particular skills plays an important role in determining an individual's social, vocational, and psychological success.[6] Consequently, in choosing the assessment techniques to be employed in the research, emphasis was placed on evaluating two kinds of changes: changes in skills (i.e., the individual's capacity to manipulate the environment) and changes in attitudes (i.e., the individual's reported feelings about himself and his social milieu). With this focus, a combination of social psychological and clinical assessment techniques were employed, with modifications necessitated occasionally by the

[6]By and large, research in the area of adolescence in general and delinquency (i.e., youths with academic, social, vocational, and behavioral difficulties) in particular has been of a twofold nature. Some investigations have concerned themselves primarily with the problem of the internal personality dynamics of the youth in trouble and with the processes of effective treatment. Others have studied the developmental aspects of the problem, generally agreeing that family relationships are the most important variable. Most recently, the role of "work experience" has been studied from the point of view of how it contributes to adolescent growth and development in terms of enabling youngsters to evolve the kinds of skills that enhance the adolescent's attitudes toward himself (i.e., self-esteem) and the world in general (Youmans, 1954). The work of Shore and Massimo (1963, 1966) with youth very similar to those served by the RYC program has indicated that vocationally oriented treatment programs may be one of the more effective ways of "reaching" so-called hard-core youngsters. Through a program somewhat similar to the RYC, they found that changes in self-esteem were necessary before a change in the ability to control aggression was noted, and that both of these changes were necessary before changes in attitudes toward authority were shown. Reckless, Dintz, and Kay (1957) report research supporting the theory that positive self-concepts insulate youths from becoming delinquents in otherwise high-delinquency areas. Given the results of previous research, it appeared that we should focus attention on both the behavioral and the attitudinal aspects of the problem within the context of what might be considered a "manpower-oriented" rehabilitative program. The choice and development of the assessment techniques utilized to evaluate the effectiveness of the RYC were predicated on this assumption.

unique nature of the program and its clients. The techniques included an open-ended interview, an attitudinal questionnaire, vocational behavior indices, and ratings of community and social behavior.

The Open-Ended Interview A lengthy interview was conducted with each resident prior to the time he became actively involved in the RYC program. Each interview was tape-recorded and included questions designed to tap the following dimensions: self-concept, social expectations, social causality, attitudes toward parents, attitudes toward authority, personal time orientation (past, present, future), alienation, hostility, reality functioning and impulse control, need for achievement, need for affiliation, task versus people orientation, dependence-independence, and social responsibility. A number of questions were semiprojective in nature and, consequently, open to personal interpretation. Although the interviews were structured, there was considerable freedom for informal discussion and clarification. The primary goal of the open-ended interview was to elicit information about the youngster's style of thinking, vocabulary, and personal philosophy.

After being interviewed, potential residents often listened to their tapes with their workers, and further comments were elicited at this time. The same interview was given to each resident again after six months. The tapes, with consent of the residents, were made available to the staff for use in discussing progress or the lack thereof. It was in this manner that the attempt was made to provide feedback to both the youngster and his worker.

The Attitudinal Questionnaire The problem of selecting and/or developing attitudinal scales for inclusion in the research was a particularly difficult one. To begin with, we were dealing with youngsters who came from "culturally and educationally disadvantaged" backgrounds. This meant that our subjects were less educated than the "usual" subjects for whom attitudinal questionnaires have been developed. Consequently, in addition to the fact that they had a limited "middle-class" vocabulary, the youngsters also had a relatively low tolerance for tests involving verbal and/or written interactions and a rather extensive and rapidly changing "slang" vocabulary. For purposes of testing, therefore, an attitudinal questionnaire had to be developed which would, on the one hand, be easily understood by inner-city youngsters but would not, on the other hand, be the kind of scale whose meaning might be apt to change readily between test administrations.

The scales finally selected for inclusion in the "RYC Opinion Questionnaire" were chosen for two reasons: first, because they measured the kinds of variables that we felt were related to, and could be affected by, the RYC experience; and second, because they had already demonstrated some sensitivity on a population somewhat similar to the youngsters for whom the RYC had been developed.[7] The scales chosen were the Marlowe-Crowne Social Desirability Scale (1960); the Gould Alienation Scale (1964); the Kenniston Trust Scale (1965); a counterbalanced version of the original Authoritarianism Scale (1950) as modified by Christie, Havel, and Seidenberg (1958) to control for acquiescence; Christie's Machiavellianism Scale (Christie, 1958; Christie and Merton, 1958); and Hoffman's "The World I Live In" Semantic Differential Test (1966).[8]

[7]Most of the scales utilized in assessing the effectiveness of the RYC with respect to its residents were drawn from those employed in a pilot educational project for disadvantaged adolescents. This project, known as the Yale Summer High School, was developed to assist underachieving youth from backgrounds of cultural, economic, and educational disadvantage. For additional information concerning the derivation and utilization of these scales, the reader is referred to the work of Klein and Gould (1965, 1969). Because the subjects used in the RYC research project were less educated than the youngsters in the Yale Summer High School project, the existing scales had to be modified.
[8]The following procedure was followed in adapting the scales for use in the RYC research design. The original scales were administered orally to 15 residents of a public housing project located in the inner city of New Haven. These residents were within the same age range (16 to 21 years of age) and socioeconomic level ("poor" as defined by the guidelines developed by the Office of Economic Opportunity) as the youngsters who would later become residents of the Center. A statement from one of the scales would be read to the subject (e.g., "Obedience and respect for authority are the most important virtues children should learn"—from the F-Scale developed by Christie, Havel, and Seidenberg). The subject would then indicate the extent to which he agreed or disagreed with the statement, and how clearly he thought

The *Marlowe-Crowne Social Desirability Scale* is a relatively new scale of social desirability independent of psychopathology. Its developers conceptualize it as measuring
"need for approval" and "defensiveness." With respect to
the RYC research design, it was intended to elicit informa-

he understood the statement. He was then asked to explain the statement in other words. When either his own certainty or the quality of
his explanation indicated a lack of comprehension, the troublesome
words or phrases would be circled (in the example above, for instance,
14 of the 15 youngsters tested had difficulty with "obedience" and
"respect for authority"). After this procedure was followed for every
item in every scale, a panel of 10 high-ability teen-agers from the same
neighborhood and background were recruited to assist with the next
step. Each went through the scales independently, substituting alternative words or phrases for those that had been circled. These alternatives
were then presented to the panel, and each selected the substitute that
came closest to the original meaning. Differences of opinion were
discussed until one substitute word or phrase was agreed upon (thus,
for example, the sentence "Obedience and respect for authority are
the most important virtues children should learn" was changed to read,
"The most important thing to teach children is to do what they are
told and to respect their elders"). The modified scales were then again
presented to the original sample of 15 youngsters. The aforementioned
procedure was followed, with each subject responding to the verbal
statement and then explaining what it meant. At this point, and with
specific reference to the example above, there were few (less than 5
percent) problems of comprehension. Inasmuch as the scales being used
were modifications of scales for which construct validity had already
been established, only the question of establishing face validity was
considered (i.e., that the verbal statements that made up the scales
were understood by the subjects and were an adequate indication of
their actual attitudes). To test the reliability of the scales, they were
administered, in written form, to two classes (N = 40) at a training
center for unemployed, disadvantaged youth. After two weeks they
were readministered to the same classes to measure the stability of the
scales over time. The test-retest correlations ranged from .50 to .78 (for
Trust and Alienation, respectively), and inasmuch as this was a fairly
severe test of stability for scales designed to be given verbally to teen-
agers with reading difficulties, this was taken as an indication of high
stability. Acting against the stability of the scales over the two-week
period was also the possibility that the youngsters actually may have
changed. Thus, the overall Spearman-Brown correlation of .68 was
reasonably high. Finally, another kind of reliability was measured: the
equivalence of the scales, to see the extent to which different versions
given to any individual at a given time would yield consistent results.
This was measured by the split-half method. The scales were divided
into two halves, and the scores on the two halves were correlated to
provide an estimate of the extent to which they were equivalent, that
is, measuring the same thing. The corrected split-half reliability of the
scales, using the Spearman-Brown formula, ranged from .52 (for the
Authoritarianism Scale) to .80 (for the Machiavellianism Scale) with an
N of 80. In summary, although rather small N's were used to establish
the reliability of the scales, in all cases the reliability approached
closely that of the original scales from which they were derived.

tion about both the individual's need for approval (presumably from the adult tester) and the degree of compliance (the willingness of the subject to accept the demand characteristics of the testing situation), which were involved in responses to the other scales.

The *Alienation Scale* is a measure of the subject's feelings of estrangement from himself and his society. It includes such statements as "There's not much use in writing letters to public officials because they aren't really interested in the problems of the average man." This measure was included because alienation was expected from a group that had had generally negative and self-deprecating experiences with those social institutions that have come to be labeled "The Establishment" (i.e., the educational system, the police, the employment system, and the welfare system). Since one of the goals of the RYC program was to help a youngster achieve a more "realistic" view of himself and the complex society he lives in, it was felt that changes in one's feeling of estrangement would be related to the degree to which the individual would be able to exercise and utilize the personal freedom that invariably accompanies a growing sense of self-determination. It was anticipated that initial changes in the experience of personal alienation would be in a negative direction—the consequence of increased openness with oneself and others, and the increased awareness of problems and the sources of these problems. Following this initial increase in alienation, a decrease was predicted as a function of subsequent successful attempts at controlling one's fate in the social and vocational world. For those youth not in the RYC program, of course, the opposite prediction was made.

The *Kenniston Trust Scale* measures the degree to which an individual is willing to place his faith in his own and other people's "words" and "comments." It includes such statements as "Just because a man makes a promise doesn't mean that he will keep it," "All men are basically and naturally good." It was expected that new RYC residents would distrust not only authority figures but people in general, including members of their own peer group. Historically, the inability to trust (be it for good reasons, bad reasons, or a combination thereof) has been related to the "self-fulfilling prophesy." Thus, for example, because of this basic lack of trust, inner-city, disadvantaged youth are often hostile to the very people who may be in a position to help them. The result, consequently, is that the offer of help is often either not made or quickly withdrawn. The net effect, at least from the point of view of the untrusting youth, is that the offer of help was from the very beginning an insincere one. Since one of the primary goals of the eventual relationship between a resident and his RYC worker was to increase the youngster's sense of trust, it was expected that this change in the youth's experience would reveal itself in a higher posttest "trust score."

The Machiavellianism Scale is an overt measure of the subject's acceptance of a cynical and distrustful orientation toward the world, coupled with a tendency to use manipulation, both of others and of the environment in general, to gain one's own ends. Thus, for example, someone high in Machiavellianism would agree with such statements as "It is usually best to tell your bosses or superiors what they really want to hear," and "It's hard to get ahead without cutting corners here and there." There are actually two factors involved: one is a view of human nature as weak and manipulatable; and the other is a tactical style designed to master the environment. Machiavellianism is not related to education, intelligence, or authoritarianism. The decision to focus attention on Machiavellianism was based on the assumption that a certain degree of manipulative control was necessary in order to succeed in many of the vocational and social settings that comprise one's practical world. In addition, the interaction of this ability with the attitude of trust was of particular interest to us since, at least on the surface of things, they seem to be such antithetical orientations, and yet both are necessary for survival in general and success in particular.

The *Authoritarianism Scale* measures, among other things, the degree to which one adheres to conventional values, is tough and rigid, and perceives the impetus for one's behavior as residing either within oneself or in the external world. The scale includes such statements as "What a boy needs most are strict rules and the determination to stand by his job, his family, and his country." One who scores high on authoritarianism is generally thought to satisfy his aggressive needs and impulses by projecting them onto "out groups," and is commonly referred to as the prejudiced personality. It was expected that the initial levels of authoritarianism would be quite high, would inhibit attempts to seek causes behind experiences, and would thus interfere with—short-circuit, so to speak—the social learning process. It was further expected that the RYC experience, if successful, would lower the level of authoritarianism among its residents.

The scales described were all administered verbally to each potential RYC resident and members of the control group. The scales were constructed in the form of statements to which the subjects indicated agreement or disagreement on a seven-point scale ranging from "agree strongly" to "disagree strongly." The scales were readministered six months after the RYC program had begun.

Indices of Vocational Behavior and Change Inasmuch as one of the major foci of the RYC program was work-related (i.e., manpower-oriented), measures for assessing vocational behavior and change were developed to evaluate some of the more "practical" effects of the program (i.e., its "cost-effectiveness"). Generally, the typical RYC resident, if he had been working at all, had spent over a year on one or more of CPI's Basic Work Crews (the most "elementary" work experience setting developed by the community action agency) without showing any significant progress and without having advanced. More often than not, his lack of progress had been accompanied by serious, chronic, and disruptive behaviors, the kinds of behaviors (e.g., poor attendance, fighting) that created difficulties for the youngster, his co-workers, and the work crew foreman. The youngster's behavior was usually interpreted as resulting from poor work habits, negative attitudes, a poor self-concept, severe family problems, and/or other factors. It was anticipated, therefore, that a youngster's success in the "world of work" while involved in the RYC program would reflect changes in many of these areas. Also, since it was explicitly understood that each youngster would get and keep a job in order to pay his rent and remain in the RYC, vocational performance could be interpreted as conformity to, or rejection of, the Center in general and the individual's worker in particular.

Included as vocational behavior indices were measures of work attendance, performance on the job, advancement, and income. The procedure for gathering this information was a relatively simple one. Each week, for both the RYC and control groups, the youngsters' employers were contacted. They were asked to submit a "time sheet" for the boys, along with whatever work-related information they felt was important. Overall group performance means were tabulated each month. Group comparisons of behavior as well as income were therefore available for evaluation both on a weekly and a monthly basis.

Indices of Community Behavior and Change   As indicated previously, the 50 youths selected for the study were chosen partly because of the nature, extent, and seriousness of their prior histories of involvement with the law. In all cases we were dealing with youngsters who had either been called "incorrigible" or who had shown persistent patterns of antisocial behavior. One of the aims of the research, therefore, was to investigate some of the attitudes and behavior patterns that provoke or control repeated and sometimes serious violations of the law. Lander (1954) suggested that delinquency is a function of the relationship between the community and the individual. According to his view, some youngsters are bound less tightly into their communities, and as a result, community norms and social controls have less effect on them. Thus, delinquents drop out of school partly because they feel less pressure to stay in. They then cease to be influenced by either "appropriate" adult authorities and role models or the prevalent school culture. In addition, it is thought that social structures and subcultures contribute to the developmental "drama" mainly in the way they shape experiences in the small groups to which an individual belongs.

Given this view, it was felt that "community behavior," in the narrowest sense of the term, could be gauged through a continuing tabulation of the relationship between youngsters and the police. For both the RYC and control groups, therefore, a regular tally was kept of the number of times they were arrested and the number of days they spent in jail as a consequence of their involvements with the law. In addition, for those youths in residence at the RYC, a record was kept of their attendance and participation in RYC House Council meetings, their violations of RYC rules, and their participation in RYC-related activities.

Results

For purposes of clarity, the research results of the first year of the RYC program have been organized into three categories: vocational functioning, attitude change, and community behavior. In addition to presenting the statistics related to these three areas of functioning, an attempt will be made to provide the reader with some initial follow-up data as well as a year-end summary of the status of the control group youngsters.

Vocational Functioning Figure 9.1 is a summary graph of the work attendance patterns of both RYC and control group youngsters from January 1966 (roughly nine months prior to the formal inception of the program) until July 1967 (approximately ten months after the program was in operation). The graph presents the data by "weeks in treatment" rather than calendar weeks. The first vertical line represents the approximate point at which the RYC staff actually began working with the RYC-bound group prior to their formal entry into the Center. The beginning of residence is represented by the second vertical line.

As can be seen, in January 1966, the control group was attending work 86.4 percent of the time, whereas the RYC-bound group was showing up for work only 66.1 percent of the time (a difference of 20.3 percent). In short, the control group youngsters were functioning better in January than the group of boys who would one day be residents of the RYC. With the passage of time, the trend is reversed. Interestingly enough, the crossover point occurs at approximately that point in time when "word got out" that an RYC would be coming into existence. The comparatively sudden "improvement" was probably due to a number of factors. To begin with, it was at that time that the staff of the RYC began working intensively with those youths who eventually would be entering the program. Initially, at least, "working with a youngster" involved preparing him for entrance into the RYC, a process that included "infusing" him with such concepts as self-help and pride. Another interpretation of the crossover point might very well involve the now classic "halo" and "Hawthorne" effects. However, as can be seen from Figure 9.1, the reversed trend was both maintained and enhanced over the succeeding weeks and months. At the point of entry into the RYC, the differences in attendance were already substantial: 85.1 percent for the RYC group and 55.4

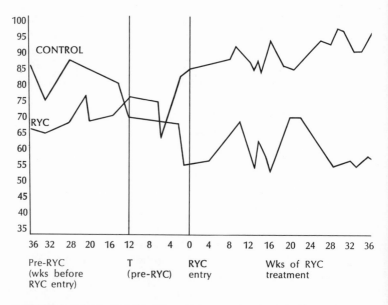

FIGURE 9.1: WORK ATTENDANCE RECORDS—RYC VS. CONTROL GROUPS

percent for the control group. The difference after 36 weeks of treatment was even more impressive: RYC = 97.5 percent, Control = 56.1 percent ($p < .001$).

The changes in work attendance noted in the figure seem to be paralleled by changes in vocational status (i.e., changes in the type and complexity of the work situation). Table 9.1 presents a pre-RYC and a six-month post-RYC comparison of changes in vocational status of the RYC and control population. The RYC youths show a large decrease in the category of "unemployed" (39.7 percent) and a correspondingly sharp increase (30 percent) in the "full-time job" category. The control group, on the other hand, shows small changes in these categories: more unemployment and fewer full-time jobs—small but negative changes in the two most important areas of vocational functioning.

With respect to income, Table 9.2 is a summary and comparison of the mean weekly wages of both RYC and control group youths. It presents the pay rates, not actual earnings, and thus does not reflect wages lost as a result of absenteeism. As can be seen, upon entry into the RYC the experimental group had an average income of $25.00 per week as com-

TABLE 9.1 VOCATIONAL STATUS CHANGES (PRE-RYC AND 6-MO. POST-RYC) OF RYC-TREATED YOUTHS AND UNTREATED CONTROLS

Work Categories		Pre-RYC (%)	Post-RYC (%)
Unemployed	RYC	46.4	6.7
	Control	40.0	50.0
Basic Work Crew*	RYC	25.0	46.7
	Control	20.0	20.0
Intermediate Work Crew	RYC	17.9	6.7
	Control	20.0	20.0
On-the-Job-Training and Full-Time Job	RYC	10.0	40.0
	Control	20.0	10.0

*As indicated previously (see Chapters 2 and 3), the Basic Work Crew program was the most elementary prevocational work setting developed by the community action agency. A member of a Basic Work Crew usually worked about 20 hours per week on a small, highly supervised work crew. He usually earned about 20 dollars per week and was expected to attend 6 to 8 hours of remedial education. An Intermediate Work Crew position, while still not a full-time or "regular" work situation, provided a youngster with more income, less supervision, and a more realistic work or work-training experience.

TABLE 9.2. GROSS WEEKLY WAGES (PRE-RYC AND 9-MO. POST-RYC) O
RYC-TREATED YOUTHS AND UNTREATED CONTROLS

Group	N	Pre-RYC Wages ($)	Post-RYC Wages ($)	Net Dif. ($)	Change (%)
RYC	36	25.00	45.11*	+20.11	80.4 (increase)
Control	30	29.00	20.72	− 8.28	28.6 (decrease)

*Adjusted to account for overall manpower program salary changes.

pared to the Control Group's $29.00 per week. Nine months
later the RYC group was averaging $45.11 per week (an in-
crease of 80.4 percent) compared to the control group's
$20.72 (a decrease of 28.6 percent).

Attitude Change Table 9.3 summarizes the results of the attitudinal questionnaire that was administered, and then readministered six months later, to both the RYC and control
groups. As can be seen, the results of the initial administration showed no significant differences between the two
groups on any of the attitudinal variables (alienation, authoritarianism, trust, Machiavellianism, social desirability) being investigated. Six months later, however, a number of important attitudinal changes can be noted between the two
sample populations. The RYC group, for example, became
significantly less alienated over that period of time ($p < .05$),
while the control group reported feeling significantly more
alienated ($p < .05$). The difference between the two populations after six months was highly significant ($p < .01$).

In contrast to a sharp decrease in authoritarianism for the
RYC group, there was little pre-post change in the control
group. Consequently, after six months the difference between
the two groups was significant at the .05 level of probability.

Although the RYC youngsters increased in Machiavellianism
and the control group youngsters decreased over the six
months, neither the changes nor the final differences approach statistical significance.

The RYC group did not show a significant change in their
feelings of trust over the treatment period, but the control
group decreased sharply ($p < .05$). This is particularly interesting because of the overlap in the Machiavellianism and trust
scales. A distrustful orientation toward the world is one of

TABLE 9.3. ATTITUDINAL VARIABLES (PRE-RYC AND 6-MO. POST-RYC) OF RYC-TREATED YOUTHS AND UNTREATED CONTROLS

Variable	Pre-RYC			Post-RYC		
	RYC	Control	Difference*	RYC	Control	Difference
Alienation	3.80	3.95	N.S.	2.20	5.75	$p < .01$
Authoritarianism	5.60	5.40	N.S.	1.80	5.60	$p < .05$
Machiavellianism	3.83	4.10	N.S.	4.80	3.60	N.S.
Trust	4.14	4.40	N.S.	4.00	1.91	$p < .10$
Social desirability	15.40	15.00	N.S.	13.00	15.40	N.S.
"World I Live In"	4.90	4.70	N.S.	3.00	5.75	$p < .05$

*N.S. = not significant.

the factors included in the Machiavellianism scale. Although there was an increase in Machiavellianism for the RYC youngsters, they did not show the concomitant decrease in trust. This, taken together with the strong decline in trust in the control population, indicates that the level of trust found in the RYC group before treatment began was maintained over the treatment period in the face of some rather severe and conflicting pressures. The final difference between the two groups approaches but does not reach significance ($p < .10$).

There were no significant group changes in social desirability over the test-retest period, although the RYC youngsters decreased slightly, thus indicating a slightly lower need to appear conforming to socially desirable behavior. The difference between the two groups does not approach significance, and the slight decrease in the RYC group might well be explained by the closer relationship that developed between the interviewer and this group over the treatment period.

With respect to the semantic differential test ("The World I Live In"), the results indicated that by and large, the control population became significantly more negative in their view of the world, while the RYC group became significantly more positive ($p < .05$). Figure 9.2 presents the responses of the RYC group to this test. The arrows indicate the direction of change from pre-RYC to post-RYC responses. As can be seen, for the RYC group the greatest change was in viewing the world as more "fair." In addition, the world for the RYC

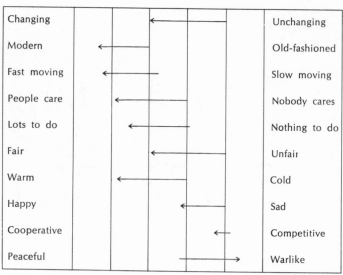

Changing			←			Unchanging
Modern	←					Old-fashioned
Fast moving	←					Slow moving
People care		←				Nobody cares
Lots to do			←			Nothing to do
Fair			←			Unfair
Warm		←				Cold
Happy				←		Sad
Cooperative					←	Competitive
Peaceful					→	Warlike

Significant change $(p < .05)$ = two spaces.

FIGURE 9.2. "THE WORLD I LIVE IN"—A COMPARISON OF ATTITUDES BEFORE ENTRY INTO THE RYC AND SIX MONTHS AFTER TREATMENT

group became significantly more "changing," was populated by more people who "cared," and was perceived as more "warlike" $(p < .05)$.

As has already been stated, most of the research undertaken and carried out at the RYC (i.e., the choice of measures to be employed, the development of scales, and the research design itself) was based on the assumption that there is an important interaction or relationship between the way an individual feels about himself and his behavior in the "world of work." Table 9.4 presents the correlations of two attitudinal variables (Machiavellianism and alienation) with two vocational behavior variables (work attendance and promotion) for the group of subjects who lived at the RYC. Promotion was defined as any change of work status in an upward direction.

Most outstanding is the correlation between work attendance and alienation (a Spearman Rank Correlation of

TABLE 9.4. VOCATIONAL BEHAVIOR–ATTITUDE CORRELATIONS
FOR YOUNGSTERS IN RESIDENCE AT THE RYC

N	Vocational Variable	Attitudinal Variable	Correlation
27	Work attendance	Machiavellianism	.30 ($p < .07$)
28	Work attendance	Alienation	.87 ($p < .01$)
30	Promotion	Machiavellianism	.44 ($p < .01$)
30	Promotion	Alienation	.70 ($p < .01$)

.867, $p < .01$): the greater the feelings of alienation, the
poorer the work attendance; the less the feelings of alienation, the better the work attendance. The alienation scale
included such statements as "People probably won't do anything to make this country a better place to live in," "Not
many people really look forward to their work," and "Most
men won't work hard unless they are forced to." With the
data now available, it is not possible, of course, to explain
the direction of the causal relationship between these two
factors. Thus, it is still unclear as to whether a youngster's
feelings of estrangement from himself and his society cause
the poor work attendance, or whether being unhappy with a
job or being unemployed determines a youngster's attitudes
toward the society he lives in.

Promotion is slightly less highly correlated with alienation
(.70, $p < .01$). Work attendance and promotion show a lower
correlation with Machiavellianism than with alienation (Machiavellianism–work attendance = .30, $p < .07$; Machiavellianism–promotion = .44, $p < .01$). It is interesting to note
the much higher correlation of Machiavellianism with promotion than with work attendance. This might be explained by
the greater success a highly Machiavellian person (i.e., someone with both the skills necessary to manipulate the environment and the cynical attitude to encourage this manipulation)

TABLE 9.5. NUMBER OF ARRESTS PER YOUTH (6 MO. PRE-RYC AND
POST-RYC) OF RYC-TREATED YOUNGSTERS AND UNTREATED CONTROLS

Group	Pre-RYC	Post-RYC	% Change
RYC	1.87	0.96	49 (decrease)
Control	1.70	2.08	22 (increase)

Research: Results and Interpretation   413

would have in obtaining new jobs or promotions on the same job. There is not as strong a tendency for a highly Machiavellian person to attend work a high percentage of the time.

Community Behavior Table 9.5 presents the average number of arrests per youngster in the RYC and control groups for the six-month periods of time before and after the Center came into existence. During the six months prior to entering the RYC, the RYC-bound youngster had 9 percent more arrests than the control group youngster. For the six-month period following the beginning of treatment, there was a sharp decrease (49 percent) in arrests for the RYC group. In contrast, the arrest incidence of control group youngsters, those without benefit of the RYC experience, increased significantly (22 percent), and they had more than twice as many arrests per boy as the RYC group. Whereas there were no significant differences in arrests during the pre-RYC period, the difference for the two groups during the six-month period after treatment began is significant at the .01 level of confidence.

The pattern described with respect to the number of arrests per youth is repeated in the record of the number of days spent in jail as a consequence of involvements with the law. Table 9.6 indicates that for the nine-month period prior to their entry into the program, the RYC-bound youngsters spent more total days in jail than their control group counterparts. This is accounted for by the more serious police involvement histories of the RYC-bound group up to that point in time. For the nine-month period following the inception of the program, however, the number of days spent in jail for the RYC group decreased 54 percent, while the control group's time in jail increased 84 percent. The difference is significant at the .01 level of confidence.

Population Summary, Status of Control Group Youngsters, and Initial Follow-up Data By the end of its first fiscal year (10 months of actual operation), the RYC had served 49 youths and 30 families (not every youngster had a family and some of the families were located out of state). A resident's average length of stay was 5.2 months, but the range extended from one

TABLE 9.6. DAYS IN JAIL (9 MO. PRE-RYC AND POST-RYC) OF
RYC-TREATED YOUTHS AND UNTREATED CONTROLS

Group	Pre-RYC	Post-RYC	% Change
RYC	153	70	54 (decrease)
Control	140	258	84 (increase)

day to 9.5 months. Median residency was 5 months. Of its 44
relatively long-term residents, 62 percent were black and 38 percent were white. The mean age at which youngsters entered the
Center was 17 years, 2 months.

Table 9.7 summarizes the status as of June 1, 1967, of the
20 members of the control group. As can be seen, half the
control group youngsters were either in jail, in mental hospitals, or living on the street. Of the 10 who were still employed, none had advanced on their jobs and three were on
the verge of losing their jobs, at least as reported by their
employers. Three of the four boys from the control group
who were in jail were serving long-term sentences for serious
crimes (felonies). Of the two who were in mental hospitals,
one was there under sentence from the court and may also
serve a long term in either the hospital or a subsequent
prison. Two of the four unemployed youngsters were dropped
from the Job Corps for serious rule infractions. The other
two have been unemployed for over 6 months.

Table 9.8 suggests that there is a relatively stable group
of employable youngsters within the control group. These
youths make up 50 percent of the group. There is also a large
group of unemployed and, at least at the present time, "un-

TABLE 9.7. STATUS OF CONTROL GROUP YOUNGSTERS AS OF
JUNE 1, 1967

Status	Number
Jail or reformatory	4
Mental hospital	2
Unemployed, on street	4
Employed, living on own	2
Employed, living at home	8
Total	20

TABLE 9.8. STATUS OF CONTROL GROUP YOUTHS BY
TWO-MONTH TIME INTERVALS

Status	October	December	February	April	June
Unknown	0	1	0	0	0
Jail or hospital	2	3	4	5	6
Unemployed	8	7	7	6	4
Employed	10	9	9	9	10

employable" youths, which remains relatively stable. Over the nine-month period covered by Table 9.8, 50 percent of this group of unemployed youths eventually wound up either in jail or in a mental institution, most of them for a fairly long period of time. It should also be pointed out that of the 50 percent of control group youngsters who were employed, the majority, at least as of June 1, 1967, were working directly for the Neighborhood Youth Corps, most of them in elementary prevocational settings (Basic Work Crews).

An initial follow-up study of 25 youngsters, all of whom had spent an average of 5.2 months at the Center, was undertaken during the RYC's second year of existence. The mean number of months since physical termination from the Center was 4.78. Among the follow-up group, unemployment was 24 percent. For the 76 percent who were employed, the average length of employment on their present jobs was 3.62 months, a relatively long period of time for youths who had once been called "unemployable" because they lacked the "work habits and attitudes"—the persistence—necessary to hold down jobs. The average hourly wage among the employed group was $1.76 an hour. Job attendance was 92 percent. The mean number of job changes among the employed group was 1.24 in a period of 4.78 months. Three of the youngsters in the follow-up group had returned to school and four were in the Armed Forces. Since termination from the Center, six of the youngsters in the follow-up group had been arrested a total of seven times, an average of .28 arrests per individual. At the time of follow-up only one of these six youths was in jail for a serious offense.

Problems of Interpreting the Data

Given the difficulties traditionally associated with working with the so-called hard-core poor, it would be only too easy to overestimate the significance of the results reported here. Clearly, the data are suggestive and encouraging. We see changes, often of a dramatic and apparently lasting quality, in a group heretofore called "unreachable" or "incorrigible." We see youngsters whom most agencies had "written off" beginning to act and feel in ways that may challenge the wisdom and validity of prior diagnoses and prognoses made about them. However, the data are tentative and warrant little more than a cautious optimism. In short, the results are neither convincing nor conclusive, and the reasons for this are once again to be found in the nature of the methodological and conceptual problems associated with most attempts to introduce, evaluate, and understand the processes of human change in highly complex and naturalistic settings.

The Problem of Numbers   To begin with, there is the "problem of numbers." Clearly, few unequivocal conclusions can or should be drawn from a study in which the combined N is less than fifty, especially a study dealing with the intricacies of human behavior and change. Given the nature of our training (be it for good or ill), it is very difficult to speak with confidence about results obtained from such a limited sample of the population. In part, of course, the number of subjects used in the study was dependent on the number of youths that could be accommodated at the RYC. Nevertheless, given the complexity of the problem, the fact remains that as sample sizes go, the research results of the first 18 months of the RYC's existence are based on an extremely small and imperfect sample of the population. Similarly, as was mentioned previously, the RYC's service responsibilities made it impossible to assign subjects to the control and experimental groups on a purely random basis. Consequently, we cannot speak of cleanly matched groups, for their matched "cleanness" was, from the very beginning, a practical and political impossibility. The RYC was funded to work with "the very worst of the worst," a mandate that not only assured service on the basis of need but also robbed the researcher of the luxury of manipulating his experimental and control groups in such a manner as to guarantee a balanced and "clean" design.

The Problem of Defining "Input" Variables   A second and certainly more critical problem has to do less with what the research "says" than with what it presently *does not* and *cannot* say; namely, *why* the RYC "works" (if, indeed, it does) and *what* there is about the setting that alone or in combination with other factors accounts for this success. Throughout this chapter we have referred repeatedly to the "RYC experience" as the treatment variable separating those youngsters who were taken into the program from those who were assigned to the control group. But clearly, the term "RYC experience" covers a multitude of variables, and we have no way, at least at this point in time, of knowing what portion of the total variance is accounted for by any or all of the interventions subsumed under that term. Thus, for example, to those of us who participated in developing the RYC's research design, the "RYC experience" meant at least four related but distinct factors: an innovative and restless staff of indigenous nonprofessionals; the development of particularly close and trusting relationships among individual RYC staff members, their youngsters, and their families; the translation of organizational theory into human terms and the implementation of an organizational structure (i.e., horizontality) geared to meet the "growth needs" of an entire staff; and finally, the development of in-service training techniques (i.e., sensitivity training) aimed at increasing individual and group competence and a sense of personal worth. At the present time, even if we were all to agree that the "RYC experience" was, indeed, a combination of these four variables, there would be no way of specifying the degree to which any one of these variables influenced the results. To be able to say anything meaningful about these variables (meaningful in the sense of delineating their individual and

collective contribution to the total variance), one would, as
a minimum, first have to translate them into operational terms
and then systematically manipulate or control their "input"
into the system. Until this is done, we can only speak in the
broadest of terms, terms indeed like "total environmental
manipulation" or the "RYC experience." To make things even
more complicated, we have no way of knowing whether or not
the variables that we considered to be an essential part of
the RYC "treatment" were, indeed, the sole factors in the
situation. Thus, for example, it was once suggested (in "jest"
of course) that Chip's "lousy cooking was driving some kids
to health" by motivating them to get out of the Center and
into their own apartments where they could obtain some
"real soul food." Ludicrous as it may seem, the point is well
taken: given the very general nature of the results to date,
we have no way of determining either the nature or the
effects of extraneous variables that were a part of the total
situation. It should also be pointed out that the complexity
of the problem might, even under the best research conditions, mitigate against our ever being able to isolate and
measure *all* the variables in the situation. Naturalistic settings,
especially those that are at once both highly complex and
extremely volatile, have rarely served as science's hand-
maidens of truth.

The Problem of Follow-up Research   A third problem is that
of follow-up research. Only after we have taken the time to
design carefully and systematically a series of longitudinal
studies of former residents will we be able to answer questions concerning the stability of the changes that seem to
have occurred as a function of residence at an RYC. Follow-up
research would also have to address itself to such problems
as the relationship between length of residence and permanence of change, the degree to which a setting such as the
RYC changes (either in orientation or in effectiveness) over
time, and the consequences for the staff of having worked
in a setting like the RYC. All these questions, questions which
in the long run may prove to be more important than any
others, still await attention. Until they are answered, until the

required follow-up research is undertaken, they will remain as gnawing reminders of the tentativeness and incompleteness of whatever has gone before.

The Problem of "Meaning" and Values Finally, there is the question of "meaning," the moral compulsion to transcend deliberately the "scientific enterprise" and deal with the data from the perspective of one's own conception of the human condition. To be sure, the question of meaning is basically a philosophical one, for it revolves around values, beliefs, and convictions that are deeply personal and highly resistant to change. But given the nature of the problem being studied, it becomes almost impossible to maintain an air of scientific detachment, especially when one senses that the data, however fragmentary and incomplete, "say something" about the quality of life in contemporary American society. It is for this reason that we cannot end this chapter without mentioning what, at least from our point of view, are some of the disquieting implications of the research to date.

There is little doubt that the youngsters in the RYC group show a marked "improvement" in functioning, an improvement presumably related to their having lived at the Center. The results indicate that they earn more money, get into less trouble, and are generally more successful in their everyday lives than those boys who were not the beneficiaries of the "RYC experience." Judging from the results of the attitudinal questionnaires, the "typical" RYC youngster is a boy who begins to feel less isolated from the society in which he lives, becomes more "inner-directed" and less rigid, and increases his ability to manipulate people and events in his own best interests without himself becoming a more trusting or spontaneous human being. It is, in short, the picture of a youngster who begins to act and feel more and more "normal" in society's terms: he works, stays out of trouble, pays his taxes (presumably), and "goes about his business" very much like the vast majority of his contemporaries in a basically affluent society. From the point of view of "society" he is a "success story"—a boy who has been "rescued" from the discarded, redirected, and is now "making it" within the framework of the existing social order without threatening or disrupting it. Clearly, however, from the point of view of those of us who have serious reservations about the "health" or even the basic humanity of that social order, the question arises as to what we have really accomplished. The answer is almost painfully clear: we have taught our youngsters how to negotiate the system, not change it; how to "adjust" and survive in it, not how to alter and influence it. We have, in short, consciously or unconsciously chosen to accept the prevailing conception of "health" as defined by society and have not sought to impose a more critical individually oriented conception of responsibility and personal action.[9] To be sure, those of us who share the view that basic institutional change (not merely greater numbers of people who "fit") is what is needed in the social order also share a similar faith with respect to our youngsters: sooner or later they, no different from ourselves, will no longer be satisfied with "making it" as individuals and will then begin to perceive an identity between their own fulfillment as human beings and the perfection of the human condition as a whole. Only then will we be able to speak of the "RYC experience" as something more than a program of partial individual remediation. At the present time, however, we must admit to a feeling of disquietude, the kind of uneasiness that prevails whenever there are no data to suggest that one has avoided the pitfall of believing that one has cured a disease with a Band-Aid.

In this chapter we have attempted to provide the reader

[9] Reiff's (1966) position that "self-determination" rather than "self-actualization" constitutes a more appropriate goal for the mental health professional working with members of the poverty population provides us with some theoretical rationale for believing that having helped youngsters to "make it" in the world of work may, in the long run, facilitate their ability and willingness to do something more than just "settle" for the existing social order. If one defines self-determination, at least in part, in terms of ending one's chronic and dehumanizing economic and social dependency, then there is some reason to believe that self-actualization may very well involve the directing of one's newly emerging sense of power and leverage toward the question of changing and acquiring a greater control of the basic social, political, and economic institutions of the society. From this point of view, institutional change becomes a self-actualizing activity, an activity predicated upon the self-determining experiences that become possible once one is able to gain a greater sense of control over one's own economic life.

with some of the descriptive and statistical data of the first 18 months of the RYC program. Because of the complexity of the program, as well as the variety of problems associated with the field of action research, we felt that the program's statistical results, coupled with the observational chronicle presented in Chapter 8, might provide the reader with as complete a picture of the RYC as possible.

The picture that finally emerges is no less complex than the undertaking itself. We are left with results that are at once both encouraging and disquieting, results that raise as many questions as they would seem to answer. It is perhaps in the nature of things that any attempt to assess the effectiveness of a setting, particularly a setting whose very existence stands as a monument to the turmoil and agony through which our society is passing, should lead ultimately to an increased awareness of just how deeply the problem of poverty cuts across the very fabric of our national existence.

In the next chapter we shall continue our examination of the RYC experience. This time, however, we shall examine the setting from the point of view of what we as its builders have learned, and continue to learn, as a consequence of having created it. In Chapter 10, therefore, we turn our attention to some of the RYC's continuing problems and the implications of these problems for the general question of the creation of settings.

Chapter 10   The Setting in 1969
Problems and Promise

A revolution is like a love affair:
it starts out with fire and passion . . .
its greatest enemy is Time.
—From the movie *The Professionals*

In Chapters 8 and 9 we reviewed much of the data concerning the effectiveness of the RYC program, particularly its
impact on the lives of those youngsters who were a part of
it. Despite the variety of questions that we ourselves raised
concerning the meaning and interpretation of the data, one
thing remains relatively clear: be it for reasons that are as
yet ill-defined or in need of further study, the program
"works"; that is to say, at least with respect to its clients, it
succeeds in reaching the supposedly "unreachable" and enables inner-city youth whom most people had given up on to
begin to function in ways that are personally less self-defeating
and socially more acceptable.

But clearly, the development and delivery of client services
was only one of the program's goals. As a setting, the Center was conceived for at least two other reasons, neither of
which had very much to do, at least directly, with providing
assistance to New Haven's ghetto youths and their families.
*The first reason had to do with the question of whether or
not a setting could be created which was at least as dedicated
to the growth of its own staff as it was to the "rehabilitation"
of its clients.* In Chapter 4 we made quite clear our belief
that if there was anything to be learned from CPI—from its
successes as well as its failures—it was that there was an
intimate relationship between the way in which a setting was
organized and the behavior of the people who populated
that setting. In terms of the RYC, therefore, the question became one of whether or not we could create the conditions,
both organizationally and interpersonally, in which people
with apparently different backgrounds and styles of life (e.g.,
professionals and nonprofessionals) could begin to experience
that sense of fulfillment so often lacking in most work situations. The development of what came to be called "horizontal structure," the sharing of administrative, clinical, and

programming responsibilities, and the decision to make "sensitivity training" an integral and ongoing part of the program were all clearly related to the attempt to create, albeit in miniature form, a "community of growth," a community predicated on the assumption that to the degree that the Center was able to meet the growth needs of its staff, to that degree it would both define itself as a setting and determine its fate as an organization.

The second question had to do with the kind of lasting impact a setting such as the RYC could have, over and above its delivery of services to chronically disadvantaged people. Cloward (1965), it will be recalled, posed the question in terms of whether the "chief target" of the federal anti-poverty program was "the victim of poverty or the sources of his victimization." In Chapter 4 we, too, discussed the problem and concluded, similarly, that the "question of impact" was indeed the fundamental ideological issue confronting those of us engaged in the War on Poverty, an issue that might be resolved if we were able to forge an alliance, however imperfect, between the goals of individual remediation and those of institutional change. Consequently, for the RYC the question of institutional impact had to be viewed on at least two additional levels. The first had to do with the effects of the program locally; that is, its impact on those conditions and agencies which in one way or another influenced the "quality of life" in the New Haven area. The second level involved an assessment of the degree to which the RYC was able to play a role in helping to shape the policies and practices of those institutions whose power and potential for generating progressive change extended far beyond the local level. In other words, the effectiveness of the program had to be gauged in terms of how well it served as a vehicle for altering the ways in which people (and professions) thought about the problems associated with "human renewal."

In this chapter we shall examine the Residential Youth Center from the point of view of how closely it came, at least during the first two years of its life, to realizing those of its goals which were not directly related to client services.

It goes without saying that any final assessment of the RYC, be it an assessment of the quality of its services or of the long-range consequences of the program as a whole, will have to await the passage of time. Nevertheless, we do feel it to be both important and appropriate to make an attempt, however preliminary and incomplete, to deal with some of the questions concerning the program's impact. In this chapter, therefore, we shall describe the RYC in terms of both the *problems* that have continually beset the setting and the *implications* of the program with respect to the question of institutional change.

The Setting and Its Problems: 1968

Perhaps the best way of beginning our analysis of the RYC as a setting would be to make the obvious statement that there are no criteria available by which one can measure the degree to which reality approximates a dream.[1] In many ways the RYC was and continues to be a dream: it is a setting dominated by the "guiding fiction" that even in these days of increased specialization and bureaucratization, it is still possible to create an organization in which people, both as individuals and as members of a group, can experience a meaningful sense of "growth"—growing being defined in the most general and human terms possible. If there was anything that bound the people who comprised the RYC's original staff, it was the fact that prior to becoming a part of the new setting they had all been members of organizations that defined growth (and, by implication, one's worth and competence) in ways that were felt to be both limited and limiting. Whether they came from Yale University, CPI, or

---

[1] Despite the patently "romantic" flavor of the wording of this statement, its intent is to focus attention not on questions of romance but on questions of science. At stake is the scientific issue of how one goes about studying and evaluating a setting like the RYC. Clearly, however, the particular criteria to be employed in such an assessment are directly related to the development of appropriate action-research methodologies. In the case of the RYC, for example, there is little doubt that a research input combining the techniques of participant observation with the "advocate" or "legal" research model suggested by Levine (1968) might yield the most useful data for generating the kind of baseline criteria necessary for future evaluations.

elsewhere, they had all been members of settings whose reward systems placed a premium on the development and demonstration of certain kinds of "technical" competencies to the relative exclusion of others. In addition, because of the dynamics that already defined these institutions, the people were rarely in positions to influence the very traditions and values that formed the ideological foundations for the organization's definitions of competence. It was, in short, a situation in which people who had spent most of their lives in organizations that in one way or another rewarded behavior that could be described as passive, noncreative, and dependent banded together to create a setting that was not only different from the ones they had already experienced but was also truly dedicated to their own development as human beings. However, the mere fact that most of us had indeed spent the greater part of our lives in "other" kinds of organizations (and had, in fact, often been rewarded for learning how to "fit in" rather than how to rebel) guaranteed that our attempt to create a "community of people" would, from the very beginning, be a task fraught with difficulty and more than a little anxiety. There was much "unlearning" that had to take place, and in the final analysis we would be able to point to the RYC as a growth-oriented setting only to the degree that we were able to unlearn patterns of behavior that were already deeply ingrained—culturally conditioned, so to speak. But the process of unlearning is far more difficult and complex than the process of learning, and as we shall indicate in the pages that follow, it is within that context that many of the setting's unresolved problems become understandable.

Problems of "Horizontality" In attempting to assess the effectiveness of the RYC's "horizontal structure," we might begin by pointing out that the concept itself involves far more than a simple redefinition of organizational roles. Fundamentally, horizontality is composed of at least two dimensions, the behavioral and the psychological, and it is not clear that the same dynamics are always at work in both instances. On the behavioral level, for example, horizontality was defined as the sharing of responsibilities and the participation by the entire staff in the Center's decision-making process. Its goal was relatively specific: to create the conditions under which people could become "creative generalists"—that is, become capable of handling a variety of different clinical and administrative functions and, in the process, begin to experience the sense of competence that accompanies the development of skills heretofore deemed unnecessary to the functioning of the organization. On the psychological level, horizontality demanded the willingness and the ability of people to commit themselves to one another and to the sharing of their experiences, problems, and concerns. Conceptually, it was based on the premise that an individual's sense of "completion" was in a variety of important ways related to the growth of the particular group of which he was an "irreplaceable" member.

Clinical Versus Administrative Duties. One of the more striking results of the RYC's horizontal structure was the degree to which people responded differentially to their "clinical" as opposed to "administrative" functions. Long before the Center became operational, during the period of time when the staff was first getting together, organizing the program, and developing its rationale, the fear was voiced: "We're not psychiatrists or social workers. We're not equipped to handle mental problems." With relatively few exceptions, the staff questioned its "clinical abilities" and its "right" to shoulder the responsibility of working with "really disturbed kids." By contrast, there was little if any evidence that the staff had similar kinds of feelings or trepidations about its administrative potential. Quite to the contrary: by and large the staff looked forward to the time when the program's overall operation and decision-making functions would be largely under its control. In time, however, there was a distinct shift, almost a reversal, in the staff's feelings concerning its clinical as opposed to administrative competence. Once the program got off the ground, especially after people became deeply involved in working with the residents and their families, the staff gradually became much less enchanted with "administrative duties" and much more enamored of the "clinical aspects" of the job. Administration became a "bore," an annoying and time-consuming interruption in an otherwise hectic and exciting life.

In retrospect, the shift in the staff's feelings about and response to their administrative and clinical duties is understandable. Despite the fact that "clinical" work is often anxiety-arousing and frightening in its complexity and implications, it does, nevertheless, bring with it something that is usually missing in the paper-and-pencil world of administration: a direct and highly personalized sense of achievement. When a youngster began to "respond" to the efforts of his worker, however tentatively and hesitatingly, the worker could in a very concrete sense point to the change in behavior and experience that indefinable exhilaration that often accompanies clinical "breakthroughs." In addition, almost every time an RYC staff member was able to point to some improvement in "his boy," two things invariably followed. First, he would receive social support and recogniton from the rest of the staff; and second, his own increasing sense of competence would gradually undermine whatever doubts he may have had regarding his "right" to work with "really disturbed kids." By contrast, the staff's administrative activities rarely met with similar responses. For this to have occurred would have required the development of a perspective broad enough that the seemingly inconsequential tasks associated with the day-to-day operation of the program could be viewed with the same enthusiasm, and accorded the same recognition, as the more dramatic or clinical aspects of the program. This heightened perspective never appeared. Tasks such as rent collection, balancing the budget, cooking, and ordering supplies never elicited a response that even remotely approached the concern accorded to clinical involvements. Despite attempts to establish parity between the two, the RYC was, and continues to be, a setting in which clinical and administrative competencies are differentially perceived and differentially related to the program's "grand design." Consequently, the question of whether or not horizontality does, indeed, create the conditions for the development of what we have called "creative generalists" remains essentially unanswered.[2]

The External Response to "Horizontality." By far the most significant and gratifying result of the RYC experience was the manner in which almost every staff member developed a sense of ownership of the setting. This sense of ownership was demonstrated in a variety of ways, among them the number of hours that people worked at the setting over and above what was expected of them. It was rare that the staff spent fewer than 14 hours a day at the Center, whether or not they were "on duty" or "on call"; as indicated in Chapter 7, it was commonplace to find staff members dropping into the RYC or spending their "spare time" there at all hours of the day and night. To many of us this quality of commitment to and concern for the setting as a whole became an operational definition of the success of what we called horizontal structure, the reasoning being that this behavior would not have occurred without the active involvement of each member in the RYC's decision-making process and their participation in every aspect of the program. But for all its positive implications, the sense of ownership created problems which, while not emanating from within the setting, were no less serious or potentially damaging to the program and its goals. Many of these problems are still unresolved, and, indeed, some may remain that way for as long as the program exists.

Intra-agency Conflict. The most serious problem had to do

[2]It should be pointed out that when we say that the question "remains essentially unanswered," we are not referring to the staff's ability to function creatively while at the setting. Despite the schism that we described between administrative and clinical duties, as a whole the staff was able to act in ways that would indicate they no longer felt constrained by the usual definitions of jobs, titles, and roles. What we do mean, however, is that the "final" answer is probably *developmental* in nature, that is, contingent upon a point of view (and a research methodology) that stresses the importance of behavioral and psychological change over time. In other words, the question of the relationship between horizontality and the emergence of the "creative generalist" will not be answered until the RYC's original staff have been "followed" over time with the aid of appropriate longitudinal studies. Only then will we be able to speak with greater certainty about the degree to which the RYC's people were able to sustain (and augment) the patterns of functioning developed at the Center.

with the conflict that the RYC's horizontality created for the community action agency as a whole, and for "downtown CPI" in particular. Here we were confronted with a situation in which the RYC's basic orientation (at least that part of its orientation regarding the role, rights, and responsibilities of its staff) was in conflict with some of the operating concepts of the "mother organization." Thus, for example, while the RYC's social structure was founded on the assumption that people could (and should) share the problems and decision-making responsibilities of the setting, CPI's central administrative body could respond only to the RYC's "leader" when a decision had to be made, and not, in his absence, to other members of the staff. It was (and continues to be) a classic example of a situation in which people within a particular organization (e.g., the RYC) react and respond to one another as equals, while the larger organization (e.g., CPI) deals with the setting in the time-honored manner prescribed by the assumptions underlying hierarchical systems. More than once was it the case that RYC staff members were told, in no uncertain terms to "butt out" whenever they sought to be "included in" on meetings or discussions that were supposed to be "for supervisors only." More often than not their desire to participate in these "high-level" meetings was interpreted as being "pushy" or as evidence that they were "overstepping" their bounds and in need of being "set straight." In the final analysis, however, the problems that beset a horizontal system, especially one that exists within a pyramidal superstructure, are problems of divergent ideologies and expectations, and to the extent that members of both organizations avoid dealing with these basic conceptual differences, the conflicts tend to become reified and increasingly difficult to resolve.

Consequently, those of us who were instrumental in developing the RYC cannot avoid the fact that the very nature of our own commitment to the concept of horizontality was, at least in part, responsible for many of the difficulties that came to define the RYC's relationship with its "mother organization."

Familial Conflict. Perhaps the most serious mistake made during the Center's first two years of existence was the degree to which the families, particularly the wives of RYC staff members, were excluded from sharing in what we have called the "sense of ownership." By focusing so much attention on ourselves, by working so hard to create the conditions for "staff ownership," we either overlooked or underestimated the effects of the setting on the lives of our own families. Thus, while the staff became more and more involved in the setting, our families (particularly the wives), unable to experience a similar sense of participation, began to feel increasingly "left out," became less and less understanding of the amount of time that was being spent away from home and "down at the RYC Club," and eventually came to view the setting with more than a little hostility and suspicion. It was only after several members of the staff began to use sensitivity sessions to talk about their "home problems" that we became acutely aware of the extent of these errors of omission. What we learned (and very forcefully) from the experience was that a setting such as the RYC can become self-defeating to a remarkable degree unless it begins to view both its workers *and* their families as constituting "the staff." If horizontality is successful, if it enables a staff to develop the kind of commitment and involvement that is usually only associated with ownership, then it also creates stresses and pressures for those (e.g., the families of staff members) who cannot be as intimately and concretely connected with the setting. Under these conditions, it becomes incumbent upon the setting, not the wives and families of its members, to develop the kind of dialogue and create the conditions that will enable a total family to share in the future of the program.

Structural Problems. Another of the RYC's unresolved problems stemmed from the fact that whatever "horizontality" the setting possessed was a "psychological" or "functional" horizontality and not a "structural" one. In other words, whereas the RYC as a setting was predicated on assumptions of "equality" and the "sharing of responsibilities," its own organiza-

tional chart and hierarchy of salaries did not even vaguely
short, a situation in which people shared the burdens and
reflect this orientation. Despite the fact that everyone carried
a case load, handled administrative duties, "lived-in," and
ran some kind of evening program, not everyone received
the same pay or had the same "job description." It was, in
problems of the setting but were not equally rewarded, either
in income or in "formal status," for their efforts. Under these
conditions it becomes difficult to refer to the RYC's horizontal
structure in anything more than "informal" or psychological
terms.

This discrepancy was destined to lead to problems. During
one of the RYC's sensitivity sessions, Butch put the problem
about as clearly as one could. He said:

Hell, all I know is I sit here and I got just as many worries
as Kelly, or Scotty, or anyone else. In fact, I probably got
more problems than both of them put together because I
carry more cases than either of those two guys; and anyone
knows that working with a kid is harder than whatever the
hell administration is. But come payday, brother, old Butch's
envelope is a whole lot skinnier than Scotty's or Kelly's.

In addition to the kind of problem reflected in Butch's out-
burst, the discrepancy between the RYC's formal structure
and its underlying assumptions facilitated the development
of what might be called "compensatory pecking-order behavior"; that is, behavior in which certain staff members,
"robbed" of the equality which would have been theirs had
the setting been structurally organized in a way that was consistent with its internal processes, sought to erect an "informal" status-hierarchy barrier between themselves and the
rest of the staff. Thus, for example, RYC workers began to
relate to live-in counselors as if they (the live-ins) were less
important to the setting. The live-ins, on the other hand, began to view themselves as increasingly left out of the Center's
decision-making process and became highly resentful of the
"high-hattedness" of the RYC workers. It was, in short, a situation in which people who were actually working in very
similar ways felt compelled to justify (and reinforce) whatever differences they could find between them.

Despite the fact that sensitivity sessions began to focus more and more attention on the reasons for this behavior, it was a relatively long time before the staff could "step back" from the situation and begin to deal with the problem in terms of its structural rather than its interpersonal implications.

It should be pointed out that the RYC's structural inequities (e.g., the differences between people's salaries and job titles) existed from the moment the program was funded, and probably long before that. There were two reasons for this. First (and this is most important), our own naïveté, coupled with the fact that our primary interests were almost exclusively directed toward questions of "psychological horizontality," made such issues as money and job titles of peripheral concern to us. In retrospect, this may have been a cardinal blunder, an excellent example of the degree to which one's interest in a particular problem can obscure or limit the attention that is paid to other areas of valid concern. Second, it is doubtful that the RYC would have been funded at all if we had demanded equal salaries and job titles for all potential employees. As it was, the funding of a proposal advocating "nonprofessional leadership" and the utilization of "untrained personnel" to deal with problems heretofore dealt with exclusively by mental health professionals was something of a milestone even in the field of community action. To have made "structural horizontality" a nonnegotiable issue might very well have resulted in no program at all.[3] In the future, however, especially for purposes of re-

[3]This is perhaps the best example of the degree to which both the RYC's nonservice and potential research contributions were limited (or at least highly influenced) by forces external to the setting. Clearly, our interest in the organizational and interpersonal implications of horizontality were neither solely nor exclusively confined to questions of service. Horizontality was, and continues to be, a research question with general implications for the field of organizational dynamics. Unlike the situation in the laboratory setting, however, we could not even modestly control the very parameters or conditions under which our investigations took place. Rather, the very opposite was the case. From the very beginning, the fact that the setting could not be organized structurally in a manner that was consistent with the assumptions underlying psychological horizontality was in many ways an example of the degree to which the setting's research potential was in-

search, it would be interesting to compare the results (and problems) of the existing RYC with those obtained in centers whose formal structures more closely approximate the assumptions underlying psychological horizontality. Such new centers might well prove invaluable as settings in which one could vary systematically the dimensions of structural horizontality. Thus, for example, one might attempt to assess the consequences of such structural "inputs" as equalized pay, the elimination of differential job titles and job descriptions, and/or the introduction of what might be called a "revolving directorship," a system in which the leadership of a setting would pass from one staff member to another on a predictable and rota ; basis. For the present, however, we must content ours̲ives with the fact that while the RYC is not truly a horizontal setting, it has made us more fully aware of some of the changes that would have to be made if it were ever to become one. What the setting "really" is might be summed up i   statement by one of its staff members, a statement made in response to a questionnaire that requested that staff members describe their understanding of the term horizontality:

To me, now, horizontal structure means no more or less than fewer levels in an organization . . . and we sure don't have that! We have maybe five or more different levels in a staff of nine people. We have a Director, a Deputy Director, RYC workers, live-ins, a cook, Yale interns, and whatnot; and every level has a different job title and a different salary. Hell, percentagewise we probably have the most vertical organization in the world. I think that Sears and Roebuck, which is one of the biggest outfits, has maybe only four different levels. But 'here are two big differences between us and Sears and Roebuck. At Sears and Roebuck the salesman on the floor can't go and tell the president of the company to go fuck himself. And second, at Sears and Roebuck the president doesn't go on the floor to ring up sales.
    I think that at the RYC we have a situation where people are in no way lim⁺ed or stereotyped by their jobs or titles. I don't know what we'd really call the RYC, but it's sure not

fluenced by demand characteristics external to the Center. In short, it was never possible to create the optimal conditions for testing fully the concept of horizontality.

a real horizontal structure. What we have here is a certain kind of freedom and a guarantee that we can be heard and be a part of things. At Sears and Roebuck I doubt that the cash-register girl can be a part of the organization's big decisions.

To the extent that we get hung up on this term "horizontal structure," I think we're missing the boat as to what we really got here. The term horizontal describes a physical situation. What we have here is something, maybe it's an idea, that goes beyond the physical or structure thing.

The Staff: Problems of Growth and Regression At this point in time, questions concerning the degree to which the RYC as a setting facilitated the personal and "professional" growth of its own staff remain essentially unanswered and open to interpretation. Once again, the reasons for this state of affairs are twofold: first, the data currently available for such an assessment are, for the most part, anecdotal and observational in nature; and second, sufficient time has not elapsed for us to make any final judgments based on adequate follow-up procedures. Nevertheless, some statements bearing on the question can be made and, although provisional, they do provide us with a way of thinking about (if not resolving) the problems associated with human development in an organization such as the RYC.

Conflicting Needs. By far the clearest, most important, and most pervasive aspect of staff life at the RYC was the continual conflict people experienced between their desires for autonomy and growth, on the one hand, and their needs for security and dependence, on the other. If the setting did little else, it created the conditions under which the ambivalent feelings usually associated with growth could no longer be kept silent or hidden. They had to "surface," and usually did, and whether they were resolved or not (they were never resolved in the sense that they ceased to exist), they influenced the setting in a variety of different and persistent ways. The most obvious of these ways was the staff's lingering tendency to seek autocratic direction, particularly during times of acute stress. At such times, much of the staff's previous "learning" experiences and accrued sense of self-determination would "come undone."[4] Crisis situations, for example, be they with respect to a particular youngster or the program as a whole, often signaled a temporary end to or limitation of the group's ability to "use itself" as the most appropriate source of help. The "crisis" often seemed to develop a dynamic of its own and would be accompanied, not by calls for immediate group decision-making responsibility but, quite to the contrary, by demands for unilateral action and direction from the "leader." This unwillingness by the staff (the leader included) to assume fully the burdens of whatever is meant by "freedom" continues to exist, and while sensitivity sessions were often used for purposes of dealing with some of the regressive implications of this behavior, observable change has been slow in coming.

Attitude Change. Given this conflict, it would be all too easy to assume (or, even worse, to conclude) that the setting failed in its attempts to create the conditions for sustained staff growth. Such a judgment would be both premature and probably inaccurate. To begin with, and as we have tried to indicate at several different points in our discussion, any attempt to assess the degree to which the RYC staff "grew" as a function of having been a part of the setting would have to take into consideration the fact that for most of us (the leader included) the RYC was a relatively new and different kind of experience; that is, most of the staff members had spent the overwhelming majority of their adult "working lives" in settings that neither stressed nor even invoked "growth" as a central organizational value. Under these conditions, it would indeed be more than a little surprising if the staff's "growth curve" were free of periodic declines and reversals. In short, two years is precious little time when

---

[4]It would be a mistake if this were interpreted as a problem peculiar to the RYC and, therefore, a singularly important criterion by which to evaluate the setting's success. Clearly, the tendency to seek autocratic direction during times of acute personal and group stress is a general phenomenon; that is, a phenomenon not limited by a setting's goals, traditions, or staff. Consequently, we discuss it here for purposes of description and explanation, not because the phenomenon of regression under stress is only typical of, or restricted to, settings like the Residential Youth Center.

compared to the number of years (and experiences) that preceded it. It should also be pointed out that research done on the RYC's original staff—research similar to that carried out on its residents—indicated attitudinal changes in the same general direction as those observed in the program's youngsters. While the results were for the most part incomplete, they did show that the staff's feelings of alienation decreased significantly from the time of initial testing (the pre-RYC days) to the time some 12 months later when the questionnaires were readministered.[5] There is some reason to believe, therefore, that despite the observable regression that occurred during periods of crisis, the setting as a whole may well be creating the conditions for sustained staff growth, albeit slow and highly "irregular."

The Question of Upgrading. Mention should be made of one final issue related to the question of growth—the issue of "upgrading" the nonprofessional. Here there is certainly little doubt that the setting made it possible for nonprofessionals to acquire the kind of training that would enable them to assume positions of responsibility and leadership in programs related to the RYC. Although we shall have more to say about this in later sections of this chapter, for the present let us point out that almost all the RYC's original full-time staff members "moved up" or were "upgraded" during the two years they spent in the program. At the present time, for example, in addition to the existing RYC, New Haven has developed a girls' residential facility (it is called

[5]The incompleteness of the pre-post attitudinal research done on the RYC's original staff is another example—similar to the one described previously with respect to structural horizontality—of the difficulties inherent in action or field research. Field researchers, for example, have absolutely no control over external events (e.g., the war in Vietnam) which, remote though they may seem, may well affect both the course and content of whatever research has been undertaken. In the case of the RYC's staff, for example, two of its seven original full-time members were drafted before the end of the program's first year of operation. Their subsequent unavailability for retesting made it more than a little difficult to speak of the attitudinal research done on the staff in anything more than tentative and incomplete ways. Whereas most laboratory studies, even those dealing with questions of attitudinal change, usually have "pools" of subjects to draw from (and can quickly go to these pools for replacement purposes), an RYC has no such "luxurious" subject-substitution possibilities.

the Young Women's Multi-Purpose Training Center) and is in the process of developing a Training and Research Institute for Residential Youth Centers (TRI-RYC). The Director of the girls' RYC was formerly an RYC worker at the boys' Center, and one of his RYC workers, Jean, used to be the secretary at the "old" RYC. The situation with respect to the new Training and Research Institute is quite similar. The Institute, which we shall discuss in more detail later in this chapter, is funded by the Department of Labor and will have as its main function the training of people from all parts of the country who are interested in establishing residential centers in their own communities. Scotty, who succeeded the author as Director of the boys' RYC, is now the Institute's Deputy Director; Butch, one of the Center's original RYC workers, is now a field trainer at the Institute; and another former RYC worker is presently the Institute's business manager.

Problems of Program Renewal and Training   In a very basic sense, the crucial test of a program's viability occurs at that point in time when its initial *rites de passage* have become fondly romanticized memories of a past that will never be relived. For the RYC, no different from most programs, the question of its own enduring "relevance" will be settled not on the basis of how well it continues to fulfill its formal goals but in terms of how appropriately it *changes* them and, in the process, changes itself. A setting such as the RYC must continually be creating and recreating itself: it cannot exist solely on the basis of some previously developed ethos, nor can it envision its own sense of renewal as a "given," contingent on nothing more than the fulfillment of its formal service responsibilities. In many ways, then, the RYC is now, even more than two years ago, at a critical point. With the "bittersweet job" of its initial "revolution" a thing of the past, and with very few of its original staff members still on the scene, the setting, if it is to maintain its relevance, must develop a new and if not totally different identity for itself, an identity tied no longer solely to its past but, hopefully, to its future. Whether or not the setting will be able to survive its own self-renewal is an open question. Its outcome will depend largely on two things. The first has to do with the way in which new staff members are selected and introduced into the setting; and the second will be contingent on the degree to which the program as a whole begins to view itself as an organically changing (and changeable) setting.

Bridging the "Generation Gap." With respect to the recruitment and training of new personnel, there is some evidence to suggest that people being brought into the setting are being hired on the basis of criteria quite different from those originally employed and, even more important, that once in the setting new staff members are not being given the kind of orientation or training that would facilitate their understanding of the program and their relationship to it. To some degree this appears to be due to a reduced flexibility on the part of the program's current leaders to recruit the kinds of people that they feel would ultimately make a significant contribution to the setting. For the most part, however, the problem seems to lie with those of us who created the setting. For most of the Center's original staff, the RYC was indeed a "love affair," an undertaking which, for all its moments of panic and uncertainty, possessed the binding qualities of a revolution. We were (or at least felt ourselves to be) a little band of rebels, scornful of tradition and duly unimpressed by the accomplishments of those who had preceded us—a group of missionaries committed to the creation of a very personal and earthbound utopia. For us, such things as sensitivity training and horizontal structure were far more than concepts: they were adventures, attempts by a "special" group of people to develop new and different patterns of relating to one another and to an organization. For those who followed us, on the other hand, there could be no immediate or self-evident identity between the setting's underlying assumptions and their own experiences. For them, concepts like horizontality and sensitivity training were just that —concepts, theoretical formulations that sounded good but had no firm foundation in a shared and mutually understandable past. Having been unable to be a part of the RYC's history, they entered the setting not as its creators but as its perpetuators, not as its founders but as its heirs. Theirs would be a far more difficult task than ours ever was, for it was a situation in which fervor would have to be replaced by more formal training: people would now have to be helped to evolve the essence of the RYC experience; it could only partially be absorbed informally . . . through the fanciful tales of the setting's "founding fathers." Whether or not this occurs will in large measure depend on the degree to which the setting's "newcomers" and "ancients" are able to look beyond themselves, are able to accept the reality that tradition and training are a part of, but never a substitute for, the future.

The Management of Flux. The second issue, that of the "organic" or changing nature of a program, is at least as complicated, if not more so, than the problem of recruiting and training new personnel. The reason is simple enough. Despite the problems associated with bringing new people into an ongoing setting, the overall question of staff selection and training is at least "manageable" in the sense that decisions concerning both the kinds of people who are ultimately brought into a setting and the nature of the formal training they will be given are embedded in a frame of reference that encompasses the long-term goals and aspirations of the setting itself. As we have tried to indicate, however, an RYC may not be the kind of setting whose goals can (or should) remain unaffected by the changing nature of the community of which it is a part. In other words, the RYC's own sense of self-renewal may very well depend on the degree to which it is able to identify itself and its own future with crises and problems that extend, at least conceptually, beyond the confines of the "block," the "neighborhood," or the "ghetto." For example, during the past six months or so there has been an ever-increasing and dramatic change in the "kinds of kids" who have become residents of the Center. At the present time a number of the RYC's residents are boys who, for want of a better term, could be called "hippies." While they do not comprise a majority of the youth currently in residence, the "flower children" either have found their way or have been referred to the Center in increasing numbers. Their presence in the house has created "problems" that have confronted the staff with the need to reexamine the very nexus of the program's intent. For some, the flower children are a welcome and long overdue addition to the house, a necessary way of introducing "variety" into an otherwise relatively homogeneous resident population. Among other staff members there is the feeling that the setting was never intended for (and should not accommodate) "spoiled middle-class kids." The situation is even further complicated by the fact that some of the RYC's newer staff members have challenged the "legitimacy" of anyone (staff or resident) to participate in the Center's work unless that person's background and past experiences have been of such a nature as to give him what they define as "the right to be here." For the most part, these staff members are black men whose power-oriented militancy is understandable either in terms of the times we live in generally or because of the experiences that preceded their entry into the setting in particular (e.g., one of the RYC's black militants became a part of the program after a series of painful and horrible experiences with white racists in Vietnam). But one way or another, the setting has arrived at that point in its life when it must deal anew with the dilemma of its own identity. The degree to which the setting and its people are able to discern the underlying existential similarities between alienated "hard-core" youth and alienated "middle-class" youth—and relate these similarities, at least conceptually, to the broader social forces currently sweeping our society as a whole—will in large measure determine both the direction and the intensity of the RYC's own evolution.

The Implications of the Setting: 1968
As indicated earlier in this chapter, two years is a hopelessly short period of time within which to gauge the institutional impact of a program such as the RYC.[6] It is also true, however

[6]While, as we have repeatedly pointed out, two years may not be the optimal amount of time to use as a basis for evaluating the setting in all its complexity and ramifications, this should not be taken to mean that the passage of two years has not provided some of the program's

(and perhaps unfortunately so), that we live in a time that makes it increasingly difficult to discuss a program's impact *without* focusing attention on the relationship between the program itself, on the one hand, and either the conditions that brought it into being or the forces that materially and continually influenced or could be affected by its development, on the other. Consequently, in the following pages an attempt will be made to describe what appears to have been the RYC's impact on the conditions and agencies that surround it locally as well as its potential influence on the thinking and planning of those who have responsibility for dealing more generally with the problems of human renewal.

The RYC in New Haven In the course of describing the RYC's "prehistory" (see Chapter 6), we repeatedly made the point that it was exceedingly difficult to speak of the New Haven community as if it were composed of groups with similar and nonconflicting values, goals, and traditions. New Haven was, and continues to be, a city populated by different agencies and power groups, each with its own enduring concerns, limitations, and spheres of influence. In this respect, it is no different from any other city. Consequently, any attempt to assess the impact of a new setting like the RYC would have to be predicated both on an appreciation of that reality and on the assumption that the concept of "impact" is itself a relatively meaningless one if applied from an "all or none" frame of reference. Clearly, there are varying degrees and kinds of impact, some being more obvious and measurable than others. The question of impact cannot be divorced from the practices and traditions—from the continuity of thinking—that characterizes and makes "distinguishable" the particular profession, agency, or setting under consideration. Beyond this, however, the issue is further complicated by the fact that for the most part, local agencies tend to respond to "innovation" more slowly than either their national counterparts or the larger "systems" of which they are local

---

early critics with new criteria by which to view the RYC's development. For some, particularly those who predicted that the setting would not survive its first month of existence, the passage of two years has proved more than a little convincing of the Center's viability.

"outposts." While local agencies may in very general ways echo rather quickly the "tones of change" that characterize their professions as a whole, rarely is it the case that their own practices change with the same or similar rapidity. Thus, for example, the fact that the thinking and policies of the Office of Education in Washington may, as a function of innovations in other fields, change rather dramatically over a relatively short period of time is no guarantee that these conceptual changes will either filter down or be implemented on the local level with anything resembling that dispatch. In many ways the situation is an understandable one, perhaps even a necessary one, but in the final analysis one factor emerges over all others: the practices of local agencies are invariably embedded in a "community dynamic" of their own, and it is this dynamic that determines (and usually retards) both the degree and speed with which traditional practices either sense or respond to the impact of new ideas.

Thus, it would be more than a little surprising if the RYC, for all its apparent success, should have had anything more than a tangential effect on the "quality of life" in New Haven—the quality of life, that is, as defined by the practices and policies of those agencies whose roots lay deep in the city's history. In actuality, it would be extremely difficult, at least at this point in time, to justify the RYC's existence on the basis of changes that it was able to engender or inspire in any of the agencies with which it came into contact.[7]

[7]One could argue, and perhaps quite persuasively, that the RYC's original or primary "mission" had little if anything to do with changing the practices and policies of existing service agencies. The RYC was not funded for purposes of social change. It came into being in order to serve a population that did not seem to be receiving or benefiting from the kinds of programs and services currently in existence in the community. Its explicit "mission," therefore, was to provide remedial and supportive services to a seemingly atypical population of youngsters and families called "hard-core" or "chronically disadvantaged." From this point of view, the RYC certainly accomplished its task, and rather well. In reality, however, and perhaps in order to fulfill these objectives, the RYC developed what might be called an "innovative model of service"; that is, a pattern of relating to both clients and the community, and a pattern that certainly seemed applicable and relevant to most agencies engaged in the activities of human service. At this point we are addressing ourselves to the question of whether or not this new "model of service" had any impact on the thinking or practices of those agencies.

For purposes of clarity we might do well to describe this impact or, perhaps more accurately, this lack of impact.

Interactions with Established Agencies. The fact that the RYC was funded to deal with youngsters labeled as "incorrigible" meant that the Center would, almost by definition, be working very closely with those institutions (e.g., the police, the mental health professions, and the social service agencies) from whose rolls the youths had either been dropped or "dropped out." It would be reasonable to assume, therefore, that whatever impact the setting and its services might have had would be felt most markedly by these very agencies. In reality, however, although the RYC did develop rather continual and for the most part good relationships with each of these agencies, it would be very difficult to say that any of these relationships caused or enabled a particular agency to reexamine (let alone change) any of its underlying assumptions about, or ways of dealing with, the so-called hard-core youngster and his family. This should not be taken to mean that no such attempts were made—quite to the contrary. Very early in the life of the RYC, in-service "training sessions" were set up with a number of the agencies with which the Center "did business." These meetings were clearly designed with the goal of creating the conditions under which participants (i.e., the RYC and whatever agency was involved) could, over a period of time, begin to relate to each other in ways that made confrontation and the reciprocal questioning of assumptions a less threatening and anxiety-producing experience. Despite the fact that these meetings proved "helpful" in a most general sense (i.e., both participants feeling that they had a better understanding of each other's problems and points of view), they rarely resulted in any significant changes in orientation or patterns of service.

By and large, whatever "good" resulted from the RYC's contacts with local agencies was largely confined to individuals; that is, certain individuals who happened to be members of various agencies did, apparently as a consequence of their involvements with RYC personnel, begin both to question some of their own underlying assumptions and to attempt to develop different strategies of service. Thus, for example, while the RYC had little if any effect on the practices and policies of the New Haven police department, it did enable a number of individual patrolmen and other law enforcement personnel to become involved in the program in ways that went beyond their "normal" police responsibilities. For these individuals, the RYC did, indeed, become a setting that facilitated a very personal kind of reexamination of the problems faced by inner-city youths and their families. The same could be said of the mental health professions. Despite the fact that in its second year of existence the RYC suddenly found itself confronted with employment applications from professional social workers, the setting as a whole had no appreciable impact on the practices of New Haven's mental health or social service agencies. One still hears professionals, often of the "community mental health" variety, referring to "that residential *treatment* center being run by people who don't know how to do treatment."

A more recent development, and one which brings with it new and potentially exciting possibilities, involves the relationship between the RYC and the New Haven public schools. During the latter part of its first year of operation, the RYC, primarily through the efforts of one of its staff members, developed a pilot program for preschool-age retarded children. Together with members of the Parents Association for Retarded Children, this RYC worker, himself the father of a retarded child, organized and coordinated a program that provided retarded children between the ages of 2 and 5 with a preschool experience oriented toward preparing them for later entrance into the public schools. The program was partly financed through Center funds, and the RYC itself became the setting for the program's planning and early implementation. Quite naturally, the program brought the RYC and members of the public school system together in a working relationship. Shortly thereafter, partly because of the success of that pilot project and the relationships that developed from it, the RYC became the "classroom" for boys who either were about to be or had already been excluded from the regular classroom situation. These youngsters (boys from the "middle" or junior high schools) were behaving in ways that were seriously undermining and disrupting their classrooms, and rather than putting them on "home bound" or suspending them entirely from the school setting (a traditional procedure with almost uniformly negative results), the decision was made to view the RYC as an "extension" of the schools, as another classroom for its students. Since the Center was, for the most part, empty during school hours (i.e., the residents, hopefully, were at work or at their job-training sites), and since the RYC was not perceived by the youngsters as a "school" (with all that that implied), it became their educational setting. They would come to the RYC, where their classes were held (in the basement) and where they could both use the Center's facilities (TV, judo room) and become involved in its evening programs. In addition, some of the RYC's staff (and one of its former residents) began to work with the youngsters in ways not too dissimilar from the ways in which they would work with full-time residents. Despite numerous problems, the program resulted in increased "school" attendance on the part of the teen-agers and provided the school system with a new and potentially helpful resource for its troubled and troublesome students. While the project by no means solved the problem of how to deal with "angry, acting-out, and resistive" adolescents, it did make it possible for members of the school system and the RYC to begin to share their ideas concerning the ways in which inner-city youths perceived school and the conditions under which the school setting could be made more relevant to their needs, concerns, and interests.[8] Finally, however, in ad-

[8]One of the most concrete results of the program involved the ex-RYC resident who participated in it. Because of his unique ability to relate to the youngsters, he was hired by the school system as a teacher-aide. When the project moved back into the schools, he remained with the youngsters and the program. At the present time, he functions within the school system as one of the program's teachers. While it would be going too far afield to deal extensively with the question, we should at least point out that the ex-resident involved, Leland (see Chapter 7), is not the kind of person who defines his role "teacher-aide" as involving the kinds of duties that have all too often become associated with that "new career" for the poor (e.g., cleaning blackboards, being a classroom policeman, or running errands for the teacher).

dition to the special programs described, the relationship between the RYC and the school system continued to grow when, for reasons which are still unclear and in need of further examination, several of the RYC's residents decided to give school "one more shot." During the RYC's second year of existence, almost half of the Center's residents returned full-time to the New Haven high schools. Once this occurred, it became natural for RYC personnel to begin visiting the high schools on a regular basis. Thus, if a particular staff member was working with a youngster who had decided to return to school, visiting his school, his classrooms, and his teachers became a regular part of the worker's schedule. If and when problems arose, the school would notify the worker, and he, in turn, would attend whatever school meetings or conferences had been set up to deal with the problem. Thus, over a period of time, RYC personnel and, by implication, the program itself gained entrance into a setting that previously had not been viewed as an area of potential impact. Whether or not this unanticipated association produces results that the school system experiences as helpful (and that the RYC views as consistent with its own concerns regarding the educational system) remains an open question. There are some signs, however, that the relationship is a promising one. During the past year, for example, several of New Haven's inner-city high schools were beset with racial tensions, which resulted in explosive and often frightening "miniriots" in school cafeterias, hallways, and grounds. At such times, RYC workers, who were not perceived by the youths (either black or white) as aligned with either the school or the city's law enforcement agencies, and whom many of the involved youngsters knew, were able to go into the schools, help quell the riots, and then, after passions had subsided sufficiently, become involved in helping both the school and its youngsters begin to reexamine the conditions that led to the outbreaks. While it is much too early to predict the long-term consequences of this involvement, one thing remains fairly clear: in the process of providing the school system with needed help, the RYC may have begun to develop the kind of relationship through which some of its own ideas concerning inner-city youth and their problems can begin to influence the thinking and practices of the New Haven educational system.

The "Revolt" Against CPI. In terms of its relationship with its "mother organization," there is no evidence that the RYC was able to effect any change in what it perceived as the agency's problems or shifting values. At one point in its second year of operation, the RYC spearheaded a fragmented and abortive revolt against the increasing distance, both physical and psychological, that had come to characterize "CPI downtown's" relationship with its "frontline troops." While the revolt may have been significant from a certain point of view (i.e., RYC personnel were both able and willing to confront very directly the administrators of the poverty agency and to accept the responsibility and the potential implications of this confrontation), it was somewhat less than effective (to put it mildly) in achieving any concrete results. If anything, the revolt worsened (at least temporarily) the relationship between the RYC and the administrative hierarchy of the community action agency.

Yale University. There is little we can say about the effects of the program on the feelings and attitudes of its participants toward the institution which in many ways dominates the New Haven scene—Yale University. With the exception of the Psycho-Educational Clinic, which was, from the very beginning, deeply committed to and involved in the development of the Residential Youth Center, the University remains, at least from the point of view of the majority of the people involved in the program, a monolithic and largely uncaring institution, an institution whose own goals are only tangentially, if at all, related to the needs and aspirations of the inner city.[9]

[9]One of our most enlightening and thought-provoking RYC experiences had to do with the results of a questionnaire that was distributed to the staff after the RYC's first year of existence. The questionnaire was devised for purposes of providing the RYC's first Director with information concerning the "progress" of the seven students whom he had brought into the Center from the University. The staff was asked to rank these students individually with respect to their "competence,"

The Development of an RYC for Girls. In terms of its impact in New Haven, perhaps the most direct and immediate result of the program was the decision on the part of the Department of Labor's Office of Manpower Policy, Evaluation and Research to use the city as the site for the development of another residential facility patterned along the lines of the boys' RYC. This facility, called the Young Women's Multi-Purpose Training Center (YWMPTC), is an experimental and demonstration project geared to meet the needs of girls between the ages of 16 and 21 years whose problems and backgrounds are similar to the population of adolescent males for whom the original RYC was created 18 months earlier. Except for the inclusion of a specific training component, the girls' center was organized and funded very much like the boys' RYC; that is, its operation was envisioned as having a basis in the ideas and practices developed at the boys' residential facility (e.g., horizontal structure, staffing by indigenous nonprofessionals, sensitivity training, and neighborhood involvement). Although the new center has been operational for less than a year—and its own problems and experiences could easily fill the pages of another book—one thing remains clear: the decision by the Department of Labor to fund another residential center, and to locate that new facility in New Haven, was in a very major, direct way influenced by

---

competence being defined as the staff member's perception of the degree to which each of the students had been able to become a part of the setting and to relate to its people (residents and staff) in helpful ways. The most outstanding result of the questionnaire was that it indicated a significant inverse relationship between the number of years a student had spent in Yale's department of psychology as a graduate student and his perceived competence in the Center. In other words, the longer a student had been in graduate school, the less competent was his rating. Before proceeding any further, we should point out that the questionnaire and its results were clearly in the nature of preliminary and descriptive pilot data. No attempts were made to control for the myriad variables which may well have influenced the outcome, and consequently, we attribute no undue significance or validity to its results. If nothing else, however, the results raise a host of compelling questions concerning graduate school education as a whole, and the kind of preparation and training being made available to potential clinical psychologists in particular. At the very least we can begin to ask ourselves whether or not current curricula and models of clinical training are adequate (or even relevant) once the clinician's setting changes from the "office" to the "community," from the confines of the university, clinic, or psychiatric ward to the world of action.

some of the results of the boys' RYC and the relationships that grew out of that experience.

In the final analysis, any attempt to assess the RYC's impact on the quality of life in New Haven would in large part depend both on one's definition of the term "impact" and on the degree to which one feels constrained to use the program's formal goals as one's point of reference. From our point of view, we take a look at New Haven now and compare it to its status two years ago when the RYC first made its appearance on the local scene. What we see is a city whose problems are essentially indistinguishable from those of most other urban settings; a city racked by divisions among its people; a city still striving to make sense out of the chaos that characterizes life in American urban society. From this perspective, the RYC contributed precious little to improving the quality of life in the city. Neither did it serve as a vehicle for attacking or changing the very conditions that necessitated its development in the first place. New Haven still has its poor, its alienated, and its disenfranchised. Also, and above all this, New Haven still has its institutions and agencies, none of whose basic orientations or patterns of service seem to have changed very much as a function of the existence of the RYC: Yale is still Yale, the Community Mental Health Center is still the Community Mental Health Center, CPI is still CPI, the police are still the police . . . and the RYC is still the RYC. Each is still striving in its own way and from its own definition of itself and its role in the community to meet the challenges to its own existence. We do not express these observations because of any desire to derogate the value of the RYC's service accomplishments or because of any need to construct a frame of reference so grandiose in its scope as to defy probability. Rather, the point we are trying to make is a simple one: If a setting (presumably one like the RYC) wishes to view itself as something more than another service agency, it must, from the very beginning, formally address itself and its energies to the question of institutional change and not expect its impact to result solely—or even primarily—from its service responsibilities.

Beyond New Haven Clearly, the RYC's most important contribution to the field of "human renewal" lies in its having developed a particular conception of services and the relationship of these services to problems of organizational structure and staff training. The extent to which this "model" proves effective over time, or succeeds in influencing the thinking and planning of those whose powers and responsibilities in the general area of human service are far-reaching in nature, will determine the long-term consequences of the program. As we have already indicated, it is much easier to report (and to question) the meaning of "service results" than it is to assess the implications of a program with respect to the broader issue of institutional change. Consequently, for purposes of achieving some additional perspective on the potential "institutional impact" of the RYC, we might describe briefly some of the more recent developments involving the program.

The Creation of a Setting to Study the Creation of Settings. At the time of this writing, the Department of Labor has again provided the funds for the development of a new and potentially exciting project. The project involves the development of something called a Training and Research Institute for Residential Youth Centers (TRI-RYC). The newly funded Institute has been given the task of developing residential youth centers in settings and with agencies outside the New Haven area. In essence, the new program will attempt to replicate and evaluate the "RYC model" in a variety of different communities, varying the model where necessary. The Institute's objective is to assess the degree to which the concepts developed at the RYC in New Haven are both applicable and generalizable to other settings in different parts of the country. In addition, however, the Institute's "mandate" is such that it need not confine itself to working solely with community action or antipoverty agencies. Thus, for example, the Institute is presently developing plans for residential facilities in conjunction with a newly emerging community mental health program in Michigan and a public school system in Indiana, in addition to working with the community action programs of several different cities along the Eastern seaboard. One will now be able to observe and study the development of these centers and to relate their individual "viability" to the particular kinds of organizations of which they are a part. Moreover, since the Institute is indeed a research facility, it will have the freedom to conduct field experiments on a number of the different variables and questions that grew out of the initial RYC experience. Thus, for example, it may now be possible to create and evaluate RYCs in which pay scales have been equalized, directorships "revolved," and job descriptions eliminated. Finally, although the Institute's primary function will be to facilitate the development of new residential centers, it will have an important additional function: to provide in-service and staff development training to any and all programs wanting or requesting such technical assistance. In essence, then, the Institute will, through its in-service training programs, have the opportunity to explore the relevance and applicability of some of its own conceptions of service with agencies that do not presently share its orientations or ideology. Again, only time will tell whether or not the Institute can make a valuable contribution to thinking and planning in the field of human renewal. What is clear, however, is that the creation of the Training and Research Institute immediately broadens the scope and, by implication, the potential impact of whatever ideas and practices were developed within the context of the RYC experience.

The Job Corps Revisited. Mention should also be made of the fact that during the time the Institute's contract was being negotiated, preliminary discussions were once again begun with the Job Corps—discussions concerning Job Corps interest in becoming involved in the new program. Unlike the situation some three years ago (see Chapters 2 and 3), representatives of the Job Corps indicated a willingness to question some of their program's underlying assumptions concerning residential facilities. In addition, they seemed favorably inclined to allocate funds to the Institute for purposes of developing small inner-city, neighborhood-based Centers as alternatives to the large Job Corps camps currently in existence. In another development, Connecticut's Commissioner of Corrections, partly because of the success of the RYC, has decided to proceed with a plan that would replace reformatories and other correctional institutions with urban residential facilities and "halfway houses."

In all of the cases described here, there appears to be a shift in the thinking and planning of agencies that are in one way or another involved in the area of human service—a shift toward viewing settings like the RYC as more appropriate for handling the kinds of problems that confront disadvantaged and/or delinquent youth. If this "new" orientation succeeds in influencing the *process* by which these new settings are created, it may then be possible to speak with far greater conviction of the "institutional impact" of the Residential Youth Center.

The War on Poverty: 1969

We could not conclude this chapter without spending a little time describing what from our point of view appears to have been the fate and implications of the War on Poverty. There are two reasons for undertaking this description. First, in a very real sense, the development of the RYC would never have taken place were it not for the War on Poverty and the community action programs to which it gave birth; and second, at the time this chapter is being written, the very existence of the poverty program itself, at least its continued existence in the form we know it, is tenuous. If the War on Poverty is dying, perhaps slowly but nonetheless surely, then there must be some meaning to its demise, and no book dealing with the creation of a setting would be complete unless it focused attention on another setting's death.

We might begin with the retrospective observation that the War on Poverty was never really intended to be a "war" at all. At its very best it was a painfully timid and overly self-conscious "assault" on the consequences rather than the causes of human misery. It was the kind of program whose "philanthropic appeal" was, from the very beginning, basically devoid of the inevitable threat that would have accompanied it had its creators touted it as a crusade against the social, economic, and institutional foundations of our society. Consequently, the initial consensus that surrounded the War on Poverty was the consensus of the unthreatened and the unembittered, the unity of purpose of those whose own lives, far from being indictments of the "American dream," were testaments to its validity. Unlike the "target population" for whom it was intended, the War on Poverty was created by people whose faith in America and its institutions was as unshaken as their belief that poverty could be eliminated through the development of a massive program of individual remediation. For better or for worse—and only history will render the final judgment—theirs was a crusade to *extend* the blessings of the system . . . not to *change* it.

But somehow, despite the infinite care that was taken to render the program as inoffensive as possible, and despite the considerable charisma and eloquence of its first spokesman-promoter, R. Sargent Shriver, something went "wrong." The alliance began to give way, and within a few short years "the war that never was a war" became its own first casualty. Now, scarcely five years after its birth—at a time when, if nothing else, the nation is more fully aware than ever of the character and extent of the misery that exists within its own borders—the War on Poverty appears to be coming to an end. Amid cutbacks and riots, "Green amendments," and attacks by local politicians, the same program whose only goal was to reaffirm the American dream has become the victim of the very system it sought to canonize.

What strikes us, perhaps more forcefully than anything else, is the possibility that if the War on Poverty is ending, it is not ending because of its failures but, quite to the contrary, because of its unintended or unanticipated successes.[10]

[10]When we speak of the War on Poverty as "ending," we do not mean to imply that all its programs will cease to exist. While some of them (e.g., Job Corps) may, indeed, be totally eliminated, most of the programs originated by OEO will continue, albeit in watered-down fashion, in one way or another. What we mean is that OEO as an agency will probably be terminated and most of its activities and programs absorbed by one or another of the more "traditional" agencies (e.g., the Departments of Labor and/or Health, Education and Welfare). This

In other words, despite what appeared to be (and probably was) its paternalistic underpinnings, the War on Poverty "succeeded," perhaps inadvertently, in creating the very conditions it so scrupulously sought to avoid: the conditions of social conflict and political unrest. By so *succeeding*, it may very well have sown the seeds of its own destruction. A few examples are in order:

1. One of OEO's first offspring, the Community Action Program, was meant to serve its local community, more or less, as a neighborhood-based manpower setting; as an agency whose primary function was to use its "indigenous-ness" as a way of developing and securing better employ-ment and training opportunities for its poor. Interestingly enough, however, local community action agencies often de-veloped as independent settings; that is, as settings not formally tied to the existing political power structure of the city. In addition, although most of these community action agencies began their existence as service-oriented settings, it was not long before many of them came to the realization that all too often the obstacles that separated poor people from job opportunities resided in the "system" as a whole and not in the individuals seeking entry into the "mainstream" of American life. Whether it was the discriminatory policies of labor unions, the hiring practices of potential employers, or the poverty-perpetuating orientations of the public schools, social service agencies, and employment services, the prob-lem of poverty was not individual in nature: it was a cancer that permeated the very length and breadth of contemporary American society. Once this became clear, coupled with the fact that most community action agencies were not "be-holden" to the good graces of local political machines for their continued existence, the conditions for conflict were

---

dissolution of the "central" poverty agency and the "farming out" of its projects constitutes, at least from our point of view, an operational definition of the "ending" of a program. By stripping OEO of its power to create and implement new programs, the independence of the agency not only is undermined, but what is also implied is the deci-sion to rely on the mechanisms of "established" agencies (i.e., agencies that have already shown themselves to be unable or unwilling to deal with the problem) to continue the "war," such as it might be.

quickly established. It was only a matter of time, therefore, before many community action agencies began "overstepping" themselves, began focusing more and more of their attention on the institutional barriers to participatory democracy. This process, however hesitatingly begun and incompletely carried through, could not help but place the entire concept of "community action" in deep peril. Therefore, it is more than a little interesting and, at least from our point of view, not at all accidental that current attempts to "dissolve" community action agencies have taken the form of trying to tie them to mayors' offices. The so-called Green amendment seeks to create the conditions under which community action agencies (local antipoverty programs like CPI) can be brought under the control of city municipalities and thereby divested of whatever independence of movement they may have had as OEO outposts. Quite naturally, the reasons given for this emasculation of poverty programs have to do with the fact that there have been misuses (and abuses) of local poverty funds. (One might argue, of course, that if fiscal sobriety was the most important reason for determining federal moneys or dictating the basic structures of "national priority" programs, then the Department of Defense would be almost penniless.) In point of fact, the attempt to place community action programs under the control of the mayor's office is a rather thinly veiled maneuver once more to render the War on Poverty as inoffensive and unthreatening as possible. Those who owe their livelihoods to the local political machine are not very likely to bite the hand that feeds them or, more important, to attack the very institutional arrangements of which they are a part.

2. The phrase "maximum feasible participation of the poor" may one day stand alongside the wording of the Supreme Court's 1954 desegregation decision ("with all deliberate speed") as one of the most controversial if not clearly conceptualized sentences in recent American history. Its effect, again perhaps inadvertently, was not only to redefine the relationship between "helping" programs and the recipients of help (see Chapter 3) but also to create the

conditions for a potential shift in political power and social control. What may very well have begun as a well-intentioned but relatively minor attempt to "involve" the poor in the planning and implementation of opportunity programs may soon be looked upon as the most significant biproduct of the War on Poverty—and, of course, a most important reason for the war's termination. For in essence, the concept of maximum feasible participation confronted ongoing systems with the need to share, and perhaps even to relinquish, a good deal of the power they had so studiously and cautiously reserved for themselves. On the other hand, by making it more possible for the heretofore powerless to determine the course of their own lives and development, the wording of the Economic Opportunity Act of 1964 opened a Pandora's box of problems and conflicts, some of which may yet change the existing social fabric of our society in some very unanticipated ways.[11]

While it began quietly enough, it soon became clear that the process by which the poor were "lobbying" for greater control of poverty funds and programs was as potentially threatening as it was irreversible. The early Resident Advisory Committees were replaced by "neighborhood corporations" as the poor quickly "turned" on their benefactors (the community action agencies) and sought what amounted to complete financial and administrative control of local poverty moneys. In addition, the rise of Black Coalitions and other militant minority groups—and the "wedding" of many of these organizations to the goal of garnering poverty funds— did little to ease the anxiety of those who came to view their initial support of the War on Poverty as having helped to

[11]Some of the unanticipated consequences of the War on Poverty may not be felt for another 10 to 15 years. We refer here to the possibility that the poor and those whose association with community action agencies (e.g., people like Scotty, Jack, Butch, and Will of the RYC staff) enabled them to amass a certain amount of power in a fairly short period of time will use that acquired leverage to form new and potentially important "urban power" blocks. Only time will tell whether community action agencies served as political springboards for those who prior to the War on Poverty would never have been able to assume positions of power and influence in the community, let alone the country as a whole.

"create a Frankenstein." And finally, the riots, the "long hot summers," and the cries of "burn, baby, burn" confronted an already shaky and frightened public with what it interpreted, among other things, as the inevitable result of America's latest "social experiment."

Undoubtedly, it will be a long time before a comprehensive history of the '60s is written, at least the kind of history that enables us to untangle the myriad and divergent threads that have shaped our recent experience. And when that history is written, it will surely have much to say about the War on Poverty. More than likely that analysis will do much to place the poverty program in its proper perspective. Perhaps only then will we be able to achieve the distance from which it becomes possible to weigh assets and liabilities, short-term consequences and long-term implications—to view the war less as an individual phenomenon and more as part of the context of our society's evolution as a whole. In the few pages we devoted to the subject, all we wished to convey was our own belief that for all its initial caution and basic conservatism, the "war that never was a war," together with events only tangentially related to poverty, may have contributed to a process of social change the ends of which are not nearly in sight. If this is true, then even if future historians tell us that in and of itself the War on Poverty was a failure, those of us who were in one way or another connected with it will still be able to feel that it failed with a modicum of grace. Perhaps little more can be expected of unintended revolutions.

In this chapter we reviewed some of the problems and implications of the RYC experience from the point of view of how close the setting came to achieving those of its goals that were not primarily "client-centered." Focusing attention on some of the setting's unresolved problems and concerns, we attempted to describe the issues (both internal and external to the Center itself) that may, in the final analysis, determine the future course and development of the program. These issues revolve around questions of change within the

RYC and the impact of setting on the thinking and planning of agencies whose powers and capabilities for creating change extend beyond the New Haven area. We concluded by offering a brief, highly personal, and admittedly incomplete analysis of the War on Poverty, an analysis predicated on the assumption that much of its significance may indeed reside not so much in its apparent and publicized failures but, to the contrary, in some of its unanticipated successes.

By way of introducing the next and final chapter of this book, we might point out that it was no accident that a clinical psychologist (the author) was a member of the group that journeyed to that mountain in Maryland. His presence in the car that rainy day in 1965, how he got there, and where the long ride finally took him are as much parts of the story of the Residential Youth Center as anything else, but the story is also much more than that. It is part of the continuing and unfinished story of how some members of the helping professions are trying to adapt themselves and their fields to the present and anticipated needs of a changing society and how, in the process of doing this, they are continuing to define themselves. History, no less than personal choice, had a hand in placing the clinician in that car, and no attempt to understand the development of the RYC would be complete unless it focused attention on much of the present-day ferment that characterizes the helping professions in general, and the field of clinical psychology in particular. It will be the purpose of our final chapter to describe this ferment and to attempt to explain its meaning.

Chapter 11   The Clinician in Times of Rapid Social Change

It is the profound tendencies of history and not the passing excitements that will shape our future.
—John F. Kennedy

No scientific discipline develops independently of, or is unaffected by, the social and political realities of its time. What men do and think, how their ideas and practices change or remain the same—these things are as much matters of historical imperative as individual choice, and it is often difficult to tell where one leaves off and the other begins. Professions, no less than individuals, are shaped by the same "profound tendencies of history" that mold the societies of which they are a part. Their orientations and practices are more often than not a reflection of the prevailing values and attitudes of the greater society in which they are embedded. They change as the needs of their societies change, and they accept as inevitable that through this process of change they will be continually defining and redefining themselves.

What we have said here is undoubtedly true to one degree or another for all professions, but it is particularly true of what we call the "helping professions" (psychiatry, clinical psychology, social work, etc.). There are probably two reasons for this, both of which have to do with the uniquely human character of the goals and processes of the helping professions. The first reason is that as clinicians our primary focus of concern is to understand the exigencies of what we call the "human condition." This being the case, our sole reason for being is to help people, and to utilize the helping relationship to develop and increase our knowledge of human behavior, all in the hope that we will someday come to understand ourselves and others better. However, unlike members of other professions, the clinician, no less than his clients, is a part of and is affected by the same human condition he seeks to understand. The simple fact of life is that no clinician can hope to be helpful unless and until he begins to understand the myriad pressures, both inside and outside the individual, that influence behavior. But once this process begins, the clinician and the client become bound in one way or another by the same values, attitudes, and even inequities, of the society in which they both live. The longer the clinician practices, the more he realizes the degree to which what he says and does is a reflection of his own participation in a societal process. Such is the fate (as well as the paradox) of the helping professions: the truth-seeker is inevitably the subject of his quest. It is therefore understandable that under these conditions the clinician can never become fully immune to the social and political pressures of his society; neither the range of his patients' problems nor the limitations of his own methodologies will allow him this luxury of disengagement.

The second reason is best stated in the form of a working assumption: a science's vulnerability to society's demands that it change its basic orientations and techniques is inversely proportional to its level of theoretical and technological sophistication at that point in time. The helping professions, unlike their more highly developed and advanced brethren in the physical sciences, have not evolved a technology sufficiently precise to hide behind or use as a buffer against the relentlessly shifting influences and needs of society.[1] Whether we wish to speak in terms of theoretical or methodological maturity, it is clear that we are far more infantile, both in age and in level of development, than our colleagues in the physical sciences. As such, our theories and techniques, the ways in which we conceptualize problems and how we go about dealing with them, are much more likely to be deeply affected by the political and social upheavals through which our society is passing.[2]

[1]Rubinstein and Parloff (1959, p. 292), after reviewing the progress in research on psychotherapy, the most prestigious of the technologies developed by the helping professions, conclude as follows: "Much has been done, but there has been relatively little progress in establishing a firm and substantial body of evidence to support very many research hypotheses. Basic problems in this field of research have remained essentially unchanged and unsolved. There is no simple, reassuring, authoritative principle which clearly supports one approach and demonstrates the invalidity of the others."
[2]Levine and Levine (1970), in a review of the history of the development of the child guidance movement in this country, have described

Therefore, it should come as no surprise to the reader to find that a clinical psychologist was among the men who journeyed to that mountain in Maryland. If nothing else, the discussion to this point should have made one thing clear: be it because of our profound concern for the human condition or the lack of comfort we can take in our theoretical and methodological sophistication, the helping professions have never been able to divorce their own development as a science from the more general and pervasive needs of their society. At other times and under different conditions, a clinical psychologist would not have been visiting mountains; he would have been doing other things and thinking other thoughts. This process of continual self-definition is not an

---

this relationship between the practices of the helping professions and the political atmosphere of the times. Their findings point to a high correlation between the particular orientations of the helping professions and the political character of the administrations in power during a specific period of time. Thus, for example, when a relatively conservative government is in power, the tendency of the helping professions is to view and to treat individual problems under the auspices of the doctrine of "intrapsychic supremacy." Levine and Levine define this doctrine in the following way:

Treatment modalities followed the basic assumption that the important events involved in those problems of living we term emotional disturbance or mental illness are intrapsychic ones. If a person was having difficulty, it was because of events within him, no change in the outside world would have very much of an important effect because the intrapsychic events were fixed in earlier experience. The assumption of intrapsychic supremacy also involves the conception, held more or less explicitly by many, that important changes in intrapsychic events could take place only within a certain set of narrow conditions, conditions normally produced only in a psychotherapeutic relationship, with a skilled, professionally trained, psychotherapist. Psychotherapy became the treatment of choice on the assumption that all one needed to do was to change the intrapsychic events, and then other matters would take care of themselves.

When, on the other hand, one finds a relatively liberal government in power, one can also expect to find a corresponding shift in the orientations and practices of mental health workers. Where liberalism dominated the political atmosphere, the focus of the mental health professions would turn to considerations of situational determinants and environmental influences on disordered patterns of living. One way or the other—whether we ourselves are liberals, conservatives, or fence-straddlers—we cannot escape the fact that as members of the helping professions what we do and say, how we think, and the techniques we use are determined, at some level, not only by our personal and theoretical predilections but also by those significant social and political events that affect our society as a whole.

easy one to accept. One would like to be able to lean back and say: "I am what I am, now and forever"; but the realities of our time will not allow us to view our profession as having reached this level of stability, permanence, and identity.

With this as our point of departure, it would seem appropriate that we describe in some detail just how closely our own professional behavior and development have mirrored what might be called the "temper of the times." If, as we would like to believe, all that is past becomes prologue, then it is to the past that we must look if we are to understand the present and illuminate the future. For the field of clinical psychology the past was not so long ago.

Clinical Psychology in the 1940s

Clinical psychology was a "war baby," the bastard child of parents called Emergency and Need. It was born at a time and under conditions that threatened the very existence of what we think of as the American society. Its birth was accompanied by havoc and its early development took place in an atmosphere of frenzy: World Wars I and II saw to that.[3] Not having natural parents, it was adopted by, or rather it grafted itself onto, that discipline (psychiatry) which needed it, wanted it, and was willing to provide it with a home in which to grow up. What happened from that point on is now history, but for the present what is important to note is that even in its earliest years, clinical psychology functioned as would anyone who was conscripted into service, doing the kinds of things and thinking the kinds of thoughts that were appropriate to facilitating the war effort. The fact that the emergency-ridden 1940s were not the kind of years that guaranteed a period of professional development that was

[3]Sarason et al. (1966) offer a detailed description of the impact of the world wars on the development of clinical psychology as a helping profession. Their analysis shows how the remedial and rehabilitative needs generated by these wars led to specific governmental policy decisions and actions that had significant consequences for the field of mental health in general, and for the development of clinical psychology in particular.

stable, calm in nature, or conducive to reflective thinking is not the issue. Not very many people or professions were, or could afford to be, stable, calm, and reflective during that time. Stability and reflection are luxuries and, like all luxuries, they are subject to rationing during a period of national emergency. A society caught in a crisis in which its very fate is in question knows only one thing—to survive; and in order to survive people do what they have to do rather than what they may want to do. In retrospect, what was most interesting about the 1940s was the degree to which clinical psychology grew up doing the kinds of things it had to do in a way that was, in principle, no different from what was characteristic of our society as a whole.

War has a way of making instant experts out of self-proclaimed amateurs. A society engulfed in a battle for self-survival must often suspend its usually held criteria for expertise in recruiting and mobilizing its human resources to fill vital manpower needs. Often, of necessity rather than choice, it must lay aside, hold in abeyance, or temporarily cease to indulge itself in many of its ancient and sometimes treasured sexual and racial prejudices.[4] The 1940s were a time when anyone, often regardless of sex, race, age, or experience, became fair game for doing things and performing jobs heretofore denied them. It was a time when women became welders and riveters in heavy-industry war plants; when Negroes and other chronically oppressed minority groups suddenly found themselves in demand; when the aged and the young donned air-raid warden helmets and scanned the evening skies; and when city dwellers and residents of our urban ghettos suddenly became farmers, tending their Victory Gardens with the same infinite love and patience as their romanticized rural brethren. The war had succeeded, albeit unintentionally, in proving once again that under conditions

[4]There is little doubt that the stage for much of the present agitation for equality by women and black people in our society was set during the period of the war years. It was during the 1940s that these chronically oppressed groups had, in many instances, their first prolonged taste of freedom and the rewards of near first-class citizenship. This taste, once acquired and savored, almost guaranteed future movements for full and equal participation in the societal process.

of emergency and need people could learn to function in ways that had not been fully anticipated or imagined.

But just as the war made heroes out of cowards and patriots out of cynics, it also made clinical practitioners out of psychologists whose prewar world was the world of academia and whose major prewar goal was to become a part of that crusading army hotly in pursuit of the holy grail called Pure Science. It is important that we not underestimate the difficulties or problems that this transformation entailed, for, as Sarason et al. (1966, p. 8) point out:

It would be correct to characterize American psychology before World War II as "academic," but this would not convey the fact that it was also anti-clinical in orientation. The Ph.D. was treasured as a symbol of scholarly and research performance untainted by practical or professional considerations.

But wars, as we have already pointed out, have a funny way of making the improbable almost commonplace, and just as anyone who could walk was a potential soldier, so too was anyone who had ever had a course in psychology a potential clinical psychologist. If women could make planes and if children could collect paper and cardboard for the war effort, it was not too much to expect academicians to leave their universities, temporarily put aside some of their research interests, and become instant mental health workers. And that, essentially, is what happened. Clinical psychology, which had lived a relatively cloistered and serene life prior to World War II, emerged from its comfortable home in the Halls of Ivy and thrust itself into the world of practical and clinical concerns. Clinical psychology was in a sense reborn as a war psychology, as a psychology of emergency in the "frantic forties."

What followed was the same adolescent exuberance and functional self-definition that characterized the activities of so many people during those years of trial and turmoil. With little preparation, and even less supervision, clinicians began to function in ways that heretofore had been almost unthinkable. They began doing things (e.g., psychodiagnostics, individual and group psychotherapy) and assuming responsibilities (e.g., making clinical decisions, developing and administering programs of rehabilitation) as needs calling for such behaviors arose, rather than because their own traditions and backgrounds had prepared them for this work. It was a time when clinical psychologists "learned while they earned" in what was for all practical purposes an OJT (on-the-job training) experience.

World War II, which placed the stamp of finality on so many lives and institutions and changed so many others, also irrevocably altered the field of clinical psychology. A profession had, like so many other citizens, responded to a national crisis; had, like so many others, functioned in a variety of different ways and undergone a host of new experiences; and would, like so many others, never again be the same.

Clinical Psychology in the 1950s

If the 1940s were "frantic" years, the 1950s had to become "silent" ones, for no society can battle endlessly without itself becoming a war casualty. A society must rest and begin to consolidate rather than continue to innovate. And so it was in the 1950s. Americans had emerged from the war victorious, but not a little tired and disillusioned, and certainly with the full realization that the "American Century" had ushered in the Bomb and the Age of Anxiety.

Under these conditions the decade of the '50s became a period of quiet desperation. It was a time of dullness and Dulles, mistrust and McCarthy, tail fins and torpor, security seeking and, above all else—silence. We became a people who either joined in the endless quest for status or withdrew into some purposely disorganized band of muted rebels and quiet insurrectionists. Schlesinger (1965, pp. 113–114) describes well this "generation which had experienced nothing but turbulence":

. . . in the fifties some sought security at the expense of identity and became organization men. Others sought identity at the expense of security and became beatniks. Each course created only a partial man.

The affluent years were upon us, and some—those who became members of The Lonely Crowd (Riesman, Glazer, and

Denny, 1950) or the *Status Seekers* (Packard, 1959)—sought in their new suburbias and packaged villages that measure of security and permanence that the world situation could no longer offer or pretend to guarantee. These were the "organization men," men who, being denied a sense of historical continuity, reached out for the instantaneous "belongingness" offered them by the beneficent organization. Whyte (1956, p. 4) puts it this way:

Listen to them talk to each other over the front lawns of their suburbia and you cannot help but be struck by how well they grasp the common denominators which bind them. Whatever the differences in their organization ties, it is the common problems of collective work that dominate their attentions, and when the Du Pont man talks to the research chemist or the chemist to the army man, it is these problems that are uppermost. The word "collective" most of them can't bring themselves to use—except to describe foreign countries or organizations they don't work for—but they are keenly aware of how much more deeply beholden they are to organizations than were their elders. They are wry about it, to be sure; they talk of the "treadmill," the "rat race," of the inability to control one's direction. But they have no great sense of plight; between themselves and organization they believe they see an ultimate harmony and, more than most elders recognize, they are building an ideology that will vouchsafe this trust.

Others, those who chose the not-so-quiet refuge offered by Kerouac's *Subterraneans* (1959) and Lipton's *Holy Barbarians* (1959), sought "nonalignment" and became the alienated hipster (the precursor of our "flower" generation) who, as Holmes (1960, pp. 18–19) described it:

. . . moves through our cities like a member of some mysterious, nonviolent Underground, not plotting anything, but merely keeping alive an unpopular philosophy, much like the Christian of the first century. He finds in bop, the milder narcotics, his secretive language and the night itself, affirmation of an individuality (more and more besieged by the conformity of our national life), which can sometimes only be expressed by outright eccentricity. But his aim is to be asocial, not antisocial; his trancelike "digging" of jazz or sex or marijuana is an effort to free himself, not exert power over others. In his most enlightened state, the hipster feels that argument, violence, and concern for attachments are

ultimately Square, and he says, "Yes, man, yes!" to the
Buddhist principle that most human miseries arise from these
emotions. I once heard a young hipster exclaim wearily to
the antagonist in a barroom brawl: "Oh, man, you don't
want to interfere with him, with his kick. I mean, man, what
a drag!"

On this level, the hipster practices a kind of passive resistance to the Square society in which he lives, and the most
he would ever propose as a program would be the removal
of every social and intellectual restraint to the expression
and enjoyment of his unique individuality, and the "kicks"
of "digging" life through it.

Schlesinger (1965, pp. 739–740), perhaps better than anyone
else, has captured the essential quality of the '50s; he describes it in the following way:

In the fifties the young men and women of the nation had
seemed to fall into two groups. The vast majority were the
"silent generation," the "uncommitted generation," the
"careful young men," the "men in the gray flannel suits"—
a generation fearful of politics, incurious about society, mis-
trustful of ideas, desperate about personal security. A small
majority, rejecting this respectable world as absurd, defected
from it and became beats and hipsters, "rebels without a
cause." Pervading both groups was a profound sense of impotence—a feeling that the social order had to be taken as
a whole or repudiated as a whole and was beyond the power
of the individual to change. David Riesman, hearing undergraduate complaints in the late fifties, wrote, "When I ask
such students what they have done about these things, they
were surprised at the very thought they could do anything.
They think I am joking when I suggest that, if things came
to the worst, they could picket! . . . It seems to me that students don't want to believe that their activities might make a
difference, because, in a way, they profit from their lack of
commitment to what they are doing."

Clinical psychology's quest in the 1950s was not discernibly
different in either its orientations or its tactics from the rest
of society's goals in the postwar era. Just as security and status
dominated the thinking and behavior of the vast majority of
postwar Americans, so did they come to characterize the actions of many clinicians. With the guns now silent and the
battlefields finally deserted, clinical psychology began its own
silent war for recognition, prestige, and professional parity.

The new adversary was psychiatry, and the prize at stake was the right to first-class citizenship in the field of mental health. It was a quiet war—even a humane one—for clinical psychologists wanted little more than to become as much like their adopted fathers in psychiatry as possible. Clinical psychologists were not concerned with developing a professional image and identity of their own. The war years had already provided them with a ready-made image with which to identify, for by doing the kinds of things psychiatrists did, psychologists had for a long time been incorporating their values and introjecting their attitudes. All psychologists wanted was "official" recognition that the practice of psychotherapy was now one of their inalienable rights rather than a temporary privilege that had been bestowed upon them by psychiatry. It was a quiet war for another reason: clinical psychologists were at the disadvantage of waging war in "their father's house," for, as Albee (1964) has pointed out, clinical psychologists were "guests in other peoples' agencies and hospitals."

To be sure, many psychiatrists were all in favor of more people becoming proficient in the practice of psychotherapy, but they somehow saw the issue in a way that was almost calculated to upset the already self-conscious clinical psychologist. The following type of interaction could, and did, often occur between a clinical psychology intern (CI) and his psychiatrist-supervisor (P-S):

P-S:
Well, I guess that just about ends our supervision time for today. I liked the way you handled the issue of transference with your patient.
CI:
Thank you. It was helpful to me to hear your ideas.
P-S:
Look, before you leave there is something I want to ask you.
CI:
Yes sir?
P-S:
Why are you so willing to settle for second best?
CI:
I don't think I understand what you mean.

P-S:
Look, you're a bright boy. Why settle for second best?
You're still young. Why don't you go to medical school, do
an internship, get your residency over with, and be a real
doctor?
CI:
But sir, I like being a clinical psychologist. I want to
be a clinical psychologist.
P-S:
You're being defensive.
CI:
I am?
P-S:
Yes. Now tell me, why don't you want to go to medical
school and become a real M.D.?
CI:
Well, to tell the truth sir, I don't think I could hack it.
P-S:
Why?
CI:
Well sir, I can't stand blood. It makes me sick.

In short, clinical psychology in the 1950s was a profession
concerned with insuring its own safety and status. The "war
for psychotherapy" was only the most obvious vehicle by
which this security and prestige could be guaranteed. While
most of our citizenry was obsessed with the idea of "keeping
up with the Joneses," installment buying, and a house in
the suburbs, clinical psychology was obsessed with the idea
of consolidating its gains in a nation that was still converting
to a peacetime economy. That clinical psychology should
have had these goals, or should have pursued them with
such laudable restraint, needs no retrospective justification
or apology. Our own professional values and practices in the
1950s were no more nor less than a reflection of the attitudes and behaviors of so many of our war-weary fellow
Americans.

Clinical Psychology in the 1960s
If the 1940s were "frantic" years, and the 1950s "silent" ones,
the decade of the 1960s sought its roots in "action." The
1960s began as a time when personal visibility, social responsibility, and the quest for a self-critical autonomy re-

placed the aimless and egocentric quietude of the previous decade.[5] America was entering a new decade, and its entrance was gradually giving birth and form to a new style, an altered orientation, and a new perspective in the conduct of public affairs. A nation began to examine itself with unsparing objectivity and candor and to understand how great a discrepancy there was between the image it tried to project abroad and the harsh imperfections of the society within its own borders. The doubting and challenging of institutions and established ways of thinking were no longer luxuries and were no longer interpreted as acts of treason: they became an imperative, an obligation, a sacred trust. There was now nothing inherently wrong with being imperfect, either as an individual or as a nation. What was morally wrong was the inability to admit imperfection and the unwillingness to do anything about it. Thought became coupled with personal action, and a nation of young people began to understand that risk-taking and the acceptance of peril in the service of ideals were the causes, rather than the effects, of freedom. More than anything else, a generation of Americans began viewing themselves as cheated so long as they lived in a society which, for all its affluence and wealth, was still incomplete and unfinished.

Kennedy, the man and the President, became a symbol of the times, for, as Schlesinger (1965, p. 114) put it:
He voiced the disquietude of the postwar generation—the mistrust of rhetoric, the disdain for pomposity, the impatience with the postures and pieties of other days, the resignation to disappointment. And he also voiced the new generation's longings—for fulfillment in experience, for the subordination of selfish impulses to higher ideals, for a link between past and future, for adventure and valor and honor. What was

[5]We are acutely aware of the fact that by labeling periods of time in the manner we have been doing, we have been speaking in the categories of a guiding fiction. No single classification of an age— even, more important, of a mere decade—can accurately reflect the upheavals and dislocations of human thought and action that took place during that span of time. Our description of the temper of the 1940s, '50s, and '60s is little more than an attempt to employ historical shorthand in depicting the feeling-tone of a limited number of years. It is, therefore, of necessity, a description that is somewhat arbitrary, unreal, and incomplete. In point of fact, none of these decades existed in and of themselves without continuity or overlapping.

forbidden were poses, histrionics, the heart on the sleeve and the tongue on the cliche. What was required was a tough, nonchalant acceptance of the harsh present and an open mind toward the unknown future.

A nation began responding to a man and through their responses gave concrete meaning to his words:

I do not want it said of our generation what T. S. Eliot wrote in his poem, *The Rock*—"and the wind shall say these were decent people, their only monument the asphalt road and a thousand lost golf balls." (John F. Kennedy, Columbus, Ohio, October 17, 1960).

The early 1960s was a time when direct action became the vehicle for the attainment of individual and group identity, autonomy, and fulfillment. Selfhood was now defined in terms of one's willingness and ability to act, and through this action to alter and influence the condition of man. It was a time when three young men (Michael Schwerner, Andrew Goodman, and James Chaney) would die, not only *with* but *for* each other, realizing that so long as one of them was not fully free, all of them were part slave.

The atmosphere that was once more making individual action a meaningful thing—an atmosphere in which, as Schlesinger puts it: "even picketing no longer appeared so ludicrous or futile"—was also infusing old movements with a new and youthful dynamism, a dynamism that their elders found at once both awe-inspiring and not a little frightening. College campuses once again began seething with political and intellectual unrest, and the movement for civil and human rights was born anew. In both cases there was a new insistence, and an impatience to wait the amount of time that had so often in the past resulted in the conversion (or subversion) of high ideals into more "mature" forms of reflection and nonaction. The concepts of partial fulfillment, half-victories, and "wait, take your time, don't go too fast" were relegated to the past, to the dunghill of worn-out ideas: "Freedom Now!" was the chant of the present.

It was in this climate of insistence and action that a plethora of new programs were born, each one seeking to fill an unfulfilled need, each one serving as both an indictment of past neglect and a challenge to prevailing orientations. In a relatively short span of time, the Peace Corps, VISTA, Operation Headstart, and, most important, the War on Poverty made their appearances.[6] In each case, despite differences in emphasis, there was a communality of intent: each program was an attempt to change the status quo and to provide a meaningful vehicle through which individual action could become the instrument of social change. The concern was now with the "condition of man," both at home and abroad. The overall focus became the community of man and, by implication, the communities in which men lived.

Clinical psychology in the '60s, no less than in the preceding decades, could not long remain unaffected by, or impervious to, the social and political changes through which our society was passing. If the "zeitgeist" of the '60s, and the programs it was giving birth to—especially the War on Poverty—was breathing new life into a society that had been too quiet too long, it was also succeeding, along with several other factors, in providing the mental health professions with a mirror through which the social bankruptcy of their own traditional modes of practice could be reflected back to them. In making this statement, we are acutely aware of the fact that what we have said is somewhat inflammatory, both in tone and in implication. To label much of our traditional clinical efforts as "socially bankrupt" has the appearance of a blanket indictment devoid of any real appreciation of the exigencies, goals, and processes that go into the formation and maintenance of that particularly delicate human situation we call the clinical relationship. Nothing could be further from the truth. The attempt to use the psychotherapeutic situation to help a troubled individual—any individual —needs no justification; it is, in and of itself, an important, laudable, and necessary clinical-human activity.

---

[6]There is little doubt that the civil rights movement, aggressive now as never before, was an important factor in the initiation of the War on Poverty. The insistence on the recognition of economic opportunity as an integral part of social freedom was for a long time one of the most powerful themes in the movement for civil and human rights in this country.

What we are saying, however, is that in the process of wedding ourselves so completely to the psychotherapeutic model of help, a very important thing occurred: we, as mental health professionals, became parties to that process which both restricted and limited our modes of conceptualization and patterns of service and simultaneously excluded us from thinking about, and dealing effectively with, a large part of our society—namely, the poor—which needed us most.

In making these statements, we have done little more than echo what some clinicians have known or felt for some time. Reiff (1966, p. 540), for example, in a paper stressing the adverse effects of our exclusively "psychotherapeutic" focus of treatment on the understanding of institutions as sources and influencers of behavior, put it the following way:

... there has been a long history of persistent alienation from mental health professionals of the lower socioeconomic group in this country. This alienation represents a critical failure. It is not merely the failure of each individual mental health professional, although there is the element of the individual's social responsibility involved here. Neither is it primarily a matter of tools and skills, although, again, this element is also involved. Basically, the problem is an ideological one. The roots of this alienation from the low-income populations lie primarily in the middle-class ideology of contemporary mental health services and secondarily in its technology.

Gordon (1967, pp. 71–73), writing from the point of view of the vocational counselor who tries to deal with the problems of culturally disadvantaged youth, comes to a similar conclusion and states:

... counseling generally assumes that the locus of problems is in the individual client, rather than in the conditions to which he has adapted. This kind of counseling, as an instrument for changing lower class boys, will at best have an uphill battle because it seeks to make them maladapted to the conditions of their lives while those conditions remain unchanged. At worst, such counseling will simply temporize by "taking the edge off" obstreperous behavior and directing it back at the individual as the locus of his problems, without revising the causes or conditions of his discontent. Most benignly, such counseling may be a palliative, helping a few individuals to move a little, but if there is no enduring structural change in the factors creating the situation, there will be no end to the counseling, and no possibility of anything but limited success. And what success is achieved will be at the price of deepening the self-blame for failure which is already so deeply enmeshed in the problems of the poor, by agreeing with the premise that the causes lie in the individual and his responses, rather than in the conditions to which he is responding.

Thus my position is that though counseling is necessary for those who are already the products of the forces indicated, the more important task is structural socio-economic change to end the production of disadvantagement, and that this goal represents a better and more productive use of the resources of counselors than a continued palliative effort to patch up the mistakes of the past without preventing the mistakes from recurring. If counselors are to be seriously concerned with the plight of the disadvantaged, they should bend their efforts toward changing the societies in which boys grow up disadvantaged.

The vocational counselor stands at the crucial intersection of individual behavior and the structure of opportunities available to the individual. If he sees his job as primarily working with the individual, so that he is presumably better able to take advantage of the limited opportunities that are available, he will be doing only half his job, and that the easier half, since it manipulates the weak and the powerless while leaving the dominant majority safe, unchanged, and protected in its preservation of the better opportunities for itself and its own children. Thus it seems to me that it is only if the counselor also sees himself as an agent of social change in the wider community of which he is a part that he can take pride in carrying out the mandate of his profession. For it is only then that he will be stimulating natural and adaptive change in his clients, instead of engaging in psychological manipulation of them; it is thus the precondition of honesty in his profession.

Focusing their attention more directly on the impact and meaning of the War on Poverty for the mental health professions, Rae-Grant, Gladwin, and Bower (1965, p. 1) conclude:

The helping professions are facing a crisis, although some professional groups seem more aware than others that their moment of truth is at hand. For mental health programs the crisis may contain the seeds of a major revolution. Like all revolutions this one could readily go too far, rooting out the good along with the bad. This is, then, a time for very careful charting of our future strategies.

The crisis with which we are faced is being precipitated by

the President's declaration of War on Poverty. The reason this represents a crisis for mental health agencies is simply that the target population in this war is composed precisely of those people whom the "helping" professions have not yet figured out how to help. If mechanisms for helping them were already available and in use, the acute distress to which the President points would already have been relieved.

Clearly, the "action '60s" were forcing the mental health professions to take a long, hard look at what they were doing, who they were doing it with, and—by implication—what they were more generally *not* doing to alter and influence the social conditions of man. This "agonizing reappraisal" brought many of us face-to-face with ourselves and with some rather painful and distressing facts that could not be dismissed easily. As much as all other professions, we were the products of our history, the victims as well as the beneficiaries of our past. It was indeed a fact that the poor in this country had been largely ignored by and had become alienated from the mental health professions (Smith and Hobbes, 1966). It was a fact that the poor, even when "treated," may have been treated in a way and with the kinds of assumptions that were irrelevant to the problems they were experiencing or the needs they had (Kelly, 1966). And, perhaps most important, it was a fact that the mental health professions had taken a basically passive stance with respect to the social, economic, and institutional inequities that existed in our society (Yolles, 1966)—the very conditions that exacted such a heavy toll in human misery and contributed so much to our "mental health" problem. In short, the movement that was now making the eradication of poverty a respectable crusade served as both an indictment of and a creative challenge to the mental health professions, and provided these professions with a new opportunity to direct their attention and talents to the wider community of which they were a part and to which they bore a responsibility.

The early 1960s saw the mental health professions begin to respond to these challenges. Attention was now focused on the "community" and on the ways in which clinicians could utilize existing resources and develop new ones to provide services that were more efficient and appropriate to the needs of the communities in which they lived or worked. What had begun as a long, hard look at existing clinical practices—as a reappraisal almost forced upon the mental health professions by events in the society as a whole—culminated in the passage of the Community Mental Health Act of 1963.[7] This

[7]It would be highly inaccurate and incorrect if, from what we have written thus far, the reader were to infer that the mental health professions in the 1960s (or at any other time) were changing their practices or orientations in a purely "reactive" manner to events taking place around them. There is, to be sure, always this element of simple reactivity to be found in processes of change. What could be all too easily overlooked, however, is the degree to which prior changes in orientation in the field itself provided a theoretical foundation for the changes in clinical practices that were being demanded by the events of the 1960s. These changes had been going on for many years before the formal advent of the community mental health movement. They were the kinds of changes in theory and practice that to some degree prepared the mental health professions for the needs of the '60s. They were also changes that had taken place in the field's natural course of development. Nowhere is this more apparent than with respect to the "community-oriented" aspects of clinical functioning. One need only look at changes and developments in the field of personality theory—that body of ideas and knowledge that forms the conceptual foundation for most existing forms of psychotherapy—to get some feeling for just how far the mental health professions had come in seeing the "community" and the world of practical affairs as settings behavior. Beginning with Freud, and extending to the present time, ideas about personality development and treatment have undergone extensive change and modification. The overall direction of this change has been one of expanding the context of settings and forces that are seen as exerting determining influences on human behavior. The movement has been one of shifting the therapists' focus of concern from purely internal dynamics concerning a relatively few significant familial relationships to viewing the client's conflicts and problems in terms of the broader social, vocational, and institutional pressures to which he is reacting and which are to some degree determining his behavior. One need only review briefly the development of personality theory since Freud to appreciate fully the magnitude of this change. One finds that each successive theorist, independent of whether he accepted or rejected Freud's basic ideas concerning the formation of personality of significant importance in the determination and alteration of human (i.e., the theory of instincts, the Unconscious, developmental stages, etc.), broadened the context of personality development and the range of variables affecting this development. Even Freud, whose primary focus of concern was the internal conflicts of the individual in his nuclear family, in a paper entitled "Analysis Terminable and Interminable" (1937), called attention to the importance of reality factors (i.e., one's job, income, and daily transactions with the environment) in the understanding of personality and its modification. Adler (1927), the first disciple to break from Freud, developed a theory of personality that broadened the concept of the family (by making the relationships between siblings crucial to individual development) and introduced the

act, coupled with the events that led up to it and the processes it gave rise to, resulted in the community mental health movement, a movement that was heralded as the "bold new approach" to the prevention and treatment of mental illness in our society. Levine (1967) has summarized some of the specific social and professional pressures that facilitated the development of the community mental health movement. He describes them in the following way:

The community mental health movement had its origins in a specific set of historical facts and in a set of social and

---

notion of "social interest" as a universal motive in human behavior. Lewin (1935) made the interaction between the person and the environment of central importance in the attempt to understand behavior. Horney (1937) continued this process by broadening the framework of personality development to include the whole host of interpersonal relations that inevitably affect individual functioning. Sullivan's (1947, 1953) ideas concerning the importance of communication and his elaboration of the .role of significant figures in personality development added necessary breadth to the understanding and explanation of human behavior. Erikson (1950), by bringing all of "culture" into personality development, by focusing attention on the development of social modalities, and by examining the concept of national character added a new dimension to the understanding of the individual. Fromm (1941, 1947), perhaps more than anyone else, served the cause of "setting expansion" with the publication of his ideas concerning the historical, political, and societal implications of man's development and behavior. It remained for the ego psychologists, primarily Hartmann (1958, 1964) and Rapaport (1959), with their emphasis on the processes of coping, adaptation, and competence to focus attention on how individuals deal with the concrete and recurring problems of everyday life in a complex society. Now, as never before, personality theorists and psychotherapists were beginning to deal with the issues and problems of the individual in the context of his daily concerns and interactions. The trend was clearly one of seeing man in relation to broader institutions. In short, the mental health professions, through their own natural and ongoing development of ideas concerning the complexity of man and personality formation, were somewhat prepared for the rise of the community mental health movement and for its orientation toward social settings. What we have said, however, should not be taken to mean that all—or even a significant percentage of—clinicians were equally impressed by or convinced of the importance of "environmental, social, or institutional" variables in the determination and alteration of human behavior. Nor do we mean that it inevitably followed that those who were convinced of the importance of these factors were equally sophisticated or concerned with examining them in any systematic manner. All we have tried to point out is the fact that, at some level, some members of the mental health professions— most particularly the personality theorists—were, over a period of time dating back to Freud, independently concerned with some of the same problems that eventuated the passage of the Community Mental Health Act of 1963.

professional pressures. These pressures had to do with the demand for new patterns of treatment which would not remove the mentally ill or the deviant from the community (Joint Commission, 1961), with the demand for preventive patterns of help (Eisenberg, 1962), with the inevitable shortage of professionally trained treatment personnel (Albee, 1959), with dissatisfactions with the efficacy of current patterns of diagnosis and therapy (Meehl, 1960; Eysenck, 1961), and with dissatisfactions concerning inequities in the distribution of services to all levels of society (Hollingshead and Redlich, 1958; Furman, 1965).

In summary, the mental health professions as a whole, in their own right and in a manner consistent with their own histories, became a part of the movements of change that were sweeping the country in the early 1960s. To be sure, there were rumblings of change among mental health workers long before the War on Poverty ever came along, and the field probably already was beginning to change or question some of its traditional directions and orientations. But the emergence of the action programs of the '60s certainly facilitated this process of self-scrutiny and, more than likely, made it imperative that much of this questioning be translated into programs of service within a relatively short period of time. More than anything else, the spirit of the times brought the mental health professions face-to-face with the necessity of developing new programs to meet chronically unmet needs, with the meaning and importance of action in a changing society, and above all, with their professional and ethical responsibility to the community as a whole.

Clinical psychology in the 1960s, in addition to responding to the pressures for change being directed at the mental health professions as a whole, was dealing simultaneously with a second crisis, a crisis most aptly termed an "identity crisis." In retrospect, it was probably the combination of these two crises that created the conditions under which it became completely appropriate for a clinical psychologist to be visiting a mountain in Maryland.

Clinical psychology's identity crisis was the natural, almost inevitable, consequence of the conditions surrounding its birth and development as a helping profession. As we have already pointed out, prior to World War II the field of psychology had neither the interest, traditions, nor facilities necessary for the development of any ongoing involvement in and concern for clinical service. Consequently, when circumstances made it imperative for clinical psychology to become involved in this area, it had to turn for help and guidance to that discipline which had already developed such traditions, practices, and training facilities. That discipline was, of course, psychiatry. It was only natural for a field, ill-equipped and ill-prepared to deal with clinical problems, to turn to that profession which, over a period of time, had concerned itself with the "mentally ill." The medical profession (psychiatry) had long since assumed the position of leadership and responsibility, had already evolved methods of training, and had over the years developed what it felt to be appropriate orientations with respect to the care and treatment of patients suffering from mental illness. It was for these reasons that the field of clinical psychology sought to identify itself with the psychiatric profession and use its facilities for training clinical personnel.

By aligning itself with psychiatry, clinical psychology, of necessity, also was tying itself to training programs that had been established in only two basic settings: the hospital (usually the Veterans Administration hospitals), and the outpatient clinic. In both of these settings the programs and orientations encompassing the training of clinicians had been developed, administered, and supervised by members of the psychiatric profession. They were—and rightly so—the acknowledged leaders and, if you will, "landlords" of the training facilities and programs into which the field of clinical psychology was seeking entry. Although it identified itself with psychiatry's traditions, orientations, and modes of practice, clinical psychology was not—nor could it expect to be —in the "driver's seat." Clinical psychology entered the psychiatric domain "by invitation," and has remained in the psychiatric setting as a "guest." In view of the historical process by which clinical psychology became aware of and accepted its newly emerging service responsibilities, its subsequent dependence on psychiatry is both clear and understandable.

However, this dependence on the field of psychiatry inevitably led to problems in terms of clinical psychology's quest for a meaningful identity of its own. No profession, especially one whose parentage is in doubt and whose development was accompanied by the chaos of having to function as an adult too soon, can long endure without a viable sense of self. Unable to exercise decisive leadership on his own and unable to assume the full range of clinical responsibilities with respect to the care and treatment of patients, the clinical psychologist could perceive himself only as an ancillary professional—albeit an important one—operating within the clinical range and limits that psychiatry had established for him. In this sense he was not essentially different from the psychiatric social worker or other allied professionals who functioned within the psychiatric setting. In many instances the difficulty in establishing an identity of his own, coupled with the need to depend on psychiatry for technical clinical training, led the clinical psychologist to experience himself and his discipline with a sense of professional inferiority. The results of this state of affairs were, among other things, the development and perpetuation of feelings of anger, resentment, frustration, and resignation. In short, clinical psychology emerged from its relationship to psychiatry without a well-defined or ego-syntonic professional identity—an identity it could live with, call its own, and hope to perpetuate.

In the 1960s, clinical psychology, perhaps spurred on by the movements for independence and autonomy taking place all around it, left its childhood and entered adolescence. In so doing, many clinical psychologists began to deal anew with the universal problem of adolescence—the identity crisis—and to seek their own place in the sun. For some (e.g., Albee, 1964) the quest for a meaningful identity necessitated a total rejection of the medical setting and a resounding "declaration of independence" from the psychiatric profession. Others (e.g., Alexander, 1966) sought to develop better training paradigms that would enable psychologists to combine their clinical and research interests within the existing framework of alliances. Still others (e.g., Sarason et al., 1966), those perhaps less concerned with formal labels, turned their attention to the implications of existing conditions for clinical psychology's future course of development and its role in fulfilling its social responsibilities.

In summary, then, clinical psychology in the 1960s, both as a part of the mental health profession and in response to its own needs to develop a meaningful and independent identity, was seeking new directions. To be sure, the search is far from over, and it is still too early to assess the long-term effects of current social crises on the practices or identity of clinical psychology. But some things are fairly clear. Born as a war psychology, clinical psychology in the 1960s was still developing in the context of upheaval and war. Now, however, the setting for the war had shifted from foreign soil to our own native land. The war was now against poverty and against those forces and institutions which were depriving a significant number of our citizens from their full and rightful participation in society.

The same historical process that had produced "instant mental health workers" in the 1940s and "silent psychotherapists" in the 1950s was now creating the conditions and making it imperative for clinical psychology to begin to explore, and become a part of, the world of the action '60s. The final path these explorations will take is still largely unknown and will certainly vary from individual to individual. But for some clinical psychologists—for us—the path inexorably led up the winding road of a lonely mountain in Maryland . . . and back down again to that very special experience that came to be called the Residential Youth Center.

Epilogue
It was raining the last time I walked out of the RYC as its Director. It was a winter rain, very cold and hard—not at all fresh and vital like the rains that would be coming later on. But somehow I didn't feel cold or hard. I was sad and tired,

perhaps even a little depressed, but certainly not despairing or bleak like the rain itself. Instead, I think I felt very much like someone who knew he had been a part of something fresh and vital—like someone who had emerged from an experience knowing he would never be the same again.

It would be foolish to pretend to know what lies ahead for the RYC. It may live and change and prosper to the beat of the different drums of those who come to possess it; it may die the premature death of a setting that comes to despise itself; or perhaps worst of all, it may remain the same, never transcending the dreams of its creators.

But whatever happens, at least on that one rainy winter's day there was a climate of hope, and I left the RYC feeling a sense of identity with the historian (Schlesinger, 1965) who said: "Revolutions accelerate not from despair but from hope."

Bibliography

Adler, A.
(1927) *Understanding Human Nature.* New York: Chilton.

Adorno, T. W., and R. N. Sanford
(1950) *The Authoritarian Personality.* New York: Harper.

Albee, G. W.
(1959) *Mental Health Manpower Trends.* New York: Basic Books.
(1964) A declaration of independence for psychology. *Ohio Psychologists,* June 1964.

Alexander, I. E.
(1966) A training paradigm for clinical psychologists. Paper presented at the annual American Psychological Association meeting, New York.

Argyris, C.
(1965) *Organization and Innovation.* Homewood, Ill.: John Irwin.
(1966) *Explorations and Issues in Laboratory Education.* Washington, D.C.: National Training Labs, National Education Association, No. 30.
(1967) How effective is the State Department? *Yale Alumni Magazine,* May 1967, pp. 38–41.

Barker, R.
(1951) *One Boy's Day.* New York: Harper.
(1960) Ecology and motivation. In M. R. Jones (Ed.), *Nebraska Symposium on Motivation.* Lincoln, Neb.: University of Nebraska Press.

Beiser, M.
(1965) Poverty, social disorganization and personality. *Journal of Social Issues,* 21: 56–78.

Benne, K. D.
(1965) The responsible behavioral scientist: An introduction. *Journal of Social Issues* 21: 1–8.

Bradford, L. P.
(Ed.) (1961a) *Group Development.* Washington, D.C.: National Training Laboratories, National Education Association.
(Ed.) (1961b) *Human Forces in Teaching and Learning.* Washington, D.C.: National Training Laboratories, National Education Association.
J. R. Gibb, and K. D. Benne (Eds.) (1964) *T-Group Theory and Laboratory Method.* New York: John Wiley & Sons.

Brooks, M. P.
(1965) The community action program as a setting for applied research. *Journal of Social Issues* 21: 37–39.

Buber, M.
(1956) *The Writings of Martin Buber.* New York: Meridian Books.

Camus, A.
(1959) *The Myth of Sysyphus and Other Essays.* New York: Vintage Books.

Caudill, W.
(1958) *The Psychiatric Hospital as a Small Society.* Cambridge, Mass.: Harvard University Press.

Christie, R.
(1958) A quantification of Machiavelli. Unpublished paper. Columbia University.

J. Havel, and B. Seidenberg
(1958) Is the F-Scale irreversible? *Journal of Abnormal and Social Psychology*, 56.
and R. K. Merton (1958) Procedures for the sociological study of the value climate of medical schools. *Journal of Medical Education*, 33.

Cloward, R. A.
(1965) Poverty, power, and the involvement of the poor. Testimony before the Senate Select Subcommittee on Poverty, Washington, D. C., June 29, 1965.

Crowne, D. P., and D. Marlowe
(1960) A new scale of social desirability independent of psychopathology. *Journal of Consulting Psychology* 24: 349–354.

Cumming, E. and J. Cumming
(1957) *Closed Ranks: An Experiment in Mental Health Education.* Cambridge, Mass.: Harvard University Press.

Eisenberg, L.
(1962) If not now, when? *American Journal of Orthopsychiatry*, 32.

Erikson, E. H.
(1950) *Childhood and Society.* New York: Norton.

Eysenck, H. J.
(1952) The effects of psychotherapy: An evaluation. *Journal of Consulting Psychologists* 16.

Ford Foundation
(1967) *Ford Foundation Evaluation Team Report.* October 1967.

Fox, E., G. Nicolau, and H. Worrord (Eds.)
(1965) *Citizen in a Time of Change: The Returned Peace Corps Volunteer.* Report of the Conference, Washington, D.C.

Frank, I. H.
(1968) Personal communication, 28 May 1968.

Freeman, H. E., and C. C. Sherwood
(1965) Research in large-scale intervention programs. *Journal of Social Issues* 21: 11–28.

Freud, S.
(1959) Analysis terminable and interminable (1937). In J. Strachey (Ed.), *The Selected Papers of Sigmund Freud.* New York: Basic Books.

Fromm, E.
(1941) *Escape from Freedom.* New York: Holt, Rinehart & Winston.
(1947) *Man for Himself.* New York: Holt, Rinehart & Winston.

Furman, S. S.
(1965) Suggestions for refocusing child guidance clinics. *Children* 12: 140–144.

Germano, D.
(1967) The Job Corps program. Paper presented at Bridgewater State Teachers College, Bridgewater, Mass.

Gladwin, T.
(1966) Social competence and clinical practice. National Institute of Mental Health, March 1966.

Glazer, N., and D. P. Moynihan
(1963) *Beyond the Melting Pot.* Cambridge, Mass.: The M.I.T. Press.

Goffman, E.
(1961) *Asylums: Essays on the Social Situation of Mental Patients and Other Inmates.* Chicago: Aldine.

Goldenberg, I. I.
(1965) The Psycho-Educational Clinic of Yale University. Paper presented at the annual American Psychological Association meeting, Chicago, Ill.
(1966) Psychotherapy: Its underlying assumptions and possible modification. Paper presented at the annual American Psychological Association meeting, New York.
(1967) The inner-city Residential Youth Center as a setting for behavioral change. Paper presented at the annual American Psychological Association meeting, Washington, D. C.
(1969) The clinician and the community: contemporary responsibilities and historical imperatives. *Transactions of the N. Y. Academy of Science,* June 1969.
and M. Levine (1969) The development and evolution of the Yale Psycho-Educational Clinic. *International Review of Applied Psychology,* Fall 1969.

Gordon, J.
(1967) The disadvantaged boy: Implications for counseling. In A. Ames (Ed.), *Counseling Culturally Disadvantaged Youth.* New York: Prentice-Hall.

Gould, J.
(1964) The alienation syndrome: Psycho-social correlates and behavioral consequences. Unpublished doctoral dissertation, University of Connecticut.

Graziano, A. M.
(1969) Clinical innovation and the mental health power structure: A social case history. *American Psychologist* 24, no. 1.

Gregory, D.
(1965) *Nigger.* New York: Pocket Books.

Harrington, M.
(1962) *The Other America.* New York: Macmillan.

Hartmann, H.
(1958) *Ego Psychology and the Problem of Adaptation.* New York: International Universities Press.
(1964) *Essays on Ego Psychology: Selected Problems in Psychoanalytic Theory.* New York: International Universities Press.

Hoffman, D.
(1966) "The world I live in": Semantic differential based on responses to Louis Harris' poll of a cross-section of U.S. teen-agers in February 1966. As reported in *Newsweek,* 21 March 1966.

Hollingshead, A. B., and R. C. Redlich
(1958) *Social Class and Mental Illness.* New York: John Wiley & Sons.

Holmes, J. C.
(1960) The philosophy of the beat generation. In S. Krim (Ed.), *The Beats.* Greenwich, Conn.: Fawcett Publications.

Horney, K.
(1937) *The Neurotic Personality of Our Times.* New York: Norton.

Iverson, W. H.
(1965) The use of the non-professional: hiring and training indigenous persons. New Haven, Conn.: Community Action Institute (CPI), Draft No. 2.

Joint Commission on Mental Illness
(1961 *Action for Mental Health*. New York: Basic Books.

Kaplan, B. H.
(1965) Social issues and poverty research: A commentary. *Journal of Social Issues* 21: 1–100.

Kelly, J. G.
(1966) Ecological constraints on mental health services. *American Psychologist* 21: 535–539.

Kenniston, K.
(1964) The alienated student. Unpublished manuscript, Yale University. (The trust scale used in the RYC research was modified by Kenniston in 1965 for use with a noncollege population.)

Kerouac, J.
(1959) *The Subterraneans*. New York: Avon Publications.

Klein, E. B., and L. J. Gould
(1965) Research report of the Yale Summer High School. Appendix II of the Report of the Director, Yale Summer High School, 1965 session.
and L. J. Gould (1969) Problems in research and evaluation of an innovative educational project. In G. B. Gottsegen and M. G. Gottsegen (Eds.), *Professional School Psychology*, Vol. III. New York: Grune and Stratton.

Kobler, J.
(1961) The Black pope. *The Saturday Evening Post*, 11 March 1961.

Krasner, L.
(1965) The behavioral scientist and social responsibility: No place to hide. *Journal of Social Issues* 21: 9–30.

Lander, B.
(1954) *Toward an Understanding of the Juvenile Delinquent*. New York: Columbia University Press.

Levine, M.
(1967a) Some postulates of community mental health practice. Prepublication report, Yale University.
(1967b) The more things change.... Paper presented at the annual American Psychological Association meeting, Washington D. C.
(1968) A social system analysis of research methods: some preliminary thoughts. Unpublished paper, Yale University.
and A. Levine (1968) Social change and human behavior; dependency, deviance or diversity. Paper presented at the Adelphi University Symposium: The Contributions of Psychoanalysis to Community Psychology, Adelphi University.
and A. Levine (1969) *A Social History of Helping Services: Clinic, Court, School and Community*. New York: Appleton-Century-Croft.

Levinson, D. J., and E. B. Gallagher
(1964) *Patienthood in the Mental Hospital*. Boston: Houghton Mifflin.

Lewin, K.
(1935) *A Dynamic Theory of Personality*. New York: McGraw-Hill.

Lippitt, G. L. (Ed.)
(1961) *Leadership in action.* Washington, D. C.: National Training Laboratories, National Education Association.

Lipton, L.
(1959) *The Holy Barbarian.* New York: Messner.

Lord, F. M.
(1967) A paradox in the interpretations of group comparisons. *Psychological Bulletins,* 68: 304–305.

McGregor, D. M.
(1961) The human side of enterprise. In E. Fleishman (Ed.), *Personnel and Industrial Psychology.* Homewood Ill.: Dorsey Press.

McIntyre, D.
(1969) Two schools, one psychologist. In F. Kaplan and S. B. Sarason (Eds.), *The Psycho-Educational Clinic: Collected Papers and Research.* Boston: The State of Massachusetts Press.

Marris, P., and M. Rein
(1967) *Dilemmas of Social Reform.* New York: Atherton Press.

Meehl, P. E.
(1960) The cognitive activity of the clinician, *American Psychologist* 15.

Mial, D., and H. C. Mial (Eds.)
(1961) *Forces in community development.* Washington D. C.: National Training Laboratories, National Education Association.

Miller, M.
(1967) The clinician and issues of public health. Paper delivered at the Yale Psycho-Educational Clinic, 19 May 1967.

Packard, V.
(1959) *The Status Seekers.* New York: David McKay.

Polsky, H. W.
(1962) *Cottage Six: The Social System of Delinquent Boys in Residential Treatment.* New York: Russell Sage Foundation.

Rae-Grant, G. A., T. Gladwin, and E. M. Bower
(1965) Personal communication.

Rapaport, D.
(1959) The structure of psychoanalytic theory: A systematizing attempt. In S. Koch (Ed.), *Psychology: A Study of a Science,* Vol. 3. New York: McGraw-Hill.

Reckless, W., S. Dintz and B. Kay
(1957) The self component in potential delinquency *American Sociological Review,* 22.

Reiff, R.
(1966) Mental health manpower and institutional change. *American Psychologist,* 21: 540–548.
Residential Youth Center (1968) *Final Report,* New Haven, Conn.

Ridgeway, J.
(1967) Treating mental illness. *The New Republic,* 10 June 1967.

Reisman, D., N. Glazer, and R. Denny
(1950) *The Lonely Crowd.* New Haven, Conn.: Yale University Press.

Reissman, F.
(1967) Strategies and suggestions for training non-professionals. *Community Mental Health Journal* 3: 103–110.
Rubinstein, E. A., and M. B. Parloff (Eds.)
(1959) *Research in Psychotherapy.* Washington, D. C.: American Psychological Association, Inc.
Salisbury, H.
(1958) *The Shook-up Generation.* New York: Harper and Row.
Sarason, S. B.
(1967) Toward a psychology of change and innovation. *American Psychologist* 22: 227–233.
(1968) The creation of settings: the beginning context. Paper presented at the Kennedy Foundation meeting, Chicago, Ill., April 1968.
and M. Levine, I. I. Goldenberg, D. L. Cherlin, and E. M. Bennett
(1966) *Psychology in Community Settings: Clinical, Educational, Vocational, Social Aspects.* New York: John Wiley & Sons.
Scheff, T. S.
(1966) *Being Mentally Ill: A Sociological Theory.* New York: Aldine.
Schein, E. H.
(1965) *Organizational Psychology.* Englewood Cliffs, N.J.: Prentice-Hall.
Schlesinger, A. M., Jr.
(1965) *A Thousand Days: John F. Kennedy in the White House.* Boston: Houghton Mifflin.
Shore, M. F., and J. L. Massimo
(1963) A comprehensive vocationally oriented psychotherapeutic program for adolescent boys. *American Journal of Orthopsychiatry* 33: 634–642.
and J. L. Massimo (1966) Comprehensive vocationally oriented psychotherapy for adolescent boys: A follow-up study. *American Journal of Orthopsychiatry* 36: 609–615.
Smith, M. B. ,and N. Hobbes
(1966) The community and the community mental health center. *American Psychologist* 21: 499–502.
Sorensen, T. C.
(1965) *Kennedy.* New York: Harper and Row.
Stanton, A. H., and M. S. Schwartz
(1955) *The Mental Hospital: A Study of Institutional Participation in Psychiatric Illness and Treatment.* New York: Basic Books.
Stevenson, R. L.
Vailima Letters. Address to the Chiefs on the opening of the Road of Gratitude, October 1894. In J. Bartlett (Ed.), *Familiar Quotations.* New York: Permabooks.
Street, D., R. D. Vinter, and C. Perrow
(1966) *Organization for Treatment: A Comparative Study of Institutions for Delinquents.* New York: The Free Press.
Suchman, A. E.
(1967) *Evaluative Research: Principles and Practices in Public Service and Social Action Programs.* New York: Russell Sage Foundation. '

Sullivan, H. S.
(1947) *Conceptions of Modern Psychiatry*. Washington D. C.:
William Alanson White Psychiatric Foundation.
(1953) *The Interpersonal Theory of Psychiatry*. New York: Norton.

Tannenbaum, A. S.
(1966) *The Social Psychology of the Work Organization*. Belmont,
California: Wadsworth.

U.S. Department of Labor (1966) Contract No. 82-07-66-64, 24 June 1966

Wechsler, J.
(1967) Scandal at Youth House. *New York Post*, March 1967.

Whyte, W. H., Jr.
(1956) *The Organization Man*. New York: Doubleday.

Yevtushenko, Y.
(1963) *A Precocious Autobiography*. New York: E. P. Dutton.

Yolles, S. F.
(1966) The role of the psychologist in comprehensive Community
Mental Health Centers. *American Psychologist* 21: 37–41.

Youmans, E. G.
(1954) Social factors in the work attitudes and interests of 12th grade
Michigan boys. *Journal of Educational Sociology* 23.

Index

T-group phenomenon, 154–157

inapplicability, 157–158

United Social Services program of
CPI, 71

Veterans Administration hospitals, 54

Walk-in clinics, 56
War on Poverty, 47, 48
  basic assumption, 116
  dilemma of change agent, 115–116
  emergence of nonprofessionals, 65
  increasing specialization, 72
  individual remediation versus
      institutional change, 76, 115
  need for ideological functional
      change, 72
  nonprofessionals, 65–67
  professional, role of, 72–73
  status in 1969, 453–458
    evaluation, 458
    maximum participation, 456
    political aspects, 453–455

Young Women's Multi-Purpose
    Training Center, 449–450